D1244393

THE COLD WORLD
THEY MADE

THE COLD WORLD
THEY MADE

The Strategic Legacy of
Roberta and Albert Wohlstetter

R ON R OBIN

Harvard University Press

Cambridge, Massachusetts
London, England
2016

First printing

Library of Congress Cataloging-in-Publication Data

Names: Robin, Ron Theodore, author.
Title: The cold world they made : the strategic legacy of Roberta
and Albert Wohlstetter / Ron Robin.
Description: Cambridge, Massachusetts : Harvard University Press, 2016. |
Includes bibliographical references and index.
Identifiers: LCCN 2016011269 | ISBN 9780674046573 (alk. paper)
Subjects: LCSH: Wohlstetter, Albert. | Wohlstetter, Roberta. |
National security—United States. | Cold War—Influence. |
United States—Military policy.
Classification: LCC UA10.5 .R62 2016 | DDC 355/.03357309045—dc23
LC record available at http://lccn.loc.gov/2016011269

Contents

THE COLD WORLD
THEY MADE

Introduction

IN THE HEADY, formative years of American strategic thought, when the bomb loomed large, the analyst was king, and the RAND Corporation ruled the policy world, America's "wizards of Armageddon" would gather at the Laurel Canyon home of Roberta and Albert Wohlstetter to share insights on existential issues. A formidable cohort of "thermonuclear Jesuits" would huddle around Albert, while Roberta played hostess.[1] A photograph, part of a fawning *Life* magazine profile, has etched this picture into the collective memory of RAND. Albert sprawls comfortably, surrounded by awkwardly seated colleagues, who appear somewhat unsettled, perhaps by the contrast between the eclectic setting of the Wohlstetter domicile and the doomsday theories that preoccupied their minds. Roberta is nowhere to be seen. She is presumably fussing around in the kitchen, just outside the frame.

In another photograph from their stunning International Style abode—a modernist masterpiece designed by their next-door neighbor, the (allegedly) card-carrying communist architect Josef Van der Kar—Albert perches on an Eames chair. Book in hand, he basks in the collective adoration of his daughter, Joan, and his wife, Roberta, who poses from a distance. The artifacts of modernism surround Albert—Eames furniture, sliding walls, a table of his own design with inverted sawhorses. The room is encased in wraparound windows, drawing the Southern California landscape into the translucent dwelling. The women in the photographs are paragons of traditional feminine domesticity. Albert graciously takes time from his reading to chat with his doting daughter; Roberta busies herself preparing appetizing delights for the ravenous intellectual.[2]

After hours, RAND Corporation analysts meet in the home of Albert Wohlstetter, 1958. *Photograph by Leonard McCombe/The LIFE Picture Collection/Getty Images.*

Joan Wohlstetter chats with her father, Albert, as her mother, Roberta, prepares a meal in their Laurel Canyon home. *Photograph by Julius Shulman. Architect: Josef Van der Kar. © J. Paul Getty Trust. Julius Shulman Photography Archive, 1936–1997. The Getty Research Institute, Los Angeles (2004.R.10).*

Histories of RAND have reinforced these images. "Albert was the guru, Roberta the den mother, Albert holding court on his views of the world, Roberta dishing out delectable soufflés," albeit "without missing a beat of the conversation."[3] Albert's dominant persona, his love of the limelight, and his gladiatorial debating style facilitated a skewed portrayal of the Wohlstetter world. But this somewhat precious 1950s vision conjured by Fred Kaplan—the cerebral husband waited on by a doting homemaker—oversimplifies a more complex reality.

To begin with, Roberta and Albert Wohlstetter were a team. At the very least, their intellectual contributions were cooperative ventures. Albert was a brilliant scholar in his own way, but he was beholden to his wife's own acumen and body of work. His intellectual achievements were built on Roberta's insight about cognitive fallibilities in war and other forms of confrontation. Albert transformed her observations into a formidable doctrinal edifice. The ideological scaffoldings of the Wohlstetter Doctrine, invariably attributed to Albert, made early appearances in Roberta's initial forays into the world of scholarship—as a social scientist, as a literary scholar, and finally as a historian of the nation at war.

Representations of the Wohlstetters' living room as either a war room or a traditional domestic hearth obscure another important aspect of the Wohlstetters' world. Like so many other members of their generation, Roberta and Albert were social experimentalists who flirted with radical ideological positions before landing in the vicinity of the Vital Center. Throughout their career, they also published controversial treatises on the nation's domestic issues. Prior to joining RAND, in particular during their tempestuous student days, they produced formidable scholarship on literature and analytical philosophy. Their intellectual inquisitiveness provides an important background for understanding the underpinnings of their later work on strategy.

Most scholars have ignored the Wohlstetters' social worldview. Their domestic concerns and personal past pop up every now and again as a curiosity or an irrelevant sideshow with no bearing on their strategic thought. And yet, Deborah Welch Larson reminds us, "social scientific theories are invariably shaped by their intellectual, social, and political contexts, and deterrence theory is no exception."[4] I argue here that disregarding the Wohlstetters' past, their cultural inquests, and their studies of the nation's social challenges is like staging *Hamlet* without the Ghost; motivation and actions become obscured by imperfect knowledge of the plot.

The Biographical Challenge

Albert and Roberta Wohlstetter are hardly household names outside policy circles. Anonymity, however, should not be confused with lack of resonance. Nor, for that matter, did the shroud of obscurity descend on the Wohlstetters by volition. Throughout much of his career, Albert, in particular, pursued the public limelight. By some accounts, Albert was "the most influential *unknown* man in the world for the past half century."[5] As the alpha male of strategic studies, he aggressively promoted his panaceas for the nation's challenges, sometimes in partnership with Roberta but often claiming center stage for himself alone.

The Wohlstetters' oeuvre grappled with the strategic uncertainties of war, in general, and of the Cold War, in particular. Roberta's study of surprise at Pearl Harbor and Albert's challenge to the dominant paradigm of a stable balance of terror between the two nuclear superpowers have provoked constant commentary and continuous reflection. Their significance, however, is disputed. Most historical assessments of the Wohlstetters tend to relegate Roberta's inquest of quintessential military surprise (*Pearl Harbor: Warning and Decision*) to the status of a period piece. The book is trotted out every now and again to chastise the short-term memory of a forgetful nation, constantly surprised by the obvious. Albert, by contrast, has claimed enduring relevance. In addition to his seminal study, in which he defied predictions of a stable equilibrium between the two superpowers, Albert is remembered as the aggressive strategist of enemy remission by devising credible threats. His unapologetic promotion of an offensive nuclear strategy and the attendant military spending spree aimed at hemorrhaging a flawed Soviet economic system were the hallmarks of what became an unnamed but highly influential Wohlstetter Doctrine during the Cold War.[6] Following the collapse of the Soviet Union, Albert maintained an angry dialogue with fainthearted leaders who demonstrated what he considered to be Hamletian hesitation in the Balkans, Iraq, and elsewhere.

Within this context, the diminished representation of Roberta as the auxiliary female strategist or muse to the intellectual giant is misplaced. When the scales of gender conventions are peeled back, Roberta appears as an equal contributor to the major themes that preoccupied the Wohlstetters. Roberta, to paraphrase Richard Klein, was the historian of the future. Her history of Pearl Harbor was anything but the reconstruction of a unique crisis. Instead of dwelling on the past, her history looked forward, offering a road map for navigating the new and confusing thermonuclear landscape. In this sense, she was the creator of a history of a conjectural event. She provided Albert with the tools to devise war-winning strategies for a hypothetical occasion of apocalyptic proportions.[7]

In addition to her Pearl Harbor inquest, Roberta produced personal contributions on a host of other strategic issues. Never a narrow scholar, she went on to write studies of Cuba under Castro. Later she explored the possibility of a symbiosis between nuclear-armed rogue states and terrorist organizations. Together with Albert, she immersed herself in

American domestic challenges, as well. Individually and as a couple, the Wohlstetters probed the United States' weltering social pathologies, identifying in the process the presence of alien vectors at the heart of social strife during the turbulent 1960s. Foreign pathogens, they implied, had infected both the mass media and the nation's universities. In fact, there were times when Roberta and Albert appeared more concerned with the Soviets' uncanny skill for domestic subversion—by means of a Cuban proxy or otherwise—than with the Soviet Union's clumsy war-making capacities.

Their construction of an exogenous threat—imperiling both the domestic and global order—was, of course, a sign of the times. The U.S.-Soviet rivalry had all the trappings of an existential struggle, and I do not for a moment wish to trivialize the fears and suspicions hovering over the American public throughout the Cold War. Nevertheless, the Wohlstetters' militancy and their warnings of alien incursions into the fault lines of domestic strife in the United States predated the Cold War and emanated from multiple intellectual and social strands embedded in their personal histories. In other words, the full meaning of their contributions on strategy and the nuclear threat requires contextualization.

I have sought to unravel the complex tapestry of the Wohlstetters' world by means of a biographical approach that weaves together the many strands of the culture and politics of their times: their intellectual awakenings within their respective families, revisionary doubts during their university years, and subsequent amendments to their worldview when fighting for the Cold War cause at the RAND Corporation, the University of Chicago, and elsewhere.

Without a biographical context, the Wohlstetter treatises on national security are reduced to artifacts, lacking in social and political contextualization; we are left at the mercy of insiders who assume license to reconstruct self-serving versions of the Wohlstetters' interaction with American society. I seek to reintroduce the Wohlstetters not as disembodied historical personae but as complex individuals who, like most of us, were confounded by distracting politics and personal passions. When viewed through the prism of their formative years as youthful intellectuals and in relation to their friendships and enmities at the heights of their careers, the contested representations of the Wohlstetters as either fearless defenders of freedom or purveyors of dangerous and costly brinkmanship become somewhat more nuanced.

Any attempt to construct a biography of the Wohlstetters is hampered, however, by their own efforts to control their past. Their few autobiographical statements were heavily redacted accounts of their intellectual journey. In the glimpses they offered of their lives prior to joining RAND in the early 1950s, the Wohlstetters edited out whole chapters of their life stories, including their youthful cultural and political experimentation and their political ambivalence during World War II, to mention but two important way stations. In fact, Roberta never offered any independent autobiographical account. Her story, as presented here, is a patchwork of the odd newspaper interview, personal papers she preserved for posterity, her brother's accounts of life in their family, and the occasional comment from friends and admirers. Reconstructing Albert's story is no less challenging. In his fascinating—and fascinatingly incomplete—oral histories, prepared at the behest of RAND and other archival projects, Albert glossed over the first leg of his intellectual journey, which took him from the disputatious alcoves of City College to the ideologically monolithic precincts of RAND, where a culture of technical expertise sought victory over the nation's enemies. In general, Albert's autobiographical sketches deny any connection between personal history and intellectual projects.

The many fine studies of the Wohlstetters are of little help on this question, suffering as they do from self-imposed disciplinary boundaries. With few exceptions, their chroniclers and historians avoid dwelling on the Wohlstetters' worldview beyond their published papers on strategic threats.[8] Discussions of the Wohlstetters typically begin and end with their prolific writings on the thermonuclear challenge, paying scant attention to their other articles and books. Most retrospectives begin with Albert's early work at RAND. The more historically inclined hark back to Roberta's seminal study of Pearl Harbor.[9] In both cases, the Wohlstetters' epistemology of strategy in the nuclear age and beyond appears as an immaculate conception, removed from the context of messy beginnings and personal politics.

A biographical approach to the Wohlstetters alters, for example, our sense of the intellectual balance of power between the two. When brought out of the shadow of her extrovert husband, Roberta is revealed as a full intellectual partner. Albert craved center stage, and he had a flair for articulating provocative policy proposals. Roberta, by contrast, offered restrained observations on the role of psychology in decisions under duress and the rising challenges of nonstate actors, while providing occasional ballast for her spouse's rococo scenarios for an imaginary war. I argue, as well, that Roberta had undue influence on the next generation of Wohlstetter warriors, described by historian Anthony David as "a new band of leaders to battle tyranny using policies that would spread liberal democratic values."[10]

The Wohlstetter students—including several prominent "neoconservatives" who led George W. Bush's post-9/11 charge into Iraq—have, indeed, garnered much public attention. In the spirit of Albert, their mentor, they have never avoided the limelight, nor have they been particularly indulgent of criticism. Beginning with the Strategic Arms Reduction talks in the 1970s and through the spectacular debacle in Iraq, a group of powerful Wohlstetter admirers muscled their way into policy circles.

I do not see their star students as merely propagating the designs of their mentors, however. Their followers imbued the Wohlstetter Doctrine with their own conceits and radical views on the nation's global predicament following the collapse of the Soviet Union. Most important, the Wohlstetters' apprentices amended their mentors' promotion of the proactive abeyance of enemy forces.

The Wohlstetters had assumed that there would *always* be an enemy lurking on the nation's doorstep. Their most influential students, by contrast, argued that an unalloyed implementation of their mentors' insights could actually break the cycle of recurring existential challenges. They preached a millenarian "end to evil," their personal riposte to the false dawn of the "end of history." While their designs for perdition in Iraq had deep roots and intimate ties to the life and times of their mentors, they bore singular responsibility for this challenging moment in the annals of American adventurism.

The Making of an Intellectual Partnership

Roberta and Albert came from different worlds. She was a child of the Cambridge, Massachusetts, academic aristocracy. He was the son of nominally Jewish immigrants in New York. They met at Columbia after two very different undergraduate experiences. At Columbia, Albert and Roberta lingered in the shadow of illustrious academics of the Left as they progressed along a familiar path from the radical persuasions of their youth to the mature, grim worldview of their later years. Their student period and their social circles, as well as the broad cultural tides sweeping through the years of their youth, shaped their work throughout their career. Literature, analytical philosophy, and art provided metaphors and similes for the worldview that they would flesh out at RAND and beyond. Roberta's early studies of *Hamlet* provide my point of departure for deciphering the Wohlstetters.

In a *Washington Post* obituary following her death in January 2007, their daughter, Joan, described her mother "as a student of both *Hamlet* and criminals," who "was fascinated with decision-making and ambiguity."[11] *Hamlet* was a recurrent presence in the Wohlstetters' world. As the clouds of war gathered in 1938, Roberta Morgan and Albert Wohlstetter worried whether the West was encumbered by the Hamlet-like affect of J. Alfred Prufrock, T. S. Eliot's decadent Western man, unable to decide on trifles, let alone existential matters.[12] In the late 1960s, when the Soviets appeared to be galloping toward nuclear parity and beyond, Albert expressed exasperation over the Air Force taking Hamlet "as a model of a modern major general"—fatally addicted to postponing decisions.[13] Later Albert wondered whether Robert McNamara's endorsement of mutually assured destruction (MAD) had been a version of Hamlet's feigned madness: Was McNamara "but MAD north-north-west?"[14]

The Wohlstetters' interpretation of Hamlet fluctuated according to circumstances and context. Roberta the scholar embraced a complex and fluid version of Hamlet, whose representation depended on the social and cultural conditions of the interpreting society. By contrast, Roberta and Albert the strategists reduced the prince of Denmark to a convenient platitude, a hollow but useful representation of the pathologies of indecisiveness. In this sense, the Wohlstetters' strategic Hamlet—the vacillating procrastinator—was an instrumental fiction rather than an authoritative interpretation of the mysteries of Shakespeare's masterpiece. Hamlet became a simulacrum of their own discontents and a metaphor for condemning the sluggishness of colleagues and statesmen in the thermonuclear age.

As for Roberta's interests in criminality, she demonstrated a similar split between her scholarly observations and the tropes driving her political observations. Roberta the scholar completed a master's thesis at Barnard on delinquency and rehabilitation. This ethnographic study of a woman's penitentiary in New Jersey described delinquency as a moving target, its definition evolving as social norms broadened to include behavior once deemed criminal. Roberta the strategist, however, experienced no difficulties in defining criminal behavior in the global arena. Most of her wrath focused on Fidel Castro, the Soviet proxy lurking off American shores. The Fidel of Roberta's studies harbored murderous tendencies. He was a pathological liar, a confidence man, and a self-hating sexual deviant to boot. His soothing advocacy of "progressive mutual restraint" was a crude ruse. Only the most gullible of American politicians failed to discern that his nostrums of peace and harmony did little to pacify his seething rage and penchant for violence.[15] Fidel was the norm rather than the exception among Soviet-inspired Latin revolutionaries. Her Che Guevara had the bedside manner of an ax murderer. Behind the thin facade of commitment to "serious ideology" lurked a pathological killer. "Guevara made his basic estimate of us plain. . . . We are 'beasts,' 'hyenas,' and for us 'there can be nothing else but hate; there can be no other thing than extermination.' "[16]

Cuba became a major obsession for the Wohlstetters. Roberta—sometimes in collaboration with Albert—produced a string of papers purporting to identify the lurking presence of Castro-inspired political infiltration in some of the major social crises affecting the United States in the 1960s, ranging from his manipulation of the American press to his impact on racial discord. They also offered strategies for undermining Soviet-style socialist planning in a soon-to-be-Castro-free Cuba. Vexing suspicions drove Roberta, at one point, to accuse Fidel of orchestrating—or at least inspiring—the John F. Kennedy assassination.[17]

Roberta's work on Cuba provided a segue to her interests in global terror. In 1976, she warned of the global threat of nonstate terrorists and of their weapons of choice. For those who feared the worst—terrorists commandeering weapons of mass destruction—Roberta explained that terror organizations did not need such drastic measures to promote their cause. Sophisticated terror organizations were engaged in what would later be called the "Theater of Terror," the execution of high-profile symbolic attacks designed to attract the attention of Western media. Weapons of mass destruction did not serve this cause.[18] Nevertheless, Roberta's tentative thoughts on the remote possibility of nuclear terrorism appeared to inspire Wohlstetter acolytes in government, fueling their post–Cold War preoccupation with the multipolar, Byzantine alliances between nuclear-brandishing rogue states and nonstate actors.

Strategy in an Age of Existential Threats

Roberta's study of the surprise attack at Pearl Harbor was the foundational document of the Wohlstetters' strategic vision. Her book was a profound historical investigation of the American military experience in the twentieth century, and it indelibly shaped Albert's thinking on nuclear strategy. It was Roberta, in fact, who was first employed by RAND. Albert, at that time the undistinguished CEO of a failing start-up, was offered a part-time consultancy at RAND as a courtesy to his much-admired spouse.

Albert's initial forays into strategic studies were provocative and innovative, but his intellectual debt to *Pearl Harbor: Warning and Decision* is quite obvious. In assessing the role of frontline bases for Air Force strategy, Albert drew on Roberta's thesis to argue that an unprotected strike force based in the vicinity of enemy lines did not provide the deterrent factor its champions promoted. The combination of provocation and vulnerability they represented would more likely spur a nervous adversary to launch a preemptive strike, as the Japanese had in 1941.

Over the course of his long career, Albert consistently berated colleagues who—much like their predecessors at Pearl Harbor, he believed—sought to divine enemy intentions but only succeeded in projecting their own wishful thinking. Roberta's study had demonstrated the limits of military intelligence to create a reliable picture of the adversary's thinking. She had argued that it was a natural human tendency to plan for enemy decisions that seem logical to oneself and to overlook any contrary evidence. Albert would subsequently continue his spouse's logic, insisting that a prudent country should prepare itself for all possible enemy capabilities—no matter how fantastic—rather than planning for the great unknown of an adversary's intentions. The focus on imaginative possibilities, rather than reasonable probabilities—one of Roberta's central insights—would become Albert's hallmark and the battle hymn of the RAND Corporation.

Albert's war-winning nuclear capabilities were ostensibly meant to thwart a Soviet enemy that only supreme threats bearing clear existential consequences could bring into abeyance. Yet evidence suggests that, by the early 1960s, the USSR as such was no longer the object of Albert's strategic thinking; it was replaced by a generic, hypothetical enemy. He was not nearly as consumed with the Soviet nuclear threat as his existing accounts might suggest. By his own admission—in RAND papers as well as in a later oral history—it was most probably the Soviets' own military and intellectual limitations, rather than American strategic choices, that precluded a surprise attack on the United States or its allies.[19]

Significant strands of evidence suggest that the Wohlstetters harbored a predominantly *economic* model of superpower confrontation. The Soviet Union's spiraling investments in military hardware may have been a threat, but one that had distinct, long-term advantages for the West. Debilitating military expenditures at the expense of the well-being of Soviet citizens provided an opportunity to bring this great adversary to its knees. The Soviets' lopsided defense expenditures, the Wohlstetters believed, would eventually bleed the enemy into an economic and political stupor. The Soviet threat was both a military and an ideological challenge. It could be undermined by encouraging—through doctrine and actual expenditures—disproportionate Soviet investments in gargantuan military ordnance that would never be used.

The Wohlstetters' understanding of Soviet intentions was driven in large part by their RAND and University of Chicago colleague Nathan Leites. Reading the texts of Russian elites, Leites produced a psychopathological model—an "Operational Code"—that fashioned the predatory behavior of the Soviet leadership. It was Leites who encouraged the Wohlstetters to avoid any serious analysis of the underlying causes of tension between the great powers beyond the ostensible ideological rift. The Leites model focused exclusively on the pent-up rage of a psychologically scarred Soviet leadership whose clinical obsession with fanatical goals could be cowed only by unremitting resolve.

Leites would eventually soften his psychocultural analysis of the politburo. In an article published in 1974, he acknowledged that trade relations and other soft-power exchanges with the United States had mellowed the Soviet leadership, although deep down they may have never relinquished their commitment to their Operational Code.[20] The Wohlstetters, by contrast, never made such a transition. Even as the Cold War dissipated before their eyes, the Wohlstetters clung to an image of an enemy that, for all practical purposes, no longer existed. Their disquisitions on Soviet behavior, in particular during the age of glasnost and perestroika, suggest their adherence to a rigid operational code of their own, one that they would share with their students and acolytes.

The Wohlstetters harped on the sacrosanct Soviet Threat well beyond its expiration date because they feared complacency. They believed that the threats of totalitarian powers would not disappear, but merely morph from one entity to another. Using history as her guide, Roberta argued that totalitarian nations—past, present, and future—were, by definition, expansionist and prone to reckless military aggression that could be abated only by unequivocal power and resolve. Roberta analyzed numerous historical instances in which Western powers had been lulled into wishful thinking by an expansionist enemy that preyed on the West's tendency to project its own status quo aspirations. Under these circumstances, history appeared to prove that a prudent nation should always prepare for the enemy's capabilities rather than its largely inscrutable intentions.

Historian Bruce Kuklick contends that such historical reasoning was, at best, superficial. It produced a "tactile" understanding of the Soviet enemy and its intentions, quite devoid of cumulative empirical evidence on Soviet society and politics. The Wohlstetters and their ilk, Kuklick argues, divined the future based only on "what they discussed in the seminar room" and on "their a priori theorizing."[21] Their allegedly solipsistic theories on Soviet intentions encouraged maniacal investments in what Mary Kaldor has called a "baroque arsenal" for confronting improbable, phantasmagoric contingencies.[22]

History and Teleology

Throughout their career, the Wohlstetters pointed to repetitive cycles of history as the main justification for their stark, Hobbesian approach to global politics. They argued for a teleological sense of the past, a theme that would become a common motif in American foreign policy circles. The conviction that some version of Pearl Harbor would always reoccur is indelibly inscribed in all of their work. Roberta and Albert believed that certain fundamental, unchanging traits of human nature—ranging from self-deception among the peace loving to the insatiable appetites of alpha predators—were the constant drivers of history. The sui generis quality of historical events held little purchase for them. Beginning with Roberta's Pearl Harbor study, the Wohlstetters' implicit assumption was that the catastrophic lack of vigilance was not related to a specific group of derelict military commanders, nor was the Japanese enemy in any way unique. The retrospective analysis of the Pearl Harbor debacle and Albert's futuristic construct of the "Delicate Balance of Terror" were both derived from the same pool of sociological and psychological insights: the lure of self-deception, on the one hand, and, on the other, the dangers of an insatiable predator when left unchecked by a vigilant West.

One of the most persistent objectives of their recourse to history was to impress upon policy makers that future Pearl Harbors, though inevitable, would not necessarily follow the 1941 pattern of sudden shock and awe. In the late 1980s, Roberta created the specter of Slow Pearl Harbors, a series of small, seemingly innocuous enemy moves that would nevertheless eventually add up to devastating cumulative consequences. This sense of repetitive historical patterns led the Wohlstetters to fan the embers of a persisting Soviet threat well past the time when the USSR began visibly crumbling. They feared that if global tensions relaxed—just as had happened after the First World War—a remissive complacency would seduce the nation. Hoping to keep the nation on alert, they clutched and clung to the rumor of the Soviet threat until such time as a new clear and present danger could be identified.[23]

The end of the Cold War did little to encourage the Wohlstetters to revise their belief in a bleak cycle of historical repetition. Their students, by contrast, approached the post–Cold War years as an opportunity to fine-tune their mentors' doctrine. In the 1990s, the Wohlstetters' acolytes focused on the abatement of "anarchy," the term used by scholars to describe the self-seeking, self-serving jostling of national ambitions in a polycentric global arena. Employing a mutation of democracy theory, the Wohlstetter students in government sought to solidify the status of the United States as the singular and supreme superpower. Their blueprint entailed a campaign of global democratization by all means possible, including intrusive regime change among hostile challengers.[24] After all, they would claim, democratic nations seldom, if ever, warred among themselves.[25]

The post–Cold War Wohlstetter Doctrine—the work more of their students than of the Wohlstetters themselves—called for the United

States to stymie all significant global and regional ambitions. It would even enforce nuclear abstinence among trusted, yet globally ambitious allies. The imposition of democracy on other political structures, coupled with the unchallenged status of a singular superpower, would break historical cycles of recurring global friction while ensuring American preeminence. The presence of the United States as an enlightened coercive power that could resolve disputes, enforce its norms, and eviscerate challenges promised to liberate the global arena from the uncertainty of anarchy.

The Wohlstetter Acolytes

It is by now a common assumption that the post–Cold War Wohlstetter Doctrine was carried into policy circuits by a "small army" of students and disciples. Moving between government, think tanks, and academia, they redeemed their mentors' theories from suspended animation in the Cold War.[26] Their apprentices transformed the Wohlstetter vision into a distinctive mix of high ambition and occult beliefs fueling the post-9/11 impulse for proactive assertion and undisputed global leadership. By virtue of their students, the Wohlstetters' combination of brilliance and conceit cascaded beyond the precincts of academic disputation and continues to shape American politics and policy to this day.

The hunt for Wohlstetter disciples in government, however, has taken on obsessive dimensions. In some screeds they appear as a secretive cabal of crypto-Zionists, while others identify massive, multifaith legions linked by a post-Soviet millenarianism. I have stepped with caution into this fray, offering short portraits of individuals who were indisputably Wohlstetter disciples: namely, Paul Wolfowitz, Zalmay Khalilzad, and Richard Perle, the three usual suspects who played pivotal roles during the George W. Bush years.

These three Wohlstetter acolytes occupied crucial decision-making positions during the transition from a relatively reclusive, pre-9/11 Republican administration to the espousal of a militant strain of global leadership. They were not, however, disciples in the biblical sense. They did not consecrate the Wohlstetters' writings as immutable texts, subject to exegesis by faithful followers of the orthodox persuasion. The Wohlstetters' fingerprints are nonetheless indelibly marked on the policies executed and designed by these three protégés.

Paul Wolfowitz was Albert's most prominent student in government, writing a dissertation under his tutelage in the early 1970s at the University of Chicago. He was the ordained theoretician among these three enforcers. As a key architect of the second American foray into Iraq, he is a necessary choice for at least a cursory glance at this crucial moment in the post–Cold War period. I have paid particular attention to Wolfowitz's view of history, and the manner in which the past informed his understanding of both the present and the future.

Second-in-command was Richard Perle. The so-called Prince of Darkness had few formal academic credentials at his disposal and seemed to relish his reputation for taking down adversaries with more distinguished academic pedigrees. Like his mentors, Perle did not earn a PhD. Indeed, he betrayed ill-concealed contempt for academics in positions of power (though he did not mind playing one in his autobiographical novel). Perle was the terminator: the man who employed all possible devices to knock Beltway counterattacks off course. My sketch of Perle focuses on the way he translated vision into action.

Among the Wohlstetter students in government, Zalmay Khalilzad served as the designated orientalist. After writing a dissertation under Albert's tutelage, he was an assistant professor of political science at Columbia University from 1979 to 1989. These were the years when the Muslim world began to consume the attention of Washington policy makers; his native Afghanistan and the Persian Gulf became the epicenter of their attention. Khalilzad took it upon himself to explain whether the paradigms of the social sciences meshed with the messy reality of the Muslim world. While all members of the invisible Wohlstetter college preached their commitment to democracy and a reformed political system in the Middle East writ large, Khalilzad provided context and insider knowledge. In addition to his published work and its dissemination during a critical period, Khalilzad served as ambassador in two of the major hot spots during the Bush years. He also served as U.S. ambassador to the United Nations.

Many inquiries have been conducted of the actions of these three individuals in government.[27] I am, therefore, absolved of the need to rush into this crowded territory. Instead of scouring the familiar terrain of their policy decisions, I seek to unpack the theory that informed their worldview. I have focused on their self-reporting, in particular the manner in which they created—individually and as a group—a mani-festo for the United States as the sole, uncontested global hegemon.

As was the case with their mentors, the acolytes had little patience for assessing probabilities—always a tenuous exercise and prone to the standard deviation of wishful thinking. Instead, they argued for possi-bilities. The *probability* that a global upstart would pursue nuclear weapons was less important than the *possibility* that it would. While dis-missive of "Western-preferred" constructions of enemy intentions, the Wohlstetter disciples created their own quite radical and solipsistic narratives.

These three Wohlstetter acolytes were prominent actors in the Reagan administration, when the Cold War reached its sudden conclu-sion. All three drew lessons from this event that provided the impetus for the push for regime change in other strategic regions. In fact, as reconstructed Wohlstetter acolyte Francis Fukuyama and others have observed, the relatively smooth and swift transition to democracy in European satellite states led them to believe that, given the application of American pressure, similar transitions could happen in other totali-tarian societies, including the Islamic world. Democracy appeared in their writings as "a kind of default condition to which societies reverted once the heavy lifting of coercive regime change occurred, rather than a long-term process of institution-building and reform." When their ex-ercise in regime change in Iraq devolved into chaos and uncertainty, its promoters asserted "they knew all along that the democratic transfor-mation of Iraq would be long and hard," although "they were clearly taken by surprise."[28]

In both theory and practice, the disciples applied the Wohlstetter stress tests for identifying regimes worthy of American attention. Disdainful of intervention in conflicts with no apparent strategic value for the consoli-dation of American power, the Wohlstetter students devised two crucial and usually interconnected conditions for American intervention. Nu-clear proliferation, the ultimate game changer in the Wohlstetter ap-proach to global conflict, became the first and foremost prerequisite for intervention. Closely related to proliferation was the presence of ambi-tious regional powers seeking to undercut American preeminence in the aftermath of the Cold War. In lieu of the Soviet threat, they identified a cluster of predatory regional upstarts with global aspirations and access to nuclear technology. When evidence of proliferation was not self-evident, it was inferred, perhaps even fabricated.

Their version of global threats recognized the presence of nonstate actors in the global arena, albeit with significant qualifications. Terrorist organizations, the ultimate nonstate actors, allegedly had no independent existence and no independent objectives. They were the proxies of nation-state enablers. Terrorists were purportedly a species of human smart bombs employed by conventional governments.[29] Terror, ostensibly the weapon of the weak and the dispossessed, was driven by rogue states with their own ulterior strategic objectives.

The language of the second generation differed from that of their mentors, too. The Wohlstetters presented their enemies as emotionally scarred psychopaths, requiring psychoanalysis to understand their motivations. By contrast, the enemy of the Wohlstetters' students was morally bankrupt, the incarnation of biblical evil. This enemy could not be contained; it needed to be annihilated and removed from civilized society.

As this shift in language suggests, the students extended and stretched their mentors' worldview. They were the bearers of a millenarian variation of the End-of-History trope. They discarded their mentors' acceptance of cyclical bouts of confrontation with predatory enemies for their own theory of stable global hegemony. The Wohlstetter acolytes, as Fred Kaplan has observed, believed that "blowing off a tyrant's lid will unleash the geyser of liberty," which for them meant the imposition—rather than the evolutionary development—of minor democratic facsimiles of the American master copy.[30]

Spinners of urban legend have made attempts to define a common worldview shared by the Wohlstetters' heirs apparent. One widespread representation paints them as charter members of a—predominately Jewish—neoconservative cabal, implying that clandestine political and ethnic allegiances motivated their ideological outlook. A harsh exchange between the journalist Michael Lind and historian Alan Wald will suffice to illustrate this theory's mendacity. Wald, the author of a definitive study of the American anti-Stalinist Left, lashed out at Lind's defamation of Bush-era foreign policy makers as "products of the largely Jewish-American Trotskyist movement of the 1930s and 1940s" who espoused "Trotsky's theory of the permanent revolution mingled with the far-right Likud strain of Zionism."[31] Wald dismissed Lind's assertion as wild and gratuitously sensationalist. He described as specious the assertion "that anyone in the group of 'neoconservative defense intellectuals' cited by Mr. Lind has ever had an organizational or ideological association with Trotskyism, or with any other wing of the Far Left." (Lind was confusing the younger cohort with the Wohlstetters' generation.) Hinting at ill-concealed innuendoes, Wald also refuted "the implications of emphasizing the 'Jewish' side of the formula, although many of these individuals may have diverse relations to the Jewish tradition—as do many leading U.S. critics of the recent war in Iraq."[32]

Others have sought a common denominator in the halls of the University of Chicago, where Wohlstetter nurtured some of his most illustrious students. Even in the Chicago connection, the bugbear of the Jewish Cabal raises its head, though coded in more genteel language. Over the years—in both the popular press and among those who should know better—both Wohlstetter and his students have been described as Straussians, the enforcers of a worldview articulated by University of Chicago philosopher Leo Strauss. None of the promoters of the Straussian connection have been able to ferret out the hidden Strauss in the work of the Wohlstetters. In fact, one would have expected the Wohlstetters to have mentioned Strauss at least once had he had any influence on their writings. The Strauss connection is association by Chicago osmosis only.[33]

At heart, Thomas Farr has observed, the Wohlstetter heirs were Kemalists rather than Straussians. Challenges, such as the religious schisms that would fan a civil war among Iraq's disaggregated communities, struck them as temporary impediments on the road to a democratic Iraqi state. In modern Turkey, they reasoned, a visionary secular actor had separated a dysfunctional religious establishment from the state. With this example in mind, the Wohlstetter disciples promoted an opportunistic, yet ineffective, Kemalist look-alike from among Iraq's pretentious but quite alienated opposition groups in exile.[34]

On Blind and Perceptive Oracles

In recent years, the question of the degree of influence the Wohlstetters and their ilk may have exercised on the nation's strategic vision has been the subject of intense debate. Were they indeed influential beyond the ivory tower? To what extent did they actually shape major policy decisions? It is within this context that I pick up the gauntlet thrown down by Bruce Kuklick in his provocative *Blind Oracles.* Assessing the role of policy intellectuals on the nation's behavior, Kuklick concluded that the Wohlstetters of this world had mostly served as useful fools, paraded about by politicians seeking validation for self-serving decisions.[35]

I do not claim the Wohlstetters induced some great shifting of the tides during their tenure as Cold War policy advisers.[36] In fact, I am agnostic on this question; it is immaterial to the argument I make in this study. Instead, I argue that the Wohlstetters did what the best intellectuals do: they spawned followers. The strategic placement of their students in positions of power, where they were able to elaborate on the mentors' doctrine, constituted this ambitious couple's ultimate triumph.

The Wohlstetters were, of course, not the only thermonuclear oracles, blind or otherwise. Among the many fine studies of this generation of scholars and policy makers, I have found Sharon Ghamari-Tabrizi's important study of Herman Kahn particularly useful.[37] Kahn's claim to fame was his uncanny ability to combine mathematical computations and bizarre Catskills humor in order to get Americans to think about the unthinkable. Moving deftly between deadpan and burlesque, this "thermonuclear Zero Mostel" created horrific scenarios of a nuclear war while offering guidance to the nation on how to prepare itself to be "struck, fight back, and survive." His dense, 651-page book, *On Thermonuclear Warfare* (1960), sold fourteen thousand copies in its first three months.[38]

When read together, the Wohlstetters appear as the straight man (and woman), the ballast for Kahn's maniacal performance in RAND's thermonuclear burlesque. Within this doomsday theater, Albert shared the marquee with Kahn. They had much in common. Both were overachieving sons of underprivileged New York Jewish families who hustled their way into a gentile defense establishment by issuing alarming clarion calls. At a purely intellectual level, Albert and Kahn shared essentially the same ideas. Both brushed aside the common assertion that merely threatening the enemy with retaliation—through MAD or other unconvincing gestures of brinkmanship—would somehow induce a stable balance of terror. Each in his own way argued that deterrence entailed convincing the enemy that the United States was fully equipped, mentally and militarily, to engage in a war-winning thermonuclear exchange that fell short of global extinction. Vulnerability—either strategic or political—would encourage a predatory enemy to strike first. Both Kahn and Albert fashioned themselves as the "clever civilian, uniquely blessed with extraordinary powers of discernment and prognostication, who could smoke out the least visible clues of fatal vulnerabilities in the national defense."[39]

Their rhetorical strategies for gaining attention were different and complementary. Herman Kahn became, in his own quip, one of the "ten most famous obscure Americans" through his comic routine and penchant for the grotesque.[40] Albert reached for the stars by claiming insights that even the Einsteins of this world would recognize. Charles Wohlstetter, Albert's entrepreneurial brother, recalled an anecdote that illustrates Albert's unbounded self-promotion. A precocious "seventeen-year-old" Albert had published an article on analytical philosophy in one of the field's most venerable journals. According to Charles—who heard the story from Albert—Albert Einstein had described the paper as "the most lucid extrapolation of mathematical logic he had ever read." Einstein subsequently invited the supposedly adolescent Albert to discuss his thesis over tea at his Princeton abode. "When my brother arrived at the great man's home, Frau Einstein arrived at the door, knitting in hand, and (no doubt expecting an elderly academic) asked after my brother's business. 'I am Albert Wohlstetter. I have an appointment with the professor.' The good lady called out over the sound of her husband's violin playing, 'Albert! Another Albert to see you!'"[41]

This vignette encapsulates the image of Albert as prodigy, allegedly ratified by no less a figure than the Princeton luminary. It likely fueled Albert's high sense of self-regard. In the story, the indisputable genius recognizes strands of brilliance in the child (though his precociousness is somewhat embellished: Albert was actually twenty-three years old when the article was published, not seventeen). In later years, Albert would go so far as to assert his own superiority over Einstein and his ilk. Looking askance at the misgivings of atomic physicists, who feared the genie they had unleashed, he disparaged the mealymouthed pieties of these "scientists and seers" as uninformed and ignorant.[42] When intellectual disputation did not silence his rivals—be they scientists or rival analysts—Albert intimidated the competition with the instincts of a barroom brawler. He impugned his adversaries by any means possible—personal and professional—all in the name of championing his version of the truth.

Examples of Albert's dismissive debating style cropped up in his relationship with Bernard Brodie, another prominent master of Cold War strategic analysis. The high stakes at play in nuclear strategy rendered the spats between Albert and Brodie more resonant than other garden-variety academic disputes of the time. As is often the case among dueling intellectuals, the principle rapidly become personal. Albert publicly derided Brodie as an intellectual lightweight, an insignificant pretender to the much-coveted position of the "Clausewitz for the nuclear age."[43] A seething Brodie found himself marginalized at RAND; he eventually retaliated by pressing charges of financial impropriety that led to Albert's dismissal. This conflict is indicative of what Michael Howard has described as Albert's "ferociously confrontational" style. "In his pursuit of adversaries, Wohlstetter showed himself at his most Calvinistic: there was at times a distinct whiff of burning in the air"—although he occasionally singed himself in the process.[44] Herman Kahn had captured public attention with gallows humor. Albert, by contrast, charged onto center stage throwing down gauntlets of fire and ice.

No man is a hero to his valet, Gertrude Himmelfarb reminds us in her ruminations on the craft of historical analysis.[45] Himmelfarb, an accomplished historian and spouse of Irving Kristol, another brawling revisionist intellectual, argues that historians retracing the steps of the dashing individuals who populate their books develop a familiarity that occasionally breeds some contempt. We know too much about the inner lives of our protagonists, their hidden habits and foibles. As I pick up after the Wohlstetters, dutifully shelving the intellectual artifacts they have strewn throughout their careers, I have developed the comfortable familiarity of a first-name basis. And yet my relationship to the Wohlstetters is ambivalent. On the one hand, I am smitten by this erudite couple. They embraced American culture in all its multilayered glory, from the tail fins of extravagant cars to the virtuosos in the nation's concert halls. At the same time, I can barely contain my horror at their nuclear brinkmanship. Their construction of an irrepressible Cold War predator and their intimidating version of cyclical challenges strike me as examples of theory run wild. The Wohlstetters—Albert in particular— were intent on winning every debate even to the point of losing the war. These reservations notwithstanding, I have made a diligent effort to provide a balanced account of their lives and intellectual contributions. I have offered clear and, to the best of my ability, nonjudgmental summaries of their work. I have allowed the protagonists to speak in their own voices. I trust that full disclosure of my ambivalence will allow readers to make their own judgments.

PART ONE

THE WOHLSTETTERS' COLD WORLD

1

The Wohlstetter Partnership

The Early Years

IN 1963 the *Los Angeles Times* named Roberta Wohlstetter "Woman of the Year," in recognition of the Bancroft Prize she had received for her study of surprise at Pearl Harbor. How does a woman deal with "such momentous matters such as crisis, warning, and decision?" a reporter asked her. "It is not a terribly feminine subject," she acknowledged, "but feminine intuition helps." When given the opportunity to invoke a feminist stance, Roberta demurred. Her message to the women of Los Angeles was domestic and tame: "Part-time work keeps a woman from going stale." She enjoyed being a housewife and a mother, as well as a part-time scholar, she reported. "It gives you a sense of balance."[1] In another *Los Angeles Times* article, she related the backhanded compliment she had received from the matronly "Mrs. Henry Steele Commager, wife of Columbia's great scholar," who had told the strikingly beautiful Roberta that she didn't "look like a historian."[2]

When pressed further, Roberta eventually addressed her unique scholarly attributes. Most students of strategy, she explained, were specialists. While such experts played an important role, the profession needed "individuals who are able to view more broadly and intuitively the combined and interrelated elements in these problems. In short, a restoration of the ancient Greek and Renaissance ideal of the rounded man"—and, presumably, woman.[3] Roberta, the elegant "foreign affairs expert and housewife" who kept "a beautiful home in the hills above Hollywood," concluded the interview with some dark thoughts. She expressed a hope that her "researches into recent history may have some future relevance for survival."[4]

Roberta the Social Scientist

Roberta, the ultimate Renaissance woman, was born into an academic family in Duluth, Minnesota, in 1912, destined to be a scholar and contrarian. She was the daughter of Elsie Smith Morgan and Edmund M. Morgan Sr., an eminent law professor who taught at Harvard and, following his retirement, at Vanderbilt. Edmund Sr. was no narrow academic. He espoused political engagement and public service beyond the confines of Harvard Yard. He drafted the first uniform military code of justice for the armed services. During World War II, he chaired a government labor panel for the Merchant Marine, and coauthored a standard textbook on judiciary evidence.[5] In the 1950s, he served as a consultant for the territory of Puerto Rico and for the state of Israel, developing codes of civil procedure for each. Edmund Sr. is remembered above all for his scathing critique of the American criminal justice system. In 1948, he published an inquest on the injustices endured by Sacco and Vanzetti, the Italian anarchists sentenced to death for a murder committed during a 1920 payroll heist in the Boston area. The study offered more than a mere jeremiad against one particular miscarriage of justice. It argued that the case revealed serious—perhaps even fatal—flaws within the American justice system.

Sacco and Vanzetti, wrote Edmund Sr., were afforded "a trial according to all the forms of law, but it was not a fair trial."[6] An incompetent defense, a compassionless, overzealous prosecutor who held back evidence favoring the defendants, and a prejudiced judge had sealed the anarchists' fate. But there was nothing unique about this travesty of justice. Roberta's father maintained that the Sacco and Vanzetti tragedy revealed significant structural faults within the legal system. A host of pathologies compromised the fair execution of ordinary criminal justice procedures: a dysfunctional, adversarial system of litigation, a scandalous resort to expert testimony for hire, and, above all, an inability to offer an impartial procedure to social pariahs—be they people of color, political misfits, or members of any other marginal group. Edmund Sr. advocated major reforms, including a trial before a panel of judges in instances when an impartial jury of peers was not a feasible option, explicit rules on the disclosure of state documents that might help defendants, and court-supervised summoning of impartial expert witnesses.

Roberta's brother, the distinguished historian Edmund S. Morgan Jr., recalled a family home of liberal leanings, where Marxist scholar Harold Laski rubbed shoulders comfortably with Supreme Court Justice Felix Frankfurter—at that time still considered by some to be a convinced liberal, but as Edmund Jr. observed, already quite conservative. He remembered the university milieu of the 1930s, when both he and Roberta were students, as saturated with Marxist sympathizers, whom he described as "simple-minded" yet impossible to ignore. He himself was a pacifist in the 1930s. He briefly became a conscientious objector and, although he abandoned pacifism, managed to avoid military service during the war.[7] Roberta and her brother were encouraged to follow in their father's footsteps and seek careers in jurisprudence. Both made faint gestures in this direction; both ultimately decided otherwise. Edmund Jr. became one of the nation's most prominent historians, best known for his studies of the Puritan past. Young Roberta's voracious intellectual curiosity led her down a broad and fascinatingly eclectic path from psychology to English literature and beyond. In 1933, after spending three consecutive summers at major academic centers—Stanford (1930), the Sorbonne (1931), and Heidelberg (1932)—she earned her BA from Vassar College.[8]

The written record of her intellectual independence dates back to 1936, when Roberta filed an MA thesis at Barnard College. Her major was psychology, but the thesis hovered on the borderlands of sociology and law. Bearing the title "One Approach to the Problem of Institutional Behavior of Delinquent Women," the monograph offered a passionate defense of translational research in the social sciences: the harnessing of scientific methodology for the solution of social problems. At its most fundamental level, the thesis delved into the debate over nature and nurture. Any attempt at reform, she argued, hinged on a scientific assessment of deviance, its sources, and its palliatives. Her work was confounded by the fact that definitions of delinquency were confusing and, at times, contradictory, the result of contested epistemological approaches. Given this state of affairs, Roberta proceeded to move beyond a limited investigation of delinquency and reform. Employing a New Jersey penitentiary as a case study, Roberta sought to dispel the shadow of doubt that had been cast over the scientific validity of the social sciences, in general, and its impact on criminology, in particular.

Her point of departure was Jerome Michael and Mortimer Adler's *Crime, Law, and Social Science* (1933), in which the two formidable scholars lashed out at the allegedly primitive nature of criminology's main intellectual founts: psychology and sociology. With the severity of hanging judges, Michael and Adler condemned the social sciences—and, by implication, criminology—to academic illegitimacy. There could be no science of criminology, they held, because neither psychology nor sociology qualified as empirical sciences. To be sure, the three disciplines had adopted quantitative methodologies and the trappings of empiricism, but it was a raw and crude empiricism, dominated by "an exclusive emphasis upon observation to the total neglect of the abstractions of analysis."[9] Lacking a theoretical framework to guide the collection of empirical data, these disciplines could not provide etiological insight. Despite a veneer of quantitative methodology, they remained primitively descriptive. In Michael and Adler's view, the claim to knowledge by quantitative methods was rendered suspect by loose data-gathering practices. "Most of the quantitative research . . . is not only insignificant; it is also unnecessary and pretentious."[10] Neither the mother disciplines nor the nascent field of criminology, therefore, provided "knowledge of either the deterrent or the reformative effects of any mode or variety of treatment."[11]

Roberta challenged this attack on the social sciences with observations of the nature of disciplinary knowledge. The history of scientific progress, she explained, was a history of trial and error. Scientific enterprises are neither immaculate conceptions nor carefully constructed, premeditated creations. Adler and Michael's critique, she contended, rested on an ahistorical if not dogmatic understanding of science. In their thinking, theories informing empirical work rise mysteriously out of nowhere. In Roberta's opposing view, cumulative evidence and theory were intimately intertwined.

The fundamental obstacle impeding the measurement of deviance, Roberta argued, was not a lack of theory. Rather, it was the ever-slippery nature of foundational definitions. In the case of criminology, for example, definitions of *deviant behavior* were the proverbial moving targets. Leaning on the natural sciences' stable universe of observable objects, Adler and Michael had nebulously defined *deviancy* as "behavior which is prohibited by the criminal code," their assumption being that social deviance was a stable concept.[12] In reality, Roberta explained, criminal codes and social norms differed over time and space. In a fluctuating social and political milieu that did not lend itself to stable definitions, criminal behavior in some settings could be seen as normative in others. In these circumstances, producing a coherent theory of deviancy became an almost insurmountable task.

As a case in point, Roberta focused on the high rate of recidivism among penitentiary inmates, their habitual relapse into criminal behavior. She found that recidivism did not result from the faulty premises of criminologists, but rather from a clash of expectations between those charged with monitoring inmates' behavior and those seeking their rehabilitation. Law enforcement officials defined *normative behavior* among penitentiary inmates in a manner that clashed with the objectives of clinical rehabilitation.

Roberta derived her empirical evidence from the lives of young female inmates in a New Jersey prison, where wardens dismissed certain pathological behaviors as irrelevant but reacted harshly and punitively toward other, more benign behaviors. The wardens' working definitions of *inmate violence* exemplified the rift separating standard penitentiary codes from professional paradigms. Prison records indicated that inmate violence against wardens was the most salient example of deviant behavior. Other manifestations of aggression, particularly violence among inmates, went mostly unrecorded, ignored by the wardens and matrons of the facility. "Slapping and fist-fights among the inmates" often served the greater purpose of keeping the peace because, "as one officer remarked, 'some of them deserved a good thrashing.'"[13]

The convoluted cultural codes of the 1930s offered another example of misrepresented deviance. A disapproving Roberta singled out, in particular, the manner in which institutional racism and rigid sexual norms criminalized the inner lives of inmates. Interracial homosexuality or even mere flirting across color lines—"playing colored girls"—ranked as a significantly more serious offense than intramural theft or violence. In fact, prison authorities did not even report what she considered to be the most obvious psychological predictors of recidivistic behavior. "Fearfulness . . . sullenness, suspiciousness, suggestibility, dependence on others, over-sensitiveness, depression"—the signs of psychological stress that, in her view, often led to recidivism—did not register among wardens because such manifestations did not disturb the peace. So long as such pathologies manifested themselves in a passive manner—sullen, submissive, or otherwise—prison officials did not report them.[14] "Since the psychiatrist and psychologist depend on the officers for observation of behavior, it is doubtful that . . . recessive behavior comes to their attention, unless pronounced enough to interfere with the routine" of the penitentiary.[15] Roberta speculated on a nexus of depression, victimization, and recurring delinquency among female inmates. Yet the disconnect between "those who diagnose and prescribe and those who effect treatment of the inmates" defeated formal efforts to rehabilitate prisoners.[16]

A tone of futility permeates the study. Roberta concluded that an unimaginative academic establishment and a criminal justice system riddled with bigotry and ignorance had conspired against any meaningful reform of rehabilitative practices. The text betrays a simmering disdain of pedestrian minds in both government and academia that would become a motif in her future studies. Roberta's disappointment was nevertheless tempered by her single-minded confidence in her major conclusion: institutional pathologies—in this case endemic delinquency—were the result of both structural and cognitive deficiencies. Delinquency was the cumulative result of psychological insecurities of individuals under duress and missed cues among their guardians. Lacking the fundamental conditions for a shift in paradigms, Roberta concluded that the phalanxes of small-minded gatekeepers would ignore the scientific road to reform, preferring, instead, to maintain a dysfunctional system until such time as it reached a state of crisis. It comes as no surprise, then, that Roberta discontinued her studies in psychology and the vocation of social reform, preferring to pursue some of her other intellectual passions.

Roberta the Literary Scholar

While working on her master's in psychology from Barnard in 1934, Roberta enrolled simultaneously at Columbia Law School. This exercise was short-lived. In 1936, at age twenty-four, she enrolled in the PhD program in English literature at Radcliffe. Roberta never publicly explained the reasons behind this abrupt change of course, though such broad interests were very much in character. As she made clear in her

MA thesis, for her no one discipline could ever explain the complexity of the human condition. Literature offered an alternative window into the human tragedy and complemented the insight she had gained from the social sciences.

Roberta's dissertation examined representations of Hamlet in Western art and literature. Based on previous work she had already published in scholarly journals, a precocious Roberta criticized contemporary scholarship's singular focus on deciphering the mind of the creator. Exploring the multitude of creative attempts to extract social meaning from classical texts was infinitely more compelling than tedious ruminations on Shakespeare's original artistic intentions. Roberta identified significant differences in the way Western artists and writers had interpreted Hamlet, thereby reflecting the shifting cultural landscape of European society and culture. A cultural artifact, she argued, was a moving target, shifting in shape and significance in accordance with the experiences and knowledge of its audience. Her fundamental premise was that shifts in culture and politics created a dialectical relationship between subject and object. Audiences constantly reinterpret and transform seemingly immutable cultural representations when they inadequately reflect new social or political conditions.

"There is a myth current about myths," Roberta wrote in the introduction, describing a misconception that "men tell the same stories . . . because human nature is eternally the same. . . . Again and again we use the same images, weave the same patterns. The task of the critic is to discover and point out these identities." Roberta rejected this, arguing that myths in general, and those represented in exemplary literary works in particular, functioned as cultural Rorschach blots. "It is false that these myths remain the same. They change as, in fact, human nature and human interests change."[17] The tragic figure of Hamlet represented a case in point. The manner in which Shakespeare's *Hamlet* had been interpreted over the ages, and in different cultural settings, offered a particularly "rich and spectacular" example of the way a cultural myth could evolve to fit the social and historical disposition of the interpreting society.[18]

Quoting T. S. Eliot, Roberta posited Hamlet as "the 'Mona Lisa' of literature," an image that had "fluctuated constantly according to the artistic and moral values of its audience." When viewed in particular national contexts, she asserted, the variations in Hamlet's representation—in both literary criticism and art—reflect "all sorts of personal and national frustrations and maladjustments."[19] To be sure, there was a conventional interpretation of Hamlet—"paralyzed by dreams . . . unstrung by the imposition of a task too great for his frail and sensitive nature," a figure who embodied all the "hesitations, the terror, the madness, the contradictions, the mystery of every human being." But at times, she insisted, the "ministrations of critics and artists" produced a Hamlet who was "quite the opposite, a heroic man of action, robust, well-balanced. Courtier, soldier, and scholar in one, he sweeps to his revenge."[20]

Scouring the presence of Hamlet in artistic representations and literary criticism in France, Germany, and Great Britain, Roberta produced an account of Hamlet's transformation from a character in a work of dramatic fiction to a reflection of cultural mood. From the Renaissance to her own day, Hamlet could appear either as a man of action or, conversely, as a reflection of crisis in Western societies during periods of intense pessimism. Writing in the shadow of World War II, Roberta observed that "our time has taken Shakespeare's hero as a most dramatic and deeply felt symbol of thought-killed action. . . . Only recently the collapse of France was explained by comparing the French leaders to Hamlets, whose capacity for action did not measure up to their intellectual schemes."[21]

The most intriguing part of the dissertation examined representations of Hamlet during the Renaissance. Here, she found confirmation of her long-held belief in the unity of theory and practice and the symbiosis of knowledge and action. Warmly endorsing the Renaissance's "contempt for sterile speculation," Roberta offered implicit praise for the "philosophic conception of the unity of thought and action."[22] Quoting Montaigne as if he were referring to contemporary events, Roberta listed the "three fundamental defects of human nature (also the three fundamental traits) . . . irresolution, presumption, and ignorance or weakness of reason."[23]

Roberta never completed her dissertation. The primary reason she abruptly abandoned this labor of love was the hostile reaction of Theodore Spencer, the distinguished Shakespearean scholar who served on her dissertation committee.[24] Spencer dismissed her work as both chronologically and thematically disjointed, and ultimately as sophomoric. The different sections, in his view, offered only "the most tenuous relation to the others; they are beads with only the wisp of a piece of string to thread them together." Her work, he wrote, belabored the obvious, at times becoming "amateurish." The selection of historical data points and artifacts for discussion was "highly arbitrary." Spencer declared that "in its present form, the thesis represents a series of tangents which fail to describe a circle, or even an ellipse."[25] Another anonymous member of the committee concurred, albeit in a more genteel fashion. "You have not altogether escaped a danger which attends the writing of *Geistesgeschichte*"—the political and social subtexts underscoring cultural manifestations at a specific time and place in history—"especially when it involves parallels between different arts—that is, isolating particular examples and making a generalized pattern therefrom, while neglecting other examples which do not harmonize with the pattern."[26]

In a series of anguished drafts of a note to another member of her thesis committee—perhaps never sent—Roberta despaired over Spencer's tongue-lashing. She admired Spencer for his scholarly accomplishments, as well as for the fact that he did not ensconce himself in the ivory tower.[27] She therefore turned to psychology, evoking "Mr. Freud" in her efforts to comprehend the vicious reaction of a mentor. "Mr. Spencer's attitude," she concluded, "recalls William James' history of the reception of a new idea. There are three stages. In the first stage, people say it is absurd. In the second stage they say it is true, but trivial, and certainly not original. . . . In the last stage, they say they've always held this view themselves. It will probably take another year before Mr. Spencer reaches the third stage with respect to my analysis."[28]

Was Spencer's critique valid or mean-spirited? Even though she dismissed his comments as fodder for psychoanalysis, Spencer had raised compelling points about the dissertation's structural coherence. In his own scholarship on *Hamlet,* Spencer argued that one could not understand the play without a firmly anchored comprehension of the historical circumstances of Shakespeare's times. *Hamlet,* he explained, was created during a period of great ruptures. In the sixteenth century, "each one of the interrelated orders—cosmological, political, and natural—which were the frame, the basic pattern, of all Elizabethan thinking, was being punctuated by a doubt. Copernicus had questioned the cosmological order, Machiavelli had questioned the political order, Montaigne had questioned the natural order. The consequences were enormous." These shifts affected Shakespeare's "emotional climate," which, in turn, produced the play's immortal representations of internal conflict, as Hamlet becomes aware of "the evil reality under the good appearance." Hamlet's realization that the kingdom was in the hands of an unworthy man, aided and abetted by the lust of his own flesh and blood, shatters "his picture of the world, the state, and the individual." The awareness of the "evil reality" lurking under "the good appearance" formed "the core of the greatness, the originality of *Hamlet.*"[29]

In a more personal article, written in the autumn of 1939, Spencer commented on the ruptured cosmological order of his times. His own ideological affiliations had been shattered when an unspeakable contemporary evil—previously hidden in appearances of good—revealed itself. The cataclysmic event was the signing of the Molotov-Ribbentrop Pact, the treaty of nonaggression between Nazi Germany and the Soviet Union, and the subsequent invasion of Poland. The pact "acted as a kind of deathblow to the belief—generally held by most intelligent young thinkers up to the time of the recent civil war in Spain—that what matters, if one is to be a human being, is the nature of the ideology in which one believes."[30] Spencer's reaction to this event was to turn away from the fallen gods and recognize that blind faith in "the pre-eminence of the mass had led to chaos." In its place, he advocated a "reawareness of the individual experience."[31]

Spencer argued that it was the responsibility of the literary scholar and teacher to illuminate such moments, "for we are the caretakers of vicarious experience; we have in our hands the nurture and development of imagination, without which we are prisoners in the dark."[32] Here, then, lay the crux of his dissatisfaction with Roberta's whirlwind tour of images of Shakespeare in Western society. She remained inattentive to historical, social, and political detail. In his appraisal, Roberta lacked the introspection to turn a laundry list of interpretations of *Hamlet* in art and literature into a coherent understanding of culture and politics in Western society.

The saving grace of this emotionally trying event was that Roberta published parts of her work in 1939 and 1941 as articles in the respectable journals *English Literary History* and *Philological Quarterly.*[33] The former is of particular interest, as it examined Roberta's fascination with Hamlet's disastrous solipsism. The article was an attempt to understand the Hamlet representation of the poet and literary scholar Ernest Hartley Coleridge (grandson of Samuel Taylor Coleridge). Strewn over multiple notes and marginalia for an 1813–1814 lecture series, Coleridge's drafts produced confusing and sometimes contradictory statements.

Coleridge accepted that Hamlet's enervation and paralysis, his endemic inability to act on any issue, had neutralized his will to avenge the death of his father. His interpretation of the causes of this paralysis, however, remained elusive. Was Shakespeare's *Hamlet* a thinly disguised diatribe against a certain type of effete intellectual, a person addicted to contemplation and disdainful of any form of involvement in the issues of "real" life? Coleridge had mused that Shakespeare may have produced *Hamlet* as a self-reflection, an attempt to articulate his own imbalance between attention paid to reality and to his inner thoughts. Roberta wondered whether *Hamlet* provided Coleridge with his own disguised self-portrait, the image of a young man of "enormous intellectual activity, and a consequent proportionate aversion to real action."[34]

She concluded that Coleridge had not defined Hamlet as an endemic condition of Western civilization; the character's indecisiveness was, rather, an abnormality. From Coleridge's thick and, at times, confusing drafts for the lecture series, she settled on an interpretation of Hamlet as an aberration, with Shakespeare wishing to show that "action is the chief end of existence—that no faculties of intellect, however brilliant, can be considered valuable, or indeed otherwise than as misfortunes, if they withdraw us from, or render us repugnant to action."[35] Hamlet, Roberta claimed, could not disentangle himself from the stranglehold of his inner beliefs until such time as the avalanche of external events brought him to his knees.

This promising entry into the world of literary scholarship was short-lived. Even though her dissertation lacked the clarity and conviction of the published articles, she rejected her advisers' criticisms. Buoyed by the angry grief of rejection that probably resonates with many struggling graduate students, she claimed a miscarriage of scholarly justice to which she would not bow. She declined the opportunity to revise and resubmit the manuscript.

Throughout her career, and in fields far removed from English literature, Roberta produced variations of the Hamlet theme: signs, signals, and symbols of reality were often obscured by the thick fog of inner conviction. A closed internal world would avoid obvious signs for action; internally driven convictions could misinterpret and reimagine cacophonous noise as ostensibly unambiguous signals. The imbalance between the real and imaginary world, the need to act even in ambiguous circumstances, would remain a central motif in her work long after this attempt to stake her claim in the world of literary scholarship.

The Young Albert

Albert was born in Manhattan in 1913. His father, a lawyer turned gramophone manufacturer, died during World War I, when Albert was four years old, leaving his mother to take care of four children on her own. His close friend and future professor of philosophy, Morton White, remembered Albert's family apartment in the west Seventies. Spacious but crowded, it housed his widowed mother and the motley extended family over which she presided: "a divorced oldest brother" and "a bachelor older brother who would later become a tycoon known as 'Wall Streeter Charlie Wohlstetter,' a divorced sister, and a spinster aunt who taught high school."[36]

The Depression years offered Albert a curious sense of liberty. "Because you couldn't get jobs anyway," he recalled, "you were really a kind of free spirit."[37] Albert abandoned himself, with delight, to expanding his intellectual horizons. His first love was music. He frequented the Metropolitan Opera House, courtesy of an uncle who was the house physician. He also immersed himself in studying calculus and mathematical logic. Given their precarious finances, Albert's family disapproved of him spinning his intellectual wheels. In White's recollection, they thought of him as "a sort of intellectual bum who should not be encouraged in his peregrinations."[38]

In the brief and carefully choreographed glimpses Albert provided of his past, he cautiously avoided digressions into his youthful politics. Although City College rippled with political activity during the Depression, Albert claimed not to have been drawn into the fray.[39] The great majority of City College students were children of immigrants who huddled between classes in factional alcoves that reflected the "fanatical ambience" and political schisms of the American Left.[40] Yet, by his account, "It wasn't until I was a graduate student that I had any political interest."[41]

Alfred Kazin, the great literary critic and interpreter of the New York Jewish experience, remembered differently. He had graduated from City College the year after Albert. According to his biographer, Kazin thought of Albert as an "outspoken radical" and a "campus leader," recalling a scene with "Albert Wohlstetter, then 'a radical program setter,' standing in the cafeteria surrounded by disciples, 'explaining things in an authoritative fashion to someone he clearly regarded as inferior.' "[42]

Albert's occlusion of his City College radicalism begs an explanation, or at least an educated guess. Presumably, he was uncomfortable with being tagged for posterity as a "New York Jewish intellectual." His associates at City College were the sons of Eastern European working-class Jews from the Lower East Side and the Brooklyn hinterlands; they huddled in the sweaty alcoves of City College, verbally bare-knuckling in both tone and tenor. Albert, by contrast, would later emphasize that he came from different, more genteel stock. His family's origins were Viennese, part of the city's German-Jewish aristocracy, patrons of high culture who felt uncomfortable in the company of the Lower East Side rabble. Judaism was an accident of birth of no great consequence; Albert never mentions it in his reminiscences. Had his father lived, and assuming more prosperous circumstances, Albert would have probably evaded the disputatious masses at City College. It may be partly for these reasons that Albert never cared to acknowledge his youthful convictions. City College defied the image he tried to present. Albert presented himself as the bearer of a consistent secular creed, as someone who had followed a straight political line, never once afflicted with radical epiphanies, either religious or ideological. The swirling world around him had changed, sometimes quite radically. He, on the other hand, had remained consistent.

Upon graduating from City College in 1934, at the age of twenty-one, Albert enrolled at Columbia Law School, apparently, like Roberta, seeking to appease his family. Bored and stifled by the plodding path to a law degree, he was quickly sidetracked back to the fields of inquiry in which he had long dabbled: music, mathematical logic—and the female sex. It was on one of his infrequent visits to the classroom that Albert met the woman who would become his life partner. "There was an extremely pretty girl there," he recalled, "and we were seated alphabetically. But I noticed that Morgan begins with 'm' and 'm' is really 'w' just upside down. So I moved there and sat next to her until we were acquainted."[43]

Courting Roberta represented a cultural shift of no small consequence. Morton White recollected that he and "Albert . . . had similar problems so far as our girls were concerned. We were both penniless Jewish New York scholars and were courting comfortable Gentile Vassar alumnae. . . . Neither Albert nor I, therefore, were exactly great catches for our girls. He was condemned for not having a job of any kind—whereas I ran into difficulties created by my parents on religious grounds."[44] Albert and Roberta would marry in 1939.

Albert abandoned law school, after a year, for a graduate program in mathematics, still at Columbia. He wrote his MA thesis under the supervision of philosopher of science Ernest Nagel and under the watchful eye of his friend, the philosopher and mathematical logician Willard Van Orman Quine.[45] While it is possible that Kazin's account of Albert's leftism at City College may be apocryphal, Albert definitely found politics, as well as romance, at Columbia. He became friends with militant philosopher Sidney Hook and found a mentor in Columbia art historian and Marxist intellectual Meyer Schapiro. Albert evoked his politicization in an oral history anecdote concerning Quine, who was as removed from the political storm engulfing the world in the late 1930s as Albert was involved in it. Strolling through Harvard Square at a conference on mathematical logic, Albert read aloud press reports to Quine "about the Spanish Civil War and he would take his pipe out of his mouth and say, "NO! Get Out!"[46] This withdrawn scientist given to abstract thought would become a die-hard conservative and an enemy of student radicalism in the 1960s.[47]

A glimpse into the worldview Albert and Roberta shared during the late 1930s appears in the couple's first collaboration, signed Roberta Morgan and Albert Wohlstetter in 1938. Published in the *Harvard Advocate,* a student journal (though a distinguished one), and prefaced with an acknowledgment of Meyer Schapiro's guidance, this voyage into the world of scholarly exposition was far removed in subject matter from their future field of glory.

"Observations on Prufrock," which grew out of Roberta's early literary studies, offered a political commentary on T. S. Eliot's "The Love Song of J. Alfred Prufrock." Roberta and Albert were fascinated—and mortified—by Eliot's rendition of the existential crisis of Prufrock, the quintessential decadent Western man, spiritually exhausted and paralyzed by an inability to reach a decision on the most trivial of matters. Prufrock is "etherized," struck immobile by an unwillingness to act forcefully for fear of disturbing his "universe," which amounts to nothing more than "a deadening succession of teas and cultures and polite leisure class formalism."[48] Encumbered by the sterile nature of his life, Prufrock lacks the will to change his destiny.

At a philosophical level, Roberta and Albert viewed Prufrock as a symbol of effete Western society. The character's existential anguish, they explained, had no drama or momentous significance. By Prufrock's own admission, he could not be compared with a Prince Hamlet; he, too, was paralyzed by indecision, but for very different reasons. Hamlet's indecision had been borne out of a momentous event and a dramatic quandary. Prufrock, by contrast, "does not delay in the performance of great deed," but instead anguishes over, and is paralyzed by, the most "banal" decision. "This ordinary, entirely conventional act he finds impossible!"[49]

Roberta and Albert implied that all human beings are in danger—as a result of nurture, rather than nature—of becoming a Prufrock, incapacitated by an aversion to bodily action and fatally attracted to spectatorship, soliloquies, and theoretical flights, even when confronted by the most urgent need to react. Albert and Roberta looked disapprovingly at some of their bookish colleagues, ensconced in ivory towers and shielded by self-infatuation and introspection from the concerns of the surrounding world. The meaning of "Hamlet's shade," Albert wrote some years later, was "that decision cannot be postponed indefinitely, that putting off the awful day frequently makes things still more awful; that we must commit ourselves."[50] They, by contrast, were involved scholars who raged against the world, both in the company they kept and in their early publications.

It was at this intersection that Albert and Roberta fell under the spell of Meyer Schapiro—"perhaps the most brilliant lecturer I have ever heard," Albert later remembered.[51] They hovered in his circle throughout their Columbia years, brushing shoulders with his other young followers, including the poet and novelist Delmore Schwartz. As his teaching assistant, Albert would "furiously take notes" while Schapiro gave his brilliant lectures with "machine gun delivery."[52]

Summarizing Schapiro's work in a few sentences is a dubious enterprise at best, as is any attempt to speculate on the degree to which he influenced his students. Schapiro viewed works of art as reflections of a distinct social and political context. Style reflects not only the aesthetics of a particular period. It also reflects the surrounding cultural, social, and political milieu. Art, he implied, was first and foremost embedded in the life and times of a unique historical moment.[53]

Meyer Schapiro's work confirmed Roberta's instincts on the differential interpretation of signals embedded in cultural artifacts. In tracing radical shifts in cultural representations, Schapiro argued that art forms change when "they are felt inadequate or uninspiring by a new wave of artists confronting new social conditions."[54] Even though artistic paradigm shifts were preceded by social riptides, they held no predestined form. All stylistic revolutions had an active ingredient of individual choice. The move from one artistic style to another would not occur without agency and choice. Cultural reactions to changing material and political circumstance did not have a predetermined trajectory. Shifts in representation could manifest themselves in a whole gamut of ways: the good, the bad, and the ugly. Material change emancipated individuals from contemporary constraints. The future, however, remained undetermined by impersonal forces of change. Individual choice mattered.

It is doubtful that Schapiro the ideologue was ever as compelling a figure for the Wohlstetters as Schapiro the art historian was. In fact, one wonders if Albert and Roberta were ever swayed by his politics. During the war years, they were witness to a fierce clash between Schapiro, their mentor, and Sidney Hook, reportedly a close friend of Albert.[55] Writing in 1943 under the pen name of David Merian in *Partisan Review,* the flagship of the era's anti-Stalinist Left, Schapiro chastised Hook for his about-face on the war, and his newfound appreciation of the Allied effort, in particular.[56] Despite Hitler's string of victories, Schapiro saw no compelling reason for the progressive forces of the Left to support the Allies. Stalin was merely Hitler's evil "identical twin," while "England and the United States are not fighting for democracy but for world domination. Their plans for the peace . . . imply the inevitable fascization of the world."[57]

Contrary to Hook, Schapiro argued that Hitler's sweeping victories had not annihilated the socialist cause. If anything, his conquests had "reawakened among the masses a revolutionary spirit." In fact, the "conquest of France radicalized the French people, revived their political will and prepared them for new struggles."[58] The grand plan to forge a common cause between the forces of socialism and capitalism for the purposes of defeating Hitler struck Schapiro as a dangerous proposition. "The lambs have nothing to gain from such seminars with the wolves, but the wolves have every reason to encourage such hopes."[59] In Schapiro's eyes, Hook had defected to the dark side of democratic liberalism.

Hook acknowledged that, following Hitler's spectacular successes, he had changed his previous condemnation of the war as an internal civil war among capitalist nations, best shunned by socialists. He dismissed as "plain foolishness," however, Schapiro's belief "that Roosevelt and Hitler are equally 'armed class opponents' . . . that it makes little difference which side wins the war, for capitalism will break down in any event; and that a revolutionary upsurge will inevitably carry the masses to socialist victory even if the Axis is triumphant."[60] For Hook, Hitler's victory spelled the annihilation of socialism, while an Allied victory would still leave space for the struggle for social justice. Jabbing Schapiro for his blindness to anything beyond his dogmatic Trotskyist cant, Hook raised Schapiro's alleged insensitivity to the persecution of Europe's Jews. "If I observe that Fascism leads to the liquidation of the Jews does it follow that I believe that the war is being fought *for* the safety of the Jews as so many anti-Semites claim?"[61]

Young Radicals

Reconstructing the Wohlstetters' politics during their graduate school days is not a simple exercise, as they consistently obfuscated what they likely considered to be youthful indiscretions. The only written document of their early political persuasion is an article written in 1939 by Albert and Morton White for *Partisan Review* offering a polemical contribution to the politically charged field of semantics. The two friends lashed out at semantic theorists and their popularizers for their politically pernicious understanding of language and society. In an essay guaranteed to evoke winces among future generations of linguistic cognoscenti, Albert and White declared that the semanticist proposition that language dictates reality was pure and utter nonsense.[62] They reserved particular scorn for Stuart Chase, author of *The Tyranny of Words*, and Jerome Frank, author of *The Folklore of Capitalism*, who had attributed all major conflicts—from Supreme Court battles to the American Civil War to the clouds of war bursting over Europe—to the abuse of language. Semanticists denied the material causes of contemporary conflicts, claiming that "endless political and economic difficulties in America have arisen and thrived on bad language." Once such "verbal monsters" become part of the public discourse, Chase professed, in prose that infuriated Albert, "no one knows how to get them out again, and they proceed to eat us out of house and home."[63]

Albert and White responded that the semanticists were trivializing materialism in order to avoid an ideological confrontation with existential issues. The concept of language dictating political reality was, they argued, scientifically unsound and politically pernicious. They heaped sarcasm on their adversaries, who, with the wave of a magic wand, had found a cure-all for the political ailments affecting the world. "Clarify the linguistic situation," they chided. "*This* is the revolutionary way out!"[64]

The two young firebrand philosophers turned their pens in particular on semanticist S. I. Hayakawa. From the pages of the liberal *New Republic,* Hayakawa had heaped derision on Sidney Hook as fatally "handicapped by the belief that a statement is either true or false." Bellowing back from the rival *Partisan Review,* Albert wrote that "Hayakawa would have us believe . . . that there are never circumstances where only two alternatives face" each other. He and White charged that the semanticists' critique of the anti-Stalinist Left was a politically motivated rejection of what nowadays we would call binary thinking: "the belief that a statement is either true or false." This carte blanche rejection of stable truths had little to do with philosophy or semantics. Instead, it was primarily a political question. The semanticists were merely seeking a linguistic legitimization for their unwillingness to evaluate empirically the stark political alternatives of the day. "Whether communism and fascism are the only alternatives facing us today, or whether there are many other alternatives, are matters which can be determined only by empirical investigation" of material conditions, rather than a "highhanded" appeal to theory.[65]

A variety of different scholars have identified Albert—and by association, Roberta, Morton White, and others—as a Trotskyist.[66] More precisely, Albert and White were associated with the post-Trotskyist Fieldite faction. White recalls being introduced to the Fieldites—known officially as the League for a Revolutionary Worker's Party—through Albert and their mutual friend Lawrence Kegan. In a dimly lit hovel off Union Square, White, Albert, and others would soak in the lectures of their leader, B. J. Field, and "his very lucid denunciations of Trotskyism."[67]

In his memoirs of Depression-era New York, Lionel Abel recalled that Albert and Morton White were among the ten or so individuals associated with this small faction claiming to adhere more strictly to Leninist principles than the Trotskyists, from whom they had broken and whom they now denounced as "utterly compromised." So harshly did they denigrate their former comrades, Abel remembered, that "when I first heard them talk about Trotskyists, I thought the party they were discussing was the Republican Party." In a manner implying both "derogation and respect," the art critic Harold Rosenberg referred to the Fieldites as "our political cubists," by which he meant the iconoclasts of the American Left.[68]

Within the closed universe of the two warring communist camps, the Trotskyists and Stalinists, the Fieldites came to reject both sides. The faction's founder, B. J. Field (born Max Gould), had been personally close to Trotsky in the early 1930s, and had headed the New York hotel and restaurant workers' union in 1934 on behalf of the (Trotskyist) Communist League of America before being expelled for lack of deference to the leadership. Field and a handful of comrades struck out on their own, claiming loyalty to the founding principles of Marxism, while framing the large issues of the day on their own terms. "All I can now remember about the League's doctrine is that . . . the Soviet Union had returned or was about to return to capitalism, whereas the Trotskyites held that Russia was at worst a degenerate workers' state," White explained in his autobiography. Unable to make itself heard amid the ideological cacophony, the League disbanded during the first months of World War II, leaving behind it the raucous but ever-diminishing ranks of American radicals.[69]

Albert and Roberta parted company with their leftist affinities sometime in the same period. The endless, amoeba-like splintering into warring factions, as well as the infatuation with argumentation rather than action among leftists of different persuasions, hastened their departure. In a veiled comment, presumably alluding to the intricacies of the American Left in the 1930s, Albert would later evoke André Gide's political interpretation of the labyrinth and the Minotaur. Gide had implied, in Albert's view, "that the reason people got lost in the Labyrinth and never returned was that they did not want to get out. The passages were full of fascination and heady odors; the food was excellent and the monster itself was beautiful." Eventually, Albert explained, the spell was broken with the realization "that the monster was quite witless," and that the meandering tour through the maze had been nothing more than an in-effectual mind game.[70] The world of New York's (mostly Jewish) radicals, caught up in the labyrinth of endlessly sterile theoretical one-upmanship, had lost its appeal.

The circumstances are obscure, but one can only surmise that they drifted along with most of the anti-Stalinist Left toward the center and, ultimately, to the right. In a 1985 interview, Albert avoided any reference to his politics of the era, but he did recall his horrified first reaction to Hiroshima and Nagasaki, convinced it was "very wrong to drop it on populations." Quoting Bertrand Russell, he remembered seeing it as an act of "cosmic impiety." It was Soviet actions of the early 1950s, he claimed, that precipitated a significant shift in his political orientation. He was "affected very much by Berlin, the fall of Czechoslovakia, and the invasion of Korea," all of which, he implied, convinced him of the du-plicitous and predatory nature of the Soviet empire.[71]

The journey from radicalism to the right began with an unremitting condemnation of Stalin as evil and depraved beyond redemption. After the war, many youthful anti-Stalinists like the Wohlstetters accom-plished a further leap by embracing the Marshall Plan as well as the Truman Doctrine and its combative, anti-Soviet stance. In his memoir of the era, fellow traveling philosopher William Barrett felt a need to "underline the irony in this situation"—something of an understate-ment. "We were Marxists and socialists, yet at this particular turn of the time, we were for measures that would stabilize the shaky capitalist economies of Western Europe; for if those economies were to collapse, the whole of Europe would slide into the grip of Stalin and the Soviet empire. We thought it preferable that the European peoples should have liberty under capitalism rather than slavery under Stalin."[72] If such left-ists criticized the United States, it was to charge that it had not acted swiftly enough to counteract the Soviet threat.

Stalin's death in 1953 hastened and broadened the general tilt in these circles toward a total rejection of the communist creed. These thinkers no longer presented Stalinism as a miscarriage of communist ideology by a single depraved individual, but rather as the inevitable re-sult of a corrupt Leninist doctrine and the Soviet system. Stalin's im-mediate heirs confirmed this position. Aside from a few intransigent anticapitalists, most intellectuals of the anti-Stalinist Left had reached a point of no return, permanently rejecting what they had come to consider the indiscretions of their youth.[73]

In the course of this ideological reconstruction, the anti-Stalinist Left developed an antipathy toward American liberalism, in particular its unwillingness to accept the existence of pure and unmitigated evil. Throughout the reign of Stalinist terror, as William Barrett observed, liberals found it "hard to believe in the reality of evil." Addicted to relativism, they regarded "evil as only relative ignorance or misunderstanding. Thus they found it hard to think of Stalin as an active and conscious agent of evil." Even when the realities of gulags, kangaroo courts, and mass murder could no longer be dismissed, liberals refused to draw a straight line between the internal Soviet regime and its international ambitions. Somehow, Barrett insisted, those of the liberal persuasion imagined that "the evil of a regime stopped at its own borders . . . a certain mentality of appeasement set in."[74]

Ideological epiphany was not, however, the only reason behind the Wohlstetters' political reconstruction. Roberta's disappointment with her dreams of achieving an academic vocation presumably distanced the couple from the bookish, liberal-leaning world of the academy. Roberta served briefly as a teaching assistant at the University of Southern California during the academic year 1937–1938, and had several teaching stints at Barnard College in the early 1940s.[75] As late as 1942, Roberta was still corresponding with her Radcliffe advisers on somehow completing her dissertation on her own terms, but to no avail. Dreams of an academic career receded even further as Albert followed Roberta in abandoning his quest for a PhD.

In the late war years, the Wohlstetters left New York. Following a brief pit stop in Washington, DC—something of a halfway house experience—they moved to Southern California in 1947. Roberta was thirty-five years old; Albert was thirty-four. By the time the Wohlstetters had settled in Santa Monica, they had accomplished a significant intellectual transformation. They had deradicalized and abandoned their affinities with the anti-Stalinist Left. They had also Americanized; their concerns were no longer aligned with any supranational political cause. Finally, they had abandoned the academic commons.

Their pathway to the West Coast was littered with scattered, unfulfilled requirements for their doctoral degrees. But in Southern California the Wohlstetters discovered stimulating alternatives to the university that were at once intellectually liberating and epistemologically confining. RAND offered a perfect place to complete their conversion experience. The politics and culture of the think tank provided a meaningful ideological alternative to these two individuals seeking a new cause following the abandonment of fallen gods.

2

Roberta Wohlstetter

The Uncertainties of Surprise

B Y 1947 ALBERT WOHLSTETTER—the argumentative "intellectual bum" devoted to cerebral meandering and political experimentation—had accomplished a major sea change. He and Roberta had moved to Santa Monica, California, and Albert had become a senior executive in a start-up housing construction company. Their changing fortunes came courtesy of Albert's doting brother, the entrepreneur Charles Wohlstetter. Albert's oral histories give short shrift to the war years, which Albert spent in graduate fellowships and then other jobs in the private and government sectors. Charlie had used his influence to procure a draft exemption for his politically unsettled, recently married sibling. According to a recent study by Robert Richardson, "Charles prevailed upon his friend, Rutgers economics professor and head of the newly formed Office of Production Management, Supplies, Priorities and Allocation Board . . . Arthur Burns, to appoint Albert to its economics research section."[1]

Charlie continued to look after his brother in the immediate postwar years. At Roberta's urging—she had become smitten with the Southern California lifestyle during a teaching stint at the University of Southern California in 1937–1938—the Wohlstetters moved to Santa Monica.[2] Charlie positioned Albert as vice president of manufacturing and construction for the Burbank-based production facility of General Panel Corporation (GPC), in which Charlie held a financial interest. Formed in 1942 to produce cutting-edge prefabricated housing primarily for war veterans, GPC was the collective brainchild of a group of architectural luminaries led by Walter Gropius, Konrad Wachsmann, and Richard Neutra. As fate would have it, Albert presided over the company's swift demise.

Histories of GPC offer numerous reasons for its misfortunes. GPC was unable to get its product on the market in time for an expansive government drive for veterans' housing in 1946–1947. A lack of investment and a dysfunctional managerial structure, divided between New York and California, plagued the company from its inception. GPC's product was too expensive, while its production line was bogged down by fastidious changes constantly initiated by the inventor of the line, "mad genius" Konrad Wachsmann.[3]

"I was always a modern architecture buff and here I was meeting Marcel Breuer, Le Corbusier, and Neutra, and all of these great architects, many of whom did designs using this modular system," Albert recalled. The daily grind of production, however, offered none of this glamour. By 1948, when Albert took over as president and general manager in a last-ditch effort to avoid bankruptcy, the company had produced a mere fifteen houses. In 1951 the company went into liquidation after manufacturing no more than two hundred of the tens of thousands of planned units. Albert placed the blame for the company's misfortunes firmly on others' shoulders. He was the altruistic and "quixotic character" intent on saving the company from the clutches of Wachsmann, an "idiot savant" whose brilliant ideas for prefabricated housing ensnared the enterprise in constant flights from market realties.[4]

Roberta delivered Albert from this dismal situation. While Albert was battling windmills at GPC, Roberta was raising their daughter, Joan, and working part time as a book reviewer at the still new and exciting RAND Corporation, an Air Force–funded think tank conveniently based in Santa Monica. Following a brief hiatus caused by RAND's budgetary constraints, Roberta rejoined RAND to work on the top secret study "Warning of Target Populations in Air War," known in RAND argot as WARBO. Roberta's work on the project had her attempting to divine possible civilian reactions to an American attack on Soviet cities by exploring reactions to the strategic bombing campaign against Nazi Germany.[5]

It was *her* job at RAND that would shape their collective future. In 1951, as GPC lurched toward liquidation, Albert proposed a return to academia, back east, but Roberta was determined to stay in California. In

Albert's recollection, "Roberta got Charlie Hitch, who headed the economics division [at RAND] to ask me to lunch to see if he could persuade
me to at least do some consulting." That year, at the age of thirty-eight,
Albert began working at RAND as a senior consultant.[6] Roberta had
rescued the Wohlstetters from expulsion from their Southern California
paradise, while, almost as an afterthought, paving their way into the
world of Cold War strategic thought.

The RAND Corporation

The story of RAND is by now well known. Created in the immediate aftermath of World War II and deriving its name from the acronym for
"research and development," RAND initially had ties to the Douglas Aircraft Company. Even after becoming nominally independent in 1948,
RAND remained intimately linked to military funders. The corporation's
original vocation was to supply the Air Force and its Strategic Air Command with "scientific planning" for national defense in the nuclear age.
With this mandate, RAND naturally brought together the type of people
who could produce research related to high-tech military ordnance,
including, but not limited to, nuclear fission. For the most part, these
were applied mathematicians and physicists.[7]

RAND's ambitious founders, however, aspired to grander goals than
establishing a group of technicians. The realization that nuclear weapons
cast a pall over every facet of modern life encouraged a significant expansion of RAND's intellectual horizons. Its unofficial mission became,
in historian David Hounshell's encapsulation, "nothing short of the
salvation of the human race."[8] First in Washington, DC, and then in Santa
Monica, RAND's founders added an impressive array of social scientists
and economists to its roster of physicists and mathematicians, bringing
the total staff to some two hundred researchers by 1949.[9]

RAND's capacious research agenda was an attempt to bypass narrow
technocracies and the pedestrian approaches they applied to the nation's
major domestic and foreign trials. The institution's decentralized style
encouraged intellectual pluralism and an interdisciplinary inquisitiveness toward addressing the multifaceted challenges facing the nation. A
major attraction to researchers was RAND's funders' willingness to let
them pursue almost any topic, as long as they could demonstrate even
a tangential relationship to major domestic or international security

issues. The faculty—some of whom were on leave from universities, others recently demobilized young PhDs—discovered at RAND a type of intellectual freedom not found in universities. Generous government grants and a research environment ostensibly free of anachronistic academic divisions produced a feverish culture of scholarly roaming that contrasted with the incapacitating rivalries of the research university.

Free of the hindrances of departmental silos, RAND's researchers could engage in more expansive research projects than could their university-bound colleagues.[10] University of Chicago sociologist Morris Janowitz—one of the itinerant scholars who would periodically shuffle between the ivory tower and the think tank—considered that "nothing short of spectacular revolutionary development" would have allowed the calcified research university to achieve a similar level of inquisitiveness.[11]

Intellectual liberation at RAND had its limitations, however. Government funders never imposed any overt restrictions on research agendas, but RAND's researchers were still the product of an obvious process of self-selection. Only mainstream thinkers—card-carrying members of what Arthur Schlesinger memorably described as the Vital Center—found their way into RAND. Beneath the celebration of pluralism lay a monolithic value system, barely concealed. Philip Green, a contemporary critic remarked that RAND was predicated on two axiomatic propositions: "that vulnerability equals provocation to an 'enemy' and that the Soviet Union and the U.S. are . . . engaged in an undeclared war, with Western Europe as one of the stakes to be defended at all costs."[12] Given the source of its funding, and the political climate of the immediate postwar years, RAND's researchers never questioned these undergirding assumptions of the Cold War. Instead, they accepted them as self-evident truths derived from prevalent political intuitions about the enemy.

To a certain degree, the sheer diversity of disciplinary viewpoints within the system mitigated RAND's underexamined value system. Yet a sameness overshadowed the diversity. Among the social scientists, for example, an orthodox strain of economics set the tone. Whether they analyzed organized crime, patterns of racism in the United States, government welfare policies, or trends in global politics, a common denominator among RAND's scholars was a prevailing antipathy to monopolies—economic, political, or ideological. Pluralism and a minimalist role for government offered a panacea for resolving economic, social, and international dilemmas. Yet the definition of pluralism espoused at RAND was a narrow and rigid one, exclusively reflecting the pride and prejudices of the nation's ruling class. Philip Green observed that RAND's board of governors resembled "a burlesque of [C. Wright] Mills' notion of the 'power elite,' not merely in who is included . . . but in who is excluded." RAND's board was staffed by public- and private-sector titans associated in one form or another with defense spending.[13]

This is the context in which Roberta, an interdisciplinary humanist and social scientist, joined RAND's ranks. Roberta's modest initial role was to read voraciously and produce succinct book reviews for the scholars of the think tank's social science division. The reviews she wrote reveal an opinionated person who maintained a measure of distance from and disdain for realism in American politics. In her survey of John McDonald's *Strategy in Poker, Business, and War* (1950), Roberta barely contained her scorn—ironically, given Philip Green's comment above—for "the group C. Wright Mills refers to as 'sophisticated conservatives,'" who projected the "Machiavellianism of the card table, aggression, cold calculation of enemies and allies, and deception" onto international affairs and the market place. A sardonic Roberta snorted at this clichéd "anti-romantic Brechtian toughness," where "poker, business, and war are all on the same level." The worldview of politics and strategy as a hard-nosed poker game struck her as "dubious, pessimistic," a shallow version "of eighteenth-century Hobbesian psychology rather than an empirical characterization of group behavior under all conditions and in all cultures."[14]

By the early 1950s, Roberta had moved beyond this support role, bringing her analytical skills to bear upon one of RAND's most significant early projects. The means by which Roberta leaped from junior apprentice to full-fledged researcher remain unclear. Her promotion paid off when, in the mid-1950s, she produced her seminal analysis of surprise attack at Pearl Harbor, by all accounts a definitive work of twentieth-century American military history. The study began as an internal RAND document based on unclassified documents drawn from the congressional record. Buoyed by its favorable reception within RAND, Roberta received permission to publish it, and she signed a book contract with Stanford University Press.[15]

To publish, however, Roberta first had to usher the book through a Kafkaesque security gauntlet, beginning with a laborious editing process to purge the text of potential security breaches, already a meaningless task for a book based on unclassified sources. Then, after she submitted a clean manuscript to Stanford, RAND received notification that the study had been classified and would be withdrawn from publication. Neither Roberta nor RAND were given any explanation—"they did not have a high enough clearance to be told." The Pentagon refused Roberta permission to revise the manuscript, claiming that the entire text was "contaminated." By September 1960, the Pentagon ordered all copies of the manuscript destroyed and placed the printer's copy in a secured vault. "Apparently not only the public, the Army, the Navy, and the government, but even the Air Force are not permitted to read it," a frustrated Roberta recounted.[16]

Much to her relief, the government eventually relented. Under the conditions of release, the manuscript could contain no mention of RAND or government sponsorship and was redacted of any overt comment on lessons drawn from Pearl Harbor for defense in the nuclear age. Writing to an anonymous Pentagon official, Roberta declared that her revised manuscript contained "*no reference to current or future intelligence operations. Pearl Harbor is compared to a few other cases of past military surprises and there is no reference to the essential relevance of the surprise attack to thermonuclear war* (changed to 'problems today')."[17]

Surprise at Pearl Harbor

Roberta's manuscript had presumably alarmed military censors because she had revealed an uncomfortable truth they wanted kept from public view, though it was hiding in plain sight. Contrary to received wisdom, Roberta's study of Pearl Harbor rejected interpretations of the debacle as the result either of incompetence or of pernicious motives. Mainstream assessments of the attack concluded that if errors borne out of stupidity or dereliction of duty had been rectified, the nation might have avoided Pearl Harbor. Roberta, by contrast, maintained that the singular focus on the failure of the human element deflected attention from the larger issue. "There were of course many errors, and some unintelligent ones, both in Washington and in the theater." However, a dispassionate examination suggested "the disaster occurred in spite of the many men . . . who were above the ordinary in ability and dedication."[18] The source of anxiety among her censors had to do with the doubt she cast over contemporary warning systems in general. "It can happen again," she wrote, "if we rely on the simple-minded belief that an intelligent decision-maker" could supersede the type of cognitive pathologies that had produced that day of infamy.[19] "Today, more than in 1941, preparations for a surprise attack can be well concealed." As such, no nation could rely on its intelligence services for security and protection against surprise attacks.[20]

"The main concept that Mrs. Wohlstetter brings to bear on these events," Warner Schilling noted in his perceptive review of the book, is that "the pictures of the world that government officials build from intelligence . . . are not so much a matter of the 'facts' their sources make available as they are a function of the 'theories' about politics already in their minds which guide both their recognition and their interpretation of said 'facts.' "[21] Displaying an almost postmodern flair, she had deflected attention away from the quality of the message—intelligence data available prior to the attack—to the mode of its reception.

It was only from the illusory vantage point of hindsight, Roberta wrote, that the surprise attack on Pearl Harbor appeared to be an anomalous event. Even though her research was based on unclassified documents, Roberta pasted together a detailed picture of precise, albeit fragmentary flows of intelligence on the eve of the attack. Disconnected slivers of evidence on Japanese intentions abounded. American intelligence services had broken the Japanese diplomatic code (known as "Magic"), and enjoyed almost unrestricted access to diplomatic traffic between Tokyo and major Japanese embassies. The U.S. ambassador in Tokyo offered prescient assessments and intelligence information, including at least one specific warning—albeit from a less than compelling source—on the impending attack in Pearl Harbor. Navy signal intelligence units pieced together important insights on Japanese naval intentions. Foreign intelligence agencies provided fragments of information, as did the many unclassified mass media reports emanating from Japan. Even the Japanese press, "rife with explicit signals of aggressive intent," was proclaiming "the Japanese government's determination to pursue its program of expansion into Southeast Asia."[22] With Magic deciphered, U.S. authorities were fully apprised of the November cutoff dates for negotiations, as well as of the "entire substance of the Japanese demands and concessions. All that we lacked was the date . . . , a precise list of targets, and—most important—an ability to estimate correctly Japanese desperation and daring."[23] The United States, Roberta argued, enjoyed the luxury of unprecedented, detailed information on enemy designs.

Given this wealth of data, the complete surprise at Pearl Harbor struck many commentators as difficult to believe, if not outright suspicious. Roberta summarily dismissed rumors of a warmongering conspiracy to delete crucial intelligence information in order to draw the United States into a then-unpopular war. She rejected, as well, attempts to impugn both military and civilian authorities for dereliction of duty. Instead, she offered a cogent explanation for the surprise attack as the result of an unmanageable—and chronic—confluence of technical, managerial, and cognitive failings, a perfect storm that would surely happen again.

Roberta cautioned that historical inquests were conducted from the vantage point of retrospection, where circumstances and outcomes were deceivingly clear. When dissected after the fact, the distinction between pertinent signals and distracting "noise"—the term she used to describe competing and contradictory information—appears to be misleadingly obvious; hindsight consistently and inevitably distorts retrospective judgment and identifies clarity where it never existed. At the time, however, the many relevant signals and their significance were imbedded in a "buzzing and blooming confusion" of contradictory data that in retrospect—and only after the fact—turned out to be irrelevant or actually deceptive.[24]

At Pearl Harbor, the nuisance factor of intelligence "noise" was somewhat more complex than "the natural clatter of useless information and competing signals" accompanying any type of intelligence enterprise.[25] In the heat of battle, Roberta's admiring disciples explained, " 'noise' has always prevailed over 'signals,' inertia over openness, and wishful thinking over realism."[26] Deception—self-induced or deliberately spread by the enemy—was almost inevitable; "there is actually *no* difference between 'signals' and 'noise'—except in retrospect," Edward Luttwak claimed in his Roberta-inspired analysis of another intelligence misreading of surprise attacks. In the heat of battle, true and false data were indistinguishable; "in a deeper sense, all strategic warning data is 'noise,' " as all information is both confusing and illuminating at the same time.[27]

Roberta identified a host of other factors contributing to this instance of monumental strategic surprise. Multiple false alarms preceded the actual attack on Pearl Harbor, which, for obvious human reasons, lowered the threshold of alertness within the government and military on the eve of the event. This lull in attentiveness in the Pacific was further exacerbated as Washington's focus was elsewhere. "The most important single thing to note about our government in the last weeks before Pearl Harbor," Roberta observed, "is the enormous absorption of almost everyone in the Atlantic and European battle areas." The lack of attention paid to Japanese actions was not, then, due to "deliberate deafness or conspiratorial silence," but resulted, rather, from an overwhelming concern with developments in Europe. "Japanese aggression was a constant threat, of course, demanding careful diplomatic attention to prevent war on two fronts; but compared to Germany's war machine, the menace of Japan seemed more remote and manageable."[28]

Heuristic American conceptual frameworks about enemy objectives and capabilities contributed to the confusion. Most U.S. officials agreed with Winston Churchill that Japan would not confront the Pacific powers prior to the weakening of Allied military might. Though some feared an attack on American bases in the Philippines, no one expected a Japanese attack on the United States so long as the Japanese were unable to annihilate Britain's Pacific bases.[29] Despite some misgivings concerning the clustering of an entire fleet in close quarters, the U.S. Pacific Fleet seemed to be a highly improbable target for a Japanese attack. According to standard American military doctrine, the fleet's powerful presence in Pearl Harbor was the ultimate deterrent. For the Japanese, however, the array of sitting ducks spread across the harbor offered an irresistible target. In the eyes of Japanese strategists, one well-planned mission would incapacitate America's major military apparatus in the Pacific while dealing a tremendous blow to American morale and prestige.

Yet for all its military brilliance, Roberta claimed, the Japanese decision to attack had been reached with no meaningful debate on its political ramification. The evidence that she had at her disposal indicated that "the Japanese decision to go to war with the United States was not clearly faced, but rather accepted as the lesser of two evils."[30] Japanese officials had acted out of political compromise and without any meaningful analysis of alternatives. Strategic considerations appeared to take a backseat to wishful political thinking. Had the Japanese truly thought through the ramifications of the Pearl Harbor attack, they would surely have anticipated its dire results. "It gives one pause to contemplate how slightly the future acted as a curb," Roberta ruminated. "With all the necessary economic and military data to predict their own defeat, the Japanese never seriously considered restraint in the pursuit of territorial expansion, with which they identified 'national honor.'"[31]

While American decision makers may have been somewhat unimaginative in forecasting the moves of their Asian enemy, the Japanese were spectacularly flippant in their assessments of American reactions to the attack. "Most unreal was their assumption that the United States, with ten times the military potential and a reputation for waging war until unconditional victory, would . . . simply accept the annihilation of a considerable part of its air and naval forces and the whole of its power in the Far East."[32] Here, then, lay one of Roberta's most important insights. Both American defenders and Japanese aggressors had allowed their preferred reaction of the enemy to inform their military strategy; both the Americans and the Japanese were quite unwilling to entertain the idea that their respective enemies would opt for strategies that differed from their own constructions. They therefore failed to prepare for contingencies.

The most meaningful insight from Pearl Harbor, Roberta concluded, was that fundamental lacunae in the human psyche, rather than individual lapses in judgment, were responsible for the surprise. Inherent cognitive flaws and self-deceptions were the most formidable enemies of all. Having decided beforehand that the Japanese would most probably carry out their major naval offensive elsewhere, the Americans either misinterpreted or ignored information to the contrary. Warnings that conflicted with well-entrenched beliefs, Roberta explained, would always be ambiguous, if not deceptive, even without elaborate deception on the part of an enemy.

Even when warning signals were strong and unambiguous, the Pearl Harbor debacle proved they could still be garbled when interpreted through the prism of preconceptions. General Douglas MacArthur received word that Pearl Harbor had been attacked about ten hours before Japanese forces struck and destroyed the entire air force under his command in the Philippines.[33] American forces in the Philippines had still not expected a second wave to hit them, and as such decided against any significant defensive maneuver. The signals were clear, but MacArthur ignored them because they clashed with American presumptions concerning the flight zones of Japan's fighter aircrafts and the military skill of the Japanese adversary. "There is a difference, then," Roberta insisted, "between having a signal available somewhere in the heap of irrelevancies, and perceiving it as a warning," Imbued with the lessons of *Hamlet* she had formulated at Radcliffe, she added that "there is also a difference between perceiving it as a warning, and acting or getting action on it."[34]

As for reforms in intelligence sharing and national security assessment, Roberta placed only perfunctory faith in reorganization. Given the fundamental perceptual barriers that kept analysts from anticipating Pearl Harbor, no structural reform could eliminate the danger of further strategic surprises. Pearl Harbor was neither an "isolated catastrophe" nor the result of a particular instance of "negligence, or stupidity, or treachery." Quite the contrary: "honest, dedicated, and intelligent men" had failed to discern enemy intentions because of chronic failures "conditions of human perception" and "uncertainties so basic that they are not likely to be eliminated, though they might be reduced."[35]

Human nature, Roberta explained, was ill equipped to deal with departures from well-entrenched preconceptions. The clients of any intelligence apparatus tend to react on a scale between extreme reluctance and indolence when confronted with information that conflicts with existing arrangements of institutional resources, attention, and commitment. "A warning signal," she pointed out, "is not likely to be heard if its occurrence is regarded as so improbable that no one is listening."[36]

The inherent difficulty of grasping how the future might differ from the past, in addition to the very human tendency to confuse expectations with wishful thinking, would always trump intelligence warnings. At Pearl Harbor, an entrenched belief that geography endowed the United States with immunity from surprise attacks blunted the resonance of all conflicting information. "Human attention is directed by beliefs as to what is likely to occur, and one cannot always listen for the right sound," she observed.[37] As Stephen Chan explains, in his analysis of Roberta's insights, radical departures from a paradigm, or challenges to ingrained "routines or interests" that entail the "reallocation of decision makers'

Roberta Morgan Wohlstetter, 1963. *Photograph by Bruce H. Cox. Originally published in "Woman of the Year: Trouble Shooter Aims High," January 15, 1964, Los Angeles Times.*

time, resources, and attention," invariably invoke extreme resistance rather than sudden awakening.[38]

Recurring Pearl Harbors

Roberta's analysis was by no means limited in time and space to Pearl Harbor. The past, she implied, was of little use if it did not provide a glimpse of the future. Her writing suggests little patience with interpretations of past events as sui generis. The significance of Pearl Harbor was too great to be left to pedantic documentarians. She was pursuing a usable past, the representation of a historical incident as an explanatory device for comprehending contemporary reality and future challenges.

The primary, practical lesson of Roberta's Pearl Harbor, therefore, was that the United States should invest in rapid and aggressive means for responding to surprise attacks. Given the fundamental human incapacity to anticipate the unfamiliar, Pearl Harbor was bound to happen again. She offered the example of Harvey DeWeerd's RAND study on strategic surprise in the Korean War as the ultimate proof of her prediction that no amount of structural reform would preclude a repeat occurrence.[39]

Released for public distribution at about the same time as Roberta's study, this RAND report documented in painful, familiar detail a rerun of American self-deception at crucial junctures of the Korean War. Despite mechanisms for intelligence sharing and analysis, and irrespective of overwhelming intelligence on the likelihood of a North Korean invasion, both the intelligence community and the National Security Council had consistently misread the signals. In a moment of supreme candor, General Douglas MacArthur explained that the unanticipated North Korean invasion was not the result of conflicting or weak intelligence. "No man or group of men could predict the North Korean attack 'anymore than you could predict such an attack as took place at Pearl Harbor.'"[40] The misinterpretation of relevant intelligence was "preconditioned by the official belief that any war in the 1950 time period would be an all-out affair involving the Soviet Union," and that, at the very most, South Korea would suffer a North Korean inspired campaign of political subversion.[41]

China's intervention in the Korean War presented yet another depressingly familiar example of the overwhelming power of preconception over reality. Civilian and military authorities, including MacArthur (who should have known better, given his experiences in World War II), disregarded the "convincing picture" of Chinese intentions and capabilities.[42] Secretary of State Dean Acheson explained that despite intelligence information to the contrary, the United States believed that there would be no Chinese intervention in the war. According to American intelligence assessments, the massive commitment of troops to such an action was unlikely, owing to Chinese fears of destabilizing its border areas. China had no real interest in such a conflict, and, barring a decision by the Soviet Union to "precipitate a global war, Chinese intervention in Korea was 'improbable.'"[43] Unlike Pearl Harbor, there were no conflicting intelligence reports. According to MacArthur, "we refused to believe what our intelligence told us was in fact happening because it was at variance with the prevailing climate of opinion in Washington and Tokyo."[44]

As far as the postwar years were concerned, Roberta predicted that any future surprise attack would have far more lethal consequences than Pearl Harbor, the Korean War, or any other attack from the annals of conventional warfare. "There have been many attempts in recent years to cheer us with the thought that the H-bomb has so outmoded general war" that it had rendered the study of surprise attacks irrelevant.

Contrary to such self-deluding expectations, she noted, the perceived benefits of surprise "have increased enormously and the penalties for losing the initiative in an all-out war have grown correspondingly."[45]

Without mentioning the Soviet Union by name, though in an apparent violation of the censorship guidelines she had accepted, Roberta explained that a contemporary aggressor did not have to hide massive troop maneuvers in order to achieve surprise. "An all-out thermonuclear attack on a Western power" would probably be launched by air, and vital, precious time "would surely have to pass before that power's allies could understand the nature of the event and take appropriate action."[46] The delivery of a single projectile would far surpass the type of limited strategic damage associated with past, pre-nuclear surprise attacks. One stealthy surprise blow, launched from a great distance with little involvement of auxiliary troops, might annihilate an adversary's entire war-making capabilities.

Surprise attacks offered an unambiguous advantage to the aggressor. "In spite of the vast increase in expenditures for collecting and analyzing intelligence data . . . the balance of advantage seems clearly to have shifted since Pearl Harbor in favor of a surprise attacker."[47]

For all of the reasons enumerated in her Pearl Harbor study—the distraction of conflicting signals, interservice rivalries, and human fallibility—Roberta asserted that no society seeking protection from aggressive predators could expect impenetrable security or infallible knowledge of enemy intentions.[48] "At the time of Pearl Harbor, the circumstances of collection in the sense of access to a huge variety of data were . . . ideal," she argued. "If our intelligence system and all our other channels of information failed to produce an accurate image of Japanese intentions and capabilities, it was not for want of the relevant materials."[49]

Roberta urged her readers to comprehend the "one major practical lesson" that emerged from her autopsy of Pearl Harbor. "Since we cannot rely on strategic warning," she warned, "our defenses . . . must be designed to function without it."[50] Instead of the futile search for invulnerability and safety through intelligence, Roberta advocated using imaginative strategies to protect against the unimaginable, although she offered no details. Surprise was inevitable, Roberta maintained, even under the best of circumstances, when policy makers enjoyed picture-perfect intelligence. "We have to accept the fact of uncertainty and learn to live with it. No magic, in code or otherwise, will provide certainty."[51]

Orthodoxy and Revisionism

Roberta's influential book spurred a cottage industry of inquests into issues of strategic surprise. Historical studies of the successful German campaigns during World War II—the German surprise attack on Norway, Operation Barbarossa, and more—reached conclusions that reflected Roberta's analysis.[52] She was, in many ways, the inspiration for an entire paradigm of strategic studies, sometimes dismissed by its disparagers as the "orthodox school" of surprise attacks.[53] Aficionados of this school offered hope for circumventing cognitive obstacles by minimizing the human hand in intelligence operations. Significant aspects of analysis, they explained, could be transferred to computers where mathematical probabilities, rather than subjectivity or intuition, would offer an important corrective to intelligence assessments.

Even though they accepted Roberta's discouraging insights on human cognition, proponents of the orthodox school did not dismiss reforms of the human and organizational elements. They proposed a solid middle ground between the Byzantine compartmentalization of intelligence services that had prevailed on the eve of Pearl Harbor and a converse monopolistic intelligence structure. Roberta's study had demonstrated the shortcomings of compartmentalized intelligence operations. Centralization, however, was equally daunting as it produced unchallenged appraisals of enemy intents and designs. The Israeli intelligence apparatus on the eve of the Yom Kippur War offered a prime example of the failure of monopoly.[54]

Not everyone accepted Roberta's thesis on intelligence and surprise.[55] Critics questioned her premise of Pearl Harbor as the archetype for surprise attacks. Ariel Levite's revisionist study of the December 7 attack suggests that, contrary to Roberta's assertion, Pearl Harbor did not even qualify as an example of strategic surprise. Pearl Harbor was not the result of faulty analysis but, instead, was the quintessential example of a lack of intelligence data. Brushing aside Roberta's examples of incriminating data that accumulated on the tables of intelligence analysts, Levite argued that the United States had been unprepared for, rather than surprised by, Pearl Harbor. Orthodox studies of surprise, including

Roberta's work, had erroneously lumped together unpreparedness, a function of a lack of pertinent information, with the notion of surprise, the misreading of available information pointing toward the obvious existence of a clear and present danger. In the case of Pearl Harbor, Levite claimed, Roberta had grossly overstated the case for surprise. Had she moved beyond her very limited sources, she would have discovered that pivotal points of her argumentation fell apart.

Levite and others questioned Roberta's claim that on the eve of the attack the United States had squandered a veritable treasure trove of warning signals on Japan's intentions. He offered evidence that the United States had not actually deciphered any key messages on an imminent attack prior to the actual Japanese onslaught. Magic had revealed major concepts of Japan's negotiating strategy, but it offered no "information of operational value on the Japanese armed forces."[56] Magic's information on diplomatic maneuvering was partial at best. The timetable for severing diplomatic relations passed through Magic only a couple of hours before the actual attack on Pearl Harbor. "Even the last, and probably also the most revealing Magic message . . . indicated no more than that the Japanese were planning a formal suspension of the negotiations with the United States for December 7, 1941."[57]

In contrast to its partial success in deciphering diplomatic traffic, the United States had made only modest dents in military channels of information. A breakthrough in cracking Japanese naval codes occurred about a week *after* Pearl Harbor. The paucity of information from signal intelligence was compounded by weak human intelligence. By his own admission, the senior American emissary in Tokyo, Joseph Grew, had no access whatsoever to privileged sources. The informant who had identified Pearl Harbor target to Ambassador Grew turned out to be an imaginative cook in the staff at the Peruvian embassy in Tokyo. Though accidentally prescient in retrospect, Grew's comments, by his own admission, were merely ruminations unsupported by evidence.

In other words, Levite showed, Pearl Harbor was the opposite of what Roberta thought: it was "essentially a failure of *collection*, not of analysis."[58] A series of financial, political, and administrative obstacles had hampered efforts to collect data on Japanese intentions. These included Victorian sensibilities concerning the morality of eavesdropping, a lag in the deciphering techniques of encoded messages, and an economically driven decision to focus intelligence efforts on the European front. The snippets of intelligence pointing toward Pearl Harbor were fragmentary, unreliable, and scattered. Pearl Harbor was, therefore, an extraordinarily poor example of the ineffectiveness of intelligence warnings in staving off surprise attacks. "The number of warnings received by the United States prior to December 7, 1941, keeps on growing and like a fine wine, so does their quality seem to improve" in the hands of historians and policy makers driven by ulterior motives.[59]

Levite and others rejected Roberta's policy recommendations, as well. Her grim prognosis posited surprise attacks as inevitable unless the price for such attacks was raised to intolerable levels. Despite the censorship that had truncated her study, she implicitly, but quite clearly, argued for a significant buildup in military might as the only realistic tool to dissuade an enemy from a surprise attack. And yet, Levite contended, "undue pessimism is no less dangerous as a policy guide than unwarranted optimism. While the latter inspires over-confidence and complacency, the former breeds either fatalism and apathy or worst-case analysis and overreaction—neither of which is conducive to national and international security."[60]

As for the lessons of history accompanying Roberta's study, her own analysis partially undermined her advocacy of deterrence and retaliatory forces as the best possible mechanism for discouraging surprise attacks. The presence of the Pacific fleet in Hawaii was supposed to have been a deterrent against Japanese aggression. The Japanese, by contrast, interpreted the presence of the fleet as a clear and present danger to its existential ambitions, a threat that demanded an immediate response. One person's deterrent is another person's target.

Critics pointed out that in contrast to Roberta's impeccable analysis of the events surrounding surprise at Pearl Harbor, her presentation of Pearl Harbor look-alikes was surprisingly shallow. In fact, Roberta's sweeping prediction of continuing vulnerability to surprise attacks was based on a singular incident in Korea. Aside from a glancing footnote at the Korean War, she did not muster any other analysis of surprise attacks to bolster her far-reaching conclusions. She dedicated no more than a page to some casual observations on other surprise attacks.[61]

Using a larger sample, a perceptive Robert Jervis reached flatly contradictory conclusions. Jervis contended that when viewed in a comparative historical context, surprise attacks were relatively rare. Intelligence apparently worked. In fact, most deterrence strategies against surprise attacks had dangerous, unintended consequences, as they were liable to be misread as threats. "There seem to be more cases of statesmen incorrectly believing others are planning major acts against their interest than of statesmen being lulled by a potential aggressor."[62]

Critics charged that Roberta with "over-representation of intelligence failures," though intelligence successes offered valuable comparative perspective.[63] Finally, Roberta stood accused of pronouncing "strategic surprise as the progenitor of disaster." In actual fact, as Levite asserted, the most salient modern examples of strategic surprise suggested that most initiators of surprise attacks—Germany, Japan, North Korea, Egypt, Syria, and Argentina—"were ultimately defeated."[64]

Roberta's *Pearl Harbor* struck Michael Howard as a somewhat flawed use of history. The quest for a usable past was a dubious enterprise at best. Analysis of the past was not a scientific venture in the classic sense. Historical events were, contrary to Roberta's sweeping declarations, sui generis. Ignoring the uniqueness of the past in the quest for meaningful lessons for the future led to an exaggerated influence of the historian's worldview. Extracting lessons from history tended to be subjective, more reflective of the historian's own mind-set than some grand discovery of design and purpose.[65]

Yet even if one accepted the notion of a usable past, Pearl Harbor offered poor material for such an exercise. The attack was indeed the most immediate and familiar example of surprise, but it was precisely for these reasons that its relevance was highly questionable. The analysis of recent events was the most treacherous enterprise of all; sources are usually incomplete and slanted by selective access to evidence. In Roberta's case, she had based her study on unclassified material only. Context is often blurred by temporal proximity; relevant data rush by unnoticed. Moreover, critics held that familiarity breeds contempt for profundity. Intimate knowledge is often mistaken for expert knowledge; such knowledge, in turn, becomes massively oversimplified.

Roberta's study did indeed omit information that may have compromised the cause of RAND's Strategic Air Command (SAC) clients. To begin with, she left out the political context of the Japanese attack. She had claimed that the decision to attack Pearl Harbor made no geostrategic sense, and that ulterior political and psychological reasons were the main motivating forces: motives of saving face and national pride, or internal power struggles. Her critics argued that, from the point of view of the Japanese leadership, the attack on Pearl Harbor was a geopolitical and military necessity. The attack, in Michael Howard's view, "was part of a desperate attempt by Japan to escape from the choice imposed on her by the American embargo of July 24, 1941, between economic strangulation and capitulation to the American demand that she should renounce her entire policy in East Asia."[66] Bernard Brodie, the Wohlstetters' RAND colleague and rival, claimed that the type of deterrent steps the Wohlstetters advocated were, in fact, counterproductive. Pearl Harbor suggested that a military buildup as a deterrent mechanism had the potential to induce desperation and provoke an enemy to "fear us too much."[67]

Moreover, Roberta had glossed over an important lesson for would-be aggressors. As far as Japan's strategic objectives were concerned, Pearl Harbor had been a fantastically unsuccessful operation. Despite the admirable execution of the attack, Japan had failed to accomplish any of its major goals. Unbeknownst to the Japanese, the prime targets of the American armada were absent from Pearl Harbor on December 7. In addition, American retaliatory capacity had far exceeded the worst-case scenarios envisioned by the Japanese.

Whatever weaknesses plagued American intelligence operations on the eve of the attack, the most spectacular failure of this formative crisis belonged to the Japanese, in particular, and, by implication, to any potential attacker. The Japanese had failed to assess the ability of the United States to regroup and ultimately retaliate. As such, Pearl Harbor's most significant intelligence failure belonged to the Japanese aggressor.

Unanticipated consequences and surprise worked both ways. While even the most efficient intelligence apparatus could not provide airtight guarantees against surprise attacks, Pearl Harbor suggested that aggressors would face equally challenging intelligence lacunae. An enemy could never hope to have a "sufficiently complete picture of our state of readiness and retaliatory capacity to make a surprise attack a rational course of action." If anything, the uncertainty confounding a would-be aggressor, Michael Howard argued, had "increased a thousandfold since 1941."[68]

In sum, Roberta's critics held that Pearl Harbor appeared first and foremost to indicate the *futility* of surprise attacks. An almost flawless execution ultimately succumbed to a misreading of the American response. Rather than a limping, demoralized post-Pearl Harbor enemy,

Japan confronted a galvanized American public and a reenergized war machine of unprecedented consequences.

Roberta's implication that strong nuclear deployments were the only meaningful manner to deter future surprise attacks struck an otherwise admiring Werner Schilling as wrongheaded. Actual political behavior in wartime situations suggested to him that the "quality of destruction" of thermonuclear war would not function as a deterrent to surprise attacks. Echoing Herman Kahn's horrific thermonuclear war scenarios, Schilling assumed that strategic choice would always be driven by "reference to relative rather than absolute costs (better World War III now than later)."[69] Under the best of circumstances, "even a peaceful and conscientious leader can frequently do no better than be guided by the crude speculation that the costs of war now will be less than the costs of war later."[70]

Contrary to Roberta, Schilling feared that a deterrent mechanism might morph with alacrity into something significantly unstable. A porous line barely separated deterrent retaliatory capability from pre-emptive force. "Think how much more damage could be avoided" by a successful *first* strike, Schilling's imaginary policy maker might think to himself.[71] By Roberta's own account, one could not rely on rational cost-benefit analysis as the ultimate deterrent. She had assigned the seemingly irrational Japanese choice to launch their strike to a particular and extraordinary case of "fuzziness," the result of unclear divisions of power between Japanese military and civilian authorities, as well as of "the mysteries of Japanese logic." Schilling disagreed. "It is the character of such choices to be fuzzy" and unpredictable, irrespective of the cultural idiosyncrasies of particular nations.[72] If anything, the Japanese decision-making process suggested that rationality was in the eyes of the subjective beholder.

The Psychology of Surprises

Pearl Harbor: Warning and Decision resonated in the halls of power. Roberta's observations on the nature of surprise attacks became a recurring motif among policy makers. Despite its shortcomings, her book entered a select list of compulsory reading for administration officials during the Cold War, and then again following 9/11, when the irreparable harm of surprise attacks became, once again, painfully evident.

Roberta's academic fortunes, by contrast, were decidedly different. Originally hailed as a foundational text, her study of surprise at Pearl Harbor slowly receded into the underworld of footnotes and then passed into silence. Richard Betts's well-received *Surprise Attack* (1980) dismissed Roberta with the faint praise of two perfunctory mentions.[73] A 1985 inquest on psychology, surprise attacks, and deterrence, compiled by the luminaries of political psychology, was equally taciturn; Roberta's work was conspicuously absent, as was the Pearl Harbor example. A perusal of the index of this collection reveals no mention of the Wohlstetters, while Pearl Harbor warranted only two glancing footnotes.[74]

One can only surmise the reasons for her study's waning academic fortunes. To begin with, Roberta's methodology might have appeared somewhat precious by the 1980s. Roberta's style of copious, blow-by-blow details may have appeared too factual and not theoretical enough. Her conventional empirical investigation, bogged down in the weeds of conflicting accounts and interpretations of motivation, appeared frozen in time, perhaps irrelevant to contemporary challenges. Left unsaid, but presumably not forgotten, was the taint of a RAND imprimatur, a study beholden to its military funders, who would leverage it to seek massive funding in anticipation of the next surprise attack, this time with nuclear weapons. Her study lacked the trappings of objectivity that were enshrined, albeit selectively, within political science and its offshoots. Reflecting on historical scholarship on the fiftieth anniversary of Pearl Harbor, Roger Dingman explained that "despite its scholarly dissection of the intricacies of intelligence gathering and evaluation," Roberta's book "was more a tract for Cold War times than an analysis of Japan's misdeeds."[75] In other words, her book was now a period piece: not without value but nevertheless quite distant from cutting-edge scholarship.

To be fair, a RAND study in the 1950s could hardly have been expected to produce a balanced account on the variety of threats facing the nation. Thermonuclear challenges emanating from powerful nation-states furnished the raison d'être of RAND's patrons in the Air Force in general, and in SAC in particular. As far as SAC in the 1950s was concerned, massive surprise attacks launched by competing nation-states were the only potential military threat facing the nation. The only meaningful preparation for them, therefore, was to create a good scholarly rationale for thermonuclear deterrence—a second-strike airborne capability that would survive a nuclear Pearl Harbor.

The core problem of Roberta's study lay in insisting on the relevance of an historic event to future warfare. Roberta had dismissed the opinions of some of her RAND colleagues who believed that the waging of war between two titans had been rendered obsolete by the nuclear revolution. Most often identified with the early writings of Bernard Brodie, this school of thought claimed that, with the advent of nuclear weapons, conventional military thought had reached a point of paradigmatic crisis.[76] Any notion of war between nuclear armed nation-states, Brodie argued, ran the risk of negating "the principle of life itself," in George Kennan's phrase.[77] Brodie cautioned against the fatal and existential error of initiating, or planning to initiate, the employment of atomic weapons, and instead counseled the development of détente with the nation's enemies, based on mutual restraint and the recognition of common existential vulnerability.

As Chapter 3 demonstrates, Albert Wohlstetter embraced Roberta's central assumptions on the imminence of the next great surprise attack and its cyclical recurrence. The lesson of Pearl Harbor for the thermonuclear age was to eliminate the temptation of an enemy first strike by providing adequate defensive shelter and the removal of the countervailing forces from immediate enemy striking range. Such moves would prove adequate only if the United States could credibly and unambiguously convey that the cost of challenging its deterrent power would exceed any imaginable gains. Beginning with that belief, Albert would stake his career on advocating for a highly lethal redundancy in weapons and their delivery systems. His strategies of deterrence were all premised on the annihilating consequences of a credible second strike. Pearl Harbor, according to the Wohlstetter Doctrine, proved that wars—past and future—occurred when a potential national predator miscalculates its relative strength. Situations such as Pearl Harbor, characterized by a roughly equal balance of power, increase the likelihood of miscalculation and heighten the probability of aggression.

Following in Roberta's footsteps, Albert would reject the reliance on intelligence warnings. Given the recurring failures in anticipating enemy notions of vulnerability, the only viable strategy to obtain security was to avoid divinations of the enemy's psyche and create, instead, an unambiguous and existential deterrent threat. At Pearl Harbor, the Pacific Fleet had failed to convey an unequivocal signal of deterrence. This sedentary and exposed target had in fact conveyed vulnerability; it had not been clear and lethal enough to discourage an enemy attack. By the same token, nuclear deterrence, if pursued weakly and fitfully, would inevitably aggravate insecurity in the anarchic world system. By contrast, a well-protected and aggressive module of deterrence would strike fear in the hearts of even the most predatory opponents. Preparation for a Roberta-inspired Pearl Harbor in the nuclear age would become Albert's main claim to fame.

Pearl Harbor in Reverse

Unbeknownst to the Wohlstetters, the historical trauma of Pearl Harbor took on a life of its own, producing unanticipated results in policy circles to which neither Roberta nor Albert were privy. The motif of Pearl Harbor—seen through the lens of the Kennedy administration—played a major role in the Cuban missile crisis, by all accounts the critical, existential moment of the Cold War. The manner in which Pearl Harbor affected the crisis circumvented, if not ignored, Roberta's analysis.

Roberta and Albert played a peripheral role during those fateful days in October 1962. Still employed at RAND, the Wohlstetters were assigned to write position papers in the Quarantine Committees, one of the several advisory panels delivering insight to those who sat with President Kennedy and his advisers in the Executive Committee of the National Security Council (the ExComm). The record of the Wohlstetters' participation is sparse. "I was naturally included as a valued advisor, sort of a junior version of Acheson at that level," Albert reported, not elaborating on Roberta's role.[78] A subset of the Wohlstetters' recommendations was published later in a RAND paper. While obviously not a full record of their input, their proposals amount to nothing more than refrains on maintaining a stiff upper lip. Apparently unaware of the actual deliberation in ExComm, they were reduced to exhorting against concessions of any kind.[79]

Looking back on the crisis, Albert deplored what he considered a transparent instance of collateral damage suffered by the United States. These thirteen days in October had eroded the resolve of the secretary of defense, Robert McNamara, beyond repair. Albert contemptuously lashed out at his allegedly weak-kneed interpretations of those tense days. The "quite extraordinary" McNamara he had admired before the missile crisis had emerged from the ExComm lacking confidence in the ability of the Great Powers to engage in a controlled conflict. Albert appeared astounded by the fact that he had rejected—or perhaps never read—the Wohlstetters' position paper on "Controlling Risks in Cuba." "McNamara and most of the principals," Albert wrote, "really thought they were practically on the edge of war" and that war—once it transpired—could not be controlled and contained from spiraling into a full-blown nuclear clash.[80]

From his vantage point of sheer ignorance, Albert found that position ludicrous. Much to Albert's chagrin, the missile crisis led the secretary of defense away from the elaborate plotting of graduated response, second strikes, and controlled nuclear warfare to the much-maligned strategy of MAD. McNamara had "moved towards Deterrence-only, which is deterring without intending to do so," abandoning in the process the Wohlstetter position of "assuring an adversary that not only *could* you retaliate, but you *would* retaliate."[81] McNamara and all the other paper tigers surrounding the president had lost their nerve, thereby jeopardizing the strategic outcome of the crisis. By Albert's account, the secretary of defense had emerged from the ExComm determined to snatch defeat from this manifest victory.

Albert was unaware that a rogue interpretation of Pearl Harbor had played a significant role in the Kennedy administration's sudden loss of interest in a military option. The secretly recorded tapes of the ExComm, released in 1997, reveal stiff resistance to the very concept of controlled escalation with a nuclear adversary, and a growing fear that any type of warfare would almost certainly deteriorate into a nuclear exchange. In response to those members of the ExComm who advocated a swift first strike against the missile sites, a cohort of advisers pushed back, defining a first strike as "a Pearl Harbor in reverse." Bobby Kennedy, Under Secretary of State George Ball, and CIA Director John McCone, as well as McNamara, had persuaded the president that any form of first strike against the missile sites would be morally analogous to the Japanese surprise attack—a venal, immoral act that would erode allied support for the American position.[82] As had been the case at Pearl Harbor, there was, as well, no certainty that such a strike could indeed wipe out all its targets, or deter a Soviet counterattack. The very idea of a surprise attack would turn allies against the United States.

Based, in part, on this argument, the ExComm rejected strategies of bellicose threats and actual acts of war, preferring instead to forge a secret agreement to remove American missiles in Turkey in exchange for the dismantling of the sites in Cuba. During those thirteen days in October, the entire laundry list of controlled warfare, first and second strikes, and American willingness to engage the Soviets directly was transformed into a hollow and unworkable pipe dream that had failed the test of reality. As the historian Dominic Tierney suggests, the moral analogy of Pearl Harbor as a devious and duplicitous strategy trumped the historical Munich analogy of the need for an unflinching response to totalitarian gestures.[83]

Never having analyzed Pearl Harbor as a moral failing of the enemy, and without any knowledge of the ExComm's deliberations or the concessions made to the Soviets, Roberta claimed victory. She deemed the Kennedy administration's military response to the Soviet challenge an unqualified ratification of the Wohlstetter paradigm of controlled threats. "The response chosen kept to a minimum the actual contact with Russian forces, but a minimum compatible with assuring Khrushchev that we meant business: quarantine, the threat of boarding, the actual boarding of one Lebanese vessel," and, eventually, "a world-wide alert of the Strategic Air Command."[84] Given the Kennedy administration's history of aggressiveness toward Castro's Cuba, and certainly convinced that their theory of credible threats and graduated response had carried the day, the Wohlstetters may be forgiven for their premature victory laps. The ethical concerns of a "Pearl Harbor in reverse" and the doubts concerning their advocacy of viable graduated threats remained hidden from view. For all practical purposes, their doctrine remained intact, vindicated by the flurry of disinformation emanating from government circles in the aftermath of the missile crisis.

3

"In Dubious Battle"

The RAND Years

IN THE WAKE OF Hiroshima and Nagasaki, one of RAND Corporation's most prominent strategists mustered John Milton's *Paradise Lost* to describe the fraught moment: "His utmost power with adverse power opposed / In dubious battle on the plains of Heaven, / And shook his throne. What though the field be lost?" Bernard Brodie prefaced his remarks on the "Atomic Dilemma" with an evocative description of Satan's "dubious battle," the war waged by rebellious seraphs against God's loyal troops "on the plains of Heaven." Following a daylong battle of futile carnage, with no clear victor in sight, Satan announces the invention of an awe-inspiring weapon capable of producing unimaginable havoc. The dreadful armament is unleashed in a surprise attack.[1]

At first, Satan's "infernal engines wreak dreadful execution." But ultimately God's acolytes respond with unanticipated ferocity. Contrary to expectations, the loyal angels "seize in the fury of the moment upon the 'absolute' weapon." They tear "the seated hills of Heaven from their roots," hurling them at God's unbowed enemies. The rebels respond in kind; Heaven turns into a smoldering wasteland. Eventually the standoff is resolved by God commanding his son to subdue Satan's army.[2]

This war in Heaven, Brodie wrote, was uncomfortably relevant. The ungodly harnessing of the atom and humankind's penchant for resolving conflicts with extreme violence had set the stage for an existential struggle with no celestial intervention in sight. As Milton's poem suggested, a doomsday weapon—whether used in an anticipatory first strike or in a retaliatory second strike—would render any type of victory hollow.

Brodie believed that the thermonuclear age ushered in a new strategic paradigm. In the past, the masters of war had feverishly planned for armed engagements that "would bring them considerable political benefits while exacting very little in the way of costs."[3] The introduction of nuclear retaliation had dramatically changed this equation. Weapons of mass destruction promised to raise the cost of strategic warfare to an unbearable level, obliterating the once clear distinction between victors and vanquished. The only alternative to such mutually assured destruction, Brodie argued, was a fundamental shift in humanity's understanding of warfare. "Thus far the chief purpose of our military establishment has been to win wars," Brodie declared. "From now on its chief purpose must be to avert them. It can have almost no other useful purpose."[4]

Brodie articulated his doctrine of nuclear deterrence in 1946, well before the Soviet Union had achieved nuclear power, but he was grimly confident that the rising nemesis would become a nuclear superpower "within a period of five to ten years."[5] He predicted that the annihilating threat of nuclear weaponry would not rule out the occasional eruption of conventional wars—by proxy or otherwise. He hoped, however, that the shadow of the bomb would "so govern the strategic and tactical dispositions of either side as to create a wholly novel form of war," defined by restraint and strictly limited objectives.[6] The mission of the strategist, therefore, was to devise strategies for employing nuclear weapons as a tool for deterrence, rather than as a functional battlefield weapon. Within this context, Brodie is rightly credited with developing the concept of "second-strike capability" as the ultimate agent of deterrence and the key to global stability in the thermonuclear age.[7]

Weapons of mass destruction had a curiously beneficial side effect, Brodie contended. Paradoxically, the specter of mutual annihilation among nuclear powers provided the key to a stable armistice. The fear of an annihilating retaliation, he speculated, would dampen the simmering impulse to solve geopolitical strife by violent means. "The first and most vital step in any American security program for the age of atomic bombs," therefore, was "to take measures to guarantee to ourselves in case of attack the possibility of retaliation in kind."[8] This threat of retaliation promised to stymie enemy military ambitions.

This timely contribution to strategic thought established Brodie as a major strategist of nuclear war and in 1951 RAND recruited his services.[9] His ascendency there proved short-lived, however. Albert Wohlstetter joined RAND's economics division the same year and swiftly supplanted Brodie as a dominant and domineering player.

Not to be outwitted by Brodie's recourse to Milton, Albert, too, found evocative imagery in poetry. Defense policy in the nuclear age struck him as a moment in which the skillful practitioner should blend inspired reading of great works of literature with formal reasoning. Quoting the poet Marianne Moore, he described the successful policy maker as an inquisitive individual who blended "imaginary gardens" with "real toads," or, as Moore put it, a "literalist of the imagination."[10]

Albert's recourse to "imaginary gardens with real toads" may have been a playful allusion to Milton's celestial landscape, where, according to literary convention, "the Satan, embodying evil, sits 'Squat like a Toad.'"[11] Albert elaborated a doctrine in which the lurking presence of real toads challenged the ephemeral tranquility of the imaginary garden, perhaps a metaphor for the illusory notion of a stable standoff propagated by Brodie. Unlike Brodie, Albert did not dwell solely on the revolutionary implications of nuclear weaponry. While Brodie pondered "the theoretical implication of the bomb in peace and war," Albert offered provocative responses to the immediate concerns of "how nuclear weapons could deter Soviet aggression."[12]

Making the Wohlstetter Doctrine

Albert's major claim to fame was his skeptical approach to stability in the thermonuclear age. Mustering quantitative and qualitative evidence, Albert dispelled notion of a durable nuclear peace. While nuclear weapons had indeed introduced a new dimension into strategic equations, Albert argued that the basic concerns and options of the strategist remained unchanged. Contrary to Bernard Brodie, for whom nuclear weaponry appeared to hold the world in the grips of a stable balance of terror, Albert set out to prove that the thermonuclear confrontation was an example of Roberta's Pearl Harbor writ large.

In many RAND studies written in the 1950s—culminating in an influential 1959 article—Albert held that, contrary to Brodie's view, the balance of terror between the two thermonuclear giants was anything but stable.[13] In reality, it was so fragile that the nation's main nuclear deterrent force—the alleged bedrock of strategic stability—was as vulnerable as the Pacific Fleet on the eve of the Japanese attack.[14] "The Japanese at Pearl Harbor attacked our fleet *not* because they wanted to occupy Hawaii, but because the fleet stood in the way of their expanding south," Albert later explained in a somewhat simplistic—and erroneous—analysis of Japanese motivation. Roberta's Pearl Harbor analysis led him to believe that the Soviets, too, would attack strategic American obstacles that stood in the way of their expansionist designs rather than target the continental United States: "They would have no hope of occupying the United States. The only reasonable place for them to occupy [might be] Europe, and . . . they might, like the Japanese, strike the U.S. before they did that."[15]

SAC, Albert argued, had based its strategic doctrine on the assumption that an agreeable enemy would obligingly follow the preferred strategy of American war planners.[16] SAC was cognitively oriented to the pre-nuclear age, where overwhelming firepower sited in proximity to the enemy were the essential prerequisites for securing the nation. Albert cautioned that SAC's insistence on basing its retaliatory force along the seams of a potential theater of war with the Soviet Union offered no obvious military advantages and actually endangered the nation's security.

Contemporary military doctrine assumed that the prime cause of war was an imbalance of fighting forces. Albert, by contrast, argued that recent debacles, particularly Pearl Harbor, proved that the major cause of wars was vulnerability—in this case the exposed nature of SAC European bases.[17] The presence of the operational wing of the nation's strategic forces close to enemy territory—ostensibly the ultimate deterrent feature of the nation's geopolitical quest for containing a ruthless adversary—was actually destabilizing. Proximity, he argued, increased the likelihood of a nuclear confrontation.[18] Albert described frontline bases as an illusory panacea created by a military establishment still blinded by a conventional wisdom that had already been discredited at Pearl Harbor. As with Pearl Harbor, unprotected arsenals stationed in bases close to enemy territory offered an almost irresistible target for an enemy seeking to tip the balance of nuclear terror in its favor.[19]

Supporters of this outmoded frontier mentality claimed that the overseas bases provided swift access to several axes of attack, as well as the overwhelming benefit of rapid refueling for numerous sorties into enemy territory. Such thinking struck Albert as myopic: it ignored the motivating force of the enemy's fear factor. A formidable American force on its territorial doorstep increased the risk of a preemptive Soviet strike, because a first strike against an American task force that was too close for comfort could be executed with little warning. After all, if American forces were close to enemy territory, then, by the same token, Soviet forces lurked nearby those ill-protected American bases. SAC's frontline strategy was, therefore, an inherently unstable and volatile state of affairs.

Albert accused his rivals within the defense establishment of diminishing the capacities of a scheming and active enemy. The military viewed the enemy much in the same way that it considered the role of terrain and other immutable obstacles. In the eyes of frontier base proponents, the enemy was a static, unimaginative entity. Albert, by contrast, posited a proactive, deceptive, and ruthlessly logical enemy who would have compelling reasons to transform liabilities—such as an adversary lurking on its frontier—into wartime advantages.

If and when the Soviets decided to launch a surprise attack, Albert predicted, SAC frontline bases would face inevitable obliteration. Proximity offered the enemy the advantage of launching a massive surprise attack with negligible warning time. Even with the relatively primitive delivery system at their disposal in the mid-1950s, Albert wrote, the Soviets could "deliver on nearby bases a freight of bombs with something like 50 to 100 times the yield that they could muster at intercontinental range. Missile accuracy would more than double."[20]

Once again, the United States appeared to be setting itself up for a repeat performance of Pearl Harbor, in which a calculating enemy would strike at the heart of the nation's fighting force with impunity. Much like the Japanese at Pearl Harbor, Albert affirmed that the Soviets could not resist attacking a poorly protected strategic force even when the odds of retaliation remained high. Yet, in contrast to Pearl Harbor, the nation's ability to recuperate from a nuclear surprise attack would be close to impossible.

The nuclear standoff was like an "old-fashioned Western gun duel" more than anything else, with each side experiencing overwhelming pressure to outdraw its opponent.[21] The Soviets, he maintained, would naturally feel obliged to allay their fears of an *American* surprise attack on the seams of their frontier by launching a preemptive strike against the fearsome but astoundingly vulnerable and underprotected enemy force. Albert also envisioned a frightening situation in which American leaders of a certain ilk would likewise find the scenario of a surprise attack tempting as a prudent preemption to stymie the designs of a ruthless enemy.[22] In fact, he concluded, without inducing significant reform, it would be extraordinarily "risky for one side *not* to attempt to destroy the other, or to delay doing so, since it not only can emerge unscathed by striking first but this is the sole way it can reasonably hope to emerge at all."[23]

In Albert's grim, Hobbesian representation of the global power play, opponents would compulsively strain at the leash to destroy their enemies; a rational military power would always seize the opportunity to incapacitate its adversary, as long as the damage inflicted entailed minimal chance of significant retaliation. It was the task of the strategic analyst to neutralize such threats by creating an intolerable price for a first strike.

Albert's scheme entailed diminishing the vulnerability of the nation's strategic forces, while simultaneously creating a punishing and invulnerable retaliatory force, capable of inflicting irreparable damage on an adversary. Bernard Brodie had articulated the problem while providing only vague and sometimes contradictory solutions. Albert, by contrast, offered detailed resolutions backed up by both theory and empirical evidence. The solution he offered for vulnerable European-based SAC airfields was to create an impenetrable retaliatory attack force based in distant "hardened shelters" in the United States.[24]

This counterintuitive solution would remove America's nuclear fighting arm from its exposed bases on the Soviet border and ensconce the planes in blast-proof hangars within the continental United States. Frontline European bases would be reduced to stations for poststrike refueling.[25] The new distance between the opposing forces would dramatically lower the risk of a surprise attack. American forces operating from bases within the United States would have ample warning following the Soviet activation of its nuclear attack force. Moreover, concrete shelters would lessen an incentive for an enemy surprise attack, because protection would raise the odds of an effective retaliation.

It was by virtue of these base studies and subsequent articles published in foreign policy journals that Albert claimed proprietary rights over the "second-strike" concept.[26] In fact, he was incensed by suggestions that it was actually Brodie who first developed "second strike." "Neither I nor any of my colleagues had ever heard, until long after all of us had left RAND, that Brodie had a role in the question of defining or emphasizing the importance of SAC's vulnerability, much less . . . the whole first-strike/second-strike distinction," Albert observed. In fact, Albert went so far as to claim that is was Roberta and other members of RAND's social science division who first came up with the idea of "alternative strategies which might hold forces in reserve" for the purposes of executing a second strike. Brodie, he complained, could claim ownership of second strike because his prose was gelatinous; one could conceivably find support for any position on the nuclear debates in such ill-conceived meanderings.[27]

Historians have seemed to take Brodie's side of the story. According to political scientist Richard Rosecrance, Albert was the most influential strategic analyst of the nuclear age, but he was not "the innovator" of the doctrines he preached. He was "not the first to recognize the need for a 'retaliatory' nuclear capability." Nor was he the first analyst to critique the implausible doctrines of Massive Retaliation and Mutually Assured Destruction (MAD), nor the first to dismiss the targeting of cities as both immoral and poor strategy.[28]

Yet to dismiss Albert's work as purely derivative surely trivializes his contribution to strategic thought and to the thermonuclear debate in government circles and beyond. The secret to Albert's success resided in his uncanny ability to translate the often untidy thoughts of others into cohesive and systematic arguments. Contrary to his nemesis, Bernard Brodie, who displayed an aversion to incorporating any form of quantitative reasoning and mathematical probability into strategic studies, Albert's work was methodical and he was quite dismissive of what he derided as the "essayist" nature of Brodie's and others' ruminations.[29]

Although Brodie may have invented second strike, Albert was its major disseminator. Albert fleshed out the theory and rendered it significantly more sophisticated. Deterrence, he explained in characteristically chilling prose, did not mean "matching or exceeding the aggressor's ability to strike first."[30] Matching explosive power had, perhaps, useful symbolic purposes for conquering the hearts and minds of allies. Such preening of weapons did not offer security, however. Only an intimidating second-strike capability could fulfill this function. The crux of this second-strike strategy thus focused on protected SAC shelters spread throughout the United States.

Many retrospective accounts of Albert's base studies offer what Mark Rix has described as a myth of acceptance: a thunderstruck SAC responding with alacrity to Albert's incisive criticism by revamping the location of the nation's strategic forces. Rix asserts that the response was, in fact, quite unfavorable.[31] The military did indeed accept the principle of dispersion and protection. However, it dismissed the base studies' underlying assumption that the nation should concentrate on its retaliatory capabilities. The Air Force rejected the idea of concrete shelters for SAC aircraft, "invoking slogans which identified concrete with the Maginot Line and with excessive defense mindedness."[32]

Contemporary military minds had difficulty coming to terms with a theory seeking to achieve "nonevents." Their most obvious difficulty with deterrence was the nagging sense that focusing on retaliation would yield "initiative to the adversary."[33] Furthermore, military planners and policy makers challenged the assumption that the primary, if not the singular, purpose of nuclear weapons was to deter enemy attacks. Rix argues that, in fact, by the mid-1950s, some of the nation's military planners maintained that the only way "to 'deter' an enemy nuclear strike was to pre-empt it."[34]

Such resistance provoked Albert to breach protocol. Shrugging off the veil of secrecy that had shrouded most debates on nuclear strategy, Albert took his case to the general public. Albert's renowned "Delicate Balance of Terror" (1959), offered an elegant refutation of conventional nuclear strategy, while sparking a more general critique of America's global posture.

Albert's point of departure was Winston Churchill's famous dictum that post–World War II peace promised to be "the sturdy child of [nuclear] terror, and survival the twin brother of annihilation."[35] Churchill appeared to suggest that nuclear weaponry had a salutary effect and would result in what John Gaddis Lewis would later call the Long Peace.[36] Albert thought otherwise. The balance of terror, he insisted, was inherently fragile. Maintaining the delicate balance would require an aggressive investment in retaliatory capabilities and across-the-board increases in their passive defense—by dispersal, hardened shelters, and other means. It also involved a reassessment of models of rational choice that informed theories of a stable nuclear confrontation between the superpowers.

Described by Wohlstetter's formidable intellectual rival Henry Kissinger as the most important contribution to latter-day strategic theory, "Delicate Balance" methodically plotted out the alarming shortcomings of a second-strike strategy as the cornerstone of stability in the nuclear age.[37] In order to successfully retaliate, Albert argued, an American second-strike force would have to muster an improbable capacity to overcome a daunting series of obstacles. To begin with, it would need to maintain command and control despite the possible destruction of communication systems, pierce formidable enemy defenses en route to the target, identify a target, and destroy it under highly adverse conditions and with notoriously inaccurate weaponry. Albert identified six obstacles in all, each one capable of foiling a meaningful second strike. "Prizes for a retaliatory capability are not distributed for getting over one of these jumps," he cautioned. "A system must get over all six."[38]

The rise of missiles as more lethal, accurate, and stealthy replacements for SAC's outmoded strategic bombers raised other, no less intimidating obstacles in the path of a plausible second-strike strategy. The most chilling problem of missiles was that they lacked the much-touted "fail-safe" mechanism. Unlike manned bombers, missiles could not be recalled in the event of a false alarm or an unintentional release. In fact, Albert warned, the measures implemented to "reduce the risk of a rational act of aggression . . . (increased alertness, dispersal, mobility)" actually "increase the risk of an irrational or unintentional act of war."[39]

Technological breakthroughs such as the rise of intercontinental ballistic missiles, the reduction in bulk of nuclear warheads, and the growth in accuracy—to mention but some of the most important ongoing developments—suggested that maintaining an equilibrium of terror was an inherently Sisyphean task. Given that control of vulnerability was tenuous, stability appeared impossible. Under these circumstances, Albert endorsed the idea of creating a strategy for controlled and discriminate warfare in which nuclear weapons would play an active role.

If an ephemeral second-strike option was a shaky foundation for a stable balance of terror, the obvious conclusion was to create a credible nuclear fighting force rather than to place blind faith in the dubious ability to strike back. "Insofar as we can limit the damage to ourselves we reduce his ability to deter us and, therefore, his confidence that we will not strike first. But decreasing his confidence in *our* not striking increases the likelihood of *his* doing so, since striking first is nearly always preferable to striking second. And so any attempt to contain the catastrophe if it comes also in some degree invites it."[40]

For those who placed little credence in the depiction of the Soviet enemy as a one-dimensional predatory power, Albert explained that he was merely advocating a pragmatic and prudent response to existential uncertainty. He argued for an American strategy based on "possibilities"—the entire spectrum of enemy options, both rational and irrational—rather than "probabilities," by which he meant preconceptions of enemy rational choice.[41] Rational choice informed the theory of decision making on which John von Neumann had founded strategic thought at RAND in the late 1940s.[42] Albert now rejected that premise, proposing instead a theory of "limited irrationality," the notion that when faced with existential dilemmas, "people aren't *always* irrational." One had to prepare for contingencies based on the assumption that the enemy may behave irrationally in contemplating a nuclear strike, but that the enemy is also "sometimes rational enough to be able to see that there is a grossly greater danger in taking the course of using nuclear weapons than if he takes the next course."[43]

Assuming, as Albert did, a Manichean world in which the adversary's values were callous and cold-blooded, the assumption that the fear of reciprocal destruction would make aggression irrational or insane lacked any empirical basis. The concept of mutually held fears—the very essence of a stable balance of terror—was predicated on a moral equivalence of values. Albert categorically rejected this conjecture. For Albert, the Cold War was the product of Soviet aggressive motives and predatory behavior rather than the fear of reciprocal obliteration. Albert's Soviets were cruel despots who would willingly sacrifice tens of millions of their citizens for the price of strategic advantage and world domination. The United States' primary strategic mission, therefore, was not to reassure the Russians by endorsing a problematic balance of terror, but to contain and tame their inherent aggressiveness by demonstrating American resolve through an unrelenting investment in arms improvement.

Given this challenging point of departure, Albert urged the government to prepare for the contingency of a strategic exchange of nuclear ordnance. "A capability to fight a general war *is* feasible—not in the sense that it could guarantee our coming out unscathed, but the sense that it could make a significant difference in *how* we would come out—in the size of the disaster to our population and economy, and in the terms on which we could force the conclusion of the war."[44] Albert believed, in other words, that war was an unavoidable tool for the achievement of political objectives, and that nuclear weaponry merely raised the price of warfare rather than obviating it.

If the balance of terror was delicate, and therefore ephemeral, the United States would have to continue its investments in nuclear technology in order to sustain the strength of its defensive capacity. Despite a growing public awareness of its terrifying destructive power, Albert placed little faith in the dread of nuclear disaster producing an ultimate revulsion against war. Echoing his colleague Herman Kahn, he wondered what the difference was "between two such unimaginable disasters as sixty and 160 million Americans dead? The only answer to that is '100 million.' Starting from the smaller losses, it would be possible to recover the industrial and political power of the United States. Even smaller differences would justify an attempt to reduce the damage to our society in the event of war."[45]

Albert's foray beyond nuclear deterrence into a strategy in which nuclear weapons might be deployed was hastened by what he considered to be ill-advised, if not defeatist, reactions to the balance of terror. In the early 1960s, a cohort of public intellectuals endorsed the theory of MAD. Fearing an arms race spiraling out of control, advocates of MAD called for a resuscitation of the balance of terror doctrine that Albert and others had demolished. The key to diminishing the threat of nuclear warfare between the superpowers, MAD supporters asserted, lay in the joint vulnerability of civilian centers in both camps. Holding vulnerable cities hostage, in their view, opened the gateway to a stable balance of terror.[46]

Conventional military doctrine had focused attention on the clash between opposing military forces. Proponents of MAD, by contrast, called for a more capacious understanding of the paradigm shift that the thermonuclear revolution had ushered in. The key to stability, they maintained, lay in the obliterating potential to wipe out entire cities with one bold stroke. The inability to protect sprawling cities on either side was the key to a stable standoff. Because cities were virtually indefensible, the sheer number of nuclear weapons and other advances in thermonuclear weaponry were of sparse significance.

In response to the reactive, "cities-only" second-strike deterrence strategy, Albert developed a competing doctrine of "counterforce."[47] The very idea of deploying a second strike on urban centers and enemy industrial concentrations, he reasoned, was morally bankrupt. It was ludicrous to suggest that a Western government would engage in the calculating annihilation of innocent bystanders. If anything, MAD would encourage an enemy to resolve encounters with a limited first strike, knowing full well that no American leader in his right mind would unleash an attack on vulnerable cities in response to a limited Soviet strike aimed exclusively at battlefield targets.

Beyond MAD's suspect moral dimensions, Albert emphasized, "cities only" was also strategically unsound. Even the most rudimentary cost-benefit analysis suggested that such a move would have no meaningful returns, as it would leave the military apparatus of a predatory enemy unscathed. Nor would the economic impact of attacking civilian centers have any immediate material effect on the enemy's military might. Looking back to recent history, Albert considered that the indiscriminate destruction of enemy infrastructure inevitably placed a heavy burden on victors. A moribund civilian infrastructure limited the extraction of retribution from defeated enemies, and it ultimately fell on the victors to pay the bill for the rehabilitation of a vanquished civilian hinterland. "Cities only" and its variations ultimately struck Albert as irresponsible, and therefore implausible. He agreed that civilian populations had a hostage value, but only after the destruction of military targets.

Contrary to the belief previously prevailing at RAND, that nuclear weapons had revolutionized the terms of military engagement, Albert concluded that the basic aims of warfare had not changed. The destruction of an opponent's fighting power remained the ultimate objective of any attempt to engage a predatory enemy. The best form of deterrence, then, would be to upgrade the bunker mentality of "second strike" in favor of a war-winning strategy of "counterforce." The only convincing deterrent to enemy designs, he now held, was the development of a full-blown nuclear strategy charged with the exclusive mission of incapacitating enemy forces, including their command and control systems. Starting from the assumption that no sane military doctrine would willfully expend the sum of its military might in one bold action, Albert transformed Bernard Brodie's vague ruminations on a second strike into a workable doctrine for destroying the enemy's thermonuclear capacity. In the event of the breakdown of deterrence, the question confronting the nation's leaders should not be whether the nation should employ its nuclear capability, but rather how the nation should conduct a nuclear campaign and for what objectives. Albert's vision of counterforce entailed fostering military capacity, organizational posture, and hardheaded mentality for engaging a gradual, precisely controlled use of nuclear weapons against strictly military targets.

Albert therefore proposed that the best defense would be a spending offense: an investment in technologically sophisticated nuclear arms that possessed both offensive and defensive capacities. Part of that strategy, he urged, was to use technological advances—in particular the rise in accuracy and the diminishing size of nuclear warheads—to create a formidable arsenal of tactical nuclear weaponry that could be deployed in contained situations.

Albert Wohlstetter in his RAND Corporation Office, 1958. *Photograph by Leonard McCombe/The LIFE Picture Collection/Getty Images.*

This shift from theorizing deterrence to actually planning for nuclear warfare was, in part, indicative of Albert's astute political skills. Cognizant of the mistrust between military clients and the cohort of civilian nuclear strategists who constantly questioned conventional military wisdom, Albert struck a different path. In order to stand out among the thickening and bickering crowd of civilian strategic mavens, he led a small group of theorists who were willing to think the unthinkable. He therefore accepted with minimal reservations the argument that, if American nuclear strategy excluded all use of the nation's nuclear arsenal, it would fail to convince, and therefore deter, the Soviets.

Opposed Systems Design

Albert's transformation into an advocate of a graduated and controlled deployment of nuclear weapons may be attributed to a number of factors, including an opportunistic political instinct, a deep personal antipathy toward a Hamlet-like inertia—in this case the nonevent of static deterrence supported by Bernard Brodie—as well the implications of improvements in the accuracy and size of warheads. Albert argued that the turn in his strategic doctrine reflected consistency, in particular his unwavering commitment to objective methodology and its application to changing strategic realities. His intellectual rivals, he implied, had no taste for matching theory with reality. Albert, in contrast, espoused a species of translational research: the application of theory to the problems of the real world. The template for this ambitious design was a theory based in economics.

Albert described his theory of "conflict systems studies" or "opposed systems designs" (OSD) as the application of theory and scientific methodology "to the analysis of political-military strategic alternatives."[48] OSD introduced two new factors into the world of weapons design and defense strategy: an active plotting of enemy designs, on the one hand, and the almost deterministic impact of modern weaponry, on the other. Previous models had always assumed unchanging enemy behavior. OSD, by contrast, offered parameters for assessing the unpredictable logic of enemy decision making in volatile crisis situations. "What I mean by conflict systems design and analysis . . . is the *explicit* outline and study of alternative systems of inter-dependent parts, where the comparative performance of a system is affected not only by the machines and the men who are elements in the system, but also by the opposing behavior of men and machines outside the system."[49]

Albert damned his colleagues with faint praise for painstaking yet pedestrian work that focused on such conventional obstacles as "difficult terrain" and "atmospheric disturbances," while treating "direct human opposition" as "only a minor concern." Strategists had tended to gloss over "man-made obstacles" even though success in the world of strategy depended on decisions made by others.[50] Albert reclaimed the human as a determinant factor in decisions to attack. The supposedly fuzzy logic of human decision making in technologically complex and existentially fraught situations could actually be divined by applying sophisticated, quantitative methodology to the world of policy making.

OSD assumed that strategic rivals would always be motivated by ideologically derived belief systems tempered by a sometimes rational assessment of marginal gain and loss. Tracking the ever-changing balance between these drivers lay at the heart of Albert's system of modeling enemy strategic behavior. OSD blended two traditions of analysis: the system analyst's focus on machines and the policy analyst's focus on human beings. OSD, Albert explained, offered answers as to a government's "choice of ends and of means to accomplish ends that stand a good chance of being opposed by other governments."[51] While operational research—OSD's closest cousin—focused on how "best to operate with given organizations and specified equipment in order to achieve various near-term goals," OSD projected its modeling into the terra incognita of human reactions and unanticipated consequences. "The sort of opposed-systems design of which I speak," Albert elaborated, "studies technologies, operations, political interactions and economic costs stretching perhaps for as much as a decade and a half into the future, and designs alternative" choices based on predictions of technological innovation and political context.[52]

OSD tracked multiple and ever-changing variables, which ranged from projected technological innovations to the ever-shifting alliances and treaty commitments between rivals and potential allies. The model discounted the notion of fixed "ends" or objectives as anachronistic. Given the complexity of thermonuclear war, it represented "a more tentative and systematic self-correcting mode of theorizing."[53] The issues of limited resources and the compelling need to avoid unbearable costs—such as irrational sacrifice in the name of a specific goal—were just two of the economics-based examples Albert offered in support of achieving a self-correcting mode of theorizing strategy. The main strength of OSD, Davis Bobrow explains, was its move away from wishful thinking about enemy designs to an acceptance that rational behavior was in the eye of the beholder. Predicting enemy behavior entailed giving an adversary "as much attention as we give ourselves; allowing them to follow their own accepted rules of the game, to act rationally and intelligently to advance their interests."[54]

Enter Nathan Leites

Albert was no prisoner of conventional economic reasoning. In his view, the universal tenets of economic behavior would always be tempered by idiosyncratic cultural codes. The key to predicting enemy choice in the nuclear arena was to decipher cultural protocols or, in RANDian argot, the "Operational Code." The concept of an Operational Code suggested that the strategic decisions of policy makers were not necessarily reactions to the external world, but rather reactions to *images* of the external world, to culturally constructed pictures of reality.

The holder of the copyright for the Operational Code and the inspiration for the Wohlstetters' construct of Soviet political behavior was Nathan Leites, RAND's resident oracle on Soviet behavior and the Wohlstetters' guide to the psychopathology of the Soviet Enemy. Roberta remembered Leites as the brilliant scholar who had forged the connection between her own "close analysis of Shakespeare's Hamlet and some of his modern counterparts" and the Bolshevik mind-set of "an extreme reaction against the fin-de-siècle moods of indecision and inertia."[55] Described by Albert as "brilliant" and "prescient," Leites gained his reputation by applying principles of psychoanalysis to the study of totalitarian societies. For a brief historical moment, he was regarded as an authority and major practitioner of this "psychopolitics."

Born in Saint Petersburg in 1912, Leites immigrated to the United States on the eve of World War II. He was associated with RAND's Social Science Division since its inception and served as a professor of political science at the University of Chicago until his death in 1987. Leites was a misanthrope, laboring in the shadows of a whole series of colorful and influential characters both at RAND and in academia. With psychoanalysis as his primary analytical tool, Leites produced a gamut of cultural studies, ranging from an appraisal of Michelangelo to a deconstruction of film noir. His reclusiveness and stubborn refusal to amend his laborious and torpid writing style limited his scholarly resonance. He was, nonetheless, one of the most influential scholars within the confines of RAND in the 1950s. His *Operational Code of the Politburo* (1951), a study of the manner in which the Soviet elite perceived events through the prism of culturally specific psychopathologies, became a seminal working manual for RAND researchers seeking to decipher the Soviet mind.[56]

The Operational Code of the Politburo provided a schema for deciphering the collective behavior of political power brokers, in general, and the curious subset of Soviet elites, in particular. Leites dismissed conventional political science as the most appropriate intellectual mechanism for anticipating behavior, arguing that neither deep ideological conviction nor political maneuvering drove political decision making among the Soviets. Instead, he proposed, their modus operandi was fundamentally a displacement of emotional pathologies particular to Russian society. Communist praxis, according to Leites, was neither an ideational creation nor the result of institutional processes. Understanding it was first and foremost a mission for the psychoanalyst. His underlying theory was that containment of the communist threat would be accomplished by capitalizing on the Soviets' psychological vulnerabilities.

For Leites, conscious articulations of political behavior did not provide reliable data for understanding motivation. Instead, he sought to uncover subconscious motivating forces derived from his subjects' collective past. Leites argued that the Soviets, in particular, did not formulate policies on the basis of a rational assessment of the external world. Instead, they focused on constructed images of realities. Political behavior was the superstructure of private emotional drivers, derived, for the most part, from early formative experiences. The grim premise of Leites's work was that fundamental political beliefs were molded in early childhood years and were, therefore, impervious to change without radical dismantling and subsequent remaking of contemporary societal structures.

Leites proposed a psychoanalytical reading of foundational documents to uncover the Soviet elites' unconscious motivations. Initially he scoured Marxist tomes and the speeches of leaders, but these conventional texts lacked the revelations into the Russian psyche that he was seeking. He therefore argued for a psychoanalytic investigation of the great works of Russian literature, where he could flesh out the pathologies of that society and its ruling class. Bolshevism, he argued, arose in the "Russian stratum known as the intelligentsia."[57] An analysis of the exemplary literature of this elite group promised to reveal what Bolshevik texts "contain in unexpressed form." Instead of wasting effort on overanalyzing overt expressions of political faith, Leites focused on "clues" hidden within literary expression that could reveal the Soviets' mostly unconscious psychopathologies.[58]

Leites's concept of an "operational code" dismissed the notion of improvisation or of realignment with changing realities. Soviet elites, he considered, were orthodox followers of a particularly stringent faith that tolerated little deviance from its inflexible dogma. Like most religions, Bolshevism espoused a teleological concept of history. Its canon was self-confirming; every historical event could be explained by resorting to foundational texts or defining events from the Russian past. Leites explained that "the present Politburo still believes a contemporary situation in international affairs to be explainable when its prototype can be found in Russian, or Party history. . . . Since the Revolution, they have continued to see themselves in the same position in relation to the outside world as they were in relation to the tsarist government, i.e., out of power and in a dangerous position. Thus, the . . . aims of the Bolsheviks tend to preserve the importance of the lessons they learned in their earlier struggles."[59] Setbacks did little to unnerve the faithful because their equivalent of sacred scriptures assured its disciples that victory—in this case, worldwide revolution—was inevitable.

Such beliefs, Leites argued, were driven primarily by a pathology of victimhood and sexual deviance. He identified the Soviet suspicion of being surrounded by enemies with "annihilatory designs" as a classic paranoid defense "against latent homosexuality," rather than some calculated move to fend off a clear and present danger.[60] "The Bolshevik insistence on, in effect, killing enemies and being killed by them is . . . an effort to ward off fear-laden and guilty wishes to embrace men and be embraced by them. This hypothesis is consistent with the existence of certain pervasive Bolshevik trends . . . the fear of being controlled and used, the fear of wanting to submit to an attack."[61]

Leites described Soviet leadership as consumed by a fanatic unwillingness to compromise, irrespective of the human price to be paid.

Bolshevik behavior was driven by the dictum of "Who-Whom?"—who will destroy whom?—and the unwavering belief that the "only safely controlled enemy is the dead (or at least politically dead) enemy."[62] Given this basic outlook, Leites warned, enemy concessions would always be tactical. The Soviets' ultimate goal was to annihilate their enemy, no matter how many temporary conciliatory gestures they might offer on the road to victory in what they perceived as a zero-sum game.

Leites's Operational Code did not apply to enemy society alone. It could be used to decipher political elites in any political setting, including the United States. In fact, Roberta employed the Leites paradigm in an early analysis of the American political character. In the late 1950s, Roberta sought to resuscitate her dissertation from oblivion by sending a revised prospectus to Sheldon Meyer, the legendary editor at Oxford University Press.[63] In notes for a chapter that was probably prepared for the Oxford Press prospectus, Roberta inquired about "Hamlet in America" through an analysis of Herman Melville's *Pierre.* The convoluted plot of Melville's stab at Greco-Shakespearean tragedy told of lovers who discover they are siblings, a strained attempt to hide the truth for the sake of family honor, and the inevitable bloodbath as reality came to light. For Roberta, this plot offered an opportunity to comment on the tragedy of the national character. Pierre, as an archetypical American persona, "is obviously a Hamlet who has no difficulty in acting," she wrote. The disastrous trajectory of events, however, demonstrated Pierre's inability to handle ambiguity. He was driven fatally by the heart, rather than the intellect, to action.

The American Hamlet, Roberta implied, was the converse of his Shakespearean cousin. In Shakespeare's play, internal conflict incapacitates the will for action. Melville's American Hamlet, on the other hand, is driven solely by action and reality, with little recourse to an inner compass. Each character, however, is deprived of balance and ballast between consciousness and cognition, and each is equally tragic. Ultimately, Roberta argued, *Pierre* fails the test of a great American novel. Its operatic conclusion—all the main characters depart in fiery death—misses the point of the American experience. The American way of resolving existential ambiguity demands detachment, requiring "less earnestness" and more common sense. "It is easy to act," Roberta philosophized. "What is difficult is to determine the morally right act to perform, and to survive its consequences."[64]

Of course, the main concern of the Wohlstetters was to anticipate the political behavior of enemy society and it is with this thought in mind that they leaned heavily of the crutch of the Operational Code. In accordance with Nathan Leites's theory, Albert observed that enemy decision making was filtered through a prism of beliefs that more or less preordained subsequent behavioral modes. With Leites as his guide, Albert predicted that the Soviets' nuclear decisions—past, present, and future—would derive from their behavioral code.[65] The decisions of the masters of war "are not always intelligently purposeful," Albert wrote. "They are not purely rational beings, and even if they were, their purposes would almost surely be blurred in transmission through the vast noisy channels of the bureaucracies informing them and executing their decisions." "If men are not always rational beings," he concluded, their behavior was still predictable, if one took into consideration the force of cultural precepts.[66] Mastering the Operational Code of enemy behavior diminished the role of imponderables by offering ways to predict enemy decisions.

As an example, Albert trotted out the Soviets' tolerance for human losses. Albert contended that the Soviet fear of "extinction" had a higher tolerance level than most Western observers were prepared to acknowledge. A country that had suffered twenty million casualties during the course of World War II had a different tolerance level for human "damage." Such capacity for casualties suggested to him that the Soviets would deem a first strike a "sensible" decision when confronted by a variety of strategic dilemmas: "disastrous defeat in peripheral war, loss of key satellites with danger of revolt spreading . . . or fear of an attack by ourselves."[67] An astute model builder, Albert argued, could factor in such behavioral codes and thereby increase the model's predictive ability.

Too many strategic studies, in Albert's view, failed to take account of the uniquely predatory nature of the Soviet enemy. Other models placed "artificial constraints" on enemy objectives and behavior. The war games driving these models, when they admitted the possibility of a Soviet first strike, expected it to commence somewhat conveniently " 'over-the-Arctic' through our Distant Early Warning line, with bombers refueled over Canada—all resulting in plenty of warning."[68] By contrast, Albert planned for more creative and significantly more ruthless Soviet first-strike strategies.

As for those who complained that Leites's model and the Wohlstetters' construct of the Soviet enemy were caricatures of a complex society, Roberta mustered history in their defense. Even if one were to view the Operational Code conceit with skepticism, Roberta claimed that the recent past provided ample empirical evidence in support of it. According to Roberta, history proved that the modus operandi of totalitarian entities was invariably predatory and expansionist and that Western leaders had ignored Leites's insights at their peril.

Roberta offered the example of the leader of "Anycountry" or "Jedesland," a modular entity created by pacifist mathematician and physicist Lewis Fry Richardson to prove that the major causes of war were due to spiraling misinterpretations of adversaries' motives. The defense minister in the Jedesland model "wanted only to defend his country but was misinterpreted as being interested in aggression and so frightened his neighbor, and was himself frightened into an arms build-up leading to war." According to critics of the Operational Code reading of Soviet behavior, the Cold War was a textbook example of the Jedesland crisis. Detractors claimed that "the United States had been forcing the reluctant Russians to spend money on arms which they would rather spend otherwise." Roberta characterized such observations as "self-destroying prophecies," a rerun of the fatal belief "that it was the Allied failure to disarm after Versailles that compelled the Germans reluctantly to rearm." In fact, she argued, all totalitarian powers—regardless of ideology—behaved in predictably aggressive fashion. History had proven that Hitler's soothing ruse "that he would much prefer to forgo armament altogether, if only the Allies would disarm completely," had brought the Free World to the edge of an existential precipice. In the nuclear age, she argued, such "vain hopes of disarmament negotiations" with a totalitarian enemy would lead to an irreversible disaster.[69]

A Trust in Numbers

Even as they paid tribute to cultural factors, the Wohlstetters' modeling equally reflected a belief in the *diminishing* role of traditional human factors in war making. Given the tremendous strides made in military technology, Albert discounted the role the human element would play once a nuclear confrontation was actually under way. In one of the most astoundingly hubristic statements of this early period of thermonuclear strategizing, Albert declared that it was "a paradox that we can do better in analyzing the potential outcomes of some sorts of conflict that have never occurred than we can do with conflicts of the sort that have been endemic for ages."[70] Technologically reliant components of warfare, "like the highly organized warning, command, control, communication, and reaction systems of aircraft and missiles, inevitably [display] many regularities and predictabilities."[71] The vagaries of troop morale, weather, and terrain, to mention but a few of the elements that introduced unpredictability into pre-nuclear warfare, faded into the background; they would have little effect on the technologically dominant wars of the future. Once thermonuclear warfare began, events would be driven by a scenario that no conscious actor could effectively modify.

The introduction of mathematical models into OSD offered correctives to outmoded strategies that were derived from battlefield folklore rather than knowledge. OSD's crisp mathematical modeling promised to remove biased subjectivity from the realms of nuclear strategy. Albert explained that "it is hard not to guess that something is feasible if you would like it to happen," and "it is hard not to prophesy a catastrophe if its imminence would make urgent an action you are recommending."[72] Only mathematical modeling by highly trained strategists, Albert argued, could produce a meaningful menu of decision options. When dealing with the existential challenges of the nuclear age, the faux clairvoyance of the strategically innocent and mathematically misinformed was a luxury that the nation could ill afford. Foresight is not gained through mysterious prescience. Instead, "it is won—precariously and intermittently, in the course of hard empirical study of the major factors" that may affect the successful execution of a wartime strategy.[73]

Mathematical models aimed at predicting enemy countermeasures also promised to eliminate the typical blind spots to which weapons systems developers and their advocates were prone. Scientists and their military allies who promoted particular weapons systems were often the prisoners of their own ingenuity. They were hamstrung by the human propensity to develop an affection for their pet projects, while practicing a "wishful negligence" of its weaknesses.[74] Mathematically driven analysis promised to overcome this blind spot.

Albert's mathematical models poked merciless holes into the conventional space-time modeling governing contemporary strategic analysis.

Citing George Kennan's dictum that "the effectiveness of the power ra-diated from any national center decreases in proportion to the distance involved," Albert offered one of his own studies as a refutation of linear understandings of global challenges.[75] According to reigning static or "classical" view, strength decreased with distance. "The case of con-temporary delivery technology," however, suggested the converse. From the safety of hardened shelters within the United States, the United States had greatly increased its military might. "The costs of a nuclear second-strike capability in the 1950s *decrease* sharply and effectiveness *increases* if operating bases are kept far back at intercontinental range."[76]

Using the tools of cost-benefit analysis, Albert added that linear dis-tance was an irrelevant economic and logistical factor even in conven-tional warfare. "Adding several thousand miles to the distance at which remote wars are fought" had no meaningful impact on costs, he wrote; distance—as measured in linear miles—posed no significant logistical barriers either. The "long distance lift capacity" of the United States would "massively" exceed "short distance" logistical bottlenecks in a U.S.-China war in the Himalayas, for example.[77]

No form of intuition, Albert stressed, could have arrived at this un-derstanding of the geopolitical space-time continuum. Only formal mathematical models could reveal such crucial information for future policy decisions.[78] These computations, he explained, were the result of painstaking and tedious empirical work blended with theory. It was through this imaginative blending of theory and practice that counter-intuitive solutions were revealed in all their glory. Infusing theoretical models with "empirical content specific to international conflict" was the ultimate test of relevance in an age of uncertainty and of a precar-ious balance of terror.[79]

In Albert's vision, a sophisticated combination of these three key factors—the constraints of a behavioral code, the deterministic role of technology, and the creative use of economic and mathematical analysis—offered American strategists the ability to imagine and create realistic strategies for both present and future confrontations. Factoring in sci-ence, technology, and a specific cultural analysis freed strategy from the constraints of capricious human vagaries and released policy makers from the deathbed of inert and unrealistic strategy.

4

"He Is but MAD North-North-West"

Albert and His Critics

In 1963, at the height of his career, Albert Wohlstetter found himself embroiled in controversy over a breach of security. Bernard Brodie, his RAND colleague and intellectual rival, accused him of failing to obtain a security clearance before sharing a draft of a RAND paper with an unauthorized individual. Albert vehemently denied the charge. After all, Albert explained, Henry (Harry) Rowen—the Defense Department official in question—had worked for RAND in the past (he had coauthored several of Albert's studies) and the paper was merely a "D," RAND's code for minimal classification. The author of the contested text was Constantin Melnik, a French student of Nathan Leites and a RAND consultant in the late 1950s who had served as chief of secret services in France from 1959 to 1962.[1] In addition to fanning the flames of the Melnik affair, Brodie had allegedly complained that Albert had abused RAND funds by extravagantly wining and dining clients and colleagues at RAND's expense. Director Frank Collbohm summarily fired Albert for breaching RAND's security protocol.[2]

Retrospective studies have showered Brodie with superlatives: "the Clausewitz of the nuclear age," "the dean of American civilian strategists" and similar accolades.[3] Albert, by contrast, described him as maniacally jealous, driven to desperate acts of vindictiveness over his growing marginalization at RAND. The height of Brodie's malice, according to Albert, was the accusation of breaching RAND's security protocol. He described Brodie's allegations as the last gasp of a disgraced practitioner who had built up a false reputation as an intrepid strategist through light plagiarism and the production of journalistic ruminations of no scholarly value.[4] Whatever the merits of the accusations, however, they nonetheless prompted Albert and Roberta to depart from RAND. After a brief way station at the University of California, they took up academic appointments at the University of Chicago and formed their own consulting company, Pan Heuristics.

The Brodie and Wohlstetter feud occurred despite, or, perhaps because of, their common background. Bernard and Albert were both liberated Jews who had linked their lives to erudite gentile women from dramatically different backgrounds. The marital relationships of both couples were sealed on prestigious university campuses, which, despite many well-documented restrictions, offered a relatively level playing field for ambitious youth of modest backgrounds.

Both of their spouses were intellectual figures in their own rights. Like Roberta, Fawn Brodie was an impressive historian. Lacking the shackles of a disciplinary PhD, she gate-crashed the narrow world of American historical biography, challenging the dominant genre of great men and their lofty thoughts. Her study of Thomas Jefferson's inner life—his sexual angst and its attendant impact on his understanding of race, class, and gender—wreaked havoc among Jefferson's mostly male cadre of hagiographers. She resurrected the abolitionist impulses of Thaddeus Stevens from some distant circle of hell, placed Richard Nixon under the scrutiny of psychoanalytical methodology, and was excommunicated from the Mormon community for daring to challenge the mythology of Joseph Smith, the founding father of her ancestral faith. She was one of the first practitioners of psychohistory in the United States, and definitely the most skilled. With Sigmund Freud as her copilot, she offered a commentary on the role of repressed emotions in human affairs at pivotal historical moments. Her disdain for the choke hold of hagiography unlocked a world of psychological symbol, allusion, and illusion. Her protagonists' every utterance, casual or otherwise, uncovered welters of sexual repression and unconscious impulses born out of distant childhood experiences.[5]

Fawn's penchant for psychoanalysis popped up in the thermonuclear oeuvre of her peevish and sometimes philandering spouse.[6] The "principles of war," he once reflected, were not unlike the pursuit of love. "For instance, if a man wishes to win a fair and virtuous maiden and if he is not too well endowed in looks and money, it is necessary for him to clarify in his mind what exactly he wants of this girl . . . and then to practice rigorously the principles of concentration of force, of the offensive, of economy of forces, and certainly of deception."[7] One of his internal memoranda at RAND employed a different set of sexual analogies for modern-day warfare. He described the strategy of limited nuclear warfare as "withdrawal before ejaculation," while all-out nuclear attack "was like going all the way."[8] He attributed Albert-like "fantasies of total war which have the United States doing all the hitting" to psychopathological "repressed rages harbored in so many breasts."[9]

RAND at midcentury offered these two driven individuals the opportunity to soar above the disciplinary divisions of the American university and ignore the often-condescending attitudes of academics who disparaged the merging of theory and practice that both espoused. Instead, they engaged in a demonstration of academic disputation at its worst. Their frequent displays of self-absorbed vindictiveness are mentioned in passing in the many histories of this period. As is often the case when confronting unpleasant personal animosity between the river gods, the chroniclers turn away in embarrassment at the sometimes juvenile spats between two great intellectuals.

Albert and Brodie's fraught exchanges flared in full view of common friends. Bernard and Fawn had met at the University of Chicago—in later years, the Wohlstetters' academic home—where they had socialized with several Wohlstetter intimates and associates. RAND colleague Nathan Leites, the purveyor of the Chicago-style merger of psychoanalysis and politics, had inspired the Brodies' own interest in psychopolitics.[10] Leites was also a close friend of the Wohlstetters, who cited with great admiration his Freudian approach to world affairs.[11]

The Brodie-Wohlstetter clash reveals much more than a disputation over the stability of the balance of terror. It is a cautionary tale of the privatization of knowledge in secretive think tanks, where vainglorious strategic experts appeared mortally afflicted by the narcissism of small differences. Their feud cannot be shrugged off as a garden-variety instance of intellectual petulance. By virtue of RAND's resonance, their unchecked vanities highlighted and heightened the existential dangers of the self-contained world of Cold War strategic studies.

Such incessant brawling did, however, call attention to the fundamental debates on grand strategy in the latter half of the twentieth century. The limits of objectivity in translational research, the role of technology in rationalizing the irrational, and the moral dilemmas of futuristic warfare were just some of the issues permeating scholarship at RAND and circulating among its critics. The following brief survey of major flashpoints offers a glimpse of the assumptions lying within the clutter of personal clashes and antipathies. Many scholars of international relations have probed the technical aspects of these raging debates.[12] In this chapter I have chosen to engage four undergirding epistemological issues: the moral dilemmas of choice in an age of existential uncertainty, technological determinism in war, the constraints of just war, and the uses of history as a path for divining the future. These four debates provide glimpses of the ideological divide separating RAND's grand strategists—Albert included—from the concerns of their critics. The epistemological disputations on the nature of culture and society in a fractured world laid bare the limits of a common cultural code and a consensual political worldview in the United States during a time of duress.

Bernard Brodie and the Delicate Balance of Terror

Over the course of their uneasy cohabitation at RAND, the Wohlstetter-Brodie rivalry simmered and periodically erupted. Brodie relentlessly picked away at inconsistencies in Albert's strategic thought, while Albert responded ad hominem. Contrary to Albert's characterization of it, however, the clash between these two RAND strategists was anything but a one-sided fight between an intellectual giant and a washed-out theorist. Brodie actually offered one of the most cogent critiques of the Wohlstetter Doctrine.

Brodie's most enduring critique of the Wohlstetter legacy focused on the legendary "Delicate Balance of Terror." Contrary to Albert's point of departure, Brodie believed that the balance of terror was quite stable and lacked the fragility claimed by Albert. Choosing to ignore the paradigmatic example of Pearl Harbor, where pertinent signals were drowned in a sea of conflicting noise, Brodie stubbornly insisted "that some kind of political warning would always be available," and that Albert's "worst case fantasies" of an "attack out of the blue" had "never happened, at least in modern times."[13]

Brodie accused Albert of exaggerating the delicacy of the balance of terror through fearsome constructions of an enemy poised to launch a

nuclear Pearl Harbor at any instant. He discounted Albert's representations of a relentless predatory enemy willing to take great risks in order
to annihilate its rivals. The enemy was a cumbersome, lumbering giant,
unable to rise to the complex challenge of deploying doomsday military
surprise. Nuclear weaponry demanded elaborate clandestine logistical
movements prior to deployment that the ungainly, doctrinaire Soviets
would be at a loss to accomplish with the necessary discretion. History
suggested that the Soviet hierarchy—both past and present—lacked the
appetite and aptitude for launching conventional surprise attacks, let
alone a nuclear Pearl Harbor.[14]

Brodie offered a significantly milder portrayal of potential enemies—
the Soviets or for that matter anyone else. "My reasons have to do
mostly with human inhibitions against taking monumental risks or
doing things which are universally detested, except under motivations
far more compelling than those suggested by Wohlstetter."[15] For Brodie
there was no enemy—outside the world of science fiction—who would
be "aggressive and imaginative enough" to make Albert's construction
of existential threats convincing. Brodie identified an impulse among
strategists to invent "interesting" and challenging opponents, while offering little thought to how closely the theoretical model actually resembled a real life opponent.[16] In Brodie's view, Albert's fixation on a
thermonuclear standoff relentlessly driven by unceasing innovation
trivialized "the inhibitory political and psychological imponderables
that might and in fact *must* affect the conditions implied by that word
delicate. . . . Many things are technologically feasible that we have
quite good reason to believe will not happen."[17]

In fact, Brodie pointed out, Albert was quite inconsistent. He wavered
between depressive warnings of a fragile balance between two nuclear
giants and manic forecasts of a futuristic, technological deterministic
battlefield governed by greater predictability and, therefore, less fragility. Albert had implied that improvement in ordnance—nuclear or
otherwise—and the automation of the modern battlefield, in general,
was an uncontainable force, and mostly for the better. According to Albert, the increasing accuracy and low payloads of modern weaponry—
both nuclear and conventional—made the plotting of the fortunes of war
more predictable, less susceptible to the whims of fickle mortals and,
therefore, less delicate. It was unclear how technological futurism interacted with the overriding concern of delicacy on the nuclear battlefields.

Albert's modeling—his statistical collations of enemy intentions and technological innovation—struck Brodie as equally phantasmagoric. Albert's modeling was ridden with biased assumptions on planning factors and betrayed willful ignorance of the dangerous vagaries of choice and the decision-making process in the heat of war.[18] Brodie lashed out at the end product, which he described as a false theory of international relations, where events conformed to models developed in the comfort of RAND offices. "In order to accomplish this end, nations have to be conceived as units . . . and of course governments and heads of government, too, have to be conceived of as units." Such reductive thinking, Brodie argued, created the false impression that men and machines acted in accordance with principles that could be deduced from data, "subject, perhaps, to minor deviations that can be handled in terms of statistical probabilities . . . that appropriate study can easily disclose."[19]

The historical example of Nazi Germany, Brodie explained, revealed the inadequacies of Albert's models. No form of modeling—not even Albert's crisp calculations—could have accounted for the Nazis' irrational and pathological behavior. No maniacal leader—a thermonuclear Hitler brandishing an H-bomb arsenal—could be neutralized by some smart algorithm.

Even if one assumed a high tolerance for millions of casualties, Brodie argued, the most ruthless of enemies would be inhibited from attacking if it could not be assured it could neutralize an annihilating counterattack. Defending his own strategic vision, Brodie held that no calculating enemy would launch such an attack against the United States "because of the numbers and variety of the American forces an enemy would need to have a high certitude of destroying in one fell swoop."[20] One surviving American bomb had the obliterating potential to inhibit any such designs.

If there was anything volatile about the balance of terror, in Brodie's view, it was the dangerous economic side effects of preaching its delicate nature. The unrealistic fear of its precariousness had led to astonishingly expensive investments in flamboyant weapon systems, most of which were rendered instantaneously obsolete by quantum leaps in technology before they could become operational. Brodie reminded his readers that, alarmist prose to the contrary, Albert had never convinced the Air Force to invest in hardened shelters for their bomber fleet, and, anyway, such protection had become a moot issue, owing to the arrival of ICBM missiles and Polaris submarines.[21]

Waving aside Albert's claim to scientific accuracy, Brodie acknowledged what few in his position were prepared to admit. The fundamental difference between competing paradigms—his own and Albert's included—was political and ideological rather than scientific. "Protagonists and opponents will take their positions on political grounds, depending on whether they harbor views inclining them towards the Committee on the Present Danger"—the powerful advocacy group of elite hawkish intellectuals—or whether they "live on lower levels of anxiety."[22]

Brodie accused Albert and his allies of adulterating the debate by asking how the Soviet Union would attack the United States, while ignoring the pertinent questions such as *"whether* some entity called the Soviet Union" was indeed driven by Albert's Hobbesian worldview, and *"who* in the Soviet Union thinks they can fight and win a nuclear war?"[23] In other words, elaborate modeling was nothing more than a flamboyant presentation of a flimsy argument. Modeling was a proverbial fig leaf for bad assumptions.

Despite technological changes and irrespective of the actual count of weaponry on either side, Brodie believed that the military and political establishments in both the Soviet Union and the United States were still driven and united by the fundamental Clausewitzian premise of war as a continuation of politics by other means. It was simply not credible to postulate an uninhibited Soviet brinkmanship. Even the sometimes dense Soviets understood that the senseless destruction of a nuclear exchange would render any valid political objective invalid.

Albert had advocated for a new generation of nuclear weaponry—light, accurate, and significantly more lethal—because such weaponry increased the number of choices available to a president during war. Brodie viewed the widening array of choices as a political liability and security nightmare. "Fallible political and military leaders have given us all too much indication" that they could not be trusted to make the right decision during uncertain times.[24] The Cuban missile crisis offered a stark demonstration on the dangers of excess choice. If the missile crisis had any lasting legacy, Brodie considered, it was the need to remove from operational considerations the pressure to experiment during an emergency with an unprecedented and untested "violent means of proving . . . resolve."[25]

Brodie remained steadfastly opposed to increasing the diversity of strategic weapons urged by Albert and others. Widening options for the president as commander in chief beyond the "straightjacketed posture of deterrence" struck Brodie as a dangerous leap into unchartered waters.[26] He believed that expanding the president's war power options was both constitutionally and pragmatically untenable. From a constitutional point of view, placing such formidable weapons in the hands of the commander in chief would upset "the limitations laid down by the Constitution upon presidential prerogatives and war-making powers." Moreover, such trends went against the grain of reducing the "pressure upon the President . . . to use the nuclear option."[27]

These differences between Albert and Brodie dwarf, however, when compared with the assumptions they shared. Brodie's advocacy of tactical nuclear weaponry serves as a case in point. Breezing past his early belief that the thermonuclear age had ushered in a paradigm shift that should preclude the employment of nuclear weapons in the battlefield, Brodie was confident that there "was no problem distinguishing between tactical and strategic bombing in World War II, and in avoiding the latter where it seemed politically desirable to do so."[28] With nary a footnote in sight, he dismissed any possibility of nuclear weapons spiraling from the tactical to the strategic. The United States, he argued, should be committed to "using tactical nuclear weapons if the Soviets use them first *or if we find ourselves losing without them.*"[29] As it was unlikely either man had ever been involved in a barroom brawl, let alone actual combat, Brodie's battlefield scenarios were no more realistic than Albert's belief in a controlled approach to nuclear war.

Normalizing Deterrence Theory

While Brodie criticized Albert from within RAND, others criticized him as a way of slamming a battering ram against RAND's doctrine of nuclear deterrence. One of his most consistent critics was the intimidating British Nobel Prize physicist P. M. S. Blackett, who lashed out at the overtly abstract qualities of "Delicate Balance." He identified a cult of numerology proposing "an excessively complicated set of theoretical and numerical arguments," and a level of abstraction that rendered them useless for implementation by mortal policy makers.[30] He also questioned Albert's characterization of the Soviet enemy as unrelentingly predatory, lacking any semblance of compassion for human lives.

Unlike Albert, who had managed to avoid conscription during World War II, Blackett had extensive combat experience and was infuriated by RAND's misunderstanding of modern warfare. He accused Albert of obsessive concoctions of theoretical capabilities, utterly lacking in empirical evidence. Such a harsh assessment of enemy mores and values was more reflective of Wohlstetter's private worldview than of any objective assessment of reality. "When Wohlstetter reaches the exact opposite conclusion, he does so by negating the conclusions of . . . common sense" and "introducing a large and arbitrary degree of moral asymmetry between the two contestants."[31]

Albert's espousal of economic reasoning offered another flashpoint for intellectual rivalry. Philip Green focused on the false god of an " 'economic conflict' model," in particular the blind faith of the economists who purveyed it in the "transferability of theory to the world of action."[32] Green decried the narrowness of such models for discounting a range of unquantifiable qualities, such as the complex, moving unquantifiable target of cultural variables and human behavior under stress. The assertion that the thermonuclear "is a calculable . . . rather than, perhaps, an incalculable nightmare" had essentially effaced the more fundamental analysis of alternatives to a thermonuclear strategy.[33] The assertions of "expertise" were, in fact, tainted by "unanalyzed and arguable political beliefs," such as Albert's "arbitrary and very questionable vision of the international political arena."[34]

Green marveled at the invocation of probabilistic reasoning "where no discoverable probabilities exist."[35] In Albert's world, choice was driven neither by moral imperatives nor ethical judgment. Choice was in the numbers. *"No conduct is absolutely prohibited,"* Green remarked with alarm, unless calculations proved them to be technically unworkable.[36] Though he expressed a begrudging admiration for the mathematical rigor in Albert's studies, Green cautioned that "rigor is not a substitute for thought, and rigorous deterrence analysis has been empty of real thought about the major problems of national policy."[37]

Albert's most exasperating accomplishment, for Green, was perhaps his ability to commandeer the terms of debate, in particular his assertion that "today it is hardly necessary to argue for deterrence."[38] Whether through self-absorption or by a Machiavellian stroke of genius, Albert had claimed for his theories "the epistemological status of the case for electromagnetism."[39]

Albert had foisted upon the policy world the normalization of RAND's questionable war-fighting paradigm. Contrary to the claims of objectivity through quantitative modeling, Green concluded, all of Albert's major work was, in itself, a pronounced value judgment on the role of war in conflict resolution. He had convinced his audiences—military authorities and civilian overseers, as well as the general public—that deterrence theory was much more than one hypothetical approach among many to superpower confrontation. In the world created by deterrence theorists, deterrence had been elevated from its modest status as one "specific political proposal" to the lofty heights of an entrenched "area of study" and an irrefutable scientific paradigm.[40] RAND, Green complained, had managed to valorize a series of contestable assumptions about global conflict and the behavior of the Soviet enemy by translating these problematic conjectures into a "complicated systematic-looking argument . . . with numbers to make the exercise look 'scientific,'" and then treating the result "as though it represented not a vague possibility but a near certainty."[41]

Because Albert's clients were first and foremost RAND's military underwriters, the premise that superpower tensions might be controlled by anything other than military means was removed from debate. The close, symbiotic relationship between researcher and funder had, in effect, militarized what was in essence a political problem. RAND had stood Clausewitz on his head. Albert knew full well that advocacy and research demanded autonomous spheres, but RAND's Air Force affiliations diminished that theory-practice divide. The RAND conceit of fusing disinterested scholarship with terrestrial problem solving had produced the worst of both worlds: "irrelevant policy advice and poor scholarship."[42]

In a 1974 debate on bias in strategic studies, Albert attempted to dispel criticism by offering an allegedly objective assessment of Soviet investment in a thermonuclear strike force. Mustering a long list of numbers, Wohlstetter claimed that "U.S. strategic budgets and the destructiveness of U.S. strategic forces have been going down, not up. U.S. strategic budgets have declined nearly exponentially from the high plateau of 1956–1961."[43] He called for massive spending in order to achieve at least technological parity with the Soviet Union. His critics countered that quantifying Soviet "strategic superiority" was moot given the Soviets' limited appetite for risk taking.[44] If anything, the Soviets had pursued a significantly more aggressive foreign policy when American strategic dominance had been incontestable; the Berlin blockade and the Korean War are two examples often cited by those claiming the irrelevance of the strategic balance to superpower policy in the global arena. In both instances, Soviet aggression had occurred despite irrefutable American advantage in arms.

Rather than approaching thermonuclear war as something that "would make sense only under the most unlikely and desperate conditions," Philip Green charged, Albert and his apostles were normalizing the nuclear option, thereby making it more likely to actually happen.[45] None of Albert's policy recommendations—hardening shelters in response to the vulnerability of nuclear ordnance or valorizing a protected retaliatory force over a first strike capability—were linked to any real-world threat. Albert had "made that judgment prematurely" without seriously weighing alternatives, and in so doing, "helped to determine the course of nuclear politics in the world."[46]

For reasons that had to do with political jostling rather than insight, Green continued, Albert's "secondary technical matters received the kiss of science," even as the assumptions underlying the creation of a bellicose nuclear strategy "were granted only the careless embrace of unanalyzed passion."[47] For all of its "deductive brilliance," Albert's theory of an inherently unstable nuclear standoff was worthless since it was premised on this one unverifiable and probably "incorrect premise."[48] Green therefore asked, rhetorically, "how much value . . . can an empirical study have when it is almost all utterly deductive?"[49]

Albert's airborne strategy for a thermonuclear clash was, for Green, a sign of conventional thinking rather than the working of a great mind. A reliance on strategic strikes represented an uninspired continuation of World War II's "easy acceptance of air war"—the carpet bombing of Dresden and Tokyo being the ultimate examples. Nuclear warfare was "a horrifying but logical extension" of what Green described as the "great moral disaster" of World War II, the normalization of indiscriminate air power, in which distinctions between innocent bystanders and enemy forces had been cavalierly ignored.[50] Tactical nuclear war would simply multiply the "bloodcurdling" aspects of World War II carpet bombing, and the indiscriminate carnage promised by both postures—the counterforce strategy aimed at military targets and the "cities only" approach—rendered the quibbling between the two irrelevant.[51]

The social scientist's claim to science, Green argued, "is to hypothesize abstract models of behavior, which are then refined through continuous testing until 'all the evidence is in' concerning the explanatory power of the final versions of the models."[52] Albert, by his own admission, had none of the data one would expect from model building. "We have no wartime operational data drawn from World War III," Albert had gibed, "and hope we never will."[53] His scenarios of strategic clashes were therefore based, in Green's view, on highly questionable assumptions and speculations regarding the diminishing role of human agency in a thermonuclear confrontation. Albert's approach, Green complained, made cavalier use of abstract constructions of theoretically "possible human behavior" in concrete solutions. Albert claimed to have gained insight from studies of enemy behavior, such as the Leites Operational Code. Greene, however, found such observations to be seriously flawed. Albert's schematic caricature of the enemy as clinically scarred individuals came at the expense of painstaking psychocultural analysis of "probable behavior of relevant persons," by which he meant actual leaders jostling in the global political arena.[54] Instead of a serious study of "the real world of, say, Soviet behavior," deterrence theory was, according to Green, dominated by "the abstract world of decision makers who all seem to think exactly like Wohlstetter" and his "abstracted, Hobbesian rationalism."[55]

By claiming that choice was often a mathematical problem of probability, Green concluded, Albert voided the moral, political, and psychological dilemmas that were endemic to any form of existential crisis. Because such variables were too messy to be translated into a mathematical model, Albert dismissed their importance with a sleight of hand. Instead, he focused attention exclusively on "what is supposedly commensurable and calculable: which is precisely what is of secondary importance compared with the political and moral questions."[56] Albert's only nonmathematical assumption was that the near future resembled the recent past. Another Pearl Harbor would always be lurking on the horizon. A rapacious enemy loitered at the nation's doorstep, and the predatory nature of that enemy was unchanging, if not static. This majestically ahistorical argument revealed more of the analyst's bias than of the enemy's intentions.

The Wohlstetter Approach to History

Albert Wohlstetter's tendency to repeatedly harp on Stalin's abuses and to conflate Stalin's modus operandi with contemporary trends in the Soviet leadership offers an important window into the Wohlstetter uses of history—their "thinking in time."[57] Contrary to their futuristic public personae, the Wohlstetters' based their reasoning on an excessively formulaic extrapolation from the annals of the recent past. The appeal of the Wohlstetters' strategic vision lay in its historical familiarity, rather than any futuristic ingenuity. Their penchant for trotting out the deceit of twentieth-century totalitarian powers was a sign of the limits of their historical reasoning. These lessons from history were not derived from any disciplined study of the past. Instead, the Wohlstetters embraced a teleological understanding of history in which one assumed—rather than proved—that the events of World War II were part of a recurring human pattern, rather than sui generis, and that little had changed since then. One could always expect a totalitarian power to have maniacal ambitions. The past, therefore, offered instruction on how to stymie the predictable ambitions of this formulaic adversary.

As for the many critics who had accused the Wohlstetters of fabricating a diabolical and unrealistic Soviet enemy, Albert countered that the question of whether the Soviets shared Western values on protecting the lives of the innocent could be assessed empirically. "We need only observe that the Soviets value military power and the means of domination at least as much and possibly more than the lives of Russian civilians." A long list of "careful scholars" had documented the manner in which the Soviets "sacrificed civilian lives for the sake of Soviet power. Their collectivization program in the 1920s gained control over the peasant at the expense of slaughtering some twelve to fifteen million of them."[58]

Albert's incessant dwelling on the Soviets' high tolerance for casualties in World War II struck Bernard Brodie as a deliberate misreading of history. The habitual illustration of the twenty to thirty million Russian lives lost implied that high casualties had been a matter of choice among the Soviet leaders at the time—a sacrifice supposedly voluntarily offered up as a maneuver to entice the Nazis to their destruction. Brodie dismissed this interpretation as a politically motivated distortion of the historical truth.[59]

As it had Brodie, the very idea that the Soviets would willingly sacri-fice tens of millions of citizens for the strategic advantage of a first strike struck P. M. S. Blackett as ahistorical and fantastically demonic. "The history of Russia," he wrote, "tells of many invasions but few military aggressions. Military caution has been a marked characteristic, even to the point, as in 1941, of nearly fatal playing for time."[60] Albert had claimed otherwise, P. M. S. Blackett observed, because the enemy of his compu-tations was a numerical construct bereft of any bearing in reality. Al-bert's Soviets were a hypothetical monster, to which he had specula-tively assigned a species of comic-book-like villainous depravity. Lacking a firm anchoring in history and contemporary social and political reality, Albert's enemy was, in Blackett's view, pure science fiction.

The role of historical events was particularly apparent in the ongoing fusion between the intellectual worlds of Roberta, the historian, and Al-bert, the analyst. The specter of Pearl Harbor encouraged a whole series of logical leaps that, in retrospect, belie the image of clear, hardheaded visions of futuristic warfare. At a loss to present any shred of evidence that the cumbersome Soviet Union had the capacity for strategic sur-prise, Albert and Roberta would later create the notion of "slow Pearl Harbors," which they employed to explain the many unforeseen threats posed by creeping violations of agreements with the Soviet Union. The Soviets' small, cumulative, stealthy breaches of treaties, the Wohlstet-ters would argue in the 1980s, threatened to culminate in a strategic surprise of monumental dimensions.[61] Even as the tides of history changed irrevocably, both Roberta and Albert expressed grave misgiv-ings over mindless "Gorbomania" and dismissed glasnost as a devious ploy to disguise preparations for a massive first strike.[62]

As Roberta so clearly explained, history proved that modern strategic crises were governed by a predictable minuet between an expansionist aggressor and a status quo victim. Writing in 1979, she identified an im-pulse for self-deception among democracies that compulsively placed faith in the good intentions of totalitarian rivals—until it was too late. "The victims in such cases may be the principal deceivers," she cau-tioned. "The adversary may only have to help the victim along a bit." Whether dealing with Germany or the Soviet Union, one could always count on the status quo power—"the victim"—to diminish "what might otherwise look like a rather menacing move." Much like the British on the eve of World War II, the impulse to trivialize and contort signs of a menacing Soviet arms buildup was "strongly affected by our strategic doctrines and political predispositions," rather than by hard data. The British survived Hitler's assault when they finally shook off the "habit of sticking one's head in the sand." Whether the West would avoid a similar fate in its confrontation with the Soviets, Roberta mused, was far from certain.[63]

One admiring historian has described the Wohlstetter oeuvre as a much needed "palliative to the fatalism that sometimes besets the nuclear age."[64] Yet the Wohlstetters' reading of history was inherently fatalistic. In their world, there would always be an enemy lurking at the doorstep for which the only remedy would be unequivocal military resolve, irrespective of the consequences. Such brinkmanship was compounded by a self-referential belief that they possessed the unique insight to tame the historical trajectory of the thermonuclear age.

"The Delicate Balance of Error"

One of Albert's less endearing qualities was his impulse to invective. His response to criticism was vengeance. He reserved particularly harsh words for the scientists who, having created thermonuclear power, had been chastened and appalled by the golem of their creation. In a merciless attack on repentant members of the scientific community who entered the fray of strategic deliberations, Albert complained that, regardless of their technical expertise, these eminent scientists were, at best, highly skilled "technologists" who were no more informed about the perils of the nuclear age than was the mostly ignorant general public. He ridiculed their declarations of concern as false intuition and alarmist divinations. They were affected by "popular fantasies relating the pursuits of science to sorcery" and delusions of supernatural abilities to predict the future.[65] "It is usual to find, at the head of petitions advocating some specific nuclear policy, sentences that run: 'As scientists we have knowledge of the dangers involved,' followed by the signatures of tens or even thousands of scientists, only a few of whom have examined the empirical evidence on one or two of the many alternative dangers involved in the policy choice. Simply as a scientist no one has a knowledge of these complex choices."[66]

If anything, the dangers defined by scientists were irrelevant, moralistic, and maudlin. Driven by phobias of a coming apocalypse, his scientist critics were invariably innocent, unaware of the many variables affecting global strategy. They trivialized the dilemmas of the nuclear world, reducing them to an imaginary dualistic choice between annihilation and global harmony, when in reality the choice was complex.

Albert viscerally attacked the qualifications of unworldly and politically naive scientists, the purveyors of self-induced delusions that they were "free of the insincerities of and dubious motives of the traditional actors on the political scene."[67] If anything, Albert asserted, their unworldliness made scientists particularly inappropriate guardians of the nation's security. They lacked the basic political acumen needed to decipher a dangerous world. By contrast, Albert lauded the nation's policy analysts, expressing confidence that well-trained, objective professionals should replace the false prophets and innocent seers with knowledge and insight garnered through hard labor rather than clairvoyance.

In a series of harsh attacks on dilettante strategists, Albert argued that the future of Western civilization hinged on scientifically verifiable analysis. Empirical analysis, however, was not to be obtained from critics within the scientific community, whom he accused of bipolar meanderings that swung erratically between ill-thought-out preemptive actions and a type of self-restraint that would inevitably invite attacks by a callous enemy.

Scientists were not the only such nuclear Hamlets. Albert singled out Robert McNamara, the secretary of defense during the Cuban missile crisis, as the prototypical vacillating politician who careened wildly between endorsing a variation of Mutually Assured Destruction (MAD) and aggressive plans to match Soviet nuclear ordnance. "Before the Cuban Missile Crisis I found Bob McNamara quite extraordinary as a secretary of defense," Albert remembered in 1986. But the crisis had left McNamara "very shaken," leading him to abandon his previous endorsement of controlled warfare in favor of a deterrence-only policy. Exasperated, Wohlstetter had failed to convince McNamara that the only way to prevent a nuclear conflagration "was by assuring an adversary that not only *could* you retaliate, but you *would* retaliate. I think [McNamara] found it hard to think about that after his experience in the Missile Crisis." Instead, McNamara "moved towards Deterrence-only, which is deterring without intending to do so."[68]

Other secretaries of defense were equally afflicted by manic-depressive swings on strategic policy. Albert accused Harold Brown—who was secretary of defense during the Carter administration and had previously been a physicist at Lawrence Livermore Labs—of being another one of those mealymouthed politicians who "oscillated between the MAD dogma" and a recognition that the Soviets would never endorse an "implicit pact for mutual suicide." Albert summoned Hamlet to describe these vacillations. Brown was "like Hamlet (and McNamara) . . . but MAD north-north-west; when the wind is southerly, he knows a hawk from a handsaw." Now that the winds had changed, these fair-weather politicians became "amazingly susceptible" to maniacal schemes of mutual deterrence that would inevitably lead to tragedy.[69]

The Morality of Nuclear War

The exchange of intellectual barrages on nuclear deterrence shifted dramatically in the early 1980s, when the National Conference of Catholic Bishops issued a pastoral letter on war and peace.[70] Individual religious leaders had expressed misgivings previously, but it was the ostensibly conservative nature of the conference of bishops that altered the nature of the debate. Deriving their views from the moral teachings of the church rather than the think tank and the laboratory, the bishops issued an unequivocally harsh condemnation of the entire corpus of deterrence theory.[71] For the nation's Catholic hierarchy, mainstream nuclear deterrence—whether the "cities-only" stream of MAD or the supposedly distinctive strategy of counterforce—offered equally untenable alternatives. Nuclear strategists of every persuasion had transgressed fundamental church teachings on the nature of free will, just wars, and the promise of an eschatological peace.

Even as they methodically punched holes through technical assertions made by secular deterrence theorists, the bishops insisted that nuclear strategy was primarily a moral and theological debate. They rejected the hardheaded realism of nuclear strategists as dangerous theoretical ruminations unhinged from both empirical reality and eternal truths. The bishops accepted their lay status and basic ignorance of many technical issues. They insisted, however, that theological insights on the hypothetical consequences of a nuclear apocalypse were as relevant as the speculative conclusions of mathematical modeling. The debate between experts and the bishops was thus, as senior Catholic adviser Francis X. Winters put it, "a skirmish between competing

schools of strategic theology," each of which claimed eternal truths derived from different belief systems, rather than clashing interpretations
of a well-defined reality. "It is by no mean self-evident that the biblical
education of the bishops is less helpful to interpreting the meaning of
deterrence than is a training in mathematics," Winters asserted.[72]

Given the fact that no empirical evidence could support any of the
conflicting models of deterrence, the bishops, like Philip Green, dismissed claims to secular omniscience as dangerous speculative exercises. Ideas had consequences, such as directing scarce resources to fight
imaginary wars, the potential for unprecedented obliteration, and a cavalier attitude toward mass killing. Nuclear weapons had the potential
to reverse a godly creation; the nuclear question therefore created an
almost biblical "moment of supreme crisis."[73]

Authoritative insight into apocalyptical crises lay first and foremost
in the scriptures and their interpretation by ordained leaders. In fact,
the bishops claimed, both the New and the Old Testament revealed a
fundamental clash between the eternal truths of the scriptures and the
false prophesies of deterrence theorists of all stripes. The bishops regarded as anathema the very concept that choice could always be reduced to a numerical equation, rather than to a moral imperative. The
immediate implication of such equations was the implicit assumption
that no strategy—however ethically questionable—could be ruled out.
The ultimate objective of survival appeared to override all moral and
religious principles.

The bishops' epistle challenged the very essence of deterrence theory
in general, and Albert's strategic vision in particular, by questioning its
framing as an unprecedented existential challenge. The champions of
deterrence theory had constructed the bipolar tensions between the superpowers as an unrivaled challenge to the body politic, with attendant
exclusive rights to massive government expenditures, in order to void
an existential threat. The bishops, by contrast, listed other existential
crises of a similar magnitude, all of which had been marginalized by
the deflection of resources to military channels. The "chasm in living
standards" between the industrialized world and developing societies
represented a moral failure that "rivals the nuclear issue in its human
significance."[74] Such moral challenges, the bishops declared, entailed a
rethinking of the meaning of "national interest," including reallocating
resources away from the bottomless pit of military research and devel-

opment.[75] "The fact of a massive distortion of resources in the face of crying human need creates a moral question," the bishops insisted. "The threats to the security and stability of an interdependent world are not all contained in missiles and bombers."[76]

The bishops approached nuclear weapons as something fundamentally new. Their lethal quality placed them in the unique category of indiscriminate weapons of mass destruction that precluded any argument for their deployment in warfare. None of Albert's reasoning regarding growing precision and smaller warheads could convince the bishops to lower their tone. In a direct challenge to the RAND mantra of controlled escalation, the bishops found the premise of tactical nuclear war untenable. No one had crossed, and no one should ever cross that threshold. Even if one were to assume growing accuracy and more discriminating use, "crossing the boundary from the conventional to the nuclear arena in any form" took humanity into "a world where we have no experience of control" but "much testimony against its possibility and therefore no moral justification for . . . this risk."[77] Nuclear weapons, as the philosopher Michael Walzer remarked, "explode the theory of Just War."[78] Advocacy of nuclear deployment—tactical, strategic, or otherwise—was inherently immoral. The bishops remained unconvinced that any form on nuclear deployment could maintain the discrimination and proportionality of a just war against a well-defined threat.

Bruce Russett, the Georgetown political scientist who had been the Catholic bishops' main adviser on the pastoral letter, in an article published in the wake of the bishops' epistle, reiterated the bishops' rejection of the idea that technological advancements, promoted by the " 'priesthood' of civilian and military strategists," trumped the authority of "Catholic teaching on peace and war."[79] Free choice, fellow Georgetown professor Francis X. Winters added, "may not legitimately be construed to include options which significantly risk abandoning future choice."[80] Strategies for waging nuclear war assumed high levels of uncertainty and were therefore morally unjustifiable. No matter how accurate new nuclear weaponry might be, a graduated nuclear exchange would surely spiral out of control, culminating in a level of destruction that would violate the severe limits of doctrinarian just war. "The schism between the bishops and the strategists on deterrence rests finally on differing views of freedom," wrote Winters. "In the Catholic tradition, at least, freedom does not mean the capacity to do whatever is feasible, but only whatever is reasonable . . . Freedom, the bishops believe, is also a self-denying faculty, in this case the capacity to say 'no' to nuclear war."[81]

Albert rejected the bishops' claim of equal partnership in the debate. Preaching from the pages of *Commentary,* the flagship of Jewish conservative intellectuals, Albert dismissed the church's authority in matters of the nuclear state. "I don't think that the differences between the strategy the bishops advocate and a strategy emphasizing discriminate and proportionate responses can be settled by an appeal to theology or even to philosophy."[82] While acknowledging that designing a strategy for warfare that had never occurred was fraught with dangers of an unimaginable quality, Albert had little tolerance for self-doubt derived from suspect moral grounds. The key to obviating the eruption of a new form of warfare, he believed, did not reside in pious homilies. When faced with "cardinal choice," he wrote, "prophecy is precarious and moral certainty hard to justify."[83] Decisions guiding war and peace should be driven by technological capacities rather than the restraints of an incoherently defined moral compass.

The bishops, Albert contended, were stuck in the paradigms of the 1950s, and "the old apparition of our spurring an arms race by doing too much."[84] Their pontifications on the "morality of bombing and deterrence" were oblivious of the manner in which the "evolution since the 1950s of technologies other than the release of nuclear energy has altered the possibilities of discrimination" between military and civilian targets. New technologies, rather than unenforceable arms agreements, promised to uphold the moral premises of just war. Discriminating technologies offered the possibility of rising above an indiscriminate arms race and of investing, instead, in weapons that could be aimed with great accuracy at exclusively military targets. Confronting credible, cutting-edge threats, rather than unearthing allegedly eternal truths from irrelevant holy scriptures, offered the key to taming an unremitting enemy who did not recognize the moral teachings of the church. Thanks to such new weaponry, there was no longer an "incompatibility of morality and statecraft in the nuclear age."[85]

Instead of recognizing this new reality, the bishops had embarked on selective cherry-picking to support an outdated argument. Their certainty of a limited nuclear clash spiraling out of control relied "heavily on a three-and-a-half-page study embodying the views of fourteen scientists who seem mainly to be specialists in public health." By the same token, the "papal study" brushed aside overwhelming evidence on the salutary effect of technological advances, devoting only "one paragraph to a 'nuclear attack directed only at military facilities.'" If only the bishops would recognize the moral nature of new weapons, Albert implied, they, too, could sit on the side of the angels.

At first glance, the pastoral letter was a continuation of ecclesiastical intervention dating back to the aftermath of the Cuban missile crisis. The American bishops were following in the footsteps of Pope John XXIII, who, in 1963, had issued his own warning on nuclear annihilation in his "Pacem in Terris."[86] But as had been the case with that encyclical, the American conference of Catholic Bishops embedded their warnings of nuclear conflagration within a broad critique of contemporary Western society. While ostensibly concerned with the role of nuclear weapons in the global arena, the American bishops ventured further. Their statement was first and foremost an appraisal of prevalent assumptions on the role of the nation-state in a perilous world.

The pastoral leaders had moved the debate out of the comfort zone of security experts who preached a maximalist police effort from a minimalist government. By expanding notions of existential threats, the bishops created a public space for debate on issues that the Wohlstetters and others aspired to limit. The pastoral letter urged centralized intervention in a gamut of social crises, domestic and global. The Wohlstetters, as we shall see, considered such thoughts a violation of the separation of church and state. As the following chapters demonstrate, the Wohlstetter Doctrine aligned itself with a minimalist role of government. Beyond the provision of domestic and national security, the state had restricted responsibilities in the lives of its citizens. A socially interventionist government, they would argue, would distort the creation of a just society through the hidden hand of unfettered economic activity. Albert urged the bishops to avoid straying down the path of the protest movements in "Protestant Northern Europe."[87] They should, instead, recognize the enemy and have faith in those ordained to maintain the integrity of an embattled Western civilization.

5

Castrophobia and the Free Market

The Wohlstetters' Moral Economy

I N THE MIDDLE OF one of her 1960s polemics on Cuba, Roberta Wohlstetter made a startling assertion. Seven months before the Warren Report was published, she had accumulated "intriguing clues" that connected Fidel Castro to the assassination of John F. Kennedy. It was "not beyond the realm of imagination," she suggested, that the *"Máximo Líder"* had "contemplated the assassination of President Kennedy, not by his own hand, but perhaps by a devoted or fanatical follower."[1]

Together with her RAND colleague and confidante Nathan Leites, Roberta had constructed a psychological composite of the Cuban dictator as a violent, conniving individual, "a wreckage of conflicts and contradictions."[2] Castro was "very far from the Bolshevik model of discipline and emotional control . . . There are large degrees of irrationality, impulsiveness, impatience, guilt and pride."[3] He boasted publicly about his machismo, while at the same time "hating confrontation, hating brute force, extremely proud and vain, confused by his homosexual tendencies."[4] This type of individual "prefers death off the stage, as in a Greek tragedy . . . if it were necessary to kill in order to preserve the revolution, he would have someone else do the killing."[5]

Roberta's first shreds of circumstantial evidence leading down a trail to the assassination were Castro's clandestine excursions to the United States. Citing a recent biography of the dictator, she reported that in 1956, in order to meet with Cuban dissidents in Texas, Castro had secretly crossed the Rio Grande "by mingling with the wetbacks."[6] A few months after his rise to power in 1959, Castro had also visited Cuban political prisoners in Texas jails. Meanwhile, Lee Harvey Oswald's trips to Texas and to the Cuban consulate in Mexico City, as well as his ties to the Fair Play for Cuba Committee in both Texas and Louisiana, made the Cuban-Oswald connection seem plausible. As supporting evidence, Roberta cited Castro's harsh diatribes against Kennedy. In one ominous pronouncement, made in reference to JFK's hit on Vietnamese dictator Ngo Dinh Diem, Castro declared that Kennedy was not "the only head of state who can order assassinations."[7] Roberta even found "characteristics of Oswald which are like Castro's and might conceivably have attracted him to Castro."[8]

Roberta's version of a conspiracy theory lionized Castro and redeemed Oswald from the ranks of the criminally insane. No longer was Oswald a lone, crazed gunman. With the stroke of a pen, he had become a fanatical black knight, a deadly proxy in a carefully orchestrated scheme to eliminate Kennedy's challenge to the Castro regime. We are left wondering how Roberta—the previous year's winner of the Bancroft Prize—could have been swept away by the siren song of international intrigue with so little evidence at her disposal.

Roberta's Oswald-Castro dossier amounted, at best, to a tattered collection of anecdotal allegations. Her flimsy "clues" were hardly damning. Nathan Leites, the RAND colleague who served as a mentor and sounding board for Roberta's Cuban phase, gently urged her to distance herself from conspiracy theory. Her accusations, he warned her, were "too strong." At most, Leites guessed, Castro "may have entertained such a thought subconsciously."[9] There was no evidence to implicate a nefarious plot with Oswald in the role of Cuban pawn.

At a purely intellectual level, Roberta acknowledged that her argument may have had psychological motives that had little to do with hard facts. "The explanation of conspiracy for an act of pure evil has one aspect which appeals to all of us. We do not want to believe that the president died by the hand of a jealous and enraged psychopath on the margin of our society, but rather that he died for his beliefs and actions. The conspiracy theory at least makes the president's murder more worthy of the march of events we call history, makes it not an accidental misfortune, but a tragedy in something like the Aristotelian sense."[10] Roberta was painfully aware that conspiracy theories were the domain of marginal groups in American society; the John Birch Society was then in full flower. Still, she was reluctant to let go of the possibility.

"As the outlines of Oswald's biography begin to be filled in," she temporized, "the act seems more and more to have been entirely his own. Nevertheless, to dismiss the notion of conspiracy, before the Warren Commission's report . . . would perhaps . . . be unwise."[11]

Many years later, Albert gave new life to Roberta's ruminations, suggesting that the Wohlstetters continued to harbor a conspiracy thesis of foreign collusion in the Kennedy assassination. During the course of a 1984 conference on "Armenian terrorism" held in Turkey, Albert dismissed the theory of Oswald as the "lone gunman" as naive. Citing approvingly an article by Joseph Sobran—who would later be removed from the staff of the *National Review* following charges of anti-Semitism and Holocaust denial—Albert argued that there was no need for an irrefutable "smoking gun" to tie Oswald to Cuba or the Soviet Union. The compatibility of Soviet and Cuban interest with Oswald's actions was proof enough. Whenever communists are involved in nefarious acts, Albert complained, "the press seems to require a direct statement from the KGB, which would still not be believed since it would be too direct."[12]

The Wohlstetters' attraction to the specter of a foreign-born conspiracy becomes more comprehensible when seen in the larger context of their approach to the American body politic. Their preoccupation with foreign maliciousness and their attendant unwillingness to look within American society for the root causes of domestic political violence was quite in character. In their extensive writings on internal American issues, the Wohlstetters consistently understated the endogenous causes of violence and dysfunction. Foreign vectors of instability—real or imaginary—deflected the Wohlstetters' attention from the structural pathologies of American society. A dysfunctional political process, student protests, racial discrimination, and the rampant recourse to violence in the American public sphere did little to disturb the Wohlstetters' quest for foreign subversion. Despite troubling evidence to the contrary, the United States remained a City on a Hill, albeit a city occasionally under siege.

Alien interventions were not the only explanation the Wohlstetters furnished for America's malaise. The heavy hand of an intrusive government, as well as any other form of monopolistic regime—social, economic, or political—stifled the free flow of creative energies that defined the United States as a nation sui generis. They identified many of the nation's root problems as the result of deviation from the self-regulation of the marketplace and its harmonious confluence of private interests. Genuine social justice, a thriving political culture, and great cultural achievements required pluralism and a minimalist central authority.

The Radicalism of the Market

In the course of a 1960 symposium on "The National Purpose," Albert argued that the marketplace, not grand governmental design, provided the basis for sustaining cultural creativity and a functioning democratic society. Entitled "No Highway to High Purpose," his essay offered a decidedly contrarian response to the theme linking most of the other essays: the notion that loss of national purpose was precipitating national decline. Unlike his fellow contributors, Albert did not endorse the pompous premise of an all-encompassing "national purpose" lying dormant in some dusty archive or ensconced in the deeds of the founding fathers. There was no singular national purpose. "To ask for our national purpose suggests that there is one high overriding aim waiting ready-made, if not to be found by leafing through some documents, perhaps to be revealed effortlessly as in a dream." For Albert, multiple visions of a collective mission, competing in a thriving and healthy marketplace of ideas, allowed the nation to flourish. The rich American tapestry of choice, in general, and cultural and political choice, in particular, militated against a single gold standard. Uniform and unchanging ideals, he argued, would be hard to justify.[13]

Albert had little patience for those who feared that rampant consumerism would lead to economic and social irresponsibility, to an inevitable descent into the abyss of a mass-market, cultural mediocrity. Midcentury America's supposedly commodified culture, he was convinced, actually presented more opportunities than challenges. Albert acknowledged his own ambivalence about certain attributes of contemporary mass culture, ranging from rock and roll to the obsession with automobile tail fins. He nevertheless insisted that despite these manifestations of cultural fluff, the free enterprise system actually fostered excellence. Albert declared that mass-produced cultural artifacts—the scourge of cultural critics on both right and left—represented unambiguously positive forces. Mass culture democratized both access to and appreciation

of hitherto restricted cultural domains. The mechanisms of mass culture, he explained, had allowed for the cheap reproduction of artistic
masterpieces in paperback and on vinyl, to mention but two of the great
achievements of the American culture industry. In the self-regulating
marketplace of ideas, aestheticism thrived. Citing the conductor Pablo
Casals, Albert observed that "when good music is easy to hear it can successfully compete with rock'n'roll."[14]

The much-maligned mediocrity of popular culture had not "sub-
merged poets such as Robert Lowell and Elizabeth Bishop, artists of the
order of Alexander Calder, the choreographers Martha Graham and
George Balanchine." In fact, the logic of the marketplace had liberated
the United States from the perils of parochialism. Using architecture as
a particular example, Albert extolled the nation's "abundance of excellent architects—Mies van der Rohe, Eero Saarinen, Gordon Bunshaft,
Marcel Breuer, Walter Gropius, Richard Neutra and many others."[15] This
pantheon of great American architects exemplified, by implication, another element of the nation's algorithm for success. With the exception
of Bunshaft, an American-born son of Jewish immigrants, these lauded
architects were all immigrants who thrived by virtue of the uniquely
American confluence of commercial opportunity and artistic genius.

The Economics of Racism and Discrimination

The Wohlstetters believed that a self-regulating, market-driven American society would correct deviations in the political and social domain,
as well. Rational economic choice among individuals, rather than the
heavy ideological hand of government policy, promised to eliminate social and political pathologies. The disturbing presence of racial inequity
in midcentury America represented a case in point. The Wohlstetters
were genuinely appalled by the blight of racism. They recognized discrimination as morally abhorrent and an embarrassment for the United
States in the global arena. They were dismayed, however, by wrongheaded diagnoses of and remedies for this vexing affliction. The injustices afflicting American society, they argued, would not be eradicated
by the revolutionary moves of a centralized authority but by the cumulative and marvelously pragmatic decisions of ordinary individuals.

The Wohlstetters declared their distaste for government intervention
by means of affirmative action on numerous occasions. If left to its own

devices, they argued, the modern marketplace would eradicate discrimination and mitigate prejudice on its own. They believed that once the dominant group in American society became cognizant of discrimination's effect on its own economic well-being, the logic of rational individualism would weaken vestiges of discrimination more effectively than government policy ever could.

Citing their eminent University of Chicago colleague Gary Becker, they contended that market forces would eventually eliminate unfairness because "the aggregate net income of the white and nonwhite 'societies' is reduced by discrimination." Economic interest would encourage white employers to seek cheaper black labor, thereby lifting African Americans out of abject impoverishment. "Firms employing Negroes tend to prosper more than firms that don't, since the former can purchase their labor at lower money cost." There was no need for the government to do battle with poverty. The drive to maximize individual profit, rather than the centralized social policies of misinformed bureaucrats, offered the most expedient route to a more equitable job market and, eventually, to racial justice.[16] In a modern economy left to its own devices, discrimination in the economic sphere would fade away.

Well-meaning efforts to level the playing field through state intervention actually lowered African Americans' living standards. "Some of the programs that have been devised specifically to aid nonwhite and other poor have frequently had an opposite effect," they claimed. "Minimum wage laws often have resulted in Negroes not getting employed at all rather than getting employed at a higher wage. Welfare payments have been coupled with means tests which reduce incentives for employment and savings and have tended to break up the Negro family."[17] Regulation and welfare were regressive, not progressive.

The Wohlstetters were not only fervent believers in the self-correcting mechanisms of markets. They also espoused an early version of what the political scientist Albert Hirschman would later call the "perversity thesis," whereby any attempt to create radical change would inevitably induce an unintended reaction in the opposite direction.[18] By this logic, the allegedly game-changing social initiatives of the 1960s—civil rights reforms and the "War on Poverty"—actually hurt the very people they intended to help by distorting market mechanisms. Lasting change, they argued, required organic social evolution rather than coercive political revolution.

On the one hand, Michael Walzer explains, in another context, intellectuals such as the Wohlstetters were profoundly convinced that there were "radical limits" to government attempts to control and direct social change. Such efforts, they argued, thwarted and distorted the organic and "radical social force," of the free market, a powerful fount of energy that "overturns all habits and customs and continually transforms daily life."[19] If there was an active role for government in ending discrimination, it was its capacity to promote equal access to education. When measured through the imperfect lens of income distribution, racial inequality decreased in proportion to the number of years of schooling completed. "Equalizing the schooling distribution," they found, "closes the average income gap by about one-third," and closes it even more for women.[20] Progress in education meant progress against discrimination.

The Wohlstetters also identified the exogenous shock of foreign war as a factor contributing to discrimination's decline. "Large advances in the status of nonwhites have occurred," they asserted, "as unintended byproducts in the conduct of foreign wars." Contrary to the common complaint that wasteful foreign wars deflected resources from domestic programs, the Wohlstetters described the counterintuitive phenomenon as a "grim paradox." As far as civil rights were concerned, foreign wars creatively disrupted patterns of racism. By historical accident, "the tangible rewards to Negroes in the form of command over goods and services grew most rapidly in absolute and relative terms during World War II, during Korea and during the expansion of the war in Vietnam."[21] National security crises hastened progress toward racial equality while exposing the ineffectual, if not negative, impact of clumsy government social engineering. To support their position, the Wohlstetters quoted the eminent black writer Ralph Ellison: "Speaking historically, our condition has been bettered in this country during periods of national disaster. . . . As much as I dislike warfare . . . I know that the people who are going to rule the South together under the new political situation there will be the black and white Southerners who are fighting together in Vietnam, getting to know one another in a manner that was not possible before, to know one another without the myths of racial inferiority or superiority."[22]

Albert and Roberta described war's allegedly positive domestic effects, both within the military and beyond, as an instructive irony.

Even though—or perhaps because—government spending on foreign wars undercut government-designed social engineering, wartime conditions significant increased employment opportunities and income levels among minorities. "If one thinks of the labor market in the form of a queue with Negroes at the end of the queue, then in a slack labor market employers don't reach the end of the queue. In a tight one, they do. Consequently, even though this war and other wars may rate strenuous disapproval on other grounds, their effect has been to improve the employment and income status of Negroes absolutely and relatively to whites."[23] Labor-market contraction far eclipsed government-designed assaults on poverty and discrimination. Emergencies, national security threats in particular, were great equalizers. These were times when employment exigencies trumped color and race.

For all of their attempts to muster empirical evidence, the Wohlstetters' road map for racial equality evinced a certain blindness to the perpetuation of racism in contemporary American society. In fact, their theory of war and social justice flew in the face of contemporary realities. Discrimination followed African American conscripts to the battlefields of Indochina, and they returned home bearing the scars of endemic military bigotry.[24] Yet the nagging persistence of social inequities, effaced by neither war nor peace, failed to shake the Wohlstetters' convictions. Instead, the couple explained away their theory's weaknesses by implicating foreign interference in American domestic affairs.

Colonialism at Home and Abroad

The violence erupting in America's urban ghettoes in the 1960s served as a case in point. While acknowledging the fundamental issues of segregation, poverty, and basic injustice, the Wohlstetters lashed out at common descriptions of this particularly fraught period in the nation's history. Metaphors derived from the condition of colonialism—in this case, an unequal exchange between an internal white-controlled center and a black periphery—had muddied the waters of American race dynamics. The intrusion of these allegedly alien concepts into the discourse on social justice in the United States was no passing intellectual fad or flippant abuse of language. Instead, the conceptual shift suggested the incursion of foreign matter into the debate on the nation's social challenges.

The Wohlstetters identified the Cuban regime as the leading foreign instigator of racial destabilization in the United States.[25] Expatriate Black Power radicals were broadcasting "incitements to revolt at the American Negro" from the safety of Cuban shores. Both Fidel Castro and Che Guevara were in active contact with the Black Muslim movement and were using their diplomatic immunity to foment racial antagonism during their visits to the United Nations General Assembly in New York. Cuban revolutionary theory did not require the presence of "objective conditions for revolutionary success" among African Americans. Conditions could be fabricated "by the guerilla revolutionary himself" through words as well as deeds.[26]

The most subversive result of the Cuban-inspired aggravation of racial tensions, the Wohlstetters argued, was the contamination of language. Outside forces were winning the battle of metaphors, saturating American racial discourse in the lexicon of decolonization, to the point that even well-meaning commentators commonly drew comparisons between the plight of African Americans and Third World struggles. In their typical belligerent manner, Albert and Roberta impugned academic innocents, black separatists, and other political radicals—both newcomers and holdouts from their own radical past—for bundling racial strife at home with postcolonialism abroad.[27] Words, they reminded their readers, had consequences. Metaphors were not merely rhetorical flourish. They were framing devices for determining root causes as well as solutions. In the Wohlstetters' eyes, the misrepresentation of urban riots as a local variation of colonial struggles had adulterated the terms of debate, while fanning the flames of the long, hot summers of the 1960s. The colonial artifact aided and abetted Marxism-Leninism as an explanation for the rampant poverty and powerlessness in Western societies. Such erroneous metaphors promoted a confusion of radical, imported solutions that impeded both minority economic progress and the advancement of civil rights.[28]

The alleged bearers of these un-American analogies amounted to an untidy crew of the naive as well as the ideologically motivated. They either lacked knowledge or willfully ignored the obvious difference between struggles abroad and the plight of minorities at home. For some, the recourse to inflammatory tropes of colonialism resulted from a combination of both political inclination and theoretical error.[29]

The Wohlstetters took on the economist Gunnar Myrdal as an example of a wolfish reformer in sheep's clothing. Myrdal had written both a pathbreaking study of racism in American society and influential examinations of the divide between the Third World and industrialized nations. He was a major proponent of centralized efforts to lift the margins of American society out of poverty and to undo the scourge of racism. As far as Myrdal was concerned, racism was firmly wedged into American society. It was a stable pattern of behavior with deep historical roots and could only be dislodged by affirmative government action.[30]

This approach, of course, was anathema to the Wohlstetters, who extolled the efficiencies and moral superiority of free enterprise and discovered false benevolence in state-run welfare programs. Following in the footsteps of the economist Gary Becker, they saw discrimination as a "taste," an ephemeral cultural artifact that would disappear with changing material conditions.[31] The key to the nation's social well-being was a robust economy. Their economic blueprint for racial equality minimized the need to examine the historical roots of discrimination in American society and discounted its embedded vestiges. The history of racial inequities had only passing bearing on the present or the future because the post–World War II economic boom had burned the bridges to the past. The rational behavior of profit-maximizing individuals in contemporary American society provided an economic trajectory that could eclipse retrogressive practices and institutions. Contrary to their long-held beliefs on the cyclical nature of history, the Wohlstetters saw no compelling reason to dig into an uncomfortable past.

Myrdal, by contrast, turned to history to discover the root causes of endemic institutional racism in the United States. Racism was not the peculiar institution of an economically regressive South, in his view. It was ingrained in the American psyche and could only be effaced through unrelenting policy interventions. Myrdal's work directly contradicted the Wohlstetters' creed of black advancement through general economic improvement. In the Wohlstetter-Becker model, there appeared to be nothing unique about discrimination toward blacks. As Becker had stated in the master text for this paradigm, the model he had developed explained discrimination against "Jews, women, or persons with 'unpleasant personalities.'"[32] The key to the dissipation of discrimination-as-taste lay in the nation's economic fortunes. Discrimination of any kind in a tight labor market would be too costly to sustain.

In Myrdal, the Wohlstetters faced a formidable intellectual rival whom they could not dismiss out of hand. Unable to dispel his resonance and public notoriety, they resorted to innuendo, insinuating that he harbored a hidden radical agenda. They placed him alongside the Fabian British economist Barbara Ward and the communist, antiapartheid activist Ronald Segal—both of whom examined racial issues in the United States within a larger global context. Roberta and Albert then attacked this amalgamated adversary for its tendency to describe the American predicament as a North-South struggle between poor nations of color and the affluent West.[33]

Myrdal and his fellow travelers, they implied, were inspired by none other than Lin Biao (then written Piao), the Maoist marshal who epitomized China's revolutionary drive into foreign lands. According to the Wohlstetters, Myrdal and his ilk had conflated America's race riots with Lin Biao's "internal war between a peasant countryside and the cities that the peasant revolutionaries besiege." This allegedly "extreme version" of "the countryside 'encircling' the city" instilled in the minds of concerned Americans the patently false understanding of race relations in the United States as part of a worldwide struggle between "colonies and the imperial power." It was thus both erroneous and dangerous.[34]

The Wohlstetters did not dismiss, in a similar fashion, everyone who employed the rhetoric of anticolonialism as ideologically contaminated. Some of the perpetrators were well-meaning academics merely exhibiting questionable intellectual rigor. A gamut of academic moderates had fallen into the slipshod vogue of confounding Third World struggles with the civil rights crisis in the United States. Not all eminent commentators on American race relations endorsed the fashionable notion of a white center of economic power and a dependent black periphery that "are inherently or irreconcilably opposed."[35] Yet many in academia still often mindlessly partook in its underlying linguistic conventions.

The Wohlstetters acknowledged that "international, cross-national and cross-temporal experience can illuminate the highly uncertain relations between American domestic inequalities and civil disorders." They felt certain, however, that most academic observers had failed to grasp the distinct qualities of these two variables. Many analysts lacked the capacity to assess the quantitative indicators of "wealth, skills, specialties," and were oblivious to the fragile equilibrium of economic indicators affecting "partially conflicting, partially common interests" of the dominant society and its struggling underclass. They had constructed, instead, a simplistic "zero-sum" world, in which the gains of one group implied a net loss for the other.[36] Ignoring the data and the quantitative analysis of it, the typical sociologist merely confused economic disparity with a false understanding of American race relations.

The black sociologist Kenneth Clark served as an example of an academic innocent led astray by careless metaphors. Swept away by the inflammatory rhetoric of militants, the manifestly moderate Clark had declared that "the dark ghettos are social, political, educational, and—above all—economic colonies."[37] In the Wohlstetters' view, Clark's position was aiding and abetting radical black separatists in the United States, even though Clark himself was aware of the economic and political futility of such movements. The Wohlstetters also called the conservatives Nathan Glazer and Daniel Moynihan to task. By mentioning—though not endorsing—the poisonous comparison of Jewish shopkeepers in Harlem and colonialist exploiters, they were echoing the conflation of domestic racial strife with irrelevant global tensions.[38]

Blinded by imprecise language that eluded the type of rigor only mathematical modeling could achieve, these intellectual enablers had assisted—by ineptitude or volition—a nefarious political agenda. Deprived of quantitative evidence that suggested otherwise, they had fallen into a trap set by American radicals and their foreign enablers. They were providing ammunition to a host of foreign-inspired domestic populists. The pantheon included Stokely Carmichael, the primary domestic agent of Che and Mao, and the indomitable Malcolm X, the high priest of separatist dogma. Metaphors of colonialism sustained the separatists' indefensible doctrine of black autarky. The "Two Nation" trope of colony and colonizer presupposed the need to free one from the other. "For militants, it implies an antagonism of interest best handled by making the separation more complete and violent."[39]

In fact, the Wohlstetters claimed, the daunting social walls that enclosed the African American ghetto were permeable and transient. And it was economic opportunity and industrial specialization that would blaze the path through them, not some version of Third World self-sufficiency. When left to their own devices, and shielded from external meddling, African Americans would follow in the footsteps of "the Italians and the Jews in the garment industry, the Italians in shoemaking, the Irish in the police . . . and so on," providing "goods and services to the larger society and not merely to their own ethnic groups."[40] The Wohlstetters did not identify the exact type of industry that would provide this magical moment for African Americans. It would presumably rise immaculately from the providence of the market.

The connection between social justice and free enterprise supported the Wohlstetters' version of a moral economy, as well. Following the path of a large group of intellectuals who had accomplished the intellectual journey from the anti-Stalinist Left to conservative values, they defined America's communist enemies—from the distant Russian Bolsheviks to their dangerously proximate Cuban proxies—as motived by a hostility to pluralism of all kinds.[41] Communists promoted the antithesis of a rational choice model of competing ideas. These ideological monopolists were singularly dedicated to the eradication of all aspects of competition—economic, political, and social. And it was monopolism that made socialist economies and political systems dysfunctional and oppressive. The Wohlstetters believed that an unfettered marketplace of ideas was the first step toward the creation of an open society. For these reasons, they concluded, one could not expect the free-flowing ingenuity associated with capitalist societies to induce change in ideologically monopolistic societies. Cuba, once again, provided an immediate illustration of the Wohlstetter paradigm.

Fat and Thin Communists

In the formative years of the Castro regime, influential commentators had cautioned against the facile conflation of Cuba with the Soviet Union. Some commentators even advocated extensive economic aid as a means of loosening the bonds between the island nation and its Bolshevik benefactors. As far as Cuba was concerned, the Wohlstetters rejected the fashionable notion of the "Fat Communist" as a tool for reducing the dangerous tensions between East and West. According to partisans of the theory, Western economic assistance to, and cooperation with, Moscow's satellites would undermine the cohesion of the communist bloc. "As long as . . . GNP increases substantially faster than population," ran the theory, "the individual totalitarian dictatorship will mellow and progress toward democracy internally and become less aggressive externally."[42] In other words, affluence would act as the solvent of communism.

Fat Communist theory, Jeffrey Engel has explained, was a variation of the Cold War paradigm of modernization.[43] Modernization theory assumed an inevitable one-way transition from tradition-bound subsistence economies to technologically intensive industrialized economies. Incremental increases in individual freedom and the ultimate demise of authoritarian political systems would accompany the trajectory. In other words, modernization was a package deal. Economic development induced, or was induced by, eurhythmic transitions in political and personal freedom.

Becoming modern entailed the acceptance of Western mores of meritocracy, individual freedom, and a benign political system. Modernization theorists assumed that even communist societies would stray from constraining artificial hindrances like political and economic monopoly and eventually converge toward prototypical Western societal arrangements.[44] Modernization, according to this logic, would produce the prototypical Fat Communists, an affluent and influential cadre of professionals for whom stability and open relations with the West would become prerequisites for their continuing prosperity. According to such logic, "contentment at home (the fat Communist) bred complacency and peaceful relations abroad."[45]

The Wohlstetters were skeptical of modernization theory and its Fat Communist offshoot. In their world, the rising fortunes of Fat Communist theory were a passing but dangerous whim, wishful rather than evidence-based thinking. It was fuzzy logic, reflecting the pipe dreams of effete French and British intellectuals who had lost their stomach for ideological confrontation. The uncritical embrace of Fat Communist theory and its derivatives, they complained, offered a deceptive theoretical prop for the belief that economic support through "trade with Communism is the way to mellow it." The unsupported notion that "Fat Communists are easier to get along with," and that "greater contact means greater means greater possibility of influence" had become a cornerstone of British and French policy. Fat Communist partisans could muster no empirical evidence to support their case.

Fat Communism, for the Wohlstetters, hinged on a series of false propositions. Offering examples of totalitarian regimes where flourishing economies had actually encouraged recklessness, Roberta and Albert found no empirical evidence "to establish such a simple relationship between 'mellowness' and 'fatness.' "[46] In fact, they considered, Western investments in Soviet bloc countries would moderate Western criticism of communist-inspired crackdowns, rather than soften its sources. They predicted that Western bankers and industrialists who were poised to gain from investment in new communist governments would pressure Western leaders to silently accept deviant communist behavior for fear of losing their loans and investments.[47]

The most disturbing aspect of Fat Communist theory, however, was its implicit assumption that some form of communism was "here to stay." The best the West could hope for, its theorists lamented, was a more malleable and splintered form of communist artifact. The notion that the United States should encourage the supposedly nonaligned "Tito variety of Communist regime" struck them as untenable. It was an offshoot of "the old-fashioned, vague, and question-begging" sphere-of-influence view of international politics. Such policies rested on the unacceptable "dogmatic assumption" that communist regimes were "permanent and irreversible."[48]

Rejecting Fat Communism, the Wohlstetters proposed, instead, their own theory of the Thin Communist. Taking Castro's Cuba as an example, they argued that continuing economic failures would eventually weaken this regime beyond reprieve. Economic mismanagement encouraged strife, power struggles, and popular resentment that would eventually reach a tipping point. Within this context, the Wohlstetters rejected the notion that the way to tame annoying enemies such as Fidel Castro was to assist in the reconstruction of his beleaguered economy. Such assistance would produce neither a less paranoid domestic posture nor a gradual "turn to democracy."[49]

Instead, they contended, "the opening up of trade between the United States and Cuba would rally a good deal of influential support on his side, [and generate] pressure by those U.S. businessmen who would be selling [goods] to and would like to expand their trade with Castro. And the pressure would be precisely for the U.S. government to furnish credits to Castro and to offer guarantees to its own nationals against the risks of dealing with him." Expansive trade "is more likely to release strong incentives and pressures for going much further and to create a substantial and respectable Castro lobby."[50] Artificial sustenance for a communist regime would provide a crutch for a system that was otherwise doomed to fail. Even without the type of rampant mismanagement that characterized the Castro regime, the inherent contradictions of the Cuban economic system spelled its ultimate demise.

A strategy of perpetuating and even aggravating the plight of the Thin Communist, in Cuba and elsewhere, offered the additional advantage of draining the master regime's resources. To maintain a friendly regime in Cuba, they explained, the Soviet Union poured an unconscionable portion of its resources into the island's faltering economy. "Cuba took two-fifths of the [Soviet] bloc's total foreign aid in 1963, and a tenth of a percent of its GNP." Such extraordinary dedication of resources rivaled the United States' most expensive foreign debacle in South Vietnam, which had cost the nation "a tenth of our own foreign aid that year and .07 percent of our GNP."[51]

Instead of modernization theory, the Wohlstetters endorsed what Jeffrey Engel has called a Lockean "catechism." This doctrine predicted that a rupture of the social contract between incompetent leaders and resentful, thin subjects would spur communism's collapse. Unable to fulfill the basic requirements of providing sustenance and protection for its citizens, embattled communist regimes would face dissent and, eventually, uprisings—such as the ones that had erupted in East Germany in 1953 and Hungary in 1956—provoked by their governments' violations of the social contract.[52] Cuba provided a vivid illustration of the paradigm. Castro's unrelenting policies of collectivization, they thought, had brought the Cuban economy to its knees and had induced an irreversible schism between the regime and its people. Castro bore responsibility for these policies. "The Cuban masses," in turn, were manifesting their disaffection through "low productivity," and would soon turn to more visible forms of resistance.[53]

The Wohlstetters did advocate aid to some vulnerable communist regimes, such as Yugoslavia, but for reasons that had little to do with fostering Fat Communism. Aid to Yugoslavia would accentuate its leaders' predisposition to distance themselves from Soviet domination. Unlike Cuba, Yugoslavia was uninterested in exporting revolution and, given its special status, was most likely to employ American aid—covert or otherwise—to further strengthen its nonaligned status.

As for Cuba, the Wohlstetters advocated a holding pattern. A prudent government, Albert wrote, would avoid the siren songs of the

political extremes. It would ignore those advocating the economic sta-
bilization of Cuba as much as it would "the right-wing elements that
urge invasion." Cuba would not be brought down by conquest, but by an
implosion caused by the sheer dysfunctionality of its economic superstructure. Given this inevitable process, the Wohlstetters were ambivalent
about American support for resistance groups. Intrusive policies such
as the hapless Bay of Pigs invasion had proven hard to control and in
any case constituted distractions that hampered the steady pace of regime disintegration. "It seems very doubtful that the government of
the United States can do very much actively to promote a democratic
revolution," they observed. "However, at the very least it can avoid . . .
seeming to support either Castro's Communism or the corrupt and stag-
nant elite against which the revolution was made."[54] Many years later,
when faced with a Castro-like dictator in Iraq, the Wohlstetters would
reverse their aversion to the use of military power against recalcitrant
tyrants. One can only surmise that Castro's astounding political lon-
gevity may have contributed to their lack of patience for the inevitable
decline of Saddam Hussein.

If, indeed, Cuba was hamstrung by its unsustainable political
economy and destined to collapse under its own weight, then Castro's
tenacious grip on power demanded an explanation. His survival, the
Wohlstetters revealed, was hardly a mystery. Castro owed it not only to
Soviet support, but also to a constant stream of useful idiots in the West.
The Wohlstetters' laundry list included London-based bankers who, they
prophesized, would soon reap a whirlwind in return for their avarice. It
also featured vainglorious French politicians seeking to assert their independence from the United States by aiding its enemies, in addition to
myopic American politicians who were the quintessential residents of a
fool's paradise.

A typical purveyor of the simplistic American bolstering Castro's
hold on power, for the Wohlstetters, was William Fulbright. The influential senator declared that Americans must choose whether Cuba constituted "a minor mischief or an extreme military threat." Given its
size, as well as its military and economic resources, Cuba was "obviously
not such a threat." It therefore could be categorized only as a trifling ir-
ritant. Fulbright's "cheerful" assessment of Cuba ignored its potential
for regional escalation, as well as its impact on the future expansion of
the Soviet bloc. The Wohlstetters bristled at the thought. "The fact that

such a new Communist outpost can so easily survive our hostility and possibly even *flourish*" would encourage, at the nation's peril, "future imitations of Castro."[55] The constant stream of such indirect support for the Castro regime, emanating from the both the political establishment as well as an incorrigibly liberal press, slackened communist Cuba's march to implosion.

Fifth Columnists of the Fourth Estate

By far the greatest impediment to the struggle against communism in Cuba allegedly lay in one of the Western world's most cherished institutions. Major American media outlets, the Wohlstetters would argue, played an important role in Castro's meteoric rise to power, as well as in his ability to drive a wedge between the United States and its allies. Blinded by an astounding misunderstanding of their role in times of existential peril, TV journalists and their counterparts in the printed press tripped over one another in a rush to humanize inhumane adversaries. The Fourth Estate, they implied, sometimes functioned as a Fifth Column.

In the Wohlstetters' view, Western media, led by the influential *New York Times*, tended to explain away unfamiliar yet nefarious political regimes by resorting to familiar yet dangerously erroneous metaphors. American media produced and disseminated an image of Castro as "the dashing, ardent young leader of the Caribbean . . . the ideal mixture of romance, courage, and at the same time respectability."[56] The dictator appeared intermittently as a Robin Hood, a John Brown, and even a Jesus Christ.

The Castro template adopted by most of the U.S. media was forged in a 1957 article by Herbert Matthews in the *New York Times*. According to Roberta, "Che Guevara correctly described Matthews's presence in the Sierra Maestra and his reports as 'more important than a military victory.'"[57] Matthews, who would later be described as "the man who invented Fidel," had discovered Fidel alive and kicking in the Sierra Maestra Mountains after the Batista regime had prematurely announced his death.[58] "The personality of the man is overpowering," Matthews had written. "It was easy to see that his men adored him and also to see why he has caught the imagination of the youth of Cuba all over the island. Here was an educated, dedicated fanatic, a man of ideals, of courage and of remarkable qualities of leadership."[59] Roberta reminded her readers that Castro had since "publicly exulted over the tricks he used to fool Matthews into believing . . . that a bandwagon is rolling" while in reality that image was "pure fantasy."[60]

Matthews's foundational portrait of Castro was particularly disturbing, Roberta believed, because the journalist pandered to the mythologies of the reading public. Matthews's breathless depiction of Castro, Roberta argued, "unites all the characteristics which would make a rebel acceptable to North American tastes. There is courage and the strength to fight against great odds, idealism, dignity, a vital self-confidence tempered with humility, and finally Christian gentleness. . . . In short, the gentle knight," who had many of the characteristics that Americans associated with their own rebel leaders who had defied the British. "Another appealing aspect for a North American audience is the Horatio Alger story of the father's rise to wealth, followed by the noble gesture of the son in sacrificing his share of that wealth to come to the aid of the peasant."[61] By virtue of its publication in the trendsetting *New York Times,* the Matthews portrait became a standard model for representations of Castro.

This template received visual ratification when Matthews's "outlines" provided the narrative structure for a May 1957 CBS documentary entitled *Rebels of the Sierra Maestra.*[62] In the documentary, Castro is "interviewed appropriately before a statue of Martí. 'This is Dr. Fidel Castro. Thirty-one. Holder of four university degrees.' . . . It was Doctor Fidel Castro then. . . . He wanted his middle-class, educated background, as well as his father's humble pick-and-shovel origin, stressed in news that would reach foreign shores." A simple exercise in fact-checking, Roberta complained, would have exploded this myth. "Since Castro attended the university for five years, it is difficult to imagine how he picked up three or four academic degrees."[63]

How did Roberta account for this infuriating and subversive portrayal of one of the nation's most persistent enemies? In part, she attributed this to Fidel's wily understanding of human vanities. "The truth will always be known," Castro declared to an allegedly vain Matthews, because of "brave reporters like you . . . willing to risk your lives to seek it out."[64] The particular "truth" that Castro wanted conveyed to Western audiences was "his middle-class, educated background." The media cooperated, even though his credentials were suspect.

Fidel's appeal was due in part to his uncanny ability to manipulate "the vocabulary of Western Liberalism" in his favor. Fidel was also a great actor who could transform himself into the role he played. In fact, Roberta wrote, Fidel "has no abiding principles, no consistent role other than being first, best, most sovereign, and always Cuban—the *Líder Máximo*. . . . He is a stunning example of a good 'method actor.' "[65] A gullible American public was "fertile ground for such propaganda. It is one of the admirable—one might say even lovable—characteristics of many Americans that they have a strong sympathy with the underdog."[66]

None of Fidel's ruses would have been possible without the support of media conglomerates in the United States. Focusing on the *New York Times* and its television counterpart, CBS—the equivalent gatekeeper of mythologies in the broadcasting world—Roberta once again discovered the destructive bias of monopolies. U.S. media monoliths, dominated by a particular ilk of liberal, left-leaning reporting, bore responsibility for the lackluster American reaction to this unpredictable, volatile, and manipulative enemy lurking off the shores of the United States. Free-flowing information was a vital instrument of maintaining a robust democracy, but it was inherently fragile and open to manipulation when concentrated in the hands of the few.[67]

The answer to such politically driven distortion resided in anti-monopolistic measures. Decentralized information systems were the only viable means of combating disinformation, distortion, and bias. Media conglomerates—most of which were controlled by a coalition of liberals and self-proclaimed realists—were gatekeepers rather than facilitators of communication.

Writing many years later in the immediate aftermath of the Soviet collapse, Albert considered that "information technology has moved in a direction opposite to that feared by Orwell in his mercilessly honest dystopia, *1984*. . . . Personal computers. Laptops. Modems. Fax machines. Copiers. Satellites. Flexible 'packet' networks." Technology was empowering "individuals to skip the bottleneck of central control to talk with each other." The vital ballasts of a robust democracy were, in sum, inherently fragile and open to manipulation in a monopolistic and hegemonic world. Only the free flow of information on a level playing field would challenge unbalanced distortion, whatever its source or motivation. Free-flowing information disrupted ossified economic systems, unleashed personal creativity and exposed the cynical and quixotic to the positive flow of reality.[68] The free flow of information was a central tranche in the functioning of a capitalist democracy, commonly defined at midcentury as a community governed by the aggregate, rational choices of its individual citizens.

Given the diffusion of liberating technology, major impediments to the spread of democracy in the Russian sphere of influence were the "cynical dreamers" in the West who had once counseled the restless nations in the Soviet Union to "give up their romantic notions about independence and face reality" under the Russian yoke.[69] In their rush to realism, Western politicians and the Western media had occluded a self-evident truth: "human capital and the institutions of ownership that encourage people to take large personal risks for big prizes, to compete, and to innovate in world markets" provided the only gateway leading from political oppression and global insecurity toward a conflict-free world of functioning democracies. Conventional media did not facilitate the breakup of a coercive Soviet empire. Instead, Albert explained, it was "the fax" that "shall make you free."[70]

6

Discriminate Interventionism

The Wohlstetters in a Multipolar World

ROBERTA AND ALBERT ACKNOWLEDGED the limitations of the rigidly bipolar Cold War paradigm as early as 1968. This "hypothetical" world, divided up into two monolithic blocs, was at best a mediocre miscomprehension of global affairs. The "real" world, Albert remarked, contained "a great many non-nuclear countries and a handful or so of countries with nuclear weapons and grossly different resources and strategic situations."[1] The Cold War paradigm allegedly ignored or trivialized menaces that lurked in multiple poles.

Despite the pallor cast by the two superpowers, Albert wrote in 1979, the "notion that nothing bad can happen to us if it is not inspired by the Russians is an enduring relic of the bipolar view."[2] Some of the most significant confrontations of the post–World War II period were internecine—between adversaries who ostensibly espoused the same worldview. "Communist Vietnam has attacked Communist Kampuchea. Communist China has fought Vietnam. And the only two nuclear-armed countries whose military forces have ever been locked in battle are Communist China and the Soviet Union."[3] The world, Albert observed, was chaotically multipolar. Living up to this insight was, however, an entirely different matter. The Wohlstetters' professional investment in the prevailing bipolar model constantly constrained their sense of adventure.

"Grave New World"

Some of the Wohlstetters' conceptual limitations beyond the closed world of superpowers are reflected in diary entries compiled during

Albert's Asian tour in the early 1960s. The ostensible reason for this trip was Albert's desire for an unmediated introduction to Asia's role in global affairs. "Trouble was popping all over; a mass exodus from China into Hong Kong, the movement of American forces into Thailand, protests against this movement in Japan, similar protests in Malaya about the movement of British units, war in South Vietnam, the West Irian madness at its peak in Indonesia, the worst financial crisis since the early 1950s in Iran, a six-week cabinet crisis in Turkey, etc., etc."[4]

This exciting agenda notwithstanding, Albert opted for a benign tourist route through the Asian thicket. In fact, he spent most of his time exchanging laborious views with individuals he could have conceivably met with anywhere. From the safety and comfort of hotel lobbies and boardrooms, Albert hunkered down with diplomats and listened avidly to jaded journalists dishing their punditry.

Only once did Albert venture out of this comfort zone. While visiting Hong Kong, an interlocutor took him on a trip to the no-man's-land separating the British colony from mainland China. The year was 1962, and Hong Kong faced waves of refugees clawing their way into the British enclave already bursting at its seams. The porous frontier with communist China was cause for great concern among the British rulers, who feared a human and political crisis spiraling out of control. In lieu of any meaningful border control on the Chinese side of the frontier, colonial officials decided to stymie the tide unilaterally. British troops roamed the landscape, hunting down the refugees and unloading their despondent cargo on the Chinese border, where they were abandoned to their own precarious fates.

On the plains beneath Albert's observation point, a nocturnal drama played itself out. Legions of Hong Kong residents scoured the landscape, shouting out names of relatives and offers of help to the columns of exhausted refugees who had completed their odyssey, only to be ensnared on the mountaintop. An emotional Albert witnessed this clamoring tragedy up close. It looked like a scene out of "an infernal landscape by Hieronymus Bosch."[5]

Hesitantly, Albert approached a truckload of detainees, where he met a young man who feared the worst. The captive refugee came from a bourgeois background and knew he would face harsh retribution upon his forced return to China. Mistaking the sympathetic white man for a colonial official, the desperate refugee pleaded for Albert's intervention. All Albert could offer were exhortations to keep the faith and a few self-evident truths. The distraught man brushed aside these nostrums and repeated his tragic story. "He was obviously intelligent," Albert observed, but too "disturbed" to listen to advice. "We left without any faith that he had understood."[6]

With the notable exception of the Hong Kong ordeal, a cautious Albert studiously avoided any other excursions into the confusing landscape of Asian politics. Instead, Albert chose the company of familiar and fawning admirers, who clamored for Albert's discursions on the Soviet menace.[7] Surrounded by polite interlocutors who asked all the right questions, Albert seized the opportunity to lecture his Asian hosts on the hermeneutics of the superpower standoff and related strategic conundrums far removed from the maelstrom raging outside his hotel window.

WMD and the Theater of Terror

Roberta offered her own take on new global challenges, one that was somewhat more innovative than Albert's regurgitation of predictable tropes. During the 1970s, she temporarily escaped from the gravitational pull of bipolarity, envisioning a surge of crises with an unfamiliar cast of actors.

Experts, she wrote, fixated on the spread of nuclear proliferation among nation-states.[8] Roberta, by contrast, examined whether a future of global instability lurked beyond the nation-state. "Why only countries?" she mused. "If a very few bombs . . . could raise a small nation to the level of a great power, what effect might one or two have in the hands of a sub-national group?"[9] Offering a rapid review of major terrorist organizations, Roberta concluded that the vast majority of such subnational actors were uninterested in mass killings; they preferred the symbolic value of targeted assassinations. The IRA was an exception, as were "extremist Arab organizations" whose "desperate character and doctrine" were "consistent with fewer qualms about large numbers of enemy deaths."[10]

The lure of terror by weapons of mass destruction (WMD) could not be dismissed out of hand. Roberta contended, however, that the probability of terrorists getting hold of nuclear weapons, let alone deploying them, remained low. Other WMD, biological weapons in particular, had been available for more than thirty years, and "could be obtained more readily . . . with smaller risks, lower costs, and more modest technical resources."[11] The fact that no one had used them suggested that WMD lacked appeal even for groups who endorsed wholesale bloodshed. The saving grace of such weapons was that they lacked the theatrics of more conventional acts of violence.

The "Theater of Terror"—the symbiotic relationship between a sensation-seeking media and this particular strain of terror groups—demanded a more palatable form of brutality.[12] Roberta herself had described how hostage crises provided the type of publicity that terror organizations sought. Cuban revolutionaries, for example, had kidnapped innocent bystanders in an attempt to gain recognition and sympathy in the United States. Such kidnappings were particularly beneficial to nonstate actors, Roberta argued, because they "violated not only internal rules of political order, but also the meagre international rules that lend some stability to relations among states: for example, the rules that concentrate relations among countries on negotiation among governments."[13]

Roberta ultimately discounted fears of nuclear terrorism as mere "premonitions." The state-based patrons of nonstate actors, she predicted, would inevitably constrain the "careless slaughter of innocents." "In the complex politics of the Middle East," for example, "Arab governments have imposed various constraints on the *Fedayeen* [Palestinian guerrillas] if only to avoid Israeli reprisals for acts of terror that are miniscule in comparison with nuclear violence." If "terror on a grand scale" was, perhaps, inevitable, the weapon of choice was unlikely to be WMD.[14] The possibility of nuclear terrorism hinged on nuclear proliferation among nation-states, not among nonstate actors. It centered, in particular, on nuclear-armed rogue states behaving "like terrorists, rather than the other way around."[15]

As far as the immediate future was concerned, Roberta concluded that terror organizations were unlikely to engage in nuclear saber rattling. Yet nonstate actors were, she recognized, a growing threat to global stability and some future resort to nuclear weapons by a combination of ambitious terrorists and reckless states could not be ruled out. The problem with the political establishment in the West lay in its reluctance to address the danger of an unchecked growth of terror.

When faced with terrorist actions, such as hostage taking, the community of nations oscillated in Hamletian fashion between incapacitating indecision and indiscriminate attack. Most nations treated their confrontations with nonstate actors as a binary choice between embarrassed capitulation or unbridled revenge. Both instances served the cause of those engaged in the theatrics of terror and obscured saner alternatives to this either-or impasse.

In her retrospective analysis of a mass kidnapping of American civilians and marine personnel in Cuba "engineered by . . . Raul Castro in 1958, the last year of Batista," Roberta demonstrated the efficacy of containing nonstate actors by a graduated escalation of military threats. In contrast to the Batista regime's reliance on unbridled violence in its confrontations with rebel forces, the United States had successfully engineered the release of hostages by gradually raising the stakes while accommodating a face-saving rebel exit strategy.

Much to the surprise of both the press and American negotiators in Cuba, the hostages were abruptly released after weeks of protracted and seemingly futile negotiations. Purportedly, Fidel's brother had set the men free to permit them to join their fellow marines in their incursion into Lebanon. Raul's "explanation that the United States needed these marines for the Lebanese crisis," Roberta wrote, "has a dream-like implausibility and irrelevance like the resolution of a comic opera plot."[16] In Roberta's analysis, the true reason a habitually intransigent Raul had accomplished this about-face was the lengthening "shadow" of American military intervention.

Raul's artful yet hasty capitulation to the controlled escalation of U.S. threats belied the assumption that the West had no strategic response to the rise of nonstate actors. "The frequent statement that the major powers in the West are powerless seems to stem from a fear that they will use power unwisely or in excess; it is a way of exhorting them not to use it. . . . a half-conscious wish, or a rationalization for inaction." There were many gradations, in fact, between "surrender" to blackmail and the "brutal display" of indiscriminate force. A discriminate use of force, as well as selectiveness among the various types of international emergencies demanding a response from the United States, was the key to the successful navigation of turbulent global times.[17]

Roberta's contribution was unusually postnationalist for its time. Her strategist-colleagues were mostly immersed in a world of nation-states;

nonstatist terror was still considered to be a relatively marginal issue unworthy of the attention of the river gods of strategic policy. At the same time, Roberta's articles toed an orthodox line. It was her fear of nuclear proliferation rather than her interest in terror that brought her to the subject of nonstate actors. The growing fear of nuclear "terror on a grand scale" served as the impetus for her article.

Roberta emphasized, moreover, that such groups did not act autonomously. Their very existence hinged on state sponsorship. The example of Arab nations' ability to control the level of violence of even the most radical Palestinian groups served as a case in point. In other words, nonstate actors could not pose independent strategic challenges to the global world order. Membership in this exclusive club was still the province of nation-states, many of whom aggressively supported these subagents of global instability.

The dilemma facing the United States in these unchartered territories was whether, and when, to intervene. The postwar challenges of nonstate actors as well as state proxies for the Soviet nemesis had all too often vacillated between damaging paralysis and thoughtless countermeasure that siphoned off resources and attention from the primary challenges of the Cold War.

The Lessons of Vietnam

The Wohlstetters' autopsy of American dilemmas received its most lucid explication in their analysis of the Vietnam War, allegedly a clear example of ill-advised intervention in a battle that ought to have been avoided. The Wohlstetters opposed, albeit after the fact, American involvement in Indochina. Albert, in particular, rejected the very notion that American interests were at stake in the conflict. He blamed both the military establishment and its civilian overseers for propagating this misconception. From there, however, he parted ways with the conventional critique of the war. Though he opposed its "indiscriminate" prosecution, the worst outcome of the violence, in his view, would be for public dissatisfaction to swing the political pendulum away from the policy option of military interventionism. The war threatened to impart the dangerous lesson that "that our problem is not to use our power discriminately and for worthy ends but the fact of power itself, that we are better off reducing the choices available to us."[18] Vietnam's deepest tragedy, for Albert, would be the "isolationist" syndrome it would leave in its wake.[19]

Albert's critique of isolationism focused on what he saw as its underlying premise: the misbegotten belief that "national interests are a function of ethnic ties and a linear function of distance."[20] Opponents of foreign wars focused impulsively and compulsively on "imperial overreach"—the classic problem of governing at a distance. Albert interpreted this error as a result of technological ignorance. There was no clear physical "overreach" now that advances in such crucial areas as transportation and communication had rendered the drawbacks of distance obsolete.

Taking the Korean War as an example, Albert demonstrated that the transport of military forces had already become relatively flawless and swift by midcentury. The bottlenecks seen in Korea were not the result of global constraints on the projection of power. Local issues pertaining to "climate, terrain, harbors, port unloading facilities, railroads and roads" had been to blame. The "long-distance lift" technology of conventional weaponry now far outstripped "that for short distance lift inside the theater" of war. In terms of potential conflicts in Asia, Albert noted that "on the Thai-Laos border, the United States can lift, from 8,500 miles away, four times as much as China can."[21] Strategic interests, in other words, rather than geographical reach, were what should dictate American involvement abroad. There were no meaningful technological constraints on the exercise of American power. If anything, the ability to move conventional military forces had led, in the case of Vietnam, to a mindless impulse to confront a strategically irrelevant enemy. Vietnam was over*kill*, not overreach.

The Indochina debacle, for Albert, showed that American decision makers had failed to comprehend the rising tide of insurgency in volatile parts of the world. Despite its unsurpassed military might, the United States needed to face two painful facts. First, sophisticated weapons technology and global command and control had proven "largely irrelevant" in the face of "revolutionary wars" like the Vietnam conflict. Second, the "ability to fight cannot be directly translated into political authority." A species of technological hubris had led to a tragic confusion between "capabilities" and "interests." While there was no material impediment to the projection of American power, the fact that the United States had globe-spanning military technology at its disposal should not have led to "the mechanical extension of American political hegemony."[22]

Albert testily denounced the impulsive, negative American reaction to every type of Third World insurgence, including those labeled communist.[23] "Communism," Hans Morgenthau had underscored in an article Albert cited, "has become polycentric, that is to say, each communist government and movement, to a greater or lesser extent, pursues its own national interests." Bearing the Hamletian title of "To Intervene or Not to Intervene," the article argued that intervention in the affairs of others "must be determined in terms not of communist ideology but of the compatibility of those interests with the interests of the United States."[24] Interests trumped ideology.

Along these same lines, Albert asserted that in Vietnam, in particular, "the nature of the threat" had been "misconceived."[25] The communism of the North Vietnamese leadership posed no threat to American interests. The available alternatives to the communists, moreover, were often even less palatable. Historical examples demonstrated the pragmatism Albert favored. "While there may be a presumption that a Communist insurgency is bad for the U.S.," he wrote, "it conceivably may be less bad than some other alternatives. Or so we thought when we aided the Russians against the Nazis. . . . Obviously, some rebellions have been the best of a bad lot of alternatives" available to a populace suffering from the repression by petty despots. "The Daughters of the American Revolution approve at least one."[26]

The tendency to side automatically with the ruling authorities and, by the same token, to automatically vilify insurgents was self-defeating and misguided.[27] The establishment, he lamented, tended to act as if every manifestation of revolution was automatically hostile to American interests.[28] An otherwise laudable effort to confront communism in Indochina had inadvertently paved the road to political instability, intermittent military coups, and the destruction of the region's political and social fiber. American support for a series of dictators—who more closely resembled Byzantine warlords than the enlightened Westernized leaders the United States hoped to implant throughout the world—neither fostered the rise of Asian democracies nor furthered any other American interests. The United States had reacted with little caution and even less intelligence. The basic question regarding American intervention in

Vietnam, he argued, should not have been "how much?" but rather "what for?"[29]

"Indiscriminate Counter-Revolution"

Vietnam, Albert, realized, had brought out the worst in his former colleagues at RAND, as well. Their analysis of the Vietnam conflict, if followed, appeared to have catastrophic implications for both foreign and domestic policy. Among the most notable of these studies was Charles Wolf and Nathan Leites's "Rebellion and Authority."[30] Focusing primarily on Vietnam, these strategists had castigated the military's flirtation with "hearts and minds"—the strategy for gaining indigenous allies by political accomplishments and social largesse among the Vietnamese peasantry.

Leites and Wolf found no empirical evidence of any correlation between socioeconomic deprivation and support for the insurgency. Enemy gains in the countryside, therefore, had little to do with any form of popular sympathy for the insurgents' cause. The Vietcong had succeeded among the masses because they approached their mission as an unadulterated military campaign and had employed ruthless coercion to gain the peasantry's acquiescence. Support for the insurgents, Wolf and Leites argued, was actually strongest among affluent peasants, those who had gained the *most* from hearts and minds. As rational actors, Vietnam's affluent peasants were bolstering their security by hedging their bets, overtly supporting the government while covertly subsidizing the rebels. If anything, for Leites and Wolf, hearts and minds conveyed a sense of weakness. The Vietnamese populace misconstrued this instance of constructive counterinsurgency as a strategy of last resort, employed because the conventional military effort was failing. Their RAND report concluded that the only effective means of winning the Vietnamese countryside would be to raise the cost of aiding and abetting the insurgency via unrelenting, punitive military violence.[31]

While their study focused primarily on counterinsurgency strategies for confronting the Vietcong, Leites and Wolf also argued that their analytical framework applied not only to insurgencies in foreign lands but also to contemporary urban disorders and campus unrest in the United States.[32] Their analysis of dissent in 1960s America denied in no uncertain terms the alleged connection between deprivation and rebellion. Poverty, they claimed to show, was no more a root cause of unrest in the United States than it was in Vietnam. Their research revealed that African American communities of Watts and Detroit, sites of riots in 1965 and 1967, respectively, were economically better off than communities untouched by uprising. "Similarly," they found, "campus rebellions have often been most severe in those academic centers (for example, Berkeley, Columbia, Wisconsin, Cornell, Harvard, and Swarthmore) where living and learning conditions were among the best."[33]

In lumping together domestic dissent and Asian insurgencies, these two prominent RAND experts rejected social and political solutions to any crisis, whether in the hamlets of Vietnam, in America's urban ghettos, or on the nation's university campuses. Tough love, RAND-style, advocated the pacification of "insurgents" of every stripe by imposing a high and painful price on those who instigated, supported, or acquiesced to challenges to authority. Hearts and minds in Vietnam and the Great Society at home merely rewarded and radicalized the target audiences. The mitigation of insurgency entailed a ruthless application of coercion, rather than any attempt at persuasion.

The Wolf-Leites model of coercive counterinsurgency at home and abroad was by no means an aberration for the era. Countless studies at RAND and elsewhere offered support for their approach. Political scientist Ted Gurr, the author of an ambitious multinational study of rebellion for the Army-funded Center for Research in the Social Sciences (CRESS), concluded that coercion was the only variable with the predictive power needed to quell both civil unrest and rebellion. Like Wolf and Leites, Gurr dismissed the notion that economic improvement was a necessary variable for maintaining "civil peace." In fact, he claimed, "among less developed nations," economic improvement was "associated with increasing strife." By contrast, "a high level of deterrent power, consistently applied, tends to inhibit civil strife."[34] Carl Rosenthal, the author of a study of "civil disturbances" in urban America, underwritten by the U.S. Army Limited War Laboratory, approached domestic unrest in the United States as a species of guerrilla warfare. Whether his study was meant to prepare the U.S. Army for the mission of controlling civil disobedience within American cites or whether the author merely felt that one could derive useful lessons on counterinsurgency abroad from the familiar terrain of the home front was never spelled out clearly.[35]

In his critique of the *Rebellion and Authority* model, Albert distanced himself from the axiomatic assumption that all forms of rebellion and insurgency were a priori negative manifestations to be crushed with unrelenting force. Albert was uneasy with Wolf and Leites's mechanical support of "the side of the authority. . . . It will identify your book as simply a contribution to the discriminate art of indiscriminate counter-revolution." He admonished Wolf and Leites for avoiding the root causes of unrest, and their automatic condemnation of any form of dissent as inherently detrimental to American interests. By presuming that U.S. policy should always maintain the status quo both domestically and abroad, he told his former colleagues, "you lapse into the lap of authority."[36]

Such conflationist theories bothered Albert. He accused his colleagues of dousing the nation's urban bonfires with flammable confrontational strategies and military metaphors. Instead of analyzing the domestic front on its own terms, as worthy of its own original policies, Leites, Wolf, and others had conflated the threat of external military attack and the threat of an internal crisis to the detriment of both.

They had swept the root causes of domestic unrest under a carpet of modular military formats that promised to aggravate rather than resolve America's afflictions.

"Mini–Brute Force"

Vietnam offered Albert an opportunity to chastise the military establishment, as well. The commanders of the nation's armed forces had committed the inexcusable blunder of basing their preparations for Vietnam on lessons gleaned from an irrelevant past. America's military establishment appeared to be prisoners of the Korean War, expecting "another conventional invasion across a parallel separating a Communist North from a non-Communist South." Forming large, conventional South Vietnamese Army (ARVN) divisions in response to this expectation, American strategists ended up creating South Vietnamese commanders "of vast independent political power," thereby increasing the threat of military coups. This led the South Vietnamese dictatorship to tighten its grip, undermining any "chance that the Vietnamese, in spite of internal attack, would be able to advance in economic and political self-development and to operate under the rule of law. That in turn encouraged subversion, terror and counter-terror and helped make a discriminate response unlikely." All of this because "our advisors were responding to a 'lesson' of Korea."[37] In fact, Albert elaborated, the military's performance in Vietnam suggested an inertia in strategic thinking that predated even Korea. Low-accuracy, World War II–style carpet bombing "exacted much too high a toll in bystanders and friendly forces."[38]

The bungled execution of the chosen strategy—however misguided— also aroused Albert's contempt. The American military establishment had two possible choices in prosecuting the war. It could effect a swift, brutal, and massive annihilation of the enemy, or it could slowly build a "viable government capable of economic and political self-development" that would "subordinate conventional military operations" to a species of hearts and minds. The military, Albert complained, had never made this necessary, if painful, choice, preferring instead to combine two tepid versions of both strategies, with spectacularly incompetent results. "In this way, it got the worst of both worlds, what might be called 'a mini– brute force policy': a slow application of brute force in the hope of achieving quickly objectives that could be achieved, if at all, only by a massive and rapid use of force. . . . While a brute force policy was mistaken, it is conceivable that in its own erroneous terms it could have been successful if it were actually massive enough." Requests for more resources or for the removal of military constraints were invariably met with hesitant, anemic responses, even though the ultimate objectives of the war, however dubious, remained unchanged. "As a result, we had the wrong objective pursued by a brute force tactic with far less than the amount of force that the objective required: in short a mini– brute force policy."[39] In opposition to this confusing morass of strategic approaches, Albert preached a "discriminate"—targeted, limited, economical—policy of American interventionism.

The Wohlstetters saw the Vietnam debacle as validating their concern with discriminating responses to security dilemmas. Yet despite such flashes of insight on the limits of a communist threat, and despite their acknowledgment of challenges and opportunities beyond the East-West divide, the Wohlstetters never fully shook off the constraints of their claim to fame. Having established their reputation as advocates of a clear and unambiguous response to the Soviet threat, the Wohlstetters ultimately remained prisoners of their obsession with the confrontation between superpowers, even as multiple conventional wars and global unrest undermined the salience of that reflex.

The Limits of Discrimination

"Once in a great while," Richard Perle announced in 1988, "a government overcomes the temptation to blandness and says something important."[40] The object of Perle's praise was *Discriminate Deterrence,* the final, declassified summation of a $1.6 million study of America's strategic aims.[41] The much-anticipated report was widely hailed as the most comprehensive strategic blueprint for American global policy since NSC-68, the ur text of Cold War policy, issued in 1950. Even to Paul Kennedy, its most trenchant critic, the report still represented "one of the most important public overviews of what American grand strategy should be, as seen by its intellectual and policy-influencing elite."[42] Albert Wohlstetter coauthored the final document with his longtime collaborator, Fred C. Iklé, then serving under Reagan as undersecretary of defense for policy. The members of its committee formed an illustrious roster; they included two former national security advisers, Henry Kissinger and Zbigniew Brzezinski; the eminent Harvard political scientist Samuel Huntington; Anne Armstrong, the former ambassador to the United Kingdom and political counselor to Presidents Nixon and Ford; and others. Despite the participation of a pantheon of strategy giants, the document read like a summary of the Wohlstetter Doctrine. It was Albert's document, and it provides a prime example both of the Wohlstetters' desire to transcend Cold War bipolarity and their inability to do so.

Discriminate Deterrence certainly aspired "to recast priorities—not to give the Soviet Union a free ride but to engage it realistically while reserving resources to meet other challenges," and was accordingly lauded as a timely corrective to a singular focus on the Soviet threat.[43] As a point of departure, the report announced its intention to assess new realities—economic, social, political, and military—and their bearing on national security priorities. Its authors promised an ambitious presentation of an "integrated" and "long-term" strategy that would prepare the United States to meet the "changing security environment'" of the late twentieth century.

"We live in a world," Albert and Iklé wrote, "whose nations are increasingly connected by their economies, cultures, and politics—sometimes explosively connected as in the repeated vast migrations since World War II of refugees escaping political, religious, and racial persecution. It is a world in which military as well as economic power will be more and more widely distributed and in which the United States must continue to expect some nations to be deeply hostile to its purposes."[44]

This era of limitations and connections, hostility and opportunity, demanded a new national security strategy based on selective weapons development, new alliances, and a discriminate approach to their employment, even at the expense of scuttling well-entrenched practices and strategies. "When spending decisions are not clearly linked to a strategic vision, then there will be heavy pressures to maintain force size and take the cuts out of modernization" and innovation.[45] Albert and Iklé's most immediate concern was to reexamine the allegedly wasteful and obsolete rituals of an outdated model of deterrence.

Given the complex task of maintaining worldwide commitments with limited resources, the report called for the reduction of the inefficient arsenal of outmoded nuclear weaponry the United States maintained in the European theater, and its replacement with precision-driven weaponry and short-range, low-impact nuclear weapons. In other words, *Discriminate Deterrence* advocated the tactical deployment of nuclear weapons in the event of a Soviet incursion into Western Europe. Nuclear weapons, according to the commission, were war-fighting devices, not props for delivering symbolic messages to the enemy. No longer would the United States maintain its nuclear weapons for the sole purpose of theatrical deterrence. For the first time since the Korean War, a broad spectrum of American policy makers endorsed the use of nuclear weapons on the modern battlefield.

The most innovative portion of the document related to the recognition of Asia's prominence. The report singled out Japan and China, who were on the verge of becoming both military and economic powers. These two Asian giants, along with an array of lesser powers, would diminish "the relative advantages of both U.S. and Soviet Forces."[46] Nevertheless, the report's authors intimated that both China and Japan would primarily threaten expansionist Soviet designs rather than American global policies.

Discriminate Deterrence also recognized the challenge of "low-intensity conflicts" in the Third World driven by "insurgencies, organized terrorism, paramilitary crime, sabotage and other forms of violence in a shadow area between peace and open warfare involving large units." It was in this area, in particular, where the report advocated for an integrated response that would include "not just [Department of Defense] personnel and materiel, but diplomats and information specialists, agricultural chemists, bankers and economists, hydrologists, criminologists," and—for some mysterious reason—"meteorologists."[47]

The report displayed an ambivalent, if not dismissive attitude toward Western European allies. The section dedicated to global economic trends accorded them a resounding silence. Its comparison of trends in GNP included only China, Japan, the Soviet Union, and the United States. No European entity was deemed important enough. NATO's military significance received a similar downgrading. Albert and Iklé offered a withering critique of the well-worn yet allegedly irrelevant strategic assumptions of the NATO alliance. Contrary to NATO's concentration on central Europe, they focused almost exclusively on Turkey and Norway—the exposed and underappreciated southern and northern flanks of the European continent.

Discriminate Deterrence pronounced the death of containment, dismissed as a modern-day Maginot line. The forty-year-old American deployment in central Europe and its thirty-five-year-old troop presence in Korea had indeed precluded Soviet encroachments in these two spots. Yet while the United States and its allies were resting on the laurels of this success, the allegedly nimble Soviet enemy had swiftly "bypassed the lines we drew and has pushed into Southern Asia, the Middle East, Africa, the Caribbean, and Central America."[48] The report therefore advocated proactive rollback, in which the United States would aid—militarily and otherwise—insurgents fighting pro-Soviet regimes. "The Free World will not remain free if its options are only to stand still or retreat."[49] In order to accomplish these goals, the United States would have to increase defense spending and revise its military doctrine.

Despite the aura of change and reconceptualization, *Discriminate Deterrence* ultimately appears rather unoriginal. The fissures eroding the Soviet empire, quite visible, did little to convince the authors that the major challenge of the future was anything more than a streamlined variation of the past. The greatest threat to the United States continued to be a bipolar military confrontation between a waffling United States and a single-minded, predatory Soviet empire. Published in 1988, on the cusp of momentous change in the Soviet empire, the report remained firmly anchored in an irrelevant paradigm: "For the foreseeable future, the United States will have to compete militarily with the Soviet Union." Yet "oddly enough," its astonished authors observed, "some Americans regard that statement as controversial."[50]

The Soviet empire appeared strong and stable. Neither the crises of Soviet society—plummeting life expectancy, rampant substance abuse within the army, and more—nor the self-evident signs of a crumbling Soviet economy registered on the report. As for overtures of political rapprochement emanating from the Soviet Union, these were declared irrelevant, if not duplicitous. Albert and his colleagues clearly acknowledged new threats and opportunities. Yet neither perestroika nor the Soviet empire's noticeably fragile fault lines left significant impressions on the study. Its authors dismissed the USSR's economic difficulties as "persistent," and therefore irrelevant.[51] The rise of Asia may have offered opportunities for global strategic realignment, but the bear was still lurking in the woods. "Even if perestroika and glasnost signal an intention" to change, *Discriminate Deterrence*'s strategists remarked, "it will not be easy to accomplish. Moscow's suspicion and hostility are rooted in seventy years of Soviet and 400 years of Tsarist history."[52]

For a document that aimed to replace NSC-68, *Discriminate Deterrence* was rather predictable and familiar. Just as had the National Security Council's 1950 study, it identified the Soviet Union as a clear and present danger eclipsing all other global challenges. The cleavage between 1950 and 1988 was technical or anecdotal: different weapons systems or unexplored hints of new global actors. Much like NSC-68, the main message of *Discriminate Deterrence* was the urgent "call to arms: America must respond with its own buildup, pushing its unrivaled productive capacity to frustrate Soviet dreams of conquest."[53] To paraphrase Søren Kierkegaard, the report's authors may indeed have desired to look forward but appeared condemned to thinking backward.

The only significant change Albert and Iklé admitted was in the battlefield and in the weapons of choice dictated by the Soviet Union. "Over the last forty years," *Discriminate Deterrence* acknowledged, "the Soviet regime has shown no signs of gravitating toward all-or-nothing gambles, much preferring instead to make gains by successive, incremental advances, below the threshold at which nuclear war would be a possibility."[54] The report therefore described the main threat inherent in future Third World conflicts as leading to "Soviet expansion in areas previously free of Soviet forces."[55] In fact, the entire world appeared to be a "Soviet periphery," where, given the lack of credible American response, "the USSR and its satellites could plausibly expect to win conventional wars and occupy other countries' territory."[56]

The report also remained firmly focused on the Soviet Union in its discussion of weapons technology. Albert and Iklé identified a significant threat of advanced Soviet military research that "continues to exceed our own," thereby eroding the paltry "qualitative edge on which we have long relied."[57] One of the report's primary conclusions rejected NATO's stubborn adherence to the doctrine of "extreme threats." Planning for the extreme—and therefore unlikely—contingency of an extensive Warsaw Pact conventional attack on the NATO central European front followed by, or coupled with, a strategic nuclear exchange with the Soviet Union, had deflected attention from more immediate challenges.[58]

At a practical level, the paradigm of "extreme threats" had ignored the less apocalyptic but more likely challenges elsewhere—the destabilization of Turkey, a Soviet incursion into Iran and the Persian Gulf, as well as low-intensity Soviet-inspired insurgencies in the third world, all of which would require a coherent and forceful American response. Yet, lacking anything aside from a hollow threat of strategic nuclear retaliation in the case of a Soviet incursion, the United States remained vulnerable to military challenges that neither militarily nor morally warranted the use of a massive nuclear response.

Without the requisite conventional weaponry to confront a Soviet incursion, NATO clung to blind faith; the empty threat of a nuclear showdown was the only device for curbing Soviet ambitions. Nuclear deployment within NATO countries, according to *Discriminate Deterrence*, had been transformed into implausible symbols of Western resolve. At best, nuclear weapons in Europe were cumbersome, archaic, and unconvincing scarecrows for psychological warfare. They were outmoded semaphores signaling into empty space "the perils of escalation" and "the apocalypse at the end of [the] road."[59] The report mocked the very idea that anyone would give credence to a retaliatory strike that would annihilate both defender and attacker. Such hollow threats would not deter a Soviet invasion. In fact, they might conceivably encourage Soviet adventurism.

Only a "credible" strategy, premised on a "controlled, discriminate," and graduated use of nuclear weapons, would deter a Soviet attack by any means.[60] A measured strategy of nuclear deployment "as an instrument for denying success to invading Soviet forces" would not lead to a "wider and more devastating war." "NATO's "nuclear posture, like its posture for conventional war," would "gain in its deterrent power from new technologies emphasizing precision and control."[61]

Based on a variation of the Wohlstetters' widely publicized aversion to MAD, the committee rejected the concept of reciprocal vulnerability as the best form of deterrence. While acknowledging the obvious—that the United States preferred deterring rather than fighting a nuclear war—the august convocation of strategy intellectuals reaffirmed the Wohlstetter claim that effective deterrence hinged on the ability and willingness to *respond,* rather than threaten, albeit in a credible and differentiated manner. "We and our allies would rather deter than defeat an aggression" with the use of nuclear weapons, "but a bluff is less effective."[62]

They thus favored replacing nuclear dinosaurs with an array of new precision-conscious weapons systems, both conventional and nuclear, that offered a wider range of strategic choices for confronting Soviet aggression, whether on the NATO front or elsewhere. Reprising a favorite Wohlstetter theme, the commission argued that immediate investments in technological innovations would allow the United States to confront its multiple strategic tasks without recourse to ultimate—and therefore empty—threats. Hence, "nuclear weapons would be used discriminately in, for example, attacks on Soviet command centers or troop concentrations." The use of nuclear weapons based on new technologies emphasizing precision and control would, according to the prognosticators of *Discriminate Deterrence,* preclude the risk of further escalation associated with the old generation of high impact but "dumb" nuclear weaponry.[63]

As for fears that the development of precision-based nuclear weapons would heighten the arms race, the report reaffirmed Albert's long-held conviction that the arms race was little more than a myth. "The Soviet-American military competition has not been much of a race," *Discriminate Deterrence* concluded. "The pattern of the past forty years is more accurately characterized by a steady, slow-paced, relentless military buildup on the Soviet side and an erratic, inconsistent . . . performance by the United States." A series of schematic graphs offered visual renditions of a steady Soviet growth in arms procurement, and an attendant decline of 67 percent in U.S. spending on strategic arms. These two contrasting trends occurred "while the myth of the arms race flourished."[64]

Ignoring the disastrous consequences of sensor-based intelligence gathering in Vietnam, the commission envisioned a system of data processing based on "networks of sensors and other microelectronic equipment" for monitoring the movements of Soviet-inspired insurgent forces and terrorist groups. The commission endorsed, as well, "low-cost space systems, long-endurance aircraft and robotic reconnaissance vehicles that make it possible to monitor large areas, day and night, regardless of weather or terrain." In sum, investments in the military sciences, which had been neglected over a long period of time, appeared essential.[65]

In sum, *Discriminate Deterrence* was mostly an exercise in creating a comfortable climate for weapons development in a period of uncertainty. While signaling an awareness of inchoate tectonic shifts on the horizon, the document clung tenaciously to traditional threats. As for future enemies, this Wohlstetter-inspired assessment bundled communist China with Japan, ostensibly a robust democracy. With the second largest economy in the world, the "key question affecting the strategic balance will be whether Japan exercises its option to become a major military power" and whether it would use its newfound power to aid and abet traditional enemies. "A Japanese decision to help in the development of Soviet technology, for example, could help increase the Soviet military potential."[66] The embers of Pearl Harbor were still smoldering in the background.

"A Not So Grand Strategy"

Discriminate Deterrence elicited a wide array of responses in the United States and abroad. European commentators interpreted the document as a significant departure from previous policies and prognoses. The emphasis on regional Asian powers, as well on as scenarios of a Soviet intrusion in the Western Hemisphere, appeared to express a diminished American concern for the European theater.

Writing in the French magazine *l'Express,* commentator Henri Eyraud described the report's call for the abandonment of massive retaliation as the scuttling of NATO. He noted that Europe appeared infrequently in the seventy-page document, and mostly as an afterthought. "'Realistic' as it is, the Iklé-Wohlstetter commission considers that Europe does not exist," Eyraud complained.[67] The report's discounting of the extreme threat paradigm appeared as an additional sign of dwindling interest in Europe, perhaps even a full-fledged American retreat from its NATO obligations. If any additional proof were needed to illustrate Europe's marginalization, numerous other commentators pointed out the "unfortunate" table on the GNP of "selected countries," from which Europe was conspicuously absent.[68]

Translations of the document into German heightened perceptions of an inherently anti-European stance, as well. Wohlstetter noticed that the word *discriminate* had been translated "in a pejorative sense, as in discriminating . . . against Europe in deciding what attacks" would elicit an American response.[69] German commentators were alarmed by the implication that a nuclear retaliatory strike would apply only in the event of an attack on the continental United States. "NATO's flexible response doctrine is obsolete," concluded *Der Spiegel.*[70] The concept of employing nuclear weapons at a tactical level against a Soviet-inspired attack in the central European theater appeared to be "a fatal concept for Germany, the potential battlefield."[71] Defense expert Lother Ruehl chided the report's faux naïveté. How could anyone believe, he mused, that rationality would prevail in the heat of battle, and that the use of tactical nuclear weapons would not lead to an inevitable employment of strategic weapons?[72] Manfred Wörner, the West German defense minister and NATO secretary general designate, summed up German misgivings when he said that *Discriminate Deterrence* was alarming because it decoupled "U.S. strategic capability from the defense of Europe." The document also legitimized the unthinkable: the concept of a "limited nuclear war," most probably to be fought on German soil.[73] Germany appeared to have been designated the role of a "nuclear firebreak."[74]

Defense officials in the United Kingdom expressed their own reservations on the apparently significant shift in the United States' nuclear doctrine. A British Foreign Office official announced that, contrary to the position articulated in the report, nuclear weapons should only be used for precisely " 'political signaling' as 'demonstrations of resolve' rather than for military effect," which "is sure to get out of control and to result in mutual destruction."[75]

Nevertheless, this particular shift in doctrine had a small, if select, share of admirers, including a fawning editorial in the London *Economist:* "Threaten a general nuclear assault on Russia if it moves across the European dividing line, and Russia is liable to remain unperturbed, because it knows that Americans know it can reply with a general nuclear assault on them. Threaten Russia with an attack on specific targets of the sort the new American report suggests . . . and the Russians face . . . unpleasant possibilities. . . . Most important it will be Russia, not America, which has to decide whether or not to make the mind-boggling next move, the jump to general holocaust. This is likelier to give pause. It is likelier, in other words, to prevent anything violent happening at all: which is what 'deterrence' means."[76]

Scandinavian reactions focused, by contrast, on the report's romancing of technology. In somewhat caustic terms, the director of the Norwegian Defense Research Establishment felt that the report had "too much confidence in the way technology can be used to solve future problems."[77] It appeared to reflect an American tendency to approach technology as a substitute for strategy.

At home, public reactions wavered between the noncommittal and the negative, with few exceptions. The *New York Times* dismissed the document as a "paean to the gods of high technology," one more fruitless attempt to invent the "silver bullet" that would bring the Soviet Union to its knees. The newspaper cited anonymous Pentagon officials "who say the commission is adoring false gods when it kneels at the altar of high technology." These anonymous critics recalled disappointments associated with the military's previous quick technological fix, the "electronic sensor barrier known as the McNamara line" that "was supposed to prevent infiltration from North Vietnam into the south. It failed along with much other exotic gadgetry."[78]

Commentators on the left found the document fantastically blind to changing global circumstances. An editorial in *The Nation* described the report as "the last-ditch effort by an aging old guard to find a convincing rationale for the globalist military posture it has championed for so many years." Contrary to most critics on the right and left, however, *The Nation* predicted that *Discriminate Deterrence* would not gather dust on some forgotten shelf. "The next Administration, whether Democratic or Republican, is likely to pursue some version of the strategy enunciated in 'Discriminate Deterrence,' in particular the emphasis on conventional precision-based weapons and the concept of flexible responses to varying contingencies. The inevitable result would be more Vietnams."[79]

Writing in the *Christian Science Monitor,* Martha Little of the liberal Committee for National Security found nothing substantially innovative in the report's philosophical underpinnings. "What these commissioners tout as new policy recommendations for the 1990s are actually anachronistic policies based on tired old thinking . . . the tendency to assess threats only in military terms, and the predilection to attribute virtually every threat to the Soviet Union."[80] Its authors, she observed, were firmly rooted in a nonoperative past.

The most withering and detailed criticism belonged to the historian Paul Kennedy. From the pages of the *New York Review of Books,* he declared a monumental anticlimax, a "not so grand strategy."[81] In Kennedy's view, *Discriminate Deterrence* failed to offer any meaningful "integrated" strategy. The document presented no more than a casual overview of contemporary economic, technological, and political developments in the United States and beyond. Despite the presence of committee members with finely tuned political antennas, the report chose to limit its concept of "integrated" strategy to purely military terms: integration of different weapons systems, integration of command and control, and so on. Despite an introductory promise to the contrary, Kennedy complained, the report focused almost exclusively on "military policy," while avoiding the incorporation of military means and ends with the nation's economic, scientific, and educational challenges.[82]

Wohlstetter and Iklé had ignored a slew of issues with a distinct bearing on national security. They imperiously ignored America's abdication of its role as "the world's greatest creditor-nation," the lack of American engineering graduates, and the levels of scientific and technological knowledge in American schools, even though all such factors were "absolutely vital parts of society's overall national strength," and had a bearing on any long-term "integrative" strategy.[83]

Discriminate Deterrence could not avoid acknowledging the very obvious shift from a "bipolar to a multipolar Great Power system," but the body of the report devoted "very little space to pondering the diplomatic and political implications of that transition in the global balances, and remains fixated on the Soviet military threat; it shows much more interest, for example, in ballistic missile defense than it does in our critically important future relations with the People's Republic of China."[84]

As for the evidence of Soviet superiority presented in the study, Kennedy accused its authors of barefaced statistical manipulation and a deceptive presentation of its graphs and tables. He pinpointed damning examples: "The sample comparison of the Soviet tank procurement of 24,300 vehicles in the years between 1978 and 1987 as against the American total of 7,580 in the same period not only ignores the issue of quality versus quantity; it also excludes the consideration of the tank totals of our NATO European allies."[85]

Faced with this barrage of negative press, U.S. government officials distanced themselves from the report, which had been commissioned by officials who were no longer part of the administration. The Reagan administration prohibited the authors, as well as Secretary of State George Schultz, from explaining the document on Worldnet, the government's overseas television network.[86] Administration officials, identified by Albert Wohlstetter as "the State Department bureaucracy," were reportedly disconcerted by the report's alleged revision of the nation's doctrine of nuclear deterrence. The authors' insistence that "NATO should use nuclear weapons in a 'discriminate way'" appeared to state department officials to contravene U.S. policy that "a nuclear war . . . must never be fought." The nation's ultimate strategic objective was "not to fight a nuclear war," but instead use the Western alliance's nuclear arsenal as a tool of deterrence.[87]

In the final analysis, *Discriminate Deterrence* reads like a lifetime summary of the Wohlstetters' contributions to national strategy, in particular their animus toward theories of MAD and their belittling of the strategic arms race (it was allegedly a one-sided process of incremental Soviet strength), as well as their advocacy of technologically based command and control of future battlefields. A cursory glance at Albert's newspaper articles offers condensed versions of *Discriminate Deterrence* many years before its actual publication. "Are we developing the right *kinds* and amount of force?" Albert had mused in a 1979 *New York Times* piece. "For years our eyes have been fixed on a possible massive attack through Germany's Fulda Gap. (Much of our Army is there and it seems almost impolite for an adversary to ignore it.) Isn't it at least as important (for Europe too) to prepare for contingencies on the flanks—in

Norway, Iceland, or Turkey? Or outside NATO, where NATO's interests are deeply engaged, like the Persian Gulf? In plans and negotiations should we shape our long-range nuclear forces for indiscriminate response . . . ? Are we saying we will use military force only after an unambiguous massive Soviet attack?"[88] As much as the document called for transcending the Cold War, *Discriminating Deterrence* maintained the persevering specter of a robust and scheming Soviet enemy well into the last twilight of the USSR.

In some sense, our recognition of this obvious anachronism may be the result of hindsight. We should, perhaps, show more charity toward the main protagonists. Nevertheless, the fear of the Soviet lurking in the report's pages typified a certain mindset. Historian Paul Edwards contends that a "closed world" of containment and binary opposition became so firmly engrained among policy makers that nothing beyond the plotting of an imaginary nuclear showdown did much to affect its iron grip.[89]

Albert offered a compelling synopsis of this cognitive dilemma in one of his early papers, where he chided his colleagues for avoiding engagement with the real world. Instead of confronting new realities, Albert observed, his colleagues immersed themselves in theoretical studies. Theory, he explained, was merely a form of procrastination, something done "to avoid actually going in and getting lost in a very dense jungle. Maps, brochures, the purchase of compasses, machetes, bush jackets and rakish tropical helmets can be used as a substitute for a hot and sweaty journey."[90]

Albert and Roberta's interest in the terra incognita beyond the pale of theory was hastened by the rise of nonstate actors, the challenges of asymmetrical warfare, and the undeniable emergence of a polycentric strategic landscape. They appeared poised to traverse new territory. Yet when the moment arrived, they hesitated—and then recoiled. The tangled path through the multipolar jungle was, to adopt Graham Greene's pertinent phrase, a "journey without maps." One could get hopelessly disoriented. Rather than venture into the unknown, the Wohlstetters chose familiar territory, interrupted every now and again by brief circular jaunts through thickets that brought them back safely to their point of departure.

7

Slow Pearl Harbors

Fear and Loathing of Glasnost

D ECEMBER 7, 1988. A landmark date in the demise of communism. Mikhail Gorbachev announced the withdrawal of five hundred thousand troops from Eastern Europe that day. By coincidence, this event transpired on the forty-seventh anniversary of the Japanese attack on Pearl Harbor. To mark the occasion, Roberta Wohlstetter returned to the defining theme of her work in speaking engagements at the National Press Club and at the National Security Forum. Rather than reiterate her analysis of the 1941 surprise attack, Roberta instead warned of a dangerous new signal she perceived amid the elusively soothing noise emanating from the Soviet Union. While Western policy makers exulted at the Soviet empire's rapid devolution, Roberta took up the role of Cassandra, reprimanding them for basking in the glow of a false dawn. A creeping, existential threat was lurking at the nation's doorstep, she warned, the menace of "slow Pearl Harbors."[1]

By "slow Pearl Harbors," Roberta meant "small, overt changes that take place steadily during an extended period of peace," such as the incremental infringements of disarmament agreements and other treaties. These barely perceptible events "discourage response . . . because each finite change is so small that we may not notice it."[2] The national security establishment, timid by nature, typically dismissed any individual incident as inconsequential. "No one of these changes seems worth responding to," either because its implications were ambiguous or because the "costs" of responding appeared to exceed the benefits of disturbing an ostensibly stable global balance of power. The accumulation of minor infringements, Roberta warned, could eventually turn into a major threat.[3]

This cumulative effect, however, remained hidden from unimaginative eyes. Roberta blamed this state of affairs on uninspired definitions of strategic surprise. Pedestrian politicians and military officials defined *strategic surprise* as an abrupt, saturated strike on a subset of targets—a result, in part, of common misapprehensions of her 1962 study of Pearl Harbor. The image of surprise attack as massive and sudden, she feared, had developed into a cognitive blind spot, eclipsing all other scenarios.

Pearl Harbor—the sudden, masterfully executed assault that demolishes an adversary's main fighting force in a stunning blitz of shock and awe—had become the monolithic model of military surprise. Yet surprise, she cautioned, could take and had taken multiple forms when planned by enterprising enemies. The most dangerous alternative to a single, unexpected assault was the incremental approach: stealthy movement into strategic positions by means of modest tactical steps, each passing largely unnoticed. Roberta's ostensibly gullible strategist colleagues remained determined to relive a selective version of history. They were looking for an immediate, mobilizing threat. Mundane documentation of small, unhurried, yet overt steps toward some version of a slow Pearl Harbor presented "a less sexy subject than signs that a surprise attack is on its way."[4] Clear and present dangers captured the imagination. Minor moves, even when carried out in broad daylight, met with drowsy complacency.

As the lauded historian of this defining event in the nation's history, Roberta posited Pearl Harbor as a metaphor for major misconceptions of contemporary Soviet designs. She had developed the slow Pearl Harbors theme some nine years earlier in a *Washington Quarterly* piece.[5] But the year 1988—the same year that Albert's much-heralded *Discriminate Deterrence* was published—offered compelling reasons to revisit the motif. In the waning months of 1988, Roberta detected ample evidence that, once again, the United States may be "surprised by the obvious." Even as signs of Soviet disintegration seemed to proliferate, and while negotiations toward a Strategic Arms Reduction Treaty (START) progressed, Roberta cautioned against the pitfalls of ill-conceived accords that could be worn away in miniscule increments of small violations. The nation was on the verge of needlessly ignoring signals of imminent danger buried in the mollifying white noise of fuzzy agreements and premature declarations of a mighty empire's decline and fall. Roberta's central insight was that deception was less the work of a conniving adversary than it was self-induced. Unlike 1941, however, there would be no redemption in the aftermath of a creeping attack in the thermonuclear age. This time, the threat was terminal.

Roberta's writings on slow Pearl Harbors emphasized—once again—the importance of focusing on capabilities over intentions, a major theme of the Wohlstetter Doctrine. If Pearl Harbor proved anything, it was that attempting to divine an enemy's intentions was a dubious prospect at best. Such predictions were mostly exercises in self-deception driven by wishful thinking, preconceptions, and a natural yet dangerous tendency to humanize even the most inhumane enemies. Reading the tea leaves in the Kremlin's samovar was an especially hopeless pursuit. The nation's security, she argued, could not depend on flimsy fortune-telling. Defense policy had to be guided by verifiable enemy capabilities, not hypothetical guesswork.

Roberta was as reluctant as Albert to publicly acknowledge the momentous events shaking the Eastern bloc. The changes that seemed to be loosening the Soviet Union's grip, they insisted, were a mirage conjured by ill-advised dilettantes and media outlets with dubious loyalties. In Roberta's world the Soviets remained as strong and as dangerous as ever. With her sights set firmly on the past—rather than on the unfolding decline of a debilitated empire—Roberta waged war on complacency. The image of a vacillating Soviet Union, she warned, was a momentary distraction. The Soviets' commitment to worldwide destabilization remained unwavering, even as their grip on satellite states appeared to be loosening.

The Late, Great Soviet Threat

Roberta's unwillingness to accept Cold War closure was derived, in part, from her teleological approach to history. Confrontation with a formidable enemy, she implied, was an inevitability, although the actors might conceivably change. Pearl Harbor and the Cold War were part of a repertoire of recurring themes in the West's fitful battle against different hues of adversarial threats. Despite obvious differences in basic ideological temperament, Roberta affirmed, historical examples of authoritarian global aggression offered instructive lessons for understanding the nature of the Soviet threat and the contemporary (1988) perils of incremental communist gains. A close look at history would provide ample evidence that pronouncements of the Soviets' demise were premature. History proved that a drop in Western vigilance would invite a latter-day version of Pearl Harbor, slow or otherwise.

Germany in the aftermath of the Great War served as a case in point. The deliberate attrition of the Treaty of Versailles, coupled with the failure of France and Great Britain to react to a series of minute moves toward incremental German rearmament, had sown the seeds of unfathomable disaster. From the moment of the treaty's inception, a determined German government had eroded its commitments by inches. The Allied committee charged with monitoring the agreement ignored the shifting strategic reality of cumulative violations, preferring, instead, to debate "whether any *single* incident 'would constitute a real danger to international security.'"[6] French foreign minister Aristide Briand dismissed the obvious evidence of transgression as petty details. Briand feared that revelations of the true nature of Germany's rearmament would frustrate his all-consuming desire to share the Nobel Prize with his German counterpart, Gustav Streseman—one of the ringleaders of German treaty infringements. By 1926, despite overwhelming evidence to the contrary, an outrageously myopic French foreign minister had declared victory. German disarmament was " 'complete.' The next year he felt it 'was even more complete.' "[7]

Versailles offered a cautionary tale for those advocating arms reduction agreements with a truculent Soviet Union, Roberta stressed. As the "experience of the 1920s illustrates, democracies find it hard to respond to a sequence of small rearmament moves by a dictatorship or even by a social democratic republic" such as Weimar Germany.[8] Versailles was a treaty enforced by victors over a vanquished state. Ostensibly, such an imbalance between signatories offered a positive environment for treaty compliance, and yet it had failed. This historical failure suggested to Roberta that monitoring an arms reduction treaty with the Soviet Union—an undefeated sovereign entity with ideological incentive and practical tools for obstructing compliance—would have disastrous consequences.

If the French, twice invaded by an aggressive German foe, were unwilling to understand the danger of cumulative changes, what could be expected from the "tolerant dreamers" who, in 1988, were gripped by a self-delusional "Gorbomania" and naive declarations on the end of the

Cold War?[9] For the self-delusional boosters who interpreted the cracks in the Soviet glacier as a triumphant end of bipolar conflict, Roberta offered condescending scorn. History—measured by Roberta as seventy years of Soviet aggression and four hundred years of paranoid "Tsarist hostility to the outside world"—provided ample evidence that receding glaciers were often an optical illusion; "glaciers advance as well as recede and in any case they tend to move at glacial rather than lightning speed."[10]

In fact, Roberta claimed, a contemporary version of Versailles-like infractions was unfolding before once-vigilant eyes, now filmed over with emotional celebrations of the "end of history." For those who considered her warnings narrow-minded and unwarranted, Roberta offered the example of a major Soviet infraction of the recently signed ABM treaty. The construction of a "football-field-size" radar in the vicinity of the Siberian city of Krasnoyarsk had led to an inevitable quandary over whether this obvious serious transgression constituted a violation, or "whether the claim of violation was a sinister U.S. preparation to denounce or violate the ABM treaty and spoil the atmosphere for START."[11] This "one violation *in and of itself* called for no response. Of course that might be said about each one of a sequence of such violations until the sequence added up to a countrywide network of radars and interceptors of the sort the treaty wanted to prohibit."[12]

Rather than incur an American reaction to a full-blown surprise attack, the Soviets were engaged in inching the strategic world—"slowly and patiently and at small risk"—in their favor.[13] The Soviets, Roberta argued, had not embarked on this strategy with the expectation that their peaceful intentions would be believed. In fact, such piecemeal strategies were a calculated device to "give us an opportunity to deceive ourselves or to save face." A "fashionably muddled" preoccupation with "crisis stability" dominated the American strategic establishment. Its members felt a constant need to reassure the "supposedly paranoid . . . bear that we are not aggressive, that there may be some misunderstanding."[14]

Roberta chastised historians of U.S.-Soviet relations for portraying poor leadership and bad decisions as great accomplishments, rather than dismal defeats that had enabled the Soviets to grow inexorably stronger. Even the Cuban missile crisis, so often misinterpreted as an American triumph, did not culminate in any significant redress of the balance of power. Beyond the self-serving "celebrations of their blinking first" lay a worrisome American impulse to produce Pollyannaish interpretations of colossal failures. Roberta reproached Kennedy hagiographers such as Theodore Sorensen and Arthur Schlesinger Jr. for perpetuating the myth that a chastened Soviet Union had acquiesced quietly to American military superiority, while accepting, de facto, a halt to the arms race. The missile crisis, she claimed, had energized Soviet leaders: "In a series of small stages," following the Cuban crisis, "they accustomed us to a new reality: that of nuclear parity." Small yet incremental infringements of the Cuban agreement were all but ignored, or relegated to the category of " 'small fusses' or non-crises."[15]

Roberta offered other examples of collusion between historians and politicians to put the best face on strategic setbacks. Truman's response to the Berlin blockade—often heralded as a singular example of American fortitude—was really the culmination of a series of slow Pearl Harbors all but ignored by inept American authorities who should have known better. The Berlin blockade was no sudden occurrence. It was preceded by multiple Soviet attempts to test the West's resolve to remain in Berlin—"harassing actions, delays of transport, or boarding of military trains. . . . At each point the Russians gave reasons which, taken alone, looked not totally implausible. . . . Cumulatively, the explanations were hard to believe" for anyone but those who were fixated on dramatic and reckless military moves, rather than the skillful erosion of American might in Berlin.[16] Historians had celebrated the ephemeral triumph of the end of the Soviet blockade as an instance of American resolve. Roberta reversed that interpretation: ultimately, the West had been forced to accept the Berlin Wall. A delusional foreign policy establishment had managed to snatch a defeat from the momentary victory of ending the blockade. "After each indecisive and bloodless engagement" in Berlin, Cuba, and elsewhere, the United States had demonstrated an alarming tendency to avoid reality, "declare a victory, and go home."[17]

As far as contemporary threats were concerned, Roberta derided her cognitively challenged colleagues for misreading a constant stream of arms control violations as discrete events with no cumulative significance. In reality, the aggregate effect had allowed the Soviet Union to achieve a "shift in the balance of nuclear forces . . . by moving slowly, overtly and steadily," creating a new strategic reality. Not a single one of these small, incremental moves generated any meaningful response;

the mediocre stewards of the nation's security were neither able nor willing to do the math. By counting such events as discrete units, these inept accountants drew up a fallacious cost-benefit analysis in which "the cost of response" to these singular infractions exceeded "the disturbance of the peace made by the response." A Hamletian aversion to decisive action exacerbated the disservice. Excuses abounded for those disinclined to act. In times of peace—such as the era of détente—they could imagine that a stern response would upset a fragile peace. "In a period of tension," on the other hand, these same analysts advocated that reaction "may seem too dangerous." But such "creep-out," she warned, would be "followed by breakout."[18]

Albert was no less concerned about an imminent Soviet threat, even as visible fissures appeared impossible to ignore. As late as July 1990, with apparent obliviousness to the unfolding of a great drama, Albert continued to invoke an image of all-powerful, cunningly deceptive Soviets: "A reasonable man, Gorbachev has said that all he wants is to negotiate, not to coerce. (While Red Army tanks and armored personnel carriers rumble through the streets of Vilnius in the middle of the night.) All he asks is that the Lithuanians—and the Estonians, and the Latvians, and the Azeris, and the Ukrainians, *et al.*—recognize the Rule of Law that binds *everyone* in the Soviet Union including himself. But he uses the word 'law' like Humpty Dumpty in *Through the Looking Glass,* who took the view that when *he* used a word it meant exactly what he chose it to mean, no more, no less."[19] All evidence to the contrary, Albert—like Roberta—persisted in insisting that the Soviets were still on the march.

The Confessions of Albert

How does one explain the Wohlstetters' unwillingness to acknowledge the writing on the crumbling wall? Why did they insist on denying the Cold War's imminent conclusion?

It is tempting to interpret the Wohlstetters' unshaken faith in the Soviet threat as a visceral reaction to the untimely demise of a pet paradigm. They certainly evinced classic symptoms of grief for the departed red menace—from denial and rage to a belated acceptance of sorts. I would argue, however, that other motives sparked this war of words between the Wohlstetters and the world.

Albert's unpublished thoughts, unlike his public pronouncements, provide a nuanced picture of the Wohlstetters' reluctance to let go. He let slip his bluntest explanation in a 1985 oral history interview. Casually offering a radically revisionist interpretation of his own doctrine, Albert divulged that he did not actually believe in the imminent Soviet threat of his public enunciations.[20]

Albert began the interview—conducted by two close friends from his RAND days—in a conventional manner. When asked to respond to recurring accusations that he had promoted a bloated and unrealistic image of the Soviet threat, he initially fell back on the probability-possibility argument. Albert recalled a 1950s argument with the arms control advocate, Raymond Garthoff, then a recently minted PhD. Garthoff's dissertation held that Russian military doctrine "deprecated surprise," and, therefore, Albert's fretting over a Soviet surprise attack was, at the very least, overkill.[21] Albert responded by presenting Garthoff with the conclusions of the Base Studies, in which he claimed to have demolished the Garthoff-like assumption that "even if the Soviets *could* deliver a surprise attack which precluded our effective response, they *would* not . . . because Soviet doctrine excludes preventive war." In his impromptu lecturing of Garthoff, Albert leaned on his collaborative studies with Henry Rowen, where he had concluded that such "predictions of Soviet behavior are suspect because they are unconditional. They do not envision circumstances in which unpleasant alternatives are thrust upon the Russians."[22] In other words, no responsible American strategist could assume that the absence of a Soviet doctrine on surprise attack precluded the use of this strategy in the future. His advocacy of an aggressive expansion of the nation's thermonuclear arsenal was justified, he insisted, by the need to address capabilities—however remote—rather than flawed constructions of Soviet intentions. The prudent strategist planned for contingencies, not personal preferences of an enemy's behavior.

The interview then veered into personal territory as Albert recalled his intellectual journey, beginning with his exposure to great thinkers at Columbia and ending with a description of his years at RAND, punctuated by his unpleasant confrontations with Bernard Brodie. At ease with his interviewers, Albert gradually let down his guard and drifted away from his self-serving image as the intrepid strategist encircled by mealymouthed appeasers. Instead he offered a glimpse of the personal and, at times, intimate motives of his public policy.

Albert intimated that disenchantment with the ideologies of his youth may have contributed to an excessively grim depiction of the Soviet adversary. Following World War II, Albert recalled the waning tug of the politics of the Left. The "enormous release of creativity" in postwar America, on the one hand, and Soviet aggression in "Berlin, the fall of Czechoslovakia, and then the invasion of Korea," on the other, were the last stations in his ideological transformation, and subsequent vilification of fallen gods.[23] Albert then moved on to describing his professional debts as another reason for aggrandizing the Soviet threat.

His fixation on a Soviet surprise attack, Albert explained, was due to Roberta's towering and, perhaps, constraining influence on his intellectual itinerary. Surprise at Pearl Harbor, Albert explained, "was implicit in the way I dealt with [the Soviet threat] and I tried to make it explicit in the theory of comparative risks which you will find expressed succinctly in R-290"—the classified RAND study on the vulnerabilities of overseas strategic bases—"and in 'The Delicate Balance' and in many other things."[24] In other words, Roberta's reconstruction of the surprise attack at Pearl Harbor was a rigid, constraining template for his elaborate modeling of Soviet behavior.

Following this homage to Pearl Harbor, Albert drifted into blunt trivializations of the Soviet enemy, much of which flew in the face of his public posturing. Throughout this portion of the interview, a relaxed and unusually candid Albert became progressively more dismissive of the Soviets. In fact, he described them as strategic midgets, albeit "normally bright midgets."[25] In this moment of candor, he acknowledged that the likelihood of an existential Soviet threat bordered on the fictitious. As adherents of a rigid doctrine, the Soviets "did not foresee living on this earth indefinitely with democracies," but instead of open war, they preferred "subversion and intimidation."[26] There was no doubt in Albert's mind that this cautious, calculating enemy would refrain from an all-out attack against the United States. "I never believed that they were likely to attack us at the strongest point." At the very most, he argued, they might attempt, as had the Japanese at Pearl Harbor, to destroy well defined American military facilities that kept them from capturing prized parts of Europe. But even these circumstances struck him as unlikely. During one of the most volatile periods of the Cold War, spanning the 1950s and early 1960s, "their bombers were *much* less ready than SAC's. When they finally got missiles, they didn't get any silos until 1965. When they got submarines, they were mostly in port and they were extremely noisy."[27] In sum, they were ill prepared for an attack of any kind, surprise or otherwise. Their modus operandi appeared to be to "forbid intervention by us" in their Eastern European domain "by the threat of war."[28]

Even in his early RAND studies Albert had acknowledged that his militant stance on counterforce capability carried "some danger of de-stabilizing the deterrent balance."[29] Yet this latter-day RAND interview suggests he had been willing to risk destabilization because he never truly believed the Soviets were as ruthless as American strategic ortho-doxy assumed. In other words, the reason Albert was comfortable with risking destabilizing strategies to address the remote *possibility* of Soviet nuclear aggression was that he had never really believed in the *proba-bility* of such a catastrophic event. The advent of progressively lethal thermonuclear weaponry had not increased the likelihood of a nuclear engagement with the Soviet Union because as far as a nuclear confron-tation was concerned, the Soviet enemy was a lethargic bully who could be intimidated into sullen inaction. Albert's Soviet adversaries were hopelessly small-minded, predictable, and unimaginative.

The Soviet enemy, Albert explained in 1963, juggled multiple chal-lenges and was "preoccupied with a good many other problems than doing us in by force of arms." The Soviets had "problems of their own development and the quarrels with their friends . . . and a good many other domestic and foreign concerns that distracted and weakened them." It was incumbent on the United States to capitalize on these is-sues with unrelenting pressure on the Cold War front. Those who feared that such pressure would ultimately escalate into a nuclear confronta-tion were driven by mindless "eschatology" rather than science or knowledge.[30]

It was ultimately the economist in Albert that drove him to publicly promote the narrative of a predatory enemy and the concomitant call for massive U.S. defense expenditures. The Soviets, he believed, were reactively investing in a perpetual production cycle of increasingly elab-orate yet increasingly also irrelevant and financially draining weapons systems. His rivals had argued that the very existence of extravagantly lethal weaponry—however irrelevant they seemed to contemporary military challenges—practically assured their eventual deployment and the inevitable advent of a nuclear holocaust. Albert dismissed such fears as unfounded. The Soviets lacked the necessary temperament for adventurous policies and were essentially pursuing a reactive war of research and development, rather than actively courting the possibility of a nuclear engagement. Albert's advocacy for a U.S. nuclear spending spree, his RAND interview suggests, was driven by his acceptance of Soviet limitations, rather than, as he had always publically claimed, his sober assessment of the enemy's predatory nature. His strategy's implicit objective was to provoke the Soviets into feckless financial hemorrhaging in their pursuit of macabre and mostly useless military accessorizing.

Albert's appraisal of the Soviet enemy as dim-witted strategists and compulsive spenders was nothing new. Such thoughts had been lurking in Albert's mind over the entire span of his career as a strategist. As early as 1959, Albert had written that the Soviet defenses were astoundingly exposed, their strategists incapable of imagining a surprise attack on their own forces. In one of his major RAND papers, written with Henry Rowen, he described the enemy's "bomber home-bases" as "quite vulnerable now (they have little radar warning, are soft and may not be highly alert) and may remain so. A considerable part of his bomber force depends on quite vulnerable staging bases."[31] Such astounding sloppiness on the enemy's part, however, was no reason to curtail aggressive expenditures. While expensive improvements to U.S. battlefield capabilities was a contentious military exercise, the aggressive research and development campaign did constitute a formidable economic weapon. A Soviet spending spree on military ordnance had the potential to bring the enemy to its knees without ever firing a single piece of doomsday weaponry. "Our object is to select feasible measures that force infeasibly expensive countermeasures" on the enemy.[32]

For the paltry sum of an additional "2.5 billion dollars more a year for four or five years," declared Albert, the United States could induce the economic implosion of the Soviet Union. At midcentury, he pointed out, American GNP was growing at a minimal rate of 3 percent a year, which translated into $15 billion a year. "We could, therefore, increase the defense budget by over $10 billion annually without retreating one iota from our present levels of consumption, investment and non-defense items in general," and with only mild inflationary effects, if any. Fully expecting a Soviet countermove, Albert claimed that any additional defense burden on the Soviet economy would wreak havoc. With a GNP no more than half as large as the United States and with a larger population to feed, "an increase of $10 billion per year in the Soviet defense budget would disrupt its investment program or deny consumers relatively important parts of their standard of living." Such a situation would provoke "social unrest and disorder." The grand plan, therefore, was to play on the Soviets' insecurities, to drive them to bankrupt themselves. "We believe that the dangers of *not* making the mild national sacrifice involved" to induce Soviet economic suicide, Albert concluded, "are very grave."[33]

In his 1985 interview, Albert offered another, somewhat startling reason for his bellicose position on weapons development. He appeared to fear that any perception of American inferiority—including the vulnerability of SAC he himself revealed in his base studies and in "Delicate Balance"—would encourage not the Russians but the Americans to behave recklessly. "I wanted people to *not* think that instead of repairing SAC's vulnerability, they could just take advantage of the Soviet vulnerability . . . [I was] afraid that discovering how vulnerable SAC was, even though we had ways of reducing it, people might do something else."[34] Insecurity and misperception, Albert believed, had the dangerous potential of fostering irresponsible policies. He appeared to have concluded that its own sense of vulnerability, rather than a ruthless Russian enemy, posed a significant threat to the security of the United States.

Albert's RAND papers and newspaper articles suggest another reason for his bellicose posture. An embellished Soviet threat served the purpose of maintaining vigilance in a nation afflicted by an attention deficit disorder. In fact, Albert expressed fears more of a generic, modular enemy—there would always be one, according to the Wohlstetter Doctrine—than of the Russian Bear. Given the context of the 1950s and 1960s, the Soviets were merely the obvious example—the usual suspect—for raising public awareness of the need for constant vigilance.

The specter of an external threat appeared to be the only narrative binding a fractious Western world. "There are many manifestations of Western weakness and vulnerability," Albert noted in 1976, including political instability among Southern European allies, the rise of isolationism, and a "reduced capacity for administrative action within the United States," by which he presumably meant the rise of racial and social unrest. The presence of an enemy—unrelenting in the pursuit of its goals—appeared, then, to be a device to hold the vacillating West together.[35]

Albert and Roberta's last collaborative exercise, a 1989 book proposal, acknowledged that their public representation of the Soviet threat was an artifact. Their construction of the Soviet enemy was born out of their distrust of the Western political class, who, for the most part, were Panglossian characters in a very dangerous world. "The democracies," they explained, appeared "to need imminent threats in order to induce them to prepare for latent long-term dangers."[36] In fact, they claimed, all of Albert's major works—"Protecting U.S. Power to Strike Back in the 1950s and 1960s," "The Delicate Balance of Terror," "The Objectives of U.S. Military Power," "No Highway to High Purpose," and other writings on the second-strike theory of deterrence—"took pains to make clear that they were directed not at the immediate likelihood of a Soviet nuclear attack. . . . None of these writings held that the Soviets were straining at the leash to launch a nuclear attack and that an adequate second-strike capability was the only thing that held them back."[37] Instead, they advocated "a new image of ourselves in a world of *persistent* danger" rather than a unique struggle with the Soviet Union.[38] From the vantage point of 1989, and tucked into a rough draft of a book proposal, the Wohlstetters acknowledged that the probability of a massive Soviet nuclear attack or a conventional invasion of the center of Europe was "never very large" and had since "been receding even further."[39] The conclusion of the Cold War did not mean the end of "fanaticism, mortal national and racial rivalries, and expansionist ambitions."[40] Quite the contrary. These lethal forces, formally contained by two great superpowers, promised to erupt with great ferocity.

The Enemy Proliferates

The Wohlstetters' constructions of future enemies, less predictable and more reckless than the Soviets, highlighted their fear of unchecked proliferation. In fact, their Cold War articles in the 1970s stated quite clearly that fixation on the Soviet Union had blinded the United States to the potential spread of nuclear weapons beyond the narrow Soviet-U.S.

axis. Long before the expiration of the Cold War, the Wohlstetters argued that nuclear proliferation among rogue states and even allies offered a significantly more challenging scenario than the Soviet-U.S. standoff.

Aligning himself with Roberta's ruminations about "Terror on a Grand Scale," Albert raised the fear of "small terror attacks by national, as well as subnational groups. Even distant small powers using freighters and short-range missiles, such as the Soviet SCUD, will be within system range of the United States." Writing in the 1970s, Albert produced a doomsday scenario of familiar, limited conflagrations spiraling out of control once nuclear weapons became the weapons of choice among hostile regional foes. If nuclear bombs were introduced into the serial wars between Israel and its Arab neighbors, he asserted, "the Arabs might suffer several million and the Israelis a million dead" before "outside powers could stop the conflict." The casualties that would result from a few hours of confrontation would far exceed the "thousands killed in the October war."[41]

Proliferation among allies offered an equally distasteful scenario. The United States was liable to find itself in the unenviable position of deciding, among allies, who the "Nth" nuclear power should be. Such a process would alienate those lacking nuclear weapons while encouraging a false sense of invincibility and entitlement among the nuclear chosen few. A gaggle of nuclear powers—even if they happened to be allies—complicated an otherwise manageable superpower confrontation. The introduction of multiple contenders, each espousing competing agendas, threatened to break the rules of what had been a comfortable, two-sided chess game.[42]

To be sure, deterrence between the United States and the Soviet Union remained precarious and far from unconditional. However, "in a many-nation world including so far five countries that have exploded nuclear devices and about 130 that have not, unconditional deterrence" became even more volatile. "If each of the nuclear countries could unconditionally deter any other, this would mean the instability of nuclear peace, not stability."[43] As Albert had written in 1961, he much preferred that the United States be "tied to complicated and uncertain negotiations with the Russians" than to depend for every strategic move on "the cooperation of potential [nuclear] Nth powers."[44]

The French were a particularly annoying example of the instability and challenges of nuclear proliferation because they espoused multiple and conflicting objectives for pursuing a nuclear arsenal. On one side stood Charles de Gaulle, who claimed that proliferation would improve the chances of disarmament: "General de Gaulle speaks of the increased effect on nuclear disarmament which France would have by becoming a nuclear power. In the limit, one might suppose that unanimity for nuclear disarmament may be achieved by distributing bombs to everybody."[45] On the other side was Pierre Gallois, the inspiration behind France's force de frappe. Gallois contended that a nuclear arsenal was the ultimate poor man's weapon, an "equalizer in international politics." According to Gallois, Albert wrote, "no nation can be counted on to defend another from atomic aggression, since in doing so it would chance annihilation. Thermonuclear weapons, however, favor the prospective victim of aggression, it is said, by making it comparatively easy to retaliate effectively. So a lesser power can deter even a major nuclear power such as the Soviet Union."[46]

The most effective way to avoid this cacophony of upstart nuclear powers—each pulling in a different direction, each adding an element of unpredictability to an already unstable environment—was to price the potential parvenus out of the market. Albert noted with satisfaction that the British, having discovered the prohibitive costs of maintaining their own arsenal, had given up on their nuclear pipe dreams. The British had realized that the dubious shield of a personal nuclear arsenal came with a staggering price tag. The "cancellation of its costly program for the Blue Streak missile marked the conscious transition from a hopefully 'independent deterrent' to the much less ambitious 'independent contribution to the deterrent.' And it is not without reason . . . that France's first 'deterrent' vehicles will be called 'Mirage.' "[47]

The Wohlstetters' antidote to the chaos of nuclear proliferation was to vigorously cry wolf over the Russian threat, while calling for the vigilant containment of regional upstarts. The gaping back door of Atoms for Peace, however, confounded such plans. "Smiling Buddha"—the curious code name of India's first nuclear detonation in 1974—was a sign of things to come.[48] India had gained the technical knowhow for creating nuclear ordnance through an Atoms for Peace program supported by both Canada and the United States. In fact, Roberta asserted in a study of the development, India's nuclear program had "slow Pearl Harbor" written all over it. The soothing "noise" of India's commitment to use atomic energy for peaceful civilian purposes, she wrote, "confused otherwise plain signals of their accumulation of separated fissile material directly usable in weapons, their capacity to separate more, the manufacture and detonation."[49]

India's entry into the nuclear club demonstrated the manner in which the spread of technology, ostensibly for the peaceful purposes of generating nuclear power, could turn plowshares into quite lethal swords, a concern that dominated the Wohlstetters' work in the 1970s and 1980s.[50] Roberta feared that with the acquisition of a bomb India had the potential to destabilize the region, if not the world. "Only a minor event is needed to tip the decision in the timing for exploding a nuclear device: for example, a mere 'tilt' toward Pakistan by the United States rather than a reversal of alliance, or a need for a distraction from transient domestic economic troubles such as a railroad strike."[51] In later years, fears of proliferation would mushroom, leading the Wohlstetter school to assign nuclear designs with abandon—Iraq being the ultimate example of this mind-set.

The War Rages On

As the Cold War faded, the fear of nuclear proliferation was adjoined by other potentially dangerous shifts in the play of global power. The triumph of decentralized markets and the flourishing of free exchange in the aftermath of the Cold War was a revolution of unanticipated consequences. Access to information and markets now occurred outside the purview of gatekeepers, the United States included. The Wohlstetters described massive changes in communication technology as the principle driving force of a booming marketplace of ideas and goods that had undermined communism. Cutting-edge communication innovations had allowed a thousand flowers to bloom, while wilting centralized alternatives. These same forces, however, challenged American power, as well.

The communication revolution, Albert told the receptive American Enterprise Institute in July 1990, "fits well the view of economics typified by Friedrich Hayek, which sees economic activities as adjusting themselves by responses to signals sent by market-clearing prices—without the need or possibility of a central plan. By improving the op-

eration of dispersed markets, the new technologies improve the operation of the system as a whole."[52] Yet such celebratory decentralization
encouraged a false sense of security. It blinded its proponents to the lingering Hobbesian environment of global politics. Since democracies
would not prepare for their long-term defense without being prompting
by "imminent threats," the post–Cold War era required a campaign to
expose lingering malignant threats, none of which were as lethal as the
hegemonic tyrannies of years past, but each in their own way quite toxic
and destructive.[53]

Invoking their most salient Cold War publications, the Wohlstetters
claimed a certain urgency in persuading skeptical colleagues of the need
to understand "ourselves in a world of persistent danger," rather than at
a tail end of a long nightmare.[54] The demise of the bipolar world did not
spell global stability. A "moral revolution" of the magnitude of the
market revolution had yet to come, a distant aspiration easily derailed
by dark energies swirling through the global arena.[55] As such, no market
triumph, however colossal, obviated the need for a vigilant gatekeeper.

As had been the case in the past, the Wohlstetters greatest fear was a
Western stampede toward disarmament and naive agreements on
arms reductions with authoritarian adversaries who cavalierly ignored
their pledges to change their evil ways. "History," Albert had cautioned
in 1960, "is replete with international agreements which have actually
encouraged aggression," thereby sowing the seeds of another global catastrophe.[56] A callous enemy, be it the Russians or some other rapacious
upstart, would approach treaties as the pursuit of war by other means,
capitalizing on a compulsive American urge to reduce defense expenditures to unimaginably low levels. Western leaders had forgotten the
most important lesson of the Second World War: the need to confront,
not to appease "the challenge of totalitarianism."[57] The Wohlstetters
feared that the widespread belief in the uniqueness of current events
had curtained off the past.

The Wohlstetters finally acknowledged victory over the communist
foe when, at last, they could no longer deny the untimely demise of the
comfortable and familiar trope that had served them so well. Waving
aside the evidence that long-term social and economic trends had debilitated the Soviet Union, the Wohlstetters and their school could claim
that it was American prescience and the impact of expensive weapons
systems, rather than internal developments in the Soviet bloc, that had

brought their opponents to their knees. Yet although the battle was won, the war still raged on. Whether dealing with the Soviet Union, the conflict in the Balkans, or threats emanating from the Persian Gulf, a slew of Hitler impressionists and Stalinist look-alikes appeared to reincarnate before their very eyes.

"Do Not Go Gentle into That Good Night"

Albert Wohlstetter after the Cold War

ALBERT WOHLSTETTER PASSED AWAY on January 10, 1997. A month later, President Bill Clinton joined a memorial ceremony at the U.S. Senate attended by Roberta, their daughter Joan, and their many students in government and academia. Senator Jon Kyl presided over the proceedings. The Republican senator from Arizona lauded the deceased as "one of the staunchest champions of 'peace through strength'—before the term became popular during the Reagan administration." Albert, he observed, had "cautioned against the folly of seeking security in arms control agreements, and advocated placing our trust in America's military strength and technological ingenuity."[1]

Kyl invoked one of Albert's last great political stands, his outspoken criticism of the American reaction to war in Bosnia. With the president sitting nearby, Kyl described Albert's deep contempt for the Clinton administration's stance on the most devastating conflict in Europe since the end of World War II. "For four long years, in countless articles, Albert reminded our leaders that with America's superpower status came not only vast military strength, but immense moral responsibility—and for those reasons, allowing a small nation in the center of Europe to become the victim of genocide was unconscionable."[2]

A somber Richard Perle delivered the eulogy. Albert, he recalled, had a particular fondness for the poems of Dylan Thomas. Perle predictably recited the poet's ode to his dying father. Albert, too, did "not go gentle into that good night." To his last days, he had raged against the alleged hypocrisies of his adversaries.

"And you, my father, there on the sad height, / Curse, bless, me now with your fierce tears, I pray."[3] As he recited these lines in front of the nation's leaders, one could only imagine Perle's reflections on his own personal struggle to live up to the expectations of his departed mentor. As the following chapters demonstrate, Wohlstetter acolytes emulated Albert in form and substance. Albert had modeled for them a unique style of subduing rivals by all means possible, formulating this strategy for cowing the opposition in the 1950s and finessing it during the 1960s as he propagated escalating investments in an arsenal of flamboyant weaponry. When arguments of substance faltered, the paterfamilias and, subsequently, his godchildren employed blasts of innuendo and defamation.

Albert bequeathed to his nuclear family a clear agenda for the challenges of the post–Cold War years. As the world moved away from the constraints of a bipolar standoff, Albert discovered new challenges in the proliferation of weapons and the rise of ambitious tyrants who threatened both regional and global stability. Yet, consistent with his public stance on the untimely demise of the Soviet empire, Albert continued to spy wisps of Russian resurgence. He lashed out at an allegedly indolent president who lacked the courage to douse the embers of a Greater Russia once more on the rise.

"Rage, Rage"

Albert's tendency to rage—on Bosnia, the Cold War, and other causes célèbres—was a centerpiece of his legacy. Never one to merely contest facts, Albert ostracized opponents and commandeered debates through intimidation, while avoiding compromise and consensus in any form or fashion. He opted for domination by overkill. When critics questioned the veracity of his data, Albert would unleash a counterstrike of biblical proportions. He did not hesitate to scorch earth and destroy critics by excommunication.

The Safeguard controversy of 1969–1972 provides an example and a template for this debating strategy and its subsequent adaptation by his most trusted students. At stake were congressional allocations for a futuristic, antiballistic missile (ABM) system—a project of staggering costs, aimed at confronting the remote possibility of a Soviet attack on Minuteman silos based in the continental United States.[4] The primary battleground was a Senate committee chaired by Albert Gore Sr. Wohlstetter led the administration's team of experts in this intense debate. Armed with tomes of data supplied by Pentagon proponents of ABM, he rattled off computations allegedly proving that 95 percent of the Minuteman system could be destroyed by a bold Soviet first strike. The subtext of Albert's argument was quite familiar and it had served him well ever since his initial proclamations on the vulnerability of strategic forces based outside the United States. With stubborn perseverance, he had argued—then and now—that every conceivable Soviet threat, no matter how remote or theoretical, deserved a robust response.

A formidable group testified against the very concept of Safeguard. The opposition's lead was Jerome Wiesner, president of MIT. Wiesner had previously served as head of MIT's Radiation Laboratory and was an electrical engineer by training. His supporting team included two MIT professors: George Rathjens, a physical chemist turned political scientist, and Steven Weinberg, the renowned physicist who would receive the Nobel Prize in Physics in 1979. Stanford University physicist Wolfgang Panofsky (son of art historian Irwin Panofsky) offered additional testimony against Safeguard.

The opposition questioned Albert's calculations, produced alternative data that implied far less threatening projections of future Soviet capacities, and ultimately diminished the argument for a strong response to a vague, futuristic Soviet threat. ABM opponents' most potent contention was the issue of timing. They projected that Minuteman would become obsolete well before the completion of expensive and time-consuming safety measures. The time lag in production assured immediate redundancy.

The measure passed by the most miniscule of margins, 51–50, leaving supporters at a momentary loss for words. Their slim victory was a virtual defeat, as it threatened to squander public support for this huge investment of contested value. Fearing the consequence of his pyrrhic victory, Senator "Scoop" Henry Jackson, Safeguard's main political proponent, enlisted Albert—a friend and ally of Jackson's other battles against compromise with the Soviet enemy.

Somewhat stymied by the argument on Minuteman's short lifespan, Albert turned his attention to a vulnerable sidebar. During the Senate hearings, George Rathjens had questioned Albert's projection of a 95 percent kill rate for a Soviet first-strike attack against Minuteman.

Rathjens's computations indicated that 25 percent of this land-based system would survive the initial onslaught—more than enough to launch a counterstrike. He projected, moreover, that other weapon systems based on land and sea would also survive in large enough numbers. This was, however, by no means the central issue at stake, as new weapons systems promised to supersede Minuteman in advance of Safeguard's activation.

In a series of letters published in the *New York Times,* an unsuspecting Rathjens fell into a trap of Albert's making. Sidestepping Safeguard's projected redundancy, Albert entangled Rathjens and other opponents in torpid computations of Russian first-strike capacities. Deftly pulling a stream of numbers out of his hat, Albert claimed that his rivals had foisted misleading data on Soviet first-strike capacity to destroy the Minuteman missiles in their silos. Rathjens, Albert bellowed in print, had deliberately manipulated the numbers. The entire brief against Safeguard was now suspect, by implication.[5]

By hinging his defense of Safeguard on the esoteric calculation of theoretical possibilities that could not be disproved, Albert had successfully reframed the debate. The issue was now integrity and mathematical competence. To bolster his case, Albert mobilized his extensive network in the burgeoning professional field of Operations Research (OR). He successfully demanded that an ad hoc committee of the Operations Research Society of America (ORSA) be convened to adjudicate the conflict of opinions over the question of Minuteman's theoretical survivability rates. At stake, Albert urged ORSA, was the professional misconduct of his debating rivals, who had transgressed fundamental academic norms of transparency and objectivity in pursuit of ideological goals. This tribunal produced a report condemning Safeguard opponents for deliberately misrepresenting evidence and promoting a partisan position that flew in the face of available data. The main exhibit of misconduct was the acrimonious exchange between George Rathjens and Albert Wohlstetter, which had little to do with Safeguard's failings.

In one bold swoop, Albert had deflected the controversy away from the lost cause of Safeguard's limitations. He had flipped the issue into a debate on partisanship in academia, claiming that opponents had deliberately misrepresented the mathematical facts. The public spotlight was now focused on highly contested and arcane computations of critical first-strike scenarios and the sensationalistic exchange of blows between a cornered Rathjens—who admittedly had committed errors of both calculation and judgment—and a relentless Albert. Safeguard's technical shortcomings remained buried from sight.

Prodded incessantly by Albert and his supporters, the ORSA committee concluded its dubious session with a sanctimonious proposal for a code of ethics, impelled, it was piously claimed, by the egregious misconduct of some of the nation's most prestigious scientists. The fact that none of Albert's opponents were actually members of ORSA, nor did they ever claim to use methodology associated with OR, was somehow lost in the censorious pieties of the majority findings.

As for the actual standoff between Rathjens and Albert, the ORSA committee accepted without debate Albert's calculations of Soviet kill ratio. The successful decimation of Minuteman predicted by Albert would have required the real-time enemy capacity to reprogram missiles that were already in flight. By all accounts such a Soviet feat bordered on the impossible, as it would have had to be accomplished in seconds under battle conditions. The ORSA report offered no meaningful evidence to support Albert's specious arguments for these "quite likely capabilities." "There are very familiar, well-known methods of arranging it so that you can reprogram missiles to replace a very large proportion of your failures," Albert asserted for the record before moving on without ever offering anything remotely resembling supporting documentation.[6] A triumphant Scoop Jackson placed the ORSA report in the *Congressional Record,* while omitting a dissenting minority report signed by five of the original twelve participants in the ORSA investigation.

The academic community, by contrast, raised concerns of a trail by a kangaroo court. The executive director of the Conference Board of Mathematical Sciences wondered how was it possible for a judicial committee convened by ORSA to pass judgment on Albert's opponents, who were neither members of ORSA "nor professional operation analysts, nor did they claim to be." The whole affair, he complained, was an orchestrated, "gratuitous and—to my mind—disgraceful attack in public on experts in other fields" based on the most obtuse of issues: the effectiveness of weapon systems that either did not exist or had never been used. "The virtual impossibility of making precise predictions of the performance of hypothetical weapons" precluded any scientifically meaningful assessments of "the weapons systems performance."[7]

An entire edition of *Management Science,* an OR flagship, followed suit by focusing on the slanted nature of the ORSA guidelines for professional conduct that had been orchestrated by Albert's handpicked committee. The contributors to this special edition, published in 1972, pounced on the platitudes of scientific objectivity that permeated the ORSA report. Hadn't anyone read Thomas Kuhn's work on the rise and fall of scientific paradigms? the critics remonstrated.[8] Where had the notion of the practitioners of OR as disinterested scientists come from? Surely the model could not be Albert, who appeared to participants as an archetype of the researcher as passionate advocate.[9]

By most accounts, the code of ethics produced by the ORSA committee was riddled with structural flaws that belied its self-representation as the gold standard for quantitative methodology. Its authors had ignored "the biases inherent in confining analysis to those parts of a problem which can be quantified." Lacking any real data on the actual implementation of nuclear missiles in the battlefield, the Safeguard debate relied on "surrogate measures" such as "assured kill levels," which were anything but assured. Such computational substitutes took on a life of their own.[10] The OR tribunal had swallowed Albert's bait: mathematical disputations of ephemeral significance. Albert was intent on winning the debate by any means possible. He prevailed by unleashing personal invectives as well as ghostwriting a report for compliant academic proxies, most of whom were the prisoners of a Pentagon-funded golden cage.

The scorched earth of the Minuteman battle was by no means an isolated incident, nor was Albert's art of war limited to Cold War debates. Tirade and invective were Albert's weapons of choice in his final frenzies against vacillating presidents and fickle politicians. In Bosnia and the Middle East, Albert raged against those who would squander the fruits of Cold War victories and thoughtlessly enable the next generation of global predators.

Well into his eighties, "when most men shed burdens rather than acquire them," as Perle put it, Albert had lashed out at U.S. policy in Iraq and at the administration's dismal response to the Bosnian tragedy.[11] He spared neither Republicans nor Democrats, although he concentrated his wrath on the Clinton administration. His parting salvo on Iraq and Bosnia offered a glimpse of Albert at his best and his worst.

Bosnia, the Cold War All Over Again

The unfolding of the Bosnian tragedy had incensed Albert, driving him to write a flurry of angry articles published in mainstream journals. He reserved particular scorn for Bill Clinton, a man who, in his eyes, was morally incapable of rising to the occasion. Lashing out at Clinton's 1992 campaign theme—"It's the Economy, Stupid"—Albert chastised both Clinton and his Republican rivals for privileging domestic issues while ignoring the opportunity to consolidate America's new and unrivaled international status.

"Clinton's final sell-out of Bosnia" reminded Albert of George Orwell's definition of political rhetoric as "designed to make lies sound truthful and murder respectable, and to give an appearance of solidity to pure wind."[12] Beneath a patina barely concealing the corrupt concept of multinational peacekeeping in Bosnia, he wrote, lurked a willfully self-deceptive approach to global challenges. To "explain away their failure to address Serbian aggression," the Clinton administration had accepted Serbia's "sham" that its vicious campaigns were merely responses to Muslim atrocities against Serbs.[13] Genocide appeared a tolerable price for avoiding any forceful American policy in the region.

The absurdity of this position, Albert thundered, was exacerbated by "an even more basic absurd assumption: that one can stop an aggression without taking sides, and that one can stop an ongoing genocidal war and enforce a peace by sending in a force sized and equipped only to keep a peace agreed to by all sides." The United States had followed the lead of the European Community and the UN by recognizing in practice "no enemy in this war of aggression."[14]

Such positions of neutrality simply did not exist in the Wohlstetters' Hobbesian world. Enemies and rivals were discrete components in any meaningful equation in international relations. Only the conceptually blind could be lured into thinking that Russia and its Serbian proxies were not inimical to American interests. "A U.S.-led coalition like that in the Gulf War, including some NATO members and some other interested countries, would clearly identify Serbia as the source of the aggression," he added.[15] When faced with obvious enemies, such as Saddam Hussein and Slobodan Milošević, the scourge "of genocidal terror can be discouraged or dealt with only by coalitions that exclude the perpetrators of genocide and their supporters and are equipped and willing to back coalition diplomacy with precise and discriminate force."[16] Avoiding this challenge would spell disaster.

Rather than assessing the Bosnian war for what it was, Albert charged, the Clinton administration forced the conflict into grotesquely irrelevant frameworks. The Bosnian tragedy was not "a spontaneous eruption of 'ancient hatreds,'" but rather a deliberate, Russian-backed campaign to establish a greater Serbia, which, in turn, would be beholden to a resurgent greater Russia.[17] Clinton allegedly explained away his inertia by clinging to the belief that any type of unilateral action would undermine the world order. Albert responded that strife-ridden multilateral bodies, driven by the logic of corrupt compromise rather than principle, inevitably produced Clinton's effete gestures of inaction.

Clinton's most egregious sin in Bosnia was squandering the Cold War's ultimate prize: the chance to sound the death knell of Soviet power in its former sphere of influence. By capitulating to Russian demands regarding the arms embargoes on Bosnian troops, and by agreeing to the outrageous "insertion of Russian 'peacekeepers'" in Bosnia, a compliant Clinton was aiding and abetting "resurgent Great Russian imperialism."[18]

Instead of capitalizing on the vacuum created by the fall of the Soviet empire, Clinton chose to blend into venal internationally brokered arms embargoes, and counterfeit multinational peacekeeping that allowed the Russians to gain a second wind. Albert claimed that only powerful American action would stymie a resurrection of the Russian empire: "The exercise of such leadership today would strengthen those democrats in Russia who oppose the resurgence of a Russian interest in dominating tens of millions of people [and] who are against such Russian domination in the now-independent former Soviet republics."[19]

The administration's policy in Bosnia, Albert argued, was even more infuriating than its strategy in the first American-led campaign against Iraq. At least a more forceful president than Clinton had taken it upon himself to destroy Iraq's military capacity. Clinton, by contrast, was ignoring the opportunity to thwart the ambitions of another menacing rogue state.

The president had capitulated to the empty threats of a saber-rattling Russia. "Serbia's threats to respond to a Western use of force . . . are empty. They are even less convincing than Saddam Hussein's threats that Western intervention in Iraq would mean 'the mother of all battles' and lead to world war." As for desperate Russian warnings that NATO's use of force would lead to an "all-out war," these too were the dying gasps of the moribund Russian imperialism that Clinton seemed intent on resuscitating.[20]

Yet even if the threats and dangers were real, Albert expected a forceful American reaction. By virtue of its overriding power, the United States was responsible for keeping the flame of a civilized world order alight. Albert demanded proactive leadership, not reflexive compromise. The United States had a duty to override conventions in extreme cases in which basic moral imperatives were threatened and civilized norms transgressed. There was a fundamental difference, Albert's star student Paul Wolfowitz explained, between "coalitions that are united by a common purpose and collections of countries that are searching for a least common denominator and the easiest way out of a problem."[21]

Having shirked its role as leader, the United States could not expect dispensation. The American-brokered arms embargo had transformed the United States into accomplices of Serbian atrocities. These agreements, according to Albert, amounted to nothing less than "genocide by mediation."[22] Despite the many tragedies warranting American attention throughout the world, he exhorted, "we should start by ending the genocides in which we are complicitous. . . . This is genocide, not another 'lifestyle choice.' "[23]

As for those who insisted that Bosnia was a regional problem, Albert claimed otherwise. Iraq and Yugoslavia presented intimately linked, globalized challenges. "The successful coalition in the Gulf War stopped too soon and . . . left in place a Baath dictatorship nearly sure to revive its programs for getting weapons of mass terror that would menace its neighbors and some countries far beyond them. That told Slobodan Milošević, who is not a slow learner, that the West would be even less likely, four months later, to stop his own overt use of the Yugoslav Federal Army to create a Greater Serbia purged of non-Serbs."[24]

Makeover in Iraq

Unlike Bosnia, Iraq offered opportunities for executing the Wohlstetter Doctrine. Desert Storm, the first U.S. campaign against Iraq, appeared to vindicate Albert's theory of "discriminate deterrence." "The revolution in technology" he advocated, in numerous publications, had "made it feasible in Desert Storm to be discriminate." The "imperfect but widespread success" of "highly accurate, discriminating weapons against military targets," as well as the exploitation of "a cumulative revolution in information technology," had won the battle—although, according to Albert's own assessment, not the war.[25] Combat operations in Iraq represented "the first war that's been fought in a way that would recognize Albert's vision for future wars," Richard Perle remarked. "That it was won so quickly and decisively, with so few casualties and so little damage, was in fact an implementation of his strategy and his vision."[26] "It was a considerable matter of personal satisfaction to watch those missiles turn right-angle corners in the Gulf War in '91, doing what Albert envisioned fifteen years before," Paul Wolfowitz observed.[27] "The myth that we must destroy a country in order to save it," as in Vietnam, received a deathblow in the Persian Gulf, Albert announced.[28]

Yet despite such triumphs, Desert Storm was also a bitter disappointment to the Wohlstetter camp. The effect of a brilliant military operation dissolved into a muddled version of realpolitik that brought the campaign for regime change in Iraq to a screeching halt. All the more reason to "rage against the dying of the light." Following the anticlimactic conclusion of Desert Storm, Albert lashed out at what he considered to be a specious and misguided policy underlying George Bush Sr.'s strategy. Albert criticized, in particular, the conventional wisdom that "an Iraqi dictatorship would be a lesser evil and the only real alternative to fundamentalist fanatics or the 'Lebanonization' of Iraq."[29] Misguided administration officials—including two consecutive presidents representing opposing political parties—clung to what Albert considered to be a misinformed understanding of the Persian Gulf, in general, and of the Iraqi predicament, in particular. To maintain stability in this particularly sensitive region, administration officials had insisted that only "the brutal Baath dictatorship . . . or its murderous Republican guards, can keep Iraq together as a peaceful 'balance' to the power of fundamentalist Iran or Syria."[30] Such predictions, Albert complained, were basically the misleading babblings of the fainthearted. These unimaginative souls were incapable of executing the United States' most crucial mission: the spread of democracy, by which Albert meant the imposition of pale reflections of the American body politic throughout the Middle East.

As for the idea of a "palace coup"—the replacement of Saddam by some other faction within the Baath regime—this idea stuck Albert as the worst possible option. An internal Baathist reshuffling would burden the United States with the responsibility of managing the unpredictable and usually brutal behavior of yet another Middle Eastern dictator. "We've been down that road before—with General Za'im in Syria, Colonel Nasser in Egypt, and General Big Minh in South Vietnam."[31] In fact, Saddam—or for that matter, any other variant of the Baath regime—would continually challenge stability and Western interests in the region.

Albert recognized that Iraq, as a sovereign state, was an artificial creation of colonial powers, bringing together a mixture of people and cultures who had little in common besides mutual enmities. He argued, however, that any splintering of Iraq into separate national or cultural entities—Shiite, Sunni, and Kurdish ministates—would have a decidedly destabilizing effect on the region. Ultimately, Albert belittled the religious and sectarian rifts within this poorly stitched national entity. The very idea that only an ironfisted dictatorship could control the weltering factional violence of the region struck him as both racist and ahistorical. "Turkey shows that, contrary to the received wisdom of many Western Arabists, Islam is not incompatible with democratic rule."[32] Why in the world, mused Albert, would the United States demand free elections in Cuba but ignore their importance in Iraq? "It would be utopian for the U.S. to demand democracy everywhere," he conceded. The call for free elections in Castro's Cuba, however, suggested "it is also utopian to support existing dictatorships everywhere."[33]

In the testy tone of a teacher confronted with a dim-witted child, Albert spelled out the fundamental difference between the Lebanese analogy and Iraq. Factional violence and terror had wreaked havoc on Lebanon, he explained, because colonial powers had imposed a government led by a Maronite minority on a Shiite majority. "What serious parallel is there in Lebanon to Iraq, where a few members of the Sunni Arab minority, making up perhaps one-fifth of the population, preside over a Shiite majority?" As for the fear that a Shiite government in Iraq would join hands with Iran in establishing a Shiite empire stretching from Teheran to Beirut, Albert reminded his readers that this very same Shiite population had resisted Iranian appeals during the Iran-Iraq

War.[34] Iraq's Shiites, moreover, would enjoy majority rule, and would therefore have no logical reason to employ violence.

Albert advocated a "loose" type of confederacy that would give the other communities in Iraq, in particular the Kurds, a certain level of autonomy. "If we are clear enough about our purposes," Albert declared, "we can use military force discriminately in ways that will avoid both chaos and the restoration of Baath totalitarian control." He did not expect full-blown Jeffersonian democracy to emerge from the present chaos. "But even a government selected by a random process" would offer greater stability and justice for all.[35] In fact, he stated as early as 1993, Iraqi dissidents had already "achieved an impressive consensus for a democratic structure representing all segments of the disparate population." The political constellation was such that he neither envisioned the need for an occupation of Iraq, nor for any substantial deployment of Coalition ground forces for keeping the peace in a post-Saddam Iraq.[36] A skillful, American-assisted construction of a democratic Iraq would, he contended, diminish the possibility of a repeat performance of Lebanon.

In making his case for Iraqi liberation, Albert challenged an incapacitating historical analogy. Iraq, he argued, did not resemble Vietnam in any meaningful sense. "The key problem in the seemingly interminable war in Vietnam was a lack of clarity in our objectives." This crucial caveat had "ensured the war would drag on, and also made it impossible to tell, for all the 'body counts' and other statistics, whether we were making any genuine progress toward achieving these objectives," whatever they may have been.[37] Somehow, during the course of that protracted war, the United States' foreign policy establishment had never recognized the obvious purpose of the war: challenging "the rule of the totalitarian government in North Vietnam."[38]

As opposed to the inchoate objectives in Vietnam, American objectives in the Iraqi standoff were "crystal clear."[39] The United States and its coalition were there to execute American-dictated UN resolutions. As time progressed, regime change was added to the list of clear objectives. In the final analysis, Albert reasoned, the most "durable problem" was the presence of a renegade "dictatorship sitting on the world's second largest pool of low-cost oil and ambitious to dominate the Gulf and the Mediterranean."[40]

As far as historical analogies were concerned, the prelude to World War II struck Albert as somewhat more appropriate than Vietnam. The

American government was engaged in classic appeasement. But, as history had proven, nothing would appease Saddam, "any more than Sudeten Czechoslovakia sated Hitler's appetites. Saddam could back his next try with much more convincing threats."[41] Given the special status of the United States in the post–Cold War period, "we can't avoid intervening." Having already intervened massively in Iraq's internal affairs— by destroying the army that served as the backbone of the regime, and targeting a "large . . . proportion of our air sorties against Iraqi industry" and civilian infrastructure—the United States had crossed the point of no return.[42]

Despite a series of allegedly doubting statements by administration and UN officials, Albert contended that Saddam's Iraq possessed the infrastructure and intent for producing WMD. Contrary to CIA assurances, Albert blustered, Iraq had a functioning program for electromagnetic isotope separation, and other telltale signs of both chemical and nuclear programs could be discerned.

Albert believed that a campaign against Saddam would garner internal support within Iraq because the Iraqi regime had inadvertently sown the seeds of its own destruction. During its halcyon years, the Baath regime had launched an aggressive and highly successful campaign to eradicate illiteracy with the ultimate aim of producing consumers for mindless Baath propaganda. The revolution in communication technology—which began with the fax and then morphed into unmediated access to Internet content—had turned the weapon of literacy against its totalitarian promoters. The end of totalitarian governments' monopoly on the flow of information then opened opportunities for the promotion of democracy by direct contact with its potential constituents.

All the ingredients necessary for Iraqi regime change were in place, Albert believed, except for support from a vacillating American president. The president still clung to the morally corrupt idea that only a dictator could keep Iraq from splintering into ethnic fiefdoms, thereby leaving Iran as the dominant regional power. The Clinton administration offered the infuriating position that it was "a mistake to 'personalize' the Coalition's conflict with Iraq."[43] Clinton was unable to grasp that predatory dictators—whether in Serbia or Iraq—would never provide the type of regional power balancing promoted by misguided administration officials and their academic sycophants.

A Waltz with Kenneth

Behind Albert's diatribes on Iraq and Bosnia lay a coherent theory of international relations that would provide a guiding light for his supporters. Like many scholars and policy makers in his time, Albert believed that the interaction between nations was driven by the nature of rulers and their domestic policies. In democracies, domestic affairs were rule driven, transparent, and privileged comprise over conflict between competing interests. One assumed that new democracies would perform in a similar peaceful manner even when their democratic frameworks had been imposed from above. By the same token, a regime that practiced internal coercion would most likely behave recklessly in the international arena, as well. Albert firmly believed that some—although not all—rampant dictatorships of the post–Cold War would inevitably destabilize international relations through their penchant for recklessness. Domestic regimes and the nature of their leaders were, according to the Wohlstetters, robust predictors of behavior in the international arena. When left unchecked, those who reigned by terror at home would use similar measures abroad. As Robert Jervis has noted, "The argument is that, as in Iraq, regime change is necessary because tyrannical governments will always be prone to disregard agreements and coerce their neighbors just as they mistreat their own citizens."[44]

This paradigm—by no means an exclusive property of the Wohlstetter clan—was first challenged in 1959 by Kenneth Waltz, in his seminal book *Man, the State, and War.* Contrary to orthodox scholarship, Waltz veered sharply away from the personalization of conflict.[45] Developing the argument further in his 1979 *Theory of International Politics,* Waltz asserted that the primary cause of war was the "anarchic" state of international relations. He defined *anarchy* in international relations as a decentralized international order, bereft of a formal strong governing authority to adjudicate between competing interests and aspirations. Anarchy, he explained, fostered a protocol of self-help in which each entity was compelled to protect its own interests, thorough fluid, Byzantine alliances that morphed in accordance with changing circumstances. The pressures of anarchy—the unrelenting promotion of self-interest by each individual actor in the global arena—rather than the nature of rulers or domestic regimes, constituted the dominant force in international relations.[46]

It is within this context that Waltz caustically dismissed, in a 1981 article, Albert's career-long caricature of the Soviet regime. "Albert Wohlstetter imagines a situation in which the Soviet Union might strike first. Her leaders might decide to do so in a desperate effort to save a sinking regime. The desperation could be produced, Wohlstetter thinks, by 'disastrous defeat in peripheral war,' by 'loss of key satellites,' by the 'danger of revolt spreading—possibly to Russia itself,' or by 'fear of an attack by ourselves.' Under such circumstances, the risk of *not* striking might appear very great to the Soviets."[47]

Albert's fevered imagination, in Waltz's view, had invented implausible scenarios for the Soviets, where, in recuperating losses from a conventional war, they would assume that the option of "striking first is bad, but presumably not striking first is even worse." Such logic struck Waltz as sophomoric. "How can the Soviet Union suffer disastrous defeat in a peripheral war?" he wondered. Peripheral defeat was just that— peripheral, as Vietnam had amply demonstrated. Waltz also found it difficult to comprehend how Albert's "imagined act" of a Soviet nuclear attack could accomplish any meaningful goal. "Some rulers will do anything to save themselves and their regimes. . . . But how a regime can hope to save itself by making a nuclear strike at a superior adversary, or at any adversary having a second-strike force, is not explained." It was "silly," he thought, "to think that the Soviet Union would strike the United States because of incipient revolt within her borders."[48]

Waltz was equally dismissive of Albert's alarmist predictions of nuclear proliferation. While Albert feared that the acquisition of nuclear weapons by upstart ruthless dictators would lead to unmitigated international chaos, Waltz argued the opposite: the more the merrier. To begin with, Waltz explained, there was nothing delicate in the nuclear balance between the superpowers, and proliferation would do little to upset the inherent stability of nuclear standoffs. Proliferation actually provided a stabilizing and retardant force because the threat of nuclear disaster mitigated the impulse to initiate war.

Using the Wohlstetter gold standard of Pearl Harbor as an example, Waltz maintained that the primary cause of war was miscalculation. "One side expects victory at an affordable price" or at least is willing to risk war if defeat "is expected to bring only limited damage." The advent of nuclear weapons, however, had changed the matrix. "In a conventional world, one is uncertain about winning or losing. In a nuclear world, one is uncertain about surviving or being annihilated." If anything, Waltz concluded, "nuclear weapons do change the relations of nations. Adversary states that acquire them are thereby made more cautious in their dealings with each other."[49]

Waltz lavished praise on Albert's nemesis, Bernard Brodie, who had "tirelessly and wisely" explained that "Clausewitz's central tenet," that war continues politics, "remains valid in the nuclear age." The presence of thermonuclear weaponry did not alter the fact that the waging of war—even among the most predatory of nations—hinged upon finding a "political objective that is commensurate with its cost. . . . Ultimately, the inhibitions lie in the impossibility of knowing for sure that a disarming strike will totally destroy an opposing force and in the immense destruction even a few warheads can wreak."[50]

Waltz was skeptical of Albert's fear of nuclear armed tyrants in the Middle East, as well. If the actual use of nuclear weapons—by tyrants or democracies, in error or deliberate—could never be dismissed, Albert's doomsday scenario of nuclear-wielding Middle Eastern potentates was baseless, nonetheless. Albert held that nuclear weapons in the hands of a rogue state would lead to rampages of blackmail, intimidation, and sheer recklessness. A "risk-acceptant and accident prone" Iraq would destabilize the international order once it acquired nuclear weaponry.[51] Waltz countered that there was little fear that a Middle Eastern tyrant armed with nuclear weapons would be more dangerous than a conventionally armed one. If anything, one could expect greater caution from the likes of a nuclear-armed Saddam Hussein. Muammar Qaddafi, another quintessential Middle Eastern tyrant, proved the point. "Would Libya try to destroy Israel's nuclear weapons at the risk of two bombs surviving to fall on Tripoli and Bengazi? And what would be left of Israel if Tel Aviv and Haifa were destroyed?"[52] Rather than focusing on Albert's "slippery notion of rationality," Waltz preferred Bernard Brodie's avoidance of theoretical measurements of sanity in poorly defined nuclear standoffs. "How do governments behave in the presence of awesome dangers?" Brodie had once asked, answering, "Very carefully."[53]

"Leviathan to the Rescue"

It is tempting to dismiss Wohlstetter's position on Bosnia and Iraq as nothing more than Machiavellian politics, bereft of the noble cause offered by its spokespersons. In Bosnia, the disbelievers observe, the pro-Israeli Wohlstetter and his cohorts had seized the moment to prove to the world in general, and the Muslim world in particular, that they were not driven by an underlying antipathy to Islam. Skeptical observers offered other ulterior motives for Albert's Bosnian tirades. Unable to shake off the fear that the Soviet threat might rise again, Albert and his followers automatically posited themselves against the Serbs, whom they viewed as Soviet pawns facilitating the revival of an evil empire. As for Iraq, commentators and critics offered a litany of ulterior motives for American intervention, Wohlstetter-style: oil interests, cronyism, and even a devious Zionist cabal of American power wielders who secretly harbored dual loyalties.

While some of these explanations have some bearing on the American entanglement in Iraq, they were contributing factors only. Albert and his followers were driven by visions more powerful than oil reserves, cronyism, or sympathy to the Zionist cause. The Wohlstetter school of strategic studies endorsed historic destiny and preached a unique role for the United States in the existential struggles of an unstable world. The United States was, to use a quite frequent metaphor, the epitome of a Leviathan unbound.

"Imagine a world in which the United States was stricken by a successful series of nuclear, biological, and chemical attacks," historian Paul Johnson—a Wohlstetter favorite—speculated in 2002. Aside from the obvious internal damage, he argues, "the global consequences would be horrifying." Lacking a superpower to uphold international law and order, the world would descend into mayhem. "Wolf and jackal states would quickly emerge to prey on their neighbors. It would be a world as described by Thomas Hobbes in his *Leviathan* . . . deprived of a giant authority figure 'to keep them all in awe,' civilization would break down, and life, for most of mankind, would be 'nasty, brutish and short.' "[54]

Some version of the Leviathan argument was the driving force behind all the Wohlstetter partisans' angry crusades. The United States, they tirelessly insisted, could ill afford to assess the impact of human rights violations, ethnic cleansing, and regional despotism in narrow domestic terms. Historical destiny had thrust the nation into a role that it could not shrug off. Efforts to explain away the nation's dereliction of duty in Iraq or Kosovo therefore struck the Wohlstetter school as trivial blather, a denial of destiny.

Iraq was a defining moment, the first step in a significant campaign to introduce structural change in the world order. It was, Lee Harris observes, a crucial event, or in "the language of Hegel, an event that is *world-historical* in its significance and scope. And it will be world-historical, *no matter what the outcome may be.*"[55] The only solution to the state of international anarchy revealed by Kenneth Waltz was the abolition of the anarchy of self-help through the creation of a supreme, global Leviathan.

The Wohlstetter school departed from this Hegelian vision in one fundamental way. The world-historical event, Harris explains, is sui generis, fraught with uncertainty, and unpredictable, "because the proper concepts for even describing the new situation have yet to be constructed."[56] For the Wohlstetters and their students, Iraq posed no such conceptual dilemma. Their constant recourse to historical comparisons suggested they felt little uncertainty in defining the parameters of the event, its optimal execution, or the outcome of the well-fought battle. Iraq was a war that had been fought before.

Armed with an arsenal of historical analogies—mostly from World War II and the Cold War—Albert and his protégés shaped the past in order to map out the future. In their eyes, the world-historical campaign in Iraq was not a reckless gamble but rather a latter-day instance of Manifest Destiny. The United States could not have allowed "a hostile power to dominate Europe or Asia" during the Cold War, Paul Wolfowitz argued, and the only way to avoid replaying that standoff—or a world war, or any other existential threat—was by "making it clear" in words and deeds that the United States would oppose any hostile action, whether in the Persian Gulf, in the Balkans, or anywhere else.[57] Concepts of compromise, stability, and containment were the flawed goods of petty politicians unable to comprehend the historical moment. The partisans of Leviathan faced down such small-minded obstructionists, much as they had throughout the Cold War.

There is no doubt that the Wohlstetters' acolytes took Albert's advice to heart. Following the Soviet implosion for which they claimed ownership, they set out to achieve a unipolar world by encouraging

American activism in the most sensitive international trouble spots. Thwarted in the former Yugoslavian Republic by a recalcitrant Bill Clinton, a more compliant and impressionable president would later give them their chance to demonstrate their new global strategy.

Events in Iraq did not follow the trajectory the Wohlstetter camp had laid out: swift victory followed by regime change, and the spread of democracy throughout the Middle East. Their utopian vision was ahistorical, landlocked in a contrived version of the past that had never transpired. Their faith-based understanding of history—an elaborate theory driven by facile simulation rather than the compilation of empirical evidence—fed a campaign fraught with unforeseen dangers that were no less precarious than the policies that they chose to dismiss.

Roberta Dissents?

A single article by Roberta suggests that she may not have been as convinced as Albert about the benefits of regime change, invasion, and the remaking of the Middle East. As she had in the past, Roberta returned to Pearl Harbor to explain her views on current crises affecting the nation. In December 1991, on the occasion of the fiftieth anniversary of the surprise attack, she published an article comparing the crisis in the Gulf with Pearl Harbor. "If our purpose in recalling Pearl Harbor is to draw 'lessons,' the main point is that we can work out useful ways of responding to signs of greater danger that may (or may not) turn out to be false alarms. And we can do it at reasonable and economic cost." Roberta went on to offer a version of counterfactual Pearl Harbor history, in which "a higher alert at Pearl Harbor in December 1941—for which the Japanese were listening—would have led them to call off the attack." Bearing this counterfactual example in mind, she then argued that similar "low-cost repeatable responses to ambiguous signals" could have averted the "Iraqi invasion and devastation of Kuwait."[58]

Instead of joining the chorus for radical regime change and ambitious makeovers of totalitarian entities, Roberta concluded this article—her very last publication—with a plea to react prudently and, by implication, avoid being sucked into military adventures. This one data point, a single article published in the *Wall Street Journal,* suggests the possibility of dissent and perhaps divergence between Albert, who appeared quite enthusiastic about the radical plans of the acolytes, and Roberta, who may have been satisfied with abeyance rather than a presumptuous remaking of the world. Was Roberta's final observation merely a distracting sliver of white noise, or was it a meaningful signal of revisionist thought? Roberta receded gently into silence, and this question remains unanswered. We are left adrift in the type of unmapped informational waters she had navigated throughout her career.

PART TWO

THE WOHLSTETTER LEGACY IN THE POST–COLD WAR ERA

9

Paul Wolfowitz

Fin de Siècle All Over Again

In 1991 the students and admirers of Roberta and Albert Wohlstetter honored their mentors with a Festschrift. Participants—Wohlstetter partisans in government, think tanks, and universities—contributed articles to an expansive anthology on strategic analysis. In addition to their learned papers, contributors reminisced about how the Wohlstetters had imparted knowledge and insight beyond the limited precincts of strategic analysis.

Participants recalled, in particular, the Wohlstetters' exquisite culinary excursions around the world. Under their mentors' tutelage, the Wohlstetters' intellectual godchildren had learned to appreciate an international cuisine transcending the bland offerings of the American breadbasket. The Festschrift contained vivid recollections of succulent food and wine—polar bear steak on a Norwegian fjord, grilled lüfer on the Bosporus, the full body of a 1924 Château Ausone under the Parisian sky, and other delectables.[1] Enthusiasm for the Wohlstetters' culinary cosmopolitanism contrasted with bemused reactions to the couple's efforts to expand their disciples' intellectual horizons. Participants poked mild fun at these didactic excursions: a guided tour of the Chartres Cathedral, a learned excursion through the streets of Prague, and other highbrow adventures. The Festschrift suggests a cosmopolitanism of the palate, and a certain lack of interest in human experiences beyond the confines of the Wohlstetters' gourmet ghetto.

Such signs of indifference to culture beyond corporeal delights not-withstanding, Wohlstetter apostles have bristled at the label of cultural know-nothings. Richard Perle's semiautobiographical fictional thriller *Hard Line* offers a self-portrait of the strategic analyst as a polyglot Har-vard professor and music aficionado who is as at home in Paris as he is in DC. Yet in the final analysis, the main character in the book—Perle's alter ego—expresses his worldliness in the kitchen, where he whips up a series of French-flavored epicurean delights.[2]

The specter of anti-intellectualism did not sit well, either, with Paul Wolfowitz—perhaps the Wohlstetters' most prominent disciple. The son of a world-renowned statistician, Wolfowitz presented himself as no less of a Renaissance man than his mentors. When the *New York Times* asked him to describe his hobbies, Wolfowitz listed "foreign lan-guages" and playing the "classical piano." He took pride in his cameo appearance in Saul Bellow's *Ravelstein,* where a thinly disguised Wolfo-witz character pays homage to a barely fictional representation of his Cornell mentor, the cultural conservative Allan Bloom.[3]

In real life, Wolfowitz had a transient brush with academia, the de-tails of which are occasionally embellished. Wolfowitz's page on the website of the American Enterprise Institute—where, as this book goes to press in 2016, he is a visiting scholar—adds rhetorical flourish to his academic career. The website ordains him "Professor, Department of Po-litical Science, Yale University, 1970–73."[4] In fact, Wolfowitz had the title of instructor at Yale from 1970 to 1972. Upon receiving his PhD from the University of Chicago in 1972, he was promoted to assistant professor. He took leave in 1973 and officially resigned in 1974.

This brief encounter notwithstanding, the trappings of academia were not foreign to Wolfowitz. Born in 1943 in Brooklyn, Wolfowitz spent the bulk of his youth in Ithaca, New York, where his father, Jacob, was a professor of statistics at Cornell University. During his under-graduate years at Cornell, he resided at the prestigious Telluride House, where a cohort of Cornell's most promising students from multiple disciplines lived and breathed a rarified intellectual atmosphere under the guidance of faculty residents. The distinguished residents included Allen Bloom, Wolfowitz's mentor during his undergraduate years. Laura, Paul Wolfowitz's sister, is listed on the Telluride website as the first female admitted to the institution.[5] His former spouse, Clare Selgin Wolfowitz, is a Telluride alumna, as well. (The couple separated in the late 1990s.) Upon graduating from Cornell, Wolfowitz entered the PhD program in political science at the University of Chicago, where he wrote a dissertation under the tutelage of Albert Wohlstetter.

Wolfowitz had other encounters with academia after his time at Yale. He held a one-year visiting professorship at the National Defense University in 1993 before serving as dean of the Paul H. Nitze School of Advanced International Studies at Johns Hopkins University from 1994 to 2001. Despite these distinguished benchmarks, Wolfowitz did not acquire—perhaps never aspired to—the gold standard of peer-reviewed scholarly articles, nor did he ever hold a tenure-track academic position. Even within academia, his signature projects were in the realm of politics rather than scholarship. His years as dean at Johns Hopkins were dedicated to fund-raising and the fostering of social networks that would serve him well in his political career.

Wolfowitz's political star began to rise during his graduate school years. In 1969, he interned at the Committee to Maintain a Prudent Defense Policy, in Washington, DC. The committee was a lobbying group and research center created by Dean Acheson and Paul Nitze to fight congressional opposition to the development of the Safeguard antiballistic missile system. The thrill of the Cold War political arena, as well as Wolfowitz's skepticism on arms control, hastened his departure from the groves of academe. One can only guess that his father's abrupt resignation from Cornell—a reaction to his disillusionment with the rising tide of student radicalism on elite campuses—may have influenced his decision, as well.[6]

From 1973 through 1977, Wolfowitz was employed by the U.S. Arms Control and Disarmament Agency. The agency's director was Fred Iklé, a Wohlstetter confidante who was deeply suspicious of arms control or freeze agreements with the Soviet Union. During these years, Wolfowitz was an active participant in Albert Wohlstetter's "New Alternatives Workshop," a policy group advocating the development of precision-guided weaponry for small-scale wars.[7] From there, a series of appointments in the Department of Defense and Department of State culminated in his appointment as U.S. ambassador to heavily Muslim Indonesia, a move that raised eyebrows given Wolfowitz's Jewish background. Clare Wolfowitz's expertise as an anthropologist and linguist specializing in Indonesian culture facilitated this unusual career move.[8]

History and the Future

For the purposes of this chapter, we will gloss over the rest of Wolfowitz's career, until his appointment as deputy secretary of defense
during the George W. Bush administration. That is when Wolfowitz
began offering the public statements on policy and strategy that are pertinent to this study.

In his early public proclamations as deputy secretary of defense, Wolfowitz intimated that a combination of rigorous academic insight and
political training had endowed him with a unique attribute: he could
bode the future. The speech he delivered to the West Point graduating
class of 2001 on the eve of 9/11 represents a notable case in point.
Standing before the army's future leaders, Wolfowitz alerted his audience to an ominous future. They would soon be put to a trial by fire, he
predicted, not unlike Americans of previous generations.

"A century ago, on a peaceful day in 1903, with great foresight, Secretary of War Elihu Root told Douglas MacArthur's graduating class:
'Before you leave the Army . . . you will be engaged in another war. It
is bound to come, and will come.'" Relating this tale before the West
Point cadets, Wolfowitz mentioned no particular threat; his prediction
was mostly an exercise in historical reasoning. History was bound to repeat itself, he informed his audience. "One day you, too, will be tested
in combat. And if you fail that test, the nation will fail, too."[9]

History looms large in Paul Wolfowitz's worldview. In 1997, he published a revealing treatise on the cyclical patterns of history and the dangers inherent in ignoring events past. Entitled "Fin de Siècle All Over
Again," it pointed out a series of structural similarities between events
on the eve of the twentieth century and those on the cusp of the new
millennium. A Pollyannaish political optimism at the turn of the century,
he found, bore striking resemblance to the nation's current false sense
of security.[10]

An "End-of-Century optimism" had sown the seeds of the tragedies
of the twentieth century, the bloodiest in human memory. Much like
the eve of the new millennium, the dawn of the twentieth century had
been "a period of exceptionally rapid economic growth" in the United
States and throughout the industrialized world. Scientific breakthroughs—an exciting "information revolution" in particular—had contributed to the fin-de-siècle euphoria. Prospects of an everlasting peace

among nations had enhanced the sense of optimism. "There had been no wars between the major powers for nearly thirty years," Wolfowitz reminded his audience. "And it had been nearly a century—marked by the end of the Napoleonic Wars—since the world had experienced war on a global or continental scale."[11]

Through a sweeping exercise in counterfactual history, Wolfowitz identified an untidy coalition of scientists, seers, and historians who were mesmerized by the false dawn of the fin de siècle. The political and cultural establishment at that time had studiously ignored the rise of two new and aggressive regional powers: Japan and, especially, Germany—"a dominant force in Europe" that "had not even existed before the end of the nineteenth century."[12] Had the Western powers reacted forcefully to these two new upstarts' aggressive early gambits, Wolfowitz claimed, the world would have been spared the horrors of two major bloodbaths.

As an example of the era's complacency, Wolfowitz offered Norman Angell's 1910 best seller *The Great Illusion*, a study predicting the end of wars between nations. Angell argued that the development of defensive technologies and military tactics had transformed the very idea of decisive victories on the battlefield into an obsolete concept. War in the modern age was, in fact, an act of national suicide, for economic as well as military reasons. The globalization of financial markets was such that a hypothetical German attack on England would wreak havoc on Germany's economy. One could therefore expect, Angell predicted, that the entire German financial and industrial community would force the hand of a putative German aggressor-government "to put an end to a situation ruinous to German trade."[13] For these vague and wishful predictions, an incredulous Wolfowitz observed, "Angell received the Nobel Prize for Peace in 1933, well after the Great War and in the year the Nazis came to power."[14]

Wolfowitz listed the ominous similarities between this early twentieth century and his own times. Much like turn-of-the-century glibness, the new millennium elicited ill-informed optimism. Its false prophets—the soul mates of the hapless Norman Angell—were Francis Fukuyama, who had trademarked "The End of History," and John Mueller, who had casually enunciated a "retreat from doomsday."[15] Like slavery and dueling before, Mueller had predicted, war was on the verge of becoming obsolete. As for Fukuyama, Wolfowitz accused him of a myopic failure to envision any lurking enemy. Following the fall of the Soviet Union, the endemic danger of a clash between competing ideological systems was, by Fukuyama's Eurocentric standards, an issue of the past. Whether Fukuyama's declaration of the victory of political and economic liberalism or Mueller's definition of war as a hopelessly blunt and economically regressive tool for conflict resolution were illusions was a matter of contention. The important issue, for Wolfowitz, was the alarming complacency of these opinion leaders and their defiant unwillingness to seek insight from history.

Leaping from the annals of the past into the contemporary world, Wolfowitz identified China as the major challenge of the new millennium, a potential reincarnation of turn-of-the-century Germany or Japan. An upstart China, he argued, was powered by a burning sense of resentment—with a "much deeper foundation than Germany's" grievance at mistreatment by the great powers. The dangers of simmering grievances were compounded by China's transition from "two decades of extremely skillful management . . . to a new leadership of uncertain quality. It was just such a transition from the statesmanship of Bismarck to the incompetence of his successors that is considered to be a principal factor leading to the tragedy of the First World War," Wolfowitz observed.[16]

Those who could not remember the unfolding of the twentieth century's tragic events, Wolfowitz cautioned, were condemned to repeat the faults of previous generations. The nation's remarkably short historical attention span "leaves us unprepared to deal even with those future events that are already casting long shadows."[17] Taiwan was China's Sudetenland, or possibly the stage for a repeat performance of Munich. It would be "a strategic as well as a moral mistake for the United States to let China have its way with Taiwan." Contrary to the cavalier musings of modern-day Chamberlains, "we will not have peace in the Taiwan Strait if this promising democracy is made to disappear."[18]

The notion of technology and rapid economic development as a double-edged sword was another strand in Wolfowitz's historical thinking. In his "fin de siècle" musings, technological and economic advances did not necessarily serve the purpose of global stability. When placed in the hands of expansionist nondemocratic regimes, technology fed insatiable appetites. Economic expansion and technological breakthroughs at the end of the nineteenth century had led to disaster rather than peace because of "the failure to deal with the emergence of . . . new powers" espousing expansionist causes.[19]

In anticipation of criticism that he was cherry-picking historical events, Wolfowitz argued that he was conducting a disciplined and critical historical exercise. He was, in fact, quite wary of the sometimes impulsive, often opportunistic way that the so-called lessons of history were mustered. "History does not tell us what to do, but it does offer us some options to ponder." The lessons of Munich, for example, were "seared into the consciousness of the Western democracies and their leaders," but with quite confusing and counterproductive results. On the one hand, Munich had reinforced the resolve of the historically conscious President Truman "to resist communist aggression in . . . 'faraway' places." By contrast, an unthinking recourse to "Munich" had led Britain and France to overreact to the perceived threat of Nasserism during the Suez Canal crisis. A false analogy to Munich led to "even worse consequences" when "Presidents Kennedy and Johnson decided that Vietnam was a similar case of aggression that had to be opposed."[20] Seeking meaningful insight from history was a serious matter best left to experts—such as himself—rather than to bungling dilettantes, opportunistic politicians, and sundry Panglossians who either mangled or ignored its lessons.

The Great Books

When properly analyzed, Wolfowitz explained, certain contemporary events did, indeed, resemble events past—except that the lessons of history could not be derived from facile recourse to the recent past. Recognizing the past's significance for the present demanded a complex and exhaustive understanding of human nature and historical events, the key to which lay in the quintessential texts—the Great Books—and their critical elucidation.

In a 2003 commencement speech delivered at the Naval War College in Newport, Rhode Island, Wolfowitz praised the school's seemingly outlandish insistence on a curriculum "that is traditional in substance, with a focus on the Great Books and history." A liberal arts education, with particular focus on the historians of classical times, was far from outmoded, he argued. Quite the contrary; their analytical acumen and deep understanding of human nature produced a "capacity for independent, critical thought and reflection and the ability to question assumptions." By dispelling "clichés about war," classical texts paradoxically offered an "advantage over your adversaries in an age of great uncertainty and rapid change."[21]

A close reading of classical history, he explained, provided an understanding of the surprises and possibilities of warfare more imaginative "than any scenario writer in the Pentagon." Contrary to the pedantic punditry of modern-day historians, the Greek and Roman historians imparted "a healthy skepticism about pat answers or easy solutions." It was only through exposure to the chroniclers of antiquity's great wars that students would become "wary about received wisdom" and cognizant of the "tremendous variety" of human experience in times of stress.[22] In another commencement speech—this time at West Point— Wolfowitz explained that to realize the hope for "world peace and prosperity" demanded a close reading of classical history, and a discriminating use of "the benefit of hindsight to replace a poverty of expectations with an anticipation of the unfamiliar and the unlikely."[23]

Future mutations in global affairs hinged on understanding the complex interaction of human nature and the affairs of state through the lens of disciplined historical analysis. History, he explained, "doesn't provide us with simple lessons or rules to tell us how to act in particular situations; it can, however, alert us to some to some of the alternatives we should consider."[24]

Charles Fairbanks Jr., Wolfowitz's close friend and fellow Wohlstetter student, recalled Wolfowitz's quest to glean insight from the historians of antiquity. Fairbanks remembers a long drive between Chicago and New York. Wolfowitz "had just been reading Livy's history of Rome. He was obviously somehow in love with political greatness, I think in the same way as the young Lincoln was. He talked for hours at a time about the ancient Romans, about what kind of men they were and what they achieved."[25]

As far as ancient history was concerned, Wolfowitz appeared to be professing that Rome's rise to greatness was not the result of some majestic imperial impulse but, rather, a matter of self-preservation. According to Livy, the great historian Edward Gibbon reminds us, "The Romans conquered the world in their own defence."[26] Livy—Wolfowitz's classical historian of choice—offered an understanding of leadership, as well. "Never mind," Livy wrote, "if they call your caution timidity, your wisdom sloth, your generalship weakness; it is better that a wise enemy should fear you than that foolish friends should praise." As it had been during the Punic Wars, so it was in modern times. Only a strong executive, unconstrained by convention—legal or political—could eviscerate the evil of predatory figures, be they Hannibal, Hitler, or Saddam Hussein.[27]

History Redux

A study of ancient Rome, Wolfowitz was convinced, demonstrated another timeless truth: that the vacuum created by the departure of one tyrant would soon be filled by another. He therefore saw no reason to recalibrate his thinking when latter-day versions of the Punic Wars were unfolding before his eyes. Contrary to the assertions of former intellectual comrades-in-arms—such as Francis Fukuyama—the historically minded Wolfowitz denied that the implosion of the Soviet Union represented history's final act. Instead of celebrating the finality of events past, Wolfowitz discovered timeless repetition of conflict issuing from the same fount of social and political discord.

According to Wolfowitz, the past offered meaningful lessons for contemporary policy makers because nothing in human experience is either unique or novel. A cyclical interpretation of history made methodological sense because human nature—its darker side in particular—remained a constant, unchanging, and dominating factor over the centuries. Despite the impact of science and technology on the machinations of human societies, Wolfowitz argued, politics and the interactions between nations were governed by the same basic passions and insecurities that had driven human affairs over the centuries.

In a speech in Poland commemorating the sixtieth anniversary of the Warsaw Uprising, Wolfowitz elaborated on his cyclical theory of the human factor by drawing historical parallels between the scourge of Nazism and contemporary challenges facing the West. "Zarqawi and Bin Laden and others like them may claim the mantle of religion," he observed before his Polish audience, "but their rhetoric is more reminiscent of the death's head of Hitler's SS." Equating Saddam Hussein's "terrorist brand of totalitarianism" with "Nazism and Communism," Wolfowitz warned that, much like the challenges of the 1940s, such depravity would "not collapse simply of its own weight. We must remain on offense." Saddam Hussein was, he assured his audience, a Hitler redux, capable of the worst acts of "genocidal repression." Like Hitler, Hussein had employed "genocidal murders" to systematical destroy Iraq. If left unchecked, he would not remain a regional tyrant; he would inevitably spread his scourge throughout the Western world. "The tragedy of World War II came about, in part, because people in my country believed that the Atlantic Ocean provided a wall behind which the United States could hide from the tragedy that was about to engulf Europe. Today I think there are some people who believe that they might escape the scourge of terrorism by building a high enough wall around their country—but that's an illusion."[28]

Wolfowitz acknowledged that he had culled much of his pessimistic view on human nature from a select, if not selective, group of writers. When queried on his reading habits, he described a formative list comprised of—in addition to the classical historians—"George Orwell. Books about the Holocaust unfortunately," and "John Hersey's *Hiroshima.*"[29] George Orwell presumably informed Wolfowitz's description of the nation's enemies who "teach that destruction is good, murder is noble."[30] As for John Hersey's chilling description of human tragedy in the atomic age, Wolfowitz somewhat counterintuitively discovered in this chronicle of destruction a confirmation of his advocacy of preventive and preemptive warfare. "One of the things that ultimately led me to leave mathematics and go into political science was thinking I could prevent nuclear war," he recalled.[31]

Wolfowitz's readings on the Holocaust were, perhaps, the driving force behind what journalist Bill Keller has described as Wolfowitz's professed "horror of standing by and watching bad things happen." Wolfowitz "often talks about Kitty Genovese, the New York woman murdered in 1964 while dozens of neighbors watched from their apartment windows without lifting a phone to call the police." It was this sense of the price of inaction that "in almost any discussion, he tends to be the one focusing on the most often overlooked variable in decision making, the cost of not acting."[32] Wolfowitz's philosophy of action—whether on the streets of New York or within the global area—had obvious undertones of his mentors' frequent recourse to Hamlet. The cost of procrastination ultimately raised the price of existential challenges.

The events of 9/11 presented Wolfowitz with what he considered to be a horrific validation of his warnings. Wolfowitz's recollection of the events was quite dramatic. "We had just had a breakfast with some congressmen," the morning of the attacks. Wolfowitz recalled warning his congressional guests that the nation was "in for some nasty surprises" from a yet unknown source and that "it's in the nature of surprise that you can't predict what it's going to be."[33] Shortly thereafter, Wolfowitz received word of the attack on the World Trade Center. Some thirty minutes later, a shock wave rocked the Pentagon. The grim coincidence of his briefing on the day of deadly attack now seemed visionary.

Such claims to prophecy notwithstanding, Wolfowitz had been seeking the enemy in the wrong direction. During the course of the briefing on 9/11, "one of the congressmen asked, 'Well, what kind of surprises do you have in mind?' I remember volunteering, 'Well, maybe Iran will test a nuclear weapon or maybe North Korea will test an intercontinental ballistic missile.'"[34] No one on Wolfowitz's list of most wanted had underwritten Al Qaeda, though this hardly prevented the administration from claiming a connection between 9/11 and Iraq. The administration made a seamless logical leap from one to the other.

Wolfowitz's boss, Secretary of Defense Donald Rumsfeld, described the logic of the Iraqi connection. It was mostly an exercise in what he colorfully described as "connect[ing] the dots" of events past to contemporary dangers. Speaking before a congressional committee on the eve of the Iraq offensive, Rumsfeld explained that "we have connected the dots as much as it is humanly possible—before the fact. Only by waiting until after the event could we have proof positive. The dots are there for all to see. The dots are there for all to connect. If they aren't good enough, rest assured they will only be good enough after another disaster—a disaster of still greater proportions. And by then it will be too late."[35] For Wolfowitz, the historian, the ancient past provided a clue. There would always be a Carthage on the horizon, and it was incumbent to act preemptively and proactively, even when guided by incomplete information.[36]

Iraq and the Cuban Missile Crisis

Wolfowitz's theory of cyclical history is instructive for understanding his latter-day, bellicose stance on Iraq. Wolfowitz linked the Cuban missile crisis and the Iraq crisis on numerous occasions as quintessential examples of the recurring nature of strategic threats.[37] "I was a Cuban missile crisis kid. I was a sophomore in college when all that happened," Wolfowitz recalled in a 2002 interview that was ostensibly about Iraq and the threat of terror. A crisis of the Cuban type was still a viable grim possibility, he declared, although "it is amazing to me to realize how remote the idea of nuclear war is to my kids' generation."[38] Contrary to his historically challenged colleagues, Wolfowitz could rattle off a list of what the Cuban crisis and the Iraqi threat had in common: presidential assassination attempts employed by the proxies of an expansionist enemy; the threat of nuclear weapons initiated by a predatory rival; and the resolute responses of two fearless presidents who brushed aside the hesitation of timid advisers.[39]

On the eve of the Cuba showdown, Wolfowitz recounted in a contested and mostly erroneous version of events, President Kennedy confronted a choice that was remarkably similar to the challenge facing American policy makers on the eve of the second U.S. invasion of Iraq. Kennedy had imperfect information regarding his adversary's intentions. His close advisers counseled caution given inadequate data on enemy intentions. Kennedy decided otherwise. He rejected traditional diplomatic negotiations in favor of an unequivocally offensive military stance. A resolute president threw caution to the wind by immediately assembling "a powerful force to demonstrate to Nikita Khrushchev that if the missiles were not removed peacefully, the United States would force their removal. That action was unquestionably risky, but without it, a peaceful resolution of the crisis would not have been possible."[40] To those who argued that the Soviets were deploying weapons for symbolic purposes, Kennedy responded that "we no longer live in a world where only the actual firing of weapons represents a sufficient challenge to the nation's security to constitute maximum peril."[41] American acquiescence to this aggressive Soviet move would destabilize the tenuous standoff between the two powers and would encourage further expansionist moves.

By occluding Kennedy's pragmatism—in particular, his dismantling of the Jupiter missile silos in Turkey in exchange for the Soviet retreat in Cuba—Wolfowitz had created a false but compelling historical artifact. In his narrative, neither containment nor patient negotiations would tame the will of such "evil people."[42] The only way to end the Iraq crisis was to adopt the confrontational stance that had allegedly served Kennedy so well during a defining moment in the Cold War.

The decision to invade Iraq was driven by Cuban-like circumstances, Wolfowitz claimed. Like Kennedy, George W. Bush did not employ the gold standard of solid empirical evidence on Iraqi intentions. Nevertheless, given the robust nature of historical examples—not least Wolfowitz's partisan version of the Cuban missile crisis—Bush wisely chose a proactive Kennedyesque path to stave off enemy capacities rather than surrender to imperfect knowledge of enemy intentions. A lack of irrefutable evidence was endemic to all forms of statecraft but was not necessarily an impediment to sound decision making. Solid theory, derived from a combination of historical analysis and a cool assessment of enemy capabilities, offered a reliable roadmap for navigating global crises.

The standoff in Iraq, according to Wolfowitz, provided textbook warning signs of an alarming repetition of the early 1960s. But if, indeed, there were similarities linking Cuba of the 1960s to Iraq of the new millennium, they resided first and foremost in the feverish minds of Wolfowitz's master teachers.

Roberta's obsession with Fidel Castro—the *Máximo Líder* who destabilized the global arena by means of presidential assassination attempts while pursuing nuclear weaponry—provided the text for inscribing Iraq on the Cuban palimpsest. Much like Roberta, who had implicated Fidel for fantasizing the Kennedy assassination, Wolfowitz maintained that the fact that Saddam Hussein had never actually executed the plot to assassinate George Bush Sr. was less significant than the ambitions the Iraqi dictator harbored.[43] By the same token, the actual presence of WMD was less important than the intent to use them. "You had a very dangerous character who played with terrorists, who had regularly declared hostile intentions toward us and toward our allies in the Persian Gulf, who definitely had the capacity to make these weapons and—absent some kind of fairly fundamental change in his attitude and policy—was extremely dangerous, and much more dangerous in the light of September 11 than before."[44]

The actual existence of WMD was a secondary issue. "The search for evidence is understandable," Wolfowitz conceded, "but at the end of the day, we are trying to judge what will happen in the future."[45] Whether Saddam Hussein harbored WMD or not was uncertain; his will to "use terrorists as an instrument of revenge" was, however, irrefutable. Wolfowitz quoted George W. Bush: "As our President has said . . . 'Saddam Hussein is harboring terrorists and the instruments of terror. . . . And he cannot be trusted. The risk is simply too great that he will use'" WMD or other nonconventional delivery systems to foist his will on his immediate surroundings and beyond.[46]

If anything, the Iraq crisis was significantly more volatile than the Cuban missile crisis had been. The Soviets had employed a proxy state, with well-defined leadership and clear territorial dimensions. Saddam Hussein, by contrast, purportedly enabled shadowy nonstate actors. The only way to contain the murky scourge of terrorism—a borderless threat that challenged the statist world of conventional international relations—was to obliterate the enablers. Imperfect knowledge of this unconventional threat was no excuse for hesitation.

An analysis of key historical crises dispelled a pervasive "intellectual notion that there is such a thing as perfect knowledge. . . . Accepting the imperfection of knowledge is a very important part of being a great decision-maker." The futile hunt for nuclear weapons was therefore not reason enough to avoid a showdown in Iraq. Saddam's rapaciousness needed to be abolished even without "perfect knowledge" of his intentions. Hamletian hesitancy in the Middle East had already led to deadly results unrecognized by the putative experts: "A fundamental flaw in the 9/11 report, absolutely fundamental, is that it assumes that if we had had perfect intelligence, we could have prevented the attacks."[47]

His Masters' Voices

Wolfowitz's interests in volatility in the Middle East had commenced many years before confrontation in Iraq. His PhD thesis, completed in 1972, provides an essential point of departure for understanding the consolidation of his views on the Middle East and its intellectual links to his Wohlstetter mentors. Ostensibly a treatise on the economic and political feasibility of Eisenhower's Atoms for Peace program in the Middle East, the manuscript offers insight into his warnings of nuclear proliferation among rogue states as well as into how he understood the broader geopolitics of the Middle East.

Written under Albert Wohlstetter's tutelage, the dissertation crisply and convincingly demolishes the economic argument for nuclear-powered desalination in the Middle East. It demonstrates the staggering costs of such an operation—whether undertaken in Israel or Egypt—and proposes, instead, desalination by other, more economical means, as well as different forms of water conservation.[48] As for the immediate political benefits, Wolfowitz dismissed the idea that an increased supply of a scarce commodity, such as water, would mitigate the likelihood of future conflagrations. Water wars were part of the Arab-Israeli conflict, he acknowledged, but in the larger scheme of events it was still a peripheral issue. Water, whether scarce or abundant, was unlikely to affect future conflicts in any meaningful way.

Wolfowitz believed that resolving the Palestinian refugee issue was the key to de-escalation. Wars in the Middle East were all driven by the problem of Palestinian refugees and their right of return to a homeland that had been transformed into the state of Israel. Until such time as Arab neighbors and the Palestinian refugees relinquished the right to return, and agreed, instead, on resettlement, the torrents of water desalination promised would have no positive impact on Middle Eastern volatility.

If anything, Wolfowitz argued, atomic-powered desalination would drive the periodic spates of violence in the Middle East into an abyss. Atoms for Peace would ignite a rush to convert civilian know-how into military use. The acquisition of nuclear weapons by either side would set off a frantic arms race, aided and abetted by outside parties, and would culminate in an untenable, extremely fragile balance of terror between Israel and its Arab foes.

Albert's fingerprints are particularly evident in this part of the dissertation. Albert had tried to stymie Israel's access to atomic desalination by trying to convince Prime Minister Levi Eshkol to avoid the prohibitive costs of such an ambitious venture.[49] Albert was not primarily concerned, however, with the fiscal solvency of the Jewish State. His main worry was proliferation. The dangers of provoking a volatile nuclear standoff through delusory endorsements of Atoms for Peace in the Middle East—a well-worn Wohlstetter theme—permeate Wolfowitz's dissertation.

Wolfowitz employed Albert's metaphor of old-style, Western gun-slinging—a central motif in "The Delicate Balance of Terror"—to describe the dynamics of nuclear weapons in the Middle East. Cognizant of the obvious advantage of a doomsday weapon, each side would seek to offset the opponent's advantage by striking first. The lack of hardened weapons shelters far removed from enemy territory—Albert's signature initiative for creating a feasible balance of terror between nuclear powers—would defeat all attempts at moderation. Ill-protected weapons in geographic proximity provided dangerously enticing incentives for a surprise attack. In the Middle East, moreover, the political stakes were especially flammable. "The fundamental reason for the explosive character of international politics in the Middle East is that the highest aspirations of the nations involved, including even physical survival, are directly and daily at stake. The hostilities are deeper and less capable of moderation than those which have divided the antagonists in the Cold War."[50] The informal doctrine of cautiousness that had defined the superpower standoff was conspicuously absent in the Middle East. Both sides in the Arab-Israeli conflict were manifestly incapable of reigning in their emotions.

In describing the dangers of nuclear weapons in Israeli hands, Wolfowitz identified the military imbalance between Israel and its multiple, hostile neighbors as the primary disruptive force. A momentary weakness on the conventional battlefield might ignite Israeli fears of an existential threat, thereby leading impulsive Israeli leaders to unleash the ultimate weapon. A technologically advanced Israel had the capacity to transform civilian reactors with relative ease. The concept of externally monitored safeguards and inspections aimed at stymieing such transformations struck Wolfowitz as pure fantasy.

As for providing nuclear technology to either Egypt or the United Arab Emirates—the two water-starved Arab states seeking access to cutting-edge desalination—Wolfowitz twice quoted the French nuclear scholar André Beaufre, who warned that such actions were tantamount to giving matches to children.[51] Arab governments were immature and inherently capricious: "Instability in the Middle East is aggravated by the instability of some of the governments in the area. Not only can this lead to sudden changes in the military balance, but may also induce some governments to recklessness."[52]

In other words, belligerent Arabs were fickle and could not be trusted with such weapons. Israelis, for their part, had existential fears—or phobias—that could induce fatally wrong decision under duress. Even without sharing General Beaufre's view on nuclear matches in the hands of immature Arabs, and regardless of the Israeli impulse to jump the gun, the glaring lack of mechanistic stabilizing devices that were central to the U.S.-Soviet standoff would inevitably lead to a nuclear conflagration.[53] Conflicts in the area had "the character more nearly of a quick-draw, Wild West gun duel than of a slow, drawn-out boxing match." It was "hard to imagine," Wolfowitz concluded, "that the introduction of nuclear weapons would be a stabilizing force in the Middle East."[54] None of the mitigating factors that had led to a species of accommodation between the United States and its Soviet adversary—however delicate—existed in the Middle Eastern tinderbox.

A Straussian Connection?

Many observers have brushed aside these manifestly robust connections between Wohlstetter and Wolfowitz. Instead they insist on creating connections between the University of Chicago philosopher Leo Strauss and the Wohlstetters' inner circle. A brief perusal of the Internet produces a flurry of alleged connections between the reclusive Leo Strauss and Paul Wolfowitz, as well as other Wohlstetter acolytes.

Wolfowitz dismisses this hypothesis: "I took two terrific courses from Leo Strauss as a graduate student. One was on Montesquieu's spirit of the laws, which did help me understand our Constitution better. And one was on Plato's laws. The idea that this has anything to do with U.S. foreign policy is just laughable." Wolfowitz identified himself foremost as a student of Albert Wohlstetter, not of Strauss. "The same fellow . . . who discovered the Straussian Conspiracy," Wolfowitz added, "kind of throws Wohlstetter in as a Straussian," when he was actually an analytical philosopher.[55] According to his daughter Joan, Albert had no more than a passing acquaintance with Leo Strauss. During their brief overlap at Chicago, their relationship never amounted to more than polite small talk in the corridors.[56]

The contrast between the Wohlstetterian and the Straussian worldviews is remarkably stark. The only common thread appears to be a putative Jewish connection, in particular a common attraction to a conservative version of the Zionist creed. A number of Wohlstetter acolytes, Wolfowitz, included, embraced the Likud's version of Zionism, which supposedly aligns with Strauss's Zionist Revisionist affinities, thereby producing a highly suspect smoking gun.[57] Aside from these philo-Zionist insinuations, there are no robust associations between the University of Chicago philosopher and the radical disciples of a colleague whom Strauss barely knew. In fact, Strauss envisioned a craft of statesmanship that none of the Wohlstetter acolytes would ever have recognized. Strauss defined the ideal leader as "free from the narrow-ness of the lawyer, the brutality of the technician, the vagaries of the visionary, the baseness of the opportunist." At the same time, Strauss advocated the acceptance of limitations in a changing world: "one's ex-pectations from politics must be moderate."[58]

The writings of the Wohlstetters' heirs suggest a collective worldview quite foreign to Strauss's advocacy of self-restraint. The demise of the Soviet Union, in particular, unleashed them from whatever wisp of moderation they may have picked up along the way. From that point onward, they pursued a visionary foreign policy, uncluttered by dis-tasteful compromise, devoid of pandering to vacillating, fainthearted allies or any acquiescence to the whims of rapacious adversaries. The Wohlstetters' students envisioned a global expansion of American-style market democracy as an alternative to the existing cacophonous world of competing political systems, where threats to worldwide security lurked in every corner.

Much like Presidents Reagan and George W. Bush—their principal enablers in the White House—the Wohlstetters' heirs in government were obsessed with expunging evil from the political arena, be it the Evil Empire or the infamous Axis of Evil. Never shy of hyperbole, they advocated nothing less than a grandiose "End to Evil."[59] This type of terminology never appeared in the writings of their mentors. Such mor-alism was their own unique creation. In fact, as Steven Smith notes, the very notion that evil could be effaced in one clean sweep was "closer to the utopian and idealistic visions of Marxism and the radical Enlight-enment than anything found in the writings of Strauss"—or of the Wohlstetters for that matter.[60] Evil, for Strauss, was a permanent fix-ture of the human condition. Indeed, he argued, "it is against nature that there should ever be a 'cessation of evils.'"[61] Statesmanship was ac-cordingly a craft "free from all fanaticism because it knows that evil cannot be eradicated."[62] Such notions were anathema to the Wohlstetter acolytes.

Francis Fukuyama does note that the Wohlstetter disciples appeared to adopt the Straussian idea "that certain political problems can be solved only through regime change." Yet, contrary to Strauss, they approached regime change as a facile panacea. Strauss had understood that regimes were not merely "power structures." The political system of any given country reflected deeply embedded cultural mores and social values, all of which would have to undergo an extreme makeover before a Western-style democracy could indeed strike roots. Such Straussian complexity eluded Wolfowitz as well as his fellow acolytes.[63]

An End to Anarchy

Like others among the Wohlstetters' intimate circle of aspiring under-studies, Wolfowitz endorsed the idea of radical regime change as a panacea for global stability. The primary tool for assuring long-term global stability, he argued, did not reside in some quick technological fix, nuclear or otherwise. Stability—whether in the Middle East or elsewhere—hinged on the introduction of a new political system. "Critics of realism, like myself, do not think that a businesslike management of the 'relations between states' should lead us to neglect issues regarding the 'nature of states.' In reality, the internal makeup of states has a huge effect on their external behavior—so it must also be a significant consideration for U.S. foreign policy."[64] Lecturing the Obama administration from the pages of *Foreign Policy,* Wolfowitz insisted that it was incumbent on any responsible administration to accept "the reality that democratic reform is a powerful force to advance U.S. interests."[65] Regime change had "benefited the U.S. national interest in so many instances—not only the peaceful collapse of the Soviet empire and the end of apartheid in South Africa, but also with the many transitions from dictatorship to democracy that have deepened security in almost every region of the world."[66] Ignoring the "nature of states" would lead to a reenactment of the fin de siècle debacle.

Wolfowitz rejected the presumption that democracy was a foreign concept foisted on supine nations by a muscular America. Democracy as a political system, he argued, was a natural state of affairs that had been corrupted by predatory regimes. The primary efforts of the United States in Iraq and elsewhere, therefore, were "to remove the shackles on democracy."[67] Though quite willing to acknowledge that the battle for the nature of states was best pursued by peaceful means, Wolfowitz nonetheless advocated the use of force, and not necessarily as a last resort. Stability in the vital Persian Gulf region, he had declared already in 1997, entailed toppling the Hussein regime by all means possible.

Wolfowitz lashed out furiously at alternatives to regime change, such as the Clinton administration's strategy of proactive containment in

Iraq. Clinton's policy of abeyance by spasmodic, surgical air strikes suggested to him a misunderstanding of the issue at hand. Clinton, he complained, did not seem to understand that "Saddam's continued rule is incompatible with peace in the Gulf."[68] Writing in the *Wall Street Journal* in 1996, Wolfowitz railed forcefully against "our passive containment policy and our inept covert operations," which might somehow last "until a tyrant possessing large quantities of weapons of mass destruction and sophisticated delivery systems strikes out at us." He defined this strategy as "Clinton's Bay of Pigs," implying a halfhearted, inept attempt to remove a clear and present danger.[69] Containment—"living with the Soviet Union" or the toleration of latter-day tyrants with global aspirations—was a subterfuge for inaction and a recipe for a disaster that would send shock waves beyond Iraq's porous borders.[70]

Wolfowitz's contempt for containment and his endorsement of regime change drew predictably on historical lessons. Suppose the British would have "successfully resisted Hitler in the Rhineland or at Munich. Germany might have then been 'contained.' But in that case, we would have been treated, would we not, to learned discourses about how the resulting 'cold war' with Germany was the unnecessary product of unwarranted Western suspicion and hostility toward a country that was legitimately supporting the right of self-determination of nationals living beyond its borders, and chafing under the harsh and unequal impositions of the Versailles Treaty."[71]

Such exercises in counterfactual history reflected the intertwining relationship of empiricism and theory in the world of Wolfowitz. Wolfowitz presented himself as a historian and theorist of international relations. His point of departure—his theory—was that, without radical change, the founts of global instability would remain constant. Within this context, Wolfowitz called for an active campaign of regime change in crucial, strategic areas of the world. The lesson of the Cold War was first and foremost that "democracy matters." In the Cold War, according to Wolfowitz, "holding the line in Berlin and Korea was not just about those places alone. It was about the resolve of the free world. Once that resolve was made clear to the Soviets, communism eventually collapsed. The same thing will happen to terrorism—and to all those who have attempted to hijack Islam and threaten America and the rest of the free world, which now includes Iraq. They will see our resolve and the resolve of the free world. Then they, too, will take their place on the ash heap of history."[72]

Mustering his own personal experience of supporting democratic reform in the Philippines, despite the presence of a pro-American despot (he had served as assistant secretary for East Asian and Pacific affairs from 1982 to 1986), Wolfowitz invoked the premise that democracies do not clash with one another.[73] As such, any long-term, viable foreign policy would have to promote—albeit with great caution—a policy of regime change and nation building in areas where the United States had both vital interests and the necessary leverage to induce change. All too frequently, he argued, misguided idealists invoked the examples of Germany and Japan as "misleading guides for the present." Germany and Japan had been ripe for transition to democracy because they were "economically advanced but, at the same time, had profoundly lost faith in their own institutions."[74] Without indigenous support, and without the necessary economic and social infrastructure to accommodate the economic, social, and political aspects of democracy, such efforts were doomed to fail.

The Role of Evil in International Affairs

At first glance, there was nothing exceptionally novel about Wolfowitz's global strategy. The inherent link between foreign and domestic policy was derived in part from the work of his mentors, the Wohlstetters. Albert, in particular, had highlighted a linear connection between the Iraqi regime's internal policies—in particular, its genocidal rampages against Iraqi minorities—and its foreign policy. A palace coup against Saddam, Albert had argued, would be nothing more than a cosmetic adjustment with no meaningful ramifications for global stability.[75] It was the nature of the regime—in Iraq, Cuba, and the former Soviet Union—that needed change. Predatory regimes, who ruled domestically with an iron fist, would inevitably behave in a similar manner in the global arena. Merely removing a despot, "trying to preserve an authoritarian regime or a dictatorship while just rearranging the personnel," would accomplish nothing. "But where it's feasible and in the U.S. interest to encourage democracy, that's something else again."[76]

On one crucial issue, Wolfowitz departed from his mentors. Following in the footsteps of their friend and RAND colleague Nathan Leites, the Wohlstetters had described rapacious regimes and their despots in terms of clinical dysfunction. The terminology Leites used to describe the Bolsheviks in his work on the Soviet elite deeply influenced them, with Roberta's description of Fidel Castro—the proverbial "wreckage of conflict and contradiction"—being a case in point.[77]

Wolfowitz thought otherwise. Rather than adopting the tone of a psychoanalyst seeking to abate clinical dysfunctionality in the political arena, he chose moralism, defining friend and foe in clear-cut ethical terms. Saddam—like Hitler, Stalin, and the rest of history's rogue gallery—was not a case study for a mental health professional. "The Cold War was about as clear a struggle between good and evil as one is likely to experience in the real world."[78] And yet, he recalled, "when Reagan denounced the Soviet Union as an 'evil empire,'" he outraged more than only those on the Left addicted to moral equivalence." Realists were equally disturbed because, in their world, "offending the Soviet Union was a dangerous business" tainted with moral imperatives that supposedly had no place in the hardheaded world of international affairs.[79]

Wolfowitz chastised the establishment for its pervasive blindness to the moral dimensions of foreign policy. The so-called realism of conventional American policy was, in fact, an instance of cultural relativism dating back, at least, to the Cold War. The establishment, in academia and along the Beltway, was in denial, he argued. The Cuban regime and the Baath party in Iraq, and by implication Iran, North Korea, and the former Soviet Union, were tangibly evil—a word the Wohlstetters never used. Evil was an eschatological challenge, a source of global instability, and a fundamental test of universal ethical precepts. "If that was true forty years ago" during the Cuban missile crisis, he asked, "a threat that was comparatively easy to observe, how much more true is it today of threats developed by evil people who use the freedoms of a democratic society to plot and plan even in our midst, in the midst of our allies in Europe and around the world?"[80]

Yet Iraq was merely the tip of the iceberg. In late 2002, Wolfowitz extended a concept George W. Bush had famously invoked earlier that year: "The United States of America, your administration, can help prevent a nuclear-armed axis of evil, including Castro, the Chavez regime in Venezuela, and the pro-Castro radical who's now leading for the presidency in Brazil, from establishing a nuclear-armed ballistic missile . . . that would help covertly destabilize neighboring countries." He accordingly urged action against Lula da Silva for his "support for terrorist organizations since 1990." Lula, he fumed, had "convened every year a group of all the terrorists from Latin America, many from Europe, many from the Middle East and official delegations from Iraq and Iran." Lula was the Latin American Saddam, another paragon of evil.[81]

This moralistic sense of history stoked Wolfowitz's antipathy toward the pursuit of a foreign policy of realism, which he described as unprincipled. "Nothing could be less realistic than the version of the 'realist' view of foreign policy that dismisses human rights as an important tool of American foreign policy."[82] Realism, according to Wolfowitz, was an affliction in which moral considerations took a backseat to fuzzy-logic expediency. Realism had deflected attention from the moral component of affairs of state. Oblivious to historical precedent, realists sought to manage existential threats rather than purge them. It was only the dispassionate scholar of world history—armed with a discriminating moral compass—who understood that evil could not be contained; it could only be expunged. In other words, Wolfowitz had uncovered an escape hatch from the recurring cycles of Carthages threatening the United States. An End to Evil—a theme picked up and elaborated by his close collaborator, Richard Perle—would transform both the nature of states and their interaction in the global arena.

Why did notions of evil—beginning with Reagan and as centerpiece in the George W. Bush administration—enter the conservative lexicon? As far as Wolfowitz is concerned, a cynical explanation would attribute his choice of words to a good copywriter. Reagan had used the catchphrase "Evil Empire" in a masterful manner, leaving his opponents sputtering for a meaningful response. There was no reason, then, to change a successful battle cry. Through the good services of speechwriters with a Reagan background, Evil became central theme in the Bush administration. One might argue, then, that Wolfowitz was merely toeing the line set by the president.

The issue of creative wordsmithing notwithstanding, the descriptor "evil" had the added value of presenting the enemy in a politic manner that would not damn the entire Muslim world as potential enemies. An entity clearly defined as "evil" exonerated, by implication, those who fell outside of its domain. Defining the enemy as malevolent usurpers of a peaceful religion distanced Wolfowitz from innuendos of Islamophobia. He was not chastising an entire religion, only its radical offshoots.

At an Iftar dinner held at the Pentagon on November 30, 2001, Wolfowitz lauded the presence of Muslim Americans in the American armed forces as well as the positive impact of Islam on the nation's moral virtues. "Through faithfulness to Islam, during the month of Ramadan, Muslim Americans encourage us all to focus our attention on God's call to brotherhood." As for the raging war in Afghanistan, Wolfowitz noted the presence of "Muslim allies" among the coalition forces "fighting an evil that arose from an irrational and ultimately selfish attempt to appropriate a great religion."[83] In this context, Wolfowitz alluded frequently to his positive interactions with Islam during tenure as ambassador to Indonesia.

Of course, Wolfowitz's and the administration's gravitation toward the imagery of objective "evil" may also have been sincere. Wolfowitz, much like the president, may very well have been a moralist at heart, engaged, he may have thought, in a primal struggle with the forces of evil stalking the earth.[84] Speaking before a mostly Jewish group, Wolfowitz described the war in Afghanistan as being led by an American battle force of "Jews, Christians, Muslims, Americans of all faiths," united in the common pursuit of "victory over the darkness of evil."[85] Contrary to his mentors, whose nemeses occupied a sliding scale between clinically irrational and psychotic, Wolfowitz's enemies appeared depraved; there was a biblical evil about them.

Terrorism and the Nuclear Connection

But Wolfowitz was not only a moralist. He claimed the mantle of rational scientist, as well. Seeking empirical evidence to back up his claims, Wolfowitz offered clear indicators of malevolent enemy designs. At times his candor embroiled him in controversy. In an interview conducted by Sam Tanenhaus in 2003, Wolfowitz allegedly "admitted that from the outset, contrary to so many claims from the White House, Iraq's supposed cache of WMD had never been the most important casus belli. It was simply one of several reasons: 'For bureaucratic reasons we settled on one issue, weapons of mass destruction, because it was the one reason everyone could agree on.' Everyone meaning, presumably, Powell and the Joint Chiefs of Staff."[86]

Attempting to dispute this uncomfortable revelation, the Department of Defense published a full transcript of the interview, claiming thereby to dispel Tanenhaus's innuendo. According to the transcript,

Wolfowitz stated that "the truth is that for reasons that have a lot to do with the U.S. government bureaucracy we settled on the one issue that everyone could agree on which was weapons of mass destruction as the core reason [for the invasion of Iraq], but . . . there have always been three fundamental concerns. One is weapons of mass destruction, the second is support for terrorism, the third is the criminal treatment of the Iraqi people. . . . The third one by itself, as I think I said earlier, is a reason to help the Iraqis but it's not a reason to put American kids' lives at risk, certainly not on the scale we did it. That second issue about links to terrorism is the one about which there's the most disagreement within the bureaucracy."[87]

A sympathetic William Kristol explained the dispute as an issue of framing. By means of a selective and incomplete quotation, Kristol explained, Tanenhaus had implied "that the Bush administration's asserted casus belli for war against Saddam Hussein—the dictator's weapons-of-mass-destruction program—was little more than a propaganda device, a piece of self-conscious and insincere political manipulation."[88]

The Department of Defense transcript and the Tanenhaus article were, in fact, quite similar in content and context. In both cases, Wolfowitz confirmed the Wohlstetterian underpinnings of American foreign policy. On the eve of 9/11—as had been the case throughout the Cold War—U.S. strategic doctrine identified nation-states as the primary actors in the global arena and the essential, if not the sole source of strategic threats facing the United States. The existence of a supranational entity that derived its power from a source other than the state struck U.S. government officials as a fantasy and a denial of international realities. According to Wolfowitz, "international terrorism is a broad network of groups of state sponsors who collaborate with one another, some in ways that we can see, and frequently in ways that are hidden from us."[89]

Within this context, policy makers insisted that the overriding strategic danger facing the United States was state-controlled nuclear proliferation. Since the Vietnam War, the threshold for any large-scale American deployment of American military force had been a threat of nuclear attack. An unprecedented war on terror therefore required the presence of a nuclear threat wielded by the nation-states that were enabling these nonstate actors. In accordance with the

Wohlstetter Doctrine, the possibility, rather than the probability, of WMD in Iraqi hands was reason enough for intervention. "What September 11th to me said was this is just the beginning of what these bastards can do if they start getting access to so-called modern weapons" (of mass destruction).[90] It was the iron grip of doctrine—rather than the devious manipulation of evidence—that drove the hunt for Iraqi WMD.

When Flight 77 struck the Pentagon on that fateful September morning, Wolfowitz recalled, "the whole building shook. I have to confess my first reaction was an earthquake." Fearing a nuclear aftershock, Wolfowitz moved to an undisclosed "bizarre location that was prepared to survive nuclear war."[91] Hunkering down in this bunker, Wolfowitz experienced a Pearl Harbor moment. As had been the case among the luckless military establishment on the eve of the Japanese strike, the strategic earthquake that had jolted Wolfowitz failed to dislodge his core assumptions. Instead it tightened the grip of powerful preconceptions, including his early thoughts on nuclear dangers in the Middle East. With a sleight of hand, Wolfowitz's dissertation on the dangers of nuclear weapons in the Arab world rose from the ashes of the Pentagon fire to become policy rather than jeremiad.

Yet, in fact, Wolfowitz was himself a victim of the very syndrome he ascribed to others. Despite the presence of clear signals, Wolfowitz had chosen to follow the distracting noise of his own preconceptions. The evocation of the Iraqi threat was probably not a deceitful marketing choice but rather, ironically, a reflection of Roberta's bitter observation that people will listen only to what they desire to hear.

Wolfowitz was by no means an outlier. He was, instead, the archetypical disciple of the Bush administration, professing the gospel while adding some moralistic amendments of his own. The major strains of his worldview—all in some way a variation of the Wohlstetter Doctrine—were common themes among the acolytes. In one form or another, they would all claim that breaking the historical cycle of global instability hinged on radical regime change for destabilizing, authoritarian regimes. Palace coups would not suffice because, in most cases, the nature of the regime, rather than any single individual tyrant, was inherently corrupted by unadulterated evil. Moralizing Wohlstetterians identified the threat of terror as a dependent variable emanating from states—albeit rogue states. And yet terror on its own was not a necessary condition for a radical, proactive intervention. The trigger for intervention was the existential threat of nuclear proliferation and its disruption of a balance of terror that had preserved the peace, delicate as it was. It was incumbent on the Wohlstetter camp to connect the proverbial dots among rogue states, transnational actors, and thermonuclear proliferation.

10

Zalmay Khalilzad

The Orientalist

I N HIS EARLY DAYS as a graduate student at the University of Chicago in the 1970s, Zalmay Khalilzad affected a radical posture. The political scientist Anne Norton, in a cranky account of "Straussians" in government and academia, recalled how he had "boasted of the demonstrations he had organized in Beirut, of the *fedayin* he knew and had worked with. . . . He went to pro-Palestinian meetings. His room had a poster of Nasser in tears."[1] Khalilzad went through a drastic transformation after he took Albert Wohlstetter's class on war in the thermonuclear age. Khalildad himself remembered his first encounter with Albert as "life-changing."[2] In Norton's telling, he discarded his revolutionary posture and joined Albert's coterie of doting graduate students. According to Norton, Khalilzad was driven by ulterior motives. He was an opportunist; it was Albert's extravagant persona and jet-setting lifestyle—rather than strategic studies per se—that enthralled him the most. In his autobiography, Khalilzad candidly recalls being intrigued when he heard that Albert called President Kennedy "Jack" and Secretary of State Kissinger "Henry." His "most enduring memory" of the "larger than life" Albert is "seeing him in one of his sports cars." He was equally impressed by the Wohlstetters' "beautiful house in Hollywood" and their apartment in Chicago's North Shore with its "stunning view of Lake Michigan" where Albert held graduate seminars, "catered by a fine restaurant."[3]

Within the Wohlstetters' orbit, Khalilzad was the designated orientalist. He offered insight on the Middle Eastern tinderbox as well as on the broader Muslim context, but his most significant contribution to the

Wohlstetter Doctrine was his resounding silence on pan-Islamic radicalism. Because of his skepticism of Islam as a motivating force beyond specific national struggles—as with Iran—Khalilzad only belatedly recognized the strategic implications of Al Qaeda and its mutations. His response to millenarianism in the Muslim world was to retreat to a paradigm he had once rejected. Upon ascending to positions of power in the George W. Bush administration, Khalilzad revoked his previous suspicions about modernization theory and abandoned his critique of the Westphalian paradigm regarding the viability of states in the Muslim world. He became a true believer in the nation-states of Afghanistan and Iraq, two artificial creations of former colonial masters.

The Nation-State in the Northern Tier

Zalmay Mamozy Khalilzad, an ethnic Pashtun, was born in 1951 in Mazar-i-Sharif, a diverse Afghani city populated primarily by Tajiks and Uzbeks.[4] His family was from the mostly rural and multiethnic province of Laghman. His father was a high-ranking government figure during the reign of King Mohammed Zahir Shah, the last king of Afghanistan, who was deposed in a coup in 1973.[5]

Khalilzad's first American experience occurred when he was a high school student at Ghazi Lycée, a private English-language school in Kabul (most private schools in Kabul, regardless of language of instruction, were called "lycées").[6] As part of an exchange program with his Afghan high school, Khalilzad spent a semester in a rural community in California's San Joaquin Valley. This first American visit was transformative. Upon returning home, he recalled in a *New Yorker* interview, "I had different values, greater interest in sports, a more pragmatic way of looking at things, and a broader horizon. I had a sense of how backward Afghanistan was. And I became more interested in how Afghanistan needed to change."[7]

Following high school, Khalilzad enrolled at Kabul University. Shortly thereafter he was offered a scholarship to attend the American University of Beirut (AUB). Khalilzad spent four years in Beirut, from 1970 to 1974, graduating with a double major in political science and the history of the Middle East. It was at AUB where Khalilzad met his wife and intellectual partner, Cheryl Benard, then a graduate student researching a dissertation on Arab nationalism.[8]

In 1975, Khalilzad entered the doctoral program in political science at the University of Chicago, where he worked under the tutelage of Albert Wohlstetter. Khalilzad, the graduate student, was also an employee of Pan Heuristics, the Wohlstetters' consulting firm, where he produced papers on nuclear proliferation.[9] Khalilzad's first and only academic appointment, as an assistant professor of political science at Columbia (1979–1989), was punctuated by frequent forays into government as an adviser on Afghani affairs for the Reagan administration.[10]

The dissertation Khalilzad wrote under Albert's guidance offers a brief window into his early aspirations (though it merited no discussion in Khalilzad's autobiography).[11] The subject was unoriginal, mostly a variation on the theme of Paul Wolfowitz's thesis on the strategic dangers of civilian nuclear proliferation. Moving beyond the Levantine Middle East, the area Wolfowitz had comfortably occupied, Khalilzad produced a censorious account of efforts to introduce nuclear power plants in Afghanistan, Pakistan, and Turkey.[12]

A welter of spelling errors and typographical mishaps leaves one wondering whether Albert ever read this paean to his own warnings on the danger of nuclear proliferation through a civilian backdoor. Indeed, a caustic Anne Norton observed, Khalilzad's adviser was an absentee professor. A serial canceler of seminars, Albert was prone to reminiscing and self-promotion rather than teaching during his sporadic classroom appearances in Chicago.[13]

As with Wolfowitz's dissertation, Khalilzad's personal contribution resided in mustering empirical evidence for a thesis that Albert had developed. He produced a quantitative analysis of the financial liabilities associated with civilian applications of nuclear technology in Iran, Iraq, Pakistan, and Turkey—at that time, all members of the Central Treaty Organization. Collectively they were known as the Northern Tier. All Northern Tier states had access to cheaper alternatives for generating power, either by fossil fuel or through hydroelectric alternatives. Khalilzad argued that rather than offering new opportunities for producing energy, the fiscal burden of nuclear power would impoverish and destabilize its unwitting clients. He described the Atoms for Peace refrain as a siren song emanating from a chorus of naive politicians and unscrupulous energy lobbyists intent on harnessing the resentment of neocolonialism that simmered locally. Third World leaders were easily mesmerized by the illusion of cheap energy as the key for unlocking the stranglehold of the West.

As with all siren songs, Khalilzad warned, such illusory hopes would end in colossal tragedy. These ostensibly civilian projects would inevitably devolve into surreptitious military schemes, which would lead, in turn, to regional turmoil with serious global implications. Each of the countries examined in his treatise had significant regional grievances. The lure of game-changing weaponry, Khalilzad contended, was liable to provoke chaotic crusades for redressing highly subjective injustices. Bereft of the balancing mechanisms—however delicate—that controlled the superpower standoff, nuclear weaponry in the Northern Tier had the potential to induce catastrophic regional destabilization. "Vulnerable nuclear systems," he argued, "are likely to increase instability and fear among rival nascent nuclear powers. They will also increase the probability of catastrophic mistakes."[14]

Toward the end of his dissertation, Khalilzad veered into divergent territory. Obviously chaffing at the Northern Tier's lack of sex appeal, Khalilzad digressed into a treatise on Iran. The triumphant return of Ayatollah Khomeini and the establishment of the Islamic Republic appeared to be of greater import than any of the mundane concerns of the drab other countries he had analyzed in his dissertation. While each of the Northern Tier countries had regional ambitions and concerns, Khomeini's Iran had messianic aspirations and would seek to impose its eschatological vision throughout the Islamic world and beyond. Iranians, he wrote, "may see nuclear weapons as a necessary ingredient of their self-image as 'a model Islamic State.' Their incentive to produce nuclear weapons may also increase substantially if any of the regional ideological and political adversaries such as Iraq acquires such weapons."[15] Such Iranian forays would eclipse any of the lurking ambitions of the less expansionist nations in the region.

The Islamic Republic of Iran, as we shall see later, would paradoxically nurture the United States' belligerent interest in Iran's Iraqi neighbor, thereby propelling Khalilzad to the forefront of the Bush administration's entanglements in the region. The American response to this regional standoff would later become Khalilzad's claim to fame, when he began divining the intentions of the two aggressive regional powers: a nominally secular Baathist dictatorship and a messianic Islamic republic.

Identity Politics in the Muslim World

Upon completing his dissertation, Khalilzad established himself as a respectable academic and policy expert on his native Afghanistan. He served as executive director of the Friends of Afghanistan, a support group for the Afghani mujahedeen who were battling their Soviet occupiers. Moonlighting for the Reagan administration during his years as an assistant professor at Columbia, Khalilzad argued forcefully for arming the Afghani mujahedeen resistance to the Soviet occupation of Afghanistan with sophisticated weaponry. He took pride in his support for providing the mujahedeen with Stinger antiaircraft missiles, which, he later claimed, was the turning point in the war. Khalilzad shrugged off the devolvement of post-Soviet Afghanistan society into a bloody civil war between radicalizing groups flush with such American weaponry.[16]

As for the rise of militant Islam in Afghanistan, he philosophically observed that retrospective criticism of American support for Afghani radicals was unfair because it did not take into account the profound fear in policy circles of a Soviet victory.[17] In fact, in the early years of post-Soviet Afghanistan, Khalilzad had expressed sympathy and support for the Taliban. Writing in the *Washington Post* in 1996, he argued that "the Taliban does not practice the anti-U.S. style of fundamentalism practiced by Iran. . . . The group upholds a mix of traditional Pashtun values and an orthodox interpretation of Islam." Khalilzad urged offering "recognition and humanitarian assistance and to promote international economic reconstruction," because "it is time for the United States to reengage" in the country, and to make the Taliban a partner.[18] The rapid transformation of the Taliban into the epitome of a global threat did not lead Khalilzad to any significant soul-searching, nor did he appear to fall out of favor in policy circles.

As a scholar, Khalilzad expressed more nuanced values and less advocacy for dubious causes. His articles on the volatility of Afghani politics and the ensuing Soviet debacle reveal a broad comprehension of the tension between the Eurocentric nation-state and the political arrangements of Muslim world. At first glance, Khalilzad's Afghani articles appear to be mere laundry lists of confusing Byzantine alliances between warlords and factional leaders, aided and abetted by Pakistan, Iran, Saudi Arabia, and its Gulf State proxies, as well as clandestine Russian agents seeking to keep an Islamic tide from seeping out of a lawless Afghanistan and into Soviet territory. In reality, his articles offered a glimpse of statist limitations: the inability of a central government to impose order on a fractious polity with no clear common cultural denominator.[19]

In Khalilzad's Afghanistan, religious affinities and enmities between Islam's multiple sects crisscrossed porous national borders, clashing and merging with militant ethnic identities, tribal loyalties, and a host of other confusing alliances. The drifting sands of ephemeral associations and duplicitous pacts were at times constrained by the nation-state, and at times superseded national borders. They were intermittently national, transnational, and antinational, but at all times quite challenging to the narrow blinders of American policy makers.[20]

Khalilzad described his colleagues in academia and government as prisoners of three interlocking intellectual constraints that encumbered attempts to gain leverage from the Afghani turmoil. To begin with, American policy makers and their academic enablers were beholden to empires and nation-states; they were unable to comprehend the divisions and alliances that transcended national affinities.

American scholars and policy makers, Khalilzad suggested, were further limited by their binary vision of international politics. He was never one to diminish the East-West conflict. He did, however, call attention to the limitations of the comfortable fiction of two rigid camps: the liberal democracies—pluralistic, egalitarian, and beholden to the public will—and the ideologically driven, totalitarian entities where elites imposed their unyielding values on a cringing populace. Beyond this conceptual, Western-preferred pale, societies were motivated by other concerns, ranging from religion to ethnicity, which had only fluid and tenuous ties to the East-West game of thrones. In post-Soviet Afghanistan, for example, the United States' blind support of Pakistan's meddling among rival mujahideen factions had exacerbated internal chaos.[21]

"Anarchy in Afghanistan," Khalilzad explained, was a petri dish for understanding anarchy among nations. In lieu of a constraining dominant power, constant shifts in factional loyalties had produced violent exercises in self-help that had torn the entire region apart, thereby facilitating the fateful Soviet intervention. Following the collapse of the Soviet invasion, the United States had been in a unique position to encourage, if not to impose, a power-sharing arrangement in the country. Instead, the nation's clueless foreign policy establishment remained beholden to devious Pakistani designs that eventually enabled the rise of the Taliban.

Chaos in Afghanistan was not only the result of factional warfare. Writing in 1997, Khalilzad observed that the Afghan civil war had "become a mini-'great game.' Pakistan is the most important outside player . . . Iran, Russia, Saudi Arabia, Uzbekistan, Turkmenistan, Tajikistan, the United States and India" also jostled for influence in Afghanistan.[22]

Khalilzad offered extensive accounts of other lost opportunities in the turbulent Northern Tier. These countries were caught in a maelstrom of economic and political convulsions that simultaneously challenged, aided, and transcended their national integrity. Soviet policy in the region fascinated Khalilzad, as the Soviets seemed so much more adroit than their flat-footed American counterparts. Published mostly in the early 1980s, his articles compared alleged Soviet nimbleness in reacting to regional realities with the inertia evident among a dazed and dispirited American foreign policy establishment still laboring under the cloud of failure in Vietnam, and now encumbered further by the recent hostage humiliation in Iran.[23]

As early as the late 1970s, the Soviets had allegedly identified the unraveling of familiar national patterns in the Northern Tier. Political fragmentation, economic crises, and the pallor of religious crusades had affected all countries in the region. While the Americans chalked up these convulsions to Soviet intervention, Khalilzad made an alternative case. The causes of unrest and disintegration were primarily internal; the Soviets were merely reacting nimbly to the opportunities and challenges of this fluid situation. By contrast, the United States demonstrated unimaginative responses, all of which had detrimentally affected American-led anti-Soviet regional pact agreements. The Soviets recognized the opportunities of ethnic disruption, as well as autonomous and supranational impulses that either bolstered or confounded the nation-state. Reacting with what Khalilzad considered skill and flexibility, the Soviet Union garnered relationships and alliances at the expense of the United States.

The key to Soviet achievements, an admiring Khalilzad observed, was political opportunism, a strategy that offended the Victorian sensibilities of their Western counterparts. Russians forged and dropped alliances with no moral compunctions other than a commitment to their own narrow interests. Gainful occasions for such enterprising actors were abundant. Opportunities arose, in Khalilzad's view, from "a crisis of national integration such as ethnic and religious conflicts; from a crisis of political and economic development, producing conflicts between groups with different ideological beliefs; from regional conflicts; from local nationalism when directed against the West; and from Islam when directed against pro-Western regimes."[24]

Khalilzad marveled at the manner in which the Soviets opportunistically reined in and unleashed local communist parties, dispensed and withheld foreign aid to extract difficult concessions, and made or broke pacts with religious entities. They cheerfully enforced policies that contravened Soviet policy and ideology when it suited their purposes. Despite their ostensible contempt for the "opium of the masses," the Soviets aligned themselves with Islamic republicanism, only to turn against such alliances when change served a larger cause. The Soviets offered selective aid to Pakistan, while simultaneously aiding and abetting separatist movements there; they fomented Kurdish separatism only to withdraw support when regional political tides changed course. "The Soviets have emphasized different goals at different times," noted Khalilzad, "depending on factors such as the ideological predisposition of indigenous ruler(s) and the Soviet preoccupation in other parts of the world."[25]

By contrast, Khalilzad continued, American policy makers reacted awkwardly and detrimentally, owing to multiple inhibitions—moral, political, and even cognitive. To begin with, administration officials and their corresponding academics seemed blind to the glaring fact that "the causes of the instabilities in the Northern Tier are largely internal."[26] The Soviets had undeniably fomented dissension and anti-American sentiment whenever possible, but the source of instability was largely independent of Soviet intervention. Lacking insight, Americans reacted poorly, he thought, to any deviation from familiar political patterns.

One of Khalilzad's favorite examples was the way the United States had mishandled the Cypriot crisis. Unable to recognize that, at times, blood is thicker than the diluted waters of multinational security pacts, and unwilling to recognize the inevitability of the Turkish invasion, the United States reacted ineptly. A weapons embargo imposed on Turkey merely drove this important ally out of regional security pacts and into a Russian bear hug. The American embargo of Turkey following the 1974 Turkish incursion into Northern Cyprus appeared disproportionate and oblivious to the power of ethnic identity politics in the world of states. Khalilzad reasoned that the United States should have reacted differently, given Turkey's "crucial contributions to Western defense . . . including protection of the southern flanks of NATO; the defense of the Persian Gulf from a potential Soviet threat; guarding the security of the Eastern Mediterranean," among other services.[27]

Modernization Theory Discredited

This severe public blow to a crucial ally illustrated for Khalilzad how the United States often proved its own worst enemy. American policy makers, he argued, were wedded to an evolutionary trajectory of nationhood, in which modern nation-states superseded primordial kinship networks and ethnic affiliations. Any global event that could not be shoehorned into the paradigm of nation-states was either ignored or interpreted as a deviant, perhaps Soviet-inspired, event. Separatist challenges to any member of the league of nation-states, therefore, led American policy makers to freeze or, even worse, to circle the wagons around a fiction of nationhood as an entity with fixed and sealed borders and unwavering internal cohesion. All other forms of collective identity were written out of the American approach to global machinations in the Northern Tier, in particular, and to the Third World, in general. A singular "focus on stability has often worked to the detriment of an effective policy," Khalilzad explained. "Concern with maintaining existing, superficially stable political systems has caused a suppression in the perception of and policy toward social changes. The result has been an alignment with those nominally in power at the cost of lost opportunities in regard to alternative political actors and currents."[28]

During his stint as full-fledged academic at Columbia, Khalilzad lambasted the deadweight of modernization theory on the American global vision. He chastised his colleagues for their facile endorsement of a eurythmic process in which democratization, industrialization, and secularization moved hand in hand in an inevitable, historical progression from primordial societies to the modern nation-state. This stupendously parochial construct, he maintained, had blinded the American policy establishment to the motivating power of religion in modern-day Iran, as well as in other momentous events in the Muslim world.[29]

Contemporary political thought assumed that the trajectory of modernization was universal in the values it instilled and in its evolutionary political arrangements. One of the central tenants of the modernization paradigm was the diminishing role in the political process it assigned to religion. A "cherished" assumption, Khalilzad noted in an article written with his wife, Cheryl Benard, was "that secularization accompanies industrialization and social change, with the traditional elites and belief systems giving way to a modern state, and religion occupying its allotted space in the private realm" only.[30] Modernization theorists expected developing countries to follow a path blazed by the developed Western exemplars, assuming that the journey toward modernization would be made somewhat smoother "by the pioneer function of the West, which had already created modern social forms and institutions and could therefore serve as a model."[31]

Any evidence to the contrary was explained away by categorizing deviancies as mere Third World variations of the dominant theme. American political scientists practiced what Samuel Huntington had defined as "accommodation": the glib transformation of divergent developments into supporting evidence for the reigning paradigm. Benard and Khalilzad quoted Huntington: "Almost anything that happens in the developing countries—coups, ethnic struggles, revolutionary wars— become part of the process of development, however contradictory or retrogressive this may appear on the surface."[32]

Iran served as a case in point. Prior to the revolution, countless academics had held up the modern Persian state as the quintessential example of successful modernization. With a burgeoning and vigorous middle class, expanding access to education, and a GNP that far outstripped its nearest competitors in the Muslim world, Iran appeared well on its way to becoming a prototypical modern state. The Shah's repressiveness was swept under the carpet as a momentary lapse in his otherwise steady leadership. Infatuation with the modernization paradigm effaced all signs of the pending religious revolution in Iran. An alienated middle class, embracing Shiism as a central part of its identity and the source of its moral values, defied the provinciality of conventional wisdom in the United States.

Flat-footed academics and government officials looked on with amazement as Iranians bypassed the premises of modernization theory and embraced, instead, primordial religious affinities. The Iranian revolution proved that there were no inherent connections between the various and allegedly interlocking notions of modernization. Solipsistic academics, Benard and Khalilzad argued, had promoted a universal theory of political development far removed from the messy forces that actually ruled the world.[33]

Modernization Theory Embraced

Khalilzad left his incisive criticism of modernization theory behind without apparent regret upon exiting the groves of academe. As a scholar Khalilzad had made his critique of modernization theory perfectly clear. When he eventually attained a position of authority in government, however, Khalilzad proved quite selective in applying what he had previously preached. Instead he accepted, promoted, and perpetuated the very same policies he had criticized in his scholarly articles. He adopted the position that Afghanistan was a normative, albeit pluralistic, nation-state that had been momentarily corrupted by exogenous forces. Writing in 2005 as he completed a two-year tenure as U.S. ambassador to Afghanistan, he asserted that the United States could smooth Afghanistan's transition to the world of functioning democracies if it would employ a light touch and not behave like the discredited Soviet conquerors.[34] Continuing this embrace of modernization theory as U.S. ambassador to Iraq and then to the United Nations, Khalilzad affirmed that "people everywhere are essentially the same in their desire for those freedoms" cherished by Americans. "They know these are the ideas and values that made the great countries what they are. That's why I often talked to the Afghans and Iraqis about the difficulties that America itself had in the beginning."[35] Afghanistan, in other words, could and should follow the path to modernized statehood that had been blazed by entities like the United States.

Khalilzad expressed similar thoughts on Iraq. Religious fissures and tumultuous ethnic divides now struck him as a natural manifestation of pluralism rather than a sign of dysfunctional identity politics. The creation of a modern, functioning Iraqi state would, he predicted, happen in a manner not unlike the theories he had debunked in his previous life as a scholar. Khalilzad chose not to question the integrity of the statist fiction of Iraq, thrown together by colonial overlords with little regard for the region's pluralism. As far as the new Khalilzad was concerned, a few structural pieces were missing from the puzzle, and it would be an American responsibility to foster these mechanisms. "First, you do need a certain set of circumstances for democracy to take root and become effective. . . . It's not just about elections. You need democratic institutions, the rule of law, and the instruments of civil society. And some of the countries in this region do start at a low level in terms of their preparation in that regard." The problem with instilling such values was that "the broader Middle East as a region is just not normal." Progression toward a functioning modernized state was stymied by dysfunctional yet powerful tugs-of-war. Mutually hostile religious divides, competing ethnic loyalties, and disruptive interventionism had corrupted the basically sound foundation of some local Iraqi variation of a functioning American-style democracy. Despite these tremendous challenges, as well as his own youthful critique of modernization theory, Khalilzad endorsed some vague variation of a Western-style democracy as the natural course for Iraq. "If Iraq were an island," protected from the meddling of aggressive neighbors such as Iran, "I think we would have seen much more progress on political reconciliation by now."[36]

As Khalilzad would make abundantly clear in some of his other writings on Iraq, the removal of a rapacious dictator—one who not only abused his own subjects but had every intent of exporting his predatory tactics—was a prerequisite for any move from the divisive tribalism of Mesopotamia to the bright horizons of a pluralistic democratic nation-state. Following in the footsteps of the senior acolyte, Paul Wolfowitz, Khalilzad approached democracy as the natural societal order even along the fractious Euphrates river. Democracy would transpire normally and even rapidly, barring impediments such as internal repression and external meddling. Iraq, as well as other authoritarian regimes in the region, would become fledgling democracies once the tyrannical layer of their present political systems was removed.

In fact, as he explained in a detailed analysis of nation building in Afghanistan, the modernization paradigm actually worked if it was turned on its head. Modernity would be achieved, but only after the imposition—usually through an enlightened intervention—of a domesticated version of Islam beholden to democracy, popular sovereignty, individual rights, and the rule of law. Afghanistan suggested that impediments to democracy could be contained, and perhaps rolled back, when an "enlightened" external force—in this case the United States—"responded to the deep aspirations" among indigenous Afghans "for normalcy, development, and democracy."[37] Afghanis viewed "the fifty years before the communist coup in April 1978 as a golden age, one in which they enjoyed peace, made slow but steady material progress, and saw their country take steps toward instituting a constitutional monarchy with real powers in Parliament."[38] In other words, according to Khalilzad, a statist democracy was the natural order even in vulnerable, disjointed societies such as Afghanistan and Iraq.

Democracy would flourish in Afghanistan, Iraq, and elsewhere if an altruistic broker would agree to resolve exogenous "sources of instability," while being constantly vigilant of the historical fact that "too large a foreign military presence has resulted in an unhealthy dependency that leads local security and other capabilities to atrophy."[39] Regional anarchy, described as "the zero-sum mindset" of geopolitical competition, had sucked a multicultural Afghanistan into a series of regional conflicts that had torn the country apart. The role of the United States was to "effectively signal our commitment, through both words and deeds, to leaders who are convinced of our short attention span."[40]

The sum of Khalilzad's comments stand in stark contradiction with his early scholarly skepticism of modernization theory and the fictions of states in the Muslim world. The major conclusion he drew from his tours of duty in Afghanistan and Iraq was that democracy was a natural state of affairs and was not governed by the one-directional trajectory associated with modernization theory. The seeds of organic democracies were present in traditional society, he now argued, but they were fragile. When the instability of regional power politics was contained, and assuming that religious tensions could be domesticated, there appeared to be no inherent clash between traditional societies and their modern statist counterparts. Modernity and tradition were not asymmetrical prospects. There was no great dichotomy between past and present, tradition and modernity. A pluralistic nation-state now appeared to replace Khalilzad's previous partiality for cohesive ethnic entities as an antidote to instability.

A number of factors may account for Khalilzad's transformation. To begin with, his newfound affinity with modernization theory and the nation-state may have been a sign of opportunism, a reaction to modernization theory's shifting fortunes in both in academia and in policy circles. Khalilzad may also have been quite sincere. As Jonathan Stevenson explains in an incisive study of post–Cold War challenges, contemporary theories of the containment of a global Caliphate hinged on "the political legitimacy" of a certain type of Islamic state as an antidote to messianic visions.[41] An Islamic version of democracy—hopefully less messianic that Shia republicanism in Iran—would provide a common denominator for the ethnic tapestry of countries like Iraq and Afghanistan. Within this context, positive economics, rather than retrograde culture, would thwart global visions of a resurgent caliphate. A prosperous Iraqi state, with expansive economic opportunity for the entire patchwork of ethnic and sectarian affinities could, in theory, resist the chaotic strains of eschatological visions. Rational economic behavior, in this case the lure of prosperity, would trump the disruptive influence of religious, cultural, and sectarian tensions.

Cheryl Benard

It is at this point that the influence of Cheryl Benard, Khalilzad's spouse, becomes quite evident. The child of an itinerant U.S. military family, Benard was born in New Orleans in 1953 and grew up between Austria and the United States. Her undergraduate degree at the American University of Beirut was in political science and Islamic studies. Upon receiving a PhD from the University of Vienna in 1975, she held several academic positions in Austria. From 2002 to 2012 Benard was a senior analyst at RAND, where she led the Initiative for Middle Eastern Youth as well as RAND's Alternative Strategies Initiative. Benard is the author of two novels: *Turning on the Girls* (2001), a feminist futuristic farce, and *Moghul Buffet* (1998), a biting indictment of political Islam and its misogynistic manifestations.[42]

Moghul Buffet is a cautionary tale of sexual repression in Pakistan, and the inability of its Islamist enforcers to live by their own harsh sexual code of conduct. Set in Peshawar, Pakistan—the Pakistani equivalent of the Wild West—Benard's ostensible murder mystery follows the fortunes of a young Pakistani woman, who becomes the mistress of an Islamic fundamentalist rabble-rouser. His illicit passions eventually lead to his downfall and her liberation. The political subtext of *Moghul Buffet* argues that the harsh version of religion sweeping through the Muslim world would collapse under the weight of its own contradictions, leaving a vacuum for different political forces to fill. The novel ends on a disturbing note, forcing the reader to wonder who will capitalize on the imminent demise of Pakistan's self-contradictory Islamic regime. Several characters seek to fill the void, including a group of sophisticated Pakistani secularists, an inept Marxist, and a lurking Taliban activist.

Beyond the world of fiction, Benard offered explicit policy recommendations for reform in the Muslim World. The most salient of these was her 2003 RAND study, *Civil Democratic Islam.* Funded by the conservative Smith Richardson Society—which also supported the Nitze School of Advanced International Studies during the tenure of Dean Paul Wolfowitz—the seventy-page document offers a blueprint for "religion building" in the Islamic world. "If 'nation building' is a daunting task, 'religion building,' " by which she meant the infusion of faith with Western values of gender equity, pluralism, and the respect for civil and human rights, "is immeasurably more perilous and complex." Religion building in the Muslim world entailed the domestication of the dark energy of Islam through the imposition of "the values of civil society and the Western vision of civilization." A necessary condition for functional statehood in the Middle East was the neutralization of "political actors in the region [who] deliberately seek to 'Islamize' the debate in a way they think will further their goals."[43] In other words, religion building would have to precede any attempts at nation building.

"Religion building" as an antidote to the hijacking of Islam by radical elements required a concerted effort to win over these impressionable youth of the Muslim world by conventional broadcasting networks, new social media, and the infusion of funds into organizations supporting "modernists" or progressive Islamists who militated against the harsh world of Islamic orthodoxy. The key to supporting modernists in the Muslim world, she argued, hinged on positioning "secularism and modernism as a 'counterculture' option for disaffected Islamic youth."[44]

Sexual liberation would be an integral part of this effort to attract youth. By ceding center stage to Islamic fundamentalists, she explained, the West had obligingly participated in the warping of the mental health of the impressionably young. The harsh repression of sexual impulse, she argued, scarred Islamic youth by violating basic "psychological needs" and channeling this pent-up sexual energy into nefarious causes.[45]

Benard identified distinct similarities between the Cold War of ideas waged by the United States and the contemporary struggle to "build free and democratic institutions and organizations" in the Muslim world. "The success of U.S. containment policy required (in addition to the military shield provided by U.S. nuclear and conventional forces) the creation of parallel democratic institutions to contest communist domination of civil society. The close link between the U.S. grand strategy and its efforts to build democratic networks was a key ingredient in the overall success of the U.S. policy of containment; as such, it provides a model for policymakers today."[46]

The Cold War experience offered a way, but, Benard complained, there was very little will. Over the years, she observed, the West has allowed a virulent strain of radical Islam to flourish in its very midst, unimpaired and without fostering alternatives for bringing domestic strains under the umbrella of Western civil society. Driven by a misguided sense of ecumenism, the West has tolerated—if not encouraged, in the name of religious freedom—extreme versions of domestic Islam. A case in point, according to Benard, was the mad rush in the United States to accept headscarves as "a minor matter of preference in dress code." This supposedly "cheap" signaling of tolerance was "unwittingly taking a major stance on a central, wildly contested issue," thereby aligning a clueless West with the most radical elements of Islam in their battle with "the modernists and the secularists."[47] In the name of tolerance, the United States was undermining its own core values and creating difficulties for its allies in the Muslim world.

Benard's recipe for religion building was ultimately quite unconvincing. This scheme to create a reformed confessional society governed by individual conviction rather than theological superstructure was ambitious to the point of being unrealistic. Her version of an Islamic society immersed in Western values and promoted by marginal groups on the periphery of Islam implicitly acknowledged a glaringly self-evident truth. Life did not imitate the art of her fictional construction of Islamic society.

If anything, Benard's unremarkable remedies for undoing centuries of religious-based community structures acknowledged the enduring power of traditional faith-based social arrangements as an unreceptive environment for change. The vast majority of believing Muslims—in Iraq, Afghanistan, and even in the Pakistan of her novel—rejected the separation of Mosque and State and her defanged version of Islam.

Her ebullient praise notwithstanding, Benard's enthusiasm seemed hollow, if not forced. Ultimately, the study read like the manifesto of a conservative foundation that would brook no dissent in its mission of spreading the benefits of Western society to a religious terra incognita. But even Benard acknowledged that the odds of success were low.

Unlike her faux faith in religion building in the Muslim world, Benard appeared more convincing in her advocacy for women's rights. Both her fiction and nonfiction identified a growing public space for women as a catalyst for, and indication of, change in the volatile social and political climate of the post–Cold War years. The spread of democracy, she argued, resided in a militant promotion of women's rights. The divide separating authoritarian societies from democratic ones was defined by "the status and condition of women. Patriarchal societies that treat women as inferior generally do the same to their ethnic and religious minorities." The "disenfranchisement and oppression of women" and accompanying male entitlement invariably fostered domestic authoritarianism as well as a rapacious engagement with the world. "Almost inevitably," the aggressive logic of unequal gender spheres extended to the domain of international politics. Societies that discriminated or excluded women from the public domain were antimeritocratic, inevitably corrupt, less prosperous, and awash with violence derived from "surplus testosterone." Gender equality, Benard argued, was the ultimate "canary-in-the-mine test. If a particular decision or compromise is bad for women, it will be bad for human security, bad for development, and detrimental to a genuine peace."[48]

The Projection of Power

Much like his spouse, Zalmay Khalilzad has also advocated for gender equity. When asked about his stance on women's rights in post-Saddam Iraq, Khalilzad offered an instrumental explanation: "Iraq wants to be a successful country and you cannot be a successful country if you discriminate against half of your population, [if] you do not give them all the opportunities that are needed for them to achieve and contribute all they can."[49] Earlier, Khalilzad took credit for a "historic milestone" in Afghan history, when the new constitution enshrined the same political rights for both men and women.[50] Yet, contrary to his wife, who approached women's rights as a tool for containing the power of organized religion, Khalilzad was more circumspect. For him, the expanded role of women in the public sphere was a tool for the rapid rehabilitation of war-battered societies rather than a device for radical social transformation.

Khalilzad's theory for the transformation of the global arena did not entail radical social transformation. Global realignment, according to Khalilzad, still resided in the conventional venues of power politics among nations. Beginning in 1990, as deputy undersecretary for policy planning in George H. W. Bush's Department of Defense, Khalilzad delved into the production of papers on the strategic dilemmas facing the nation in the post–Cold War world. He had no compunctions, moreover, about sharing his thoughts with the public beyond the Beltway.

In April 1992 *New Yorker* correspondent Nicholas Lemann met with a "senior official" from the outgoing Bush Sr. administration who handed him a confidential strategic paper. The document did not sit well with Lemann. Given the sheer amount of energy invested in climbing the ladder in Washington, Lemann was shocked to discover that the leaked item was a "bland, opaque document" that was "physically indistinguishable from a high-school term paper."[51] This sophomoric report, Lemann announced, amounted to sad evidence of the declining imagination of the American political class. The document in question was a sanitized version of a position paper prepared by Zalmay Khalilzad in his role as deputy undersecretary for policy planning and later published by RAND in a different format some years after his departure from government.[52]

The creation of the document was a textbook example of the not-so-invisible college of Wohlstetter acolytes in action. At the time, Khalilzad was serving under Scooter Libby, a Princeton student of and principal deputy to Paul Wolfowitz, the undersecretary for policy in Dick Cheney's Department of Defense. Abram Shulsky, the director of special plans in the Department of Defense, was a principal participant in the drafting of the document.[53] Shulsky had roomed with Wolfowitz during the undergraduate Telluride years, had received his doctorate in political science from the University of Chicago in 1972, and had served under Richard Perle when he was assistant secretary of defense during the Reagan years. All of these individuals were linked to Albert Wohlstetter, who, by some accounts, had seen this document before its circulation.[54]

The original document was leaked to the *New York Times,* prompting a political furor and intense embarrassment within the Bush administration.[55] Most of the criticism centered on the document's explicit recipe for American preeminence. The United States, according to the draft, would not only contain the rise of inimical rivals; the nation would preempt possible allied challenges, as well.

Khalilzad's spruced-up and expanded RAND version of the report—questioningly entitled *From Containment to Global Leadership?*—provided a series of ostensibly frightening but actually rather unimaginative alternatives to a world governed by an unrivaled American superpower.[56] Khalilzad argued that the United States faced several unappealing options in the wake of the Soviet Union's collapse. It could accept a return to the state of anarchy envisioned by the "realists," which had prevailed prior to the bipolarity of the Cold War. This state of affairs, he warned, was unappealing. Anarchy in a post–Cold War environment, where nuclear technology was widespread, threatened to elevate the precarious equilibrium among the nuclear powers to intolerable levels. As Robert Jervis wrote, in an article Khalilzad cited, there was a distinct possibility that countries such as "Germany and Japan, freed from the security and constraints of the Cold War, will seek nuclear weapons," following the rule whereby "great powers seek the most prestigious and powerful weapons available even in the absence of a clear threat."[57] It stood to reason that other regional powers with global ambitions would follow suit. The sheer number of contacts points for precipitating thermonuclear warfare—"dyads," in political science argot—would therefore ultimately dilute even the fragile stability that had existed during the standoff between two superpowers.

One alternative to the return to anarchy would be a resurgence of some new iteration of the Cold War. An ambitious power in either Europe or Asia "might seek global hegemony and the United States would face another global Cold War and the risk of a world war even more catastrophic than the last."[58] The return of a bipolar world governed by a resurgent delicate balance of terror would mean a new "Great Trade-

Off," in which peace hinged on the somewhat optimistic assumption that future leaders would behave at least as logically as the Soviet leadership.[59]

The report concluded that the regime of self-help in international politics, in which all players focused exclusively on their own interests regardless of the consequences for other players, would be infinitely more volatile than any past scenario. Even if a nuclear arms race among aspiring global powers could be avoided—and even if, somehow, a new Cold War did not materialize—the number of regional conflicts and friction points in a rudderless global arena could still have disastrous implications for the United States.

As a case in point, Khalilzad envisioned that even a momentary absence of superpower dominance in the Persian Gulf would eventually alter regional alliances and disrupt the integrity of sovereign states, all to the detriment of American interests. In a world of regional power struggles unchecked by global hegemons, either Iran or Iraq might come to dominate the Gulf region and, inevitably, attempt to bring the rest of the Arab Middle East under its orbit. In addition to the damage this regional hegemon could inflict on the economies of the Western world, other crucial American interests would be affected, as well. "Israeli security problems would multiply . . . increasing the risk of war between the Arabs and the Israelis." Such a crisis in the Middle East, spiraling out of control and cascading into other arenas, would inflict devastating economic consequences on the United States. Even if actual conflict in the region could be avoided, "higher oil prices would reduce the U.S. standard of living. Turmoil in Asia and Europe would force major economic adjustments in the United States."[60]

The means of avoiding these two grim scenarios, Khalilzad proposed, was to defy balance-of-power predictions, either in their multipolar or bipolar versions. Instead of wallowing in the paradigms of the past, the United States should instead take advantage of this brief window of opportunity to assert itself as the singular global hegemon. The United States should "seek to retain global leadership and to preclude the rise of a global rival or a return to multipolarity for the indefinite future."[61] While maintaining such a posture would not be cost-free, the payoff would be game changing. Under the auspices of its hegemonic stature, the United States could foster the rise of free-market, pluralistic democracies in the Muslim world and beyond. Stability would prevail instead of volatile friction because war among democratic nations committed to free trade was "unthinkable."[62]

This type of strategic daydreaming—which had struck Nicholas Lemann as sophomoric—was premised on a rare historic moment. The collapse of its Soviet rival appeared to have left the United States with undisputed preeminence in every measurable sense. Its robust economy, military might, cutting-edge technology, and geopolitical preeminence had produced the foundation for a new global system without the need to contend with peer powers. "For several centuries," Khalilzad wrote in another article, "the international order had been characterized by multipolarity and a balance of power."[63] In the new millennium, the United States could conceivably enjoy solitary and unprecedented preeminence without a war and with no budding "hostile alliance" in sight.[64]

Khalilzad was suggesting that the collapse of the Soviet Union—the result of insolvent investments in empire building—was a unique moment in the annals of statehood as it left one power, the United States, in a position of primacy in just about every dimension of power possible. Given this revolutionary shift in power distribution, Khalilzad envisioned new global political arrangements. Contrary to the enunciations of the unimaginative and fainthearted, unipolar preeminence was not an ephemeral illusion. Instead, it was a momentary opportunity to move out of the shadow of balance-of-power paradigms. If the nation's stewards failed to seize it, this "fleeting, once-in-a-lifetime" opportunity to shape the fate of the Free World would be squandered and lost.[65]

Contemporary theory in academia and in Washington, Khalilzad complained, militated against seizing the day. The policy establishment was constrained by the axiomatic assumption that international order is inherently unstable, and that the rise to a unipolar status would prove transient at best. Conventional knowledge assumed that hegemony would linger for an indeterminate period until it produced a dissatisfied countervailing entity with the capacity to challenge the single superpower. Khalilzad, by contrast, remonstrated against entrapment within this paradigm. Alternatives were contingent on the will of policy makers, not some hidden hand. The United States could remain bounded by the rules of balance of power at its own peril—or the nation could break the cycle and create a stable *Pax Americana*.

A first crucial move in this direction would be to step out of the cave of prevailing wisdom and acknowledge that a perpetual state of anarchy among nations was not inevitable. Academic mandarins had proclaimed that only myopic cheerleaders refused to recognize that a return to multipolarity began the very day that the Soviet Union collapsed and the United States hastily declared victory.[66] Khalilzad professed the contrary. The United States controlled its own destiny. The nation could, indeed, remain within the comfort zone of the balance-of-power paradigm. After all, it was a matter of choice. Were the United States to decide against asserting its preeminence for fear of arousing dormant rivals or for any other reason, then the familiar struggles for power and security among nations—bipolar, multipolar, or any other variation— would reoccur as predicted by the guardians of the paradigm.

Khalilzad acknowledged that in a post–Cold War world it would be tempting for Americans to go back to the future. There were compelling reasons to withdraw into a comfortable isolationist shell. A reduced military budget would allow the country to tend to its own domestic challenges, lower taxes, and rely on its regional sphere of influence. History, he argued, had proven otherwise. The annals of the twentieth century suggested that such disengagement would inevitably lead to some form of instability that would affect the United States directly. Power vacuums would be filled by upstarts—by which he meant nations whose economic and military capacities were linked to deeply ingrained expansionist ambitions.

Those upstarts might be a resurgent Germany or Japan, a predatory dictator from the Middle East, or, most probably, an Asian tiger. Khalilzad dedicated a long treatise to the rise of China following the demise of the Soviet Union. The level of uncertainty on China's future led Khalilzad to hedge his bets. Given its tremendous economic surge, China could conceivably generate a robust middle class that would push it into the community of peaceful relations. Conversely, an insurgent China, still in the grips of its doctrinaire Communist Party, could conceivably fill the void vacated by the Soviet Union. The broad spectrum of possibilities did little to settle the raging battle of policy experts. They pushed in divergent directions toward either aggressive containment or, conversely, engagement with the emerging Chinese giant, in the hope of nurturing incipient democratic trends. Khalilzad's rather cagey conclusion was to hedge his bets and advocate for "congagement," a flexible policy that could go either way, according to whatever circumstances might face the United States.[67]

Khalilzad's most salient conclusion in both his China study and his more comprehensive surveys of strategic challenges was neither the re-surgence of a bipolar standoff nor a return to the anarchy of states. Given America's unrivaled global preeminence, the most predictable threat would be regional powers asserting themselves over areas of strategic importance to the United States. "During the Cold War, the United States and its allies faced a global adversary" with an insatiable reach. "The absence of such a global rival has improved the global security environ-ment for the United States and its allies qualitatively. Now the greatest threats are regional."[68]

In the case of communist China, Khalilzad did not anticipate the re-incarnation of Soviet expansionism. At worst, he expected an attempt to assert sovereignty over contested areas, such as Taiwan. Beyond China, the greatest threat to regional stability, he asserted, was in the Persian Gulf. "The Persian Gulf is one of the primary regional fronts of the new era. It is in the United States' interest to keep the threats small and pre-clude the domination of critical regions, like the Gulf, by hostile re-gional powers."[69]

At no point did Khalilzad envision a strategic threat emanating from an entity other than a nation-state. To the degree that he recognized nonstate actors, he assigned to them limited territorial ambitions. Osama bin Laden's preaching was rarified noise rather than a pertinent signal of trouble in the offing. In 1995 Khalilzad defined bin Laden's presence in Afghanistan as a localized threat primarily effecting American in-terests in the Gulf. He expressed concern over Afghanistan's granting of asylum to "a Saudi businessman known to sponsor anti-U.S. terror in Saudi Arabia."[70] On the eve of 9/11, bin Laden was assigned dimin-ished, regional status in Khalilzad's analysis of Afghanistan as a "rogue state" controlled by religious extremists. "Clearly, bin Laden is a dan-gerous terrorist who must be captured and prosecuted. Yet the U.S. focus on him, rather than the trend he represents, is misguided."[71] The core issue, Khalilzad insisted, was not a globalized radical Islam, but, the lo-calized threat of rogue states who provided support for such marginal characters.

In the spring 2001 edition of *RAND Review,* Khalilzad, together with his RAND colleague Robert Hunter and RAND trustee and former de-fense secretary Frank Carlucci, presented the executive summary of a bipartisan committee on foreign relations advising the transition team of George W. Bush. The document identified the three most "critical issues" facing the nation as "(1) national missile defense, (2) a modernized defense program, and (3) Arab-Israeli peacemaking." In addition they added that the president should "be ready to meet crises that might erupt in places like Iraq, the Taiwan Strait, the Korean Peninsula, and Colombia."[72] The final report, entitled "Taking Charge," contained one paragraph on the threat of terrorism out of its seventy-eight pages. With the exception of the unlikely use of WMD by terrorists, the committee concluded that nonstate actors did not "pose serious threats to the U.S. or its allies."[73] The report contained an appendix of dissenting views and amendments by various members of the committee. Khalilzad, at the time the chair for international security studies at RAND, saw no reason to add a friendly amendment of any kind on the threat of nonstate actors in the Middle East or elsewhere.

Iraq and the Containment of Islamic Republicanism

Khalilzad's most important contributions to strategic studies focused mainly on the oil-rich Gulf. His constructions of Gulf power plays offer important clues for understanding the fixation on regime change in Iraq, even though—or because—a revivified Iran posed significantly greater dangers to both regional and global stability.

Within this context, the archival record suggests that Khalilzad may have laid the foundations for the Wohlstetter school's latter-day fixation on Iraq. In a series of internal memoranda prepared for "Albert Wohlstetter and the Power Projection Group" at RAND, Khalilzad described Iraqi ambitions in the region, with particular emphasis on Kuwait. Written in the late 1970s, the reports describe the multiple strategic opportunities available for an Iraq poised to conquer Kuwait. Such an enterprise, Khalilzad considered, might be accomplished by sheer brute force, or more likely by fomenting internal dissension within Kuwait—strife between native Kuwaitis and the country's large Palestinian community, for example—or by aiding and abetting a palace coup by Kuwait military officers sympathetic to the Baathist cause. The most likely scenario, he thought, did not involve any actual belligerent acts, but rather coercion though a projection of Iraqi power. "A man will usually hand a mugger his wallet upon seeing his gun. Similarly, the weaker side in a conflict will often make concessions without being physically forced to do so."[74]

Iraq's projection of power in the strategically important Persian Gulf region had become particularly ominous given the challenges of imposing a countervailing hegemony, in any region, in the post-Vietnam era. "The recent strain in U.S.-Saudi relations," Khalilzad wrote, "largely reflects a serious doubt by Saudi officials about such a U.S. capability and resolve."[75] The perception in the Gulf was that, since the Vietnam War, the United States had projected weakness and irresolution and could not be counted on to contain the destabilizing forces rumbling through the Middle East.

Khalilzad consistently argued that it was Iran, rather than Iraq, that posed the most lethal threat to regional stability. He identified in the Islamic Republic of Iran many of the attributes of the former Soviet empire.[76] The Republic embraced a messianic vision bearing remarkable similarities to the Soviet regime that had preoccupied the United States during most of the second half of the twentieth century. It espoused an "elaborate and totalistic ideology," maintaining and sustaining a "system of one-party rule" through "the creation of an image of the leader as an incarnation of supreme wisdom and indomitable will power." The party and its leader solidified power by creating "conditions of external stress, in part because of domestic political considerations," and in part as an extension of an internationalist ideology of "world rebellion" and the "belief in the inevitability of one's victory." Iran's hardline leaders promoted a bellicose extension of their messianic republicanism and "the inevitable spread of 'liberating Islamic ideology,'" first to neighboring countries, and, by extension, throughout the world.[77]

The Iran-Iraq War had slowed down the implementation of this doctrine and had kept Iran's predatory vision at bay. In Khalilzad's view, it was in American interests to nurture and sustain a balance of power between Iraq and Iran as a relatively cheap manner of constraining Iranian designs. Much to American policy makers' chagrin, Saddam Hussein became the proverbial spoiler of this strategy, which aimed to achieve regional tranquility by balancing local powers. In theory, the only way to contain Iran was by aiding and abetting its Iraqi nemesis. Given Saddam's aggressive impulse and the lack of any fundamental change in the Iraqi regime following Desert Storm, any attempt to sustain the balance of power by maintaining Iraq's relative strength was "politically impossible."[78]

It was this dilemma that had produced the Clinton administration's concept of "dual containment," containing both countries through a combination of international sanctions and embargoes. For Khalilzad, this strategy was inconsistent with American objectives. "The concept implies that U.S. objectives towards Iran and Iraq are the same— which they are not." American policy toward Iran did "not seek the overthrow of the Islamic government, but rather, its containment," with the ultimate hope that, much like the Soviet Union, the regime might collapse under the weight of unsustainable economic commitments and imperial overstretch. By contrast, Khalilzad wrote in 1995, "the unstated American goal with respect to Iraq appears to be the overthrow of the regime."[79] In other words, a friendly regime in Iraq was the only feasible manner of controlling the much greater threat of an ideologically expansive Iran. Regime change in Iraq was an indispensable condition for resisting Iran's relentless march.

The marketing of this convoluted design for the assertion of an American dominion in Iraq was placed in the hands of a third member of the Wohlstetters' inner circle. Armed with Khalilzad's insight on Middle East power politics, and having endorsed the paradigm of cyclical historical trends, a pugnacious Richard Perle accepted the task of normalizing a Middle Eastern realignment by hegemonic design. Arguably the most trusted of the Wohlstetters' disciples, Perle moved beyond ponderous tracts on Gulf power politics. His intense vilification of the Iraqi rogue state energized visions of a clash of civilizations that only an American hegemon could control.

11

Richard Perle

Prejudice as a Cultural Weapon

P REJUDICE, ZALMAY KHALILZAD and Cheryl Benard observed, "is often taken to mean a kind of defect of reason, a prior judgment based on excessive or incorrect generalization." Their own analysis of seething waves of prejudice along the Western-Islamic divide suggested otherwise. Prejudice "is not just a kind of arbitrary ignorance," they found. "It performs important social and political functions" ranging from creating the "cohesiveness of the group, to maintain[ing] a certain order, to defend[ing] a power relationship, or to challeng[ing] it."[1]

In the Middle East and throughout the developing world, Khalilzad and Benard argued, "prejudicial images . . . facilitated the pursuit of the one goal the U.S. ultimately decided it valued most highly in the Third World: stability. The contradiction between the democratic intentions with which policy makers justified U.S. presence," and their acquiescence to injustices, "was bridged by theories" of inferiority, barbarism, and immorality of the Islamic Other.[2] Prejudice as theory, Benard and Khalilzad explained in a moment of insight predating the flames of 9/11, swept the "excessive burden of historic fact" under a proverbial orientalist rug.[3]

Richard Perle, the most uninhibited of the Wohlstetters' acolytes, tapped into this great "reservoir of prejudice" with panache, brushing aside all protestations to the contrary.[4] Wielding both fiction and nonfiction, Perle employed stereotype and innuendo to defend America's unipolar moment from its detractors. His oeuvre is made up of intermittent bursts of rage, sarcasm, and the selective mobilization of prejudice. His aggressive style contrasts with the more measured prose of Wolfowitz and Khalilzad. While sharing their same basic worldview, Perle eschewed debate, preferring, instead, to scorch the earth under his critics' feet.

Following the events of 9/11, and on the eve of the Iraq invasion, Perle unleashed rampages against a certain construct of militant Islam and its enablers in the West. He accused European allies of collaboration with a willful enemy and reproached a U.S. president for compromising America's security through heedless concessions to the enemy. Even supposedly solid American allies were not spared his tongue-lashings. Perle's rage against the threat of militant Islam and its appeasers was, in itself, a nonevent. Mainstream America shared many of his views on the threat of militant Islam. They were normative, to a large degree, for their times. If he can be faulted, it is for his merciless defamation of character and his use of guilt by association.

Perle was at his most bellicose when defending the turf of his Wohlstetter mentors. He was far more than a mundane disciple. The self he curated in his writing and public presentations was that of a virtual family member, closer to the Wohlstetters than any other member of the inner circle. He considered it his duty to sustain their legacy by all means possible. Within this context, Perle's impulse was to circle the wagons and respond with maximum firepower. He accepted with equanimity and some pride his reputation as the "Prince of Darkness."

Perle entered politics in 1969 as a member of Senator Henry "Scoop" Jackson's team, where he was later joined by Paul Wolfowitz and Abram Shulsky, at the time both were graduate students at the University of Chicago. All three had been recommended by Albert Wohlstetter. As a staffer for the Democratic senator from Washington State, he participated in forging the 1972 "Russian Wheat Deal" negotiated by Richard Nixon and the Soviet Union, which linked a major trade agreement with the Soviet Union to emigration rights for Soviet Jewry. Together with Paul Wolfowitz, he led Jackson's militant campaigns against strategic arms reduction initiatives with the Soviet Union.[5] Perle and Wolfowitz were instrumental in orchestrating the blocking of Senate ratification of the SALT II arms reduction agreement with the Soviet Union during the Carter administration (although its terms were honored by both sides).

For the most part, Perle preferred to work behind the scenes. His most prominent government assignment was as assistant secretary of defense for international security policy from 1981 to 1987, during the Reagan administration. In the first year of the George W. Bush administration, Perle was named chairman of the Pentagon's advisory Defense Policy Board by Defense Secretary Donald Rumsfeld, a position he was forced to resign following revelations of his ties with the defense arm of Hollinger International, the business empire of media mogul and convicted felon Conrad Black.[6] But by far Perle's most important political assignment began as a teenager, when he first met his mentor, Albert Wohlstetter.

The Wohlstetter Swimming Pool

Perle formed his bond with the Wohlstetters at their Laurel Canyon abode in the late 1950s. "I was in the eleventh grade at Hollywood High School when I had my first Wohlstetter tutorial, standing by the swimming pool at Woodstock Road," Perle reminisced in his funeral oration for Albert. "'The Delicate Balance of Terror' had recently appeared in *Foreign Affairs,* and Albert had just completed eighty or ninety classified briefings over many weeks in Washington. What a marvel of precision and compression that article was, and how intricate and subtle was the underlying analysis. I would never have pursued a career in strategic policy without Albert's patient, gentle, generous teaching which began one day in 1958 and continued for forty wonderful years. And I might be a good deal thinner if Albert had been less successful instructing me in the joys of the Michelin Guide."[7]

Given the story's ubiquity, it is instructive to linger momentarily at that poolside, as this vignette has taken on a life of its own. The Wohlstetters' only child, their daughter, Joan, who had invited her classmate to the Wohlstetter pool, now appears in countless websites as the indelible link between Perle and Albert. Seeking to cement the neocons' genealogical connections, and apparently not satisfied with a chance meeting at a swimming pool, the *New York Times* concocted matrimonial ties between Joan and Richard. A sheepish retraction reproduced another common falsehood, the claim that Albert had been Perle's doctoral adviser at the University of Chicago. In fact, Perle had never studied at Chicago, nor did he ever complete a PhD of any kind.[8] These errors are unsurprising, as Perle was an intimate confidante, much more than a mere disciple.

The Wohlstetters' Laurel Canyon Home, 1954. *Photograph by Julius Shulman. Architect: Josef Van der Kar. © J. Paul Getty Trust. Julius Shulman Photography Archive, 1936–1997. The Getty Research Institute, Los Angeles (2004.R.10).*

One can only imagine the sense of wonder that must have struck the young Richard Perle upon entering the Wohlstetter abode at 2805 Woodstock Road. The house was the epitome of modernism, wrapped in glass and seemingly suspended in the air over vistas of Laurel Canyon. Never shy of the camera, Albert invited the press into the Eames-furnished home, dubbed by the *Los Angeles Herald Examiner* as "the house that hangs in the sky."[9]

A voyeuristic press was particularly fascinated by the bonds of friendship between the Wohlstetters and their next-door neighbor, Josef Van der Kar, the architect of the Wohlstetters' stunning home. Van der Kar, who had worked for Albert in the abortive General Panels enterprise, was not only a talented craftsman but also, allegedly, a card-carrying communist and a victim of the House Un-American Activities investigations. The swimming pool and gardens, exuding sophistication and modernity, were the work of famed landscaper Garrett Eckbo.

Joan Wohlstetter and the Laurel Canyon swimming pool, 1954. *Photograph by Julius Shulman. Architect: Josef Van der Kar. © J. Paul Getty Trust. Julius Shulman Photography Archive, 1936–1997. The Getty Research Institute, Los Angeles (2004.R.10).*

Into this world of epicurean refinement, intellectual chic, and high-brow Angelino hedonism arrived young Richard Perle, eager to fit in both intellectually and socially. His incessant retelling of the poolside encounter between the precocious teenager and the master theorist im-plies a bond that none of the other acolytes could claim. Perle, the story informs us, had access to Albert at an early, formative age, and not only in formal policy settings.

Unlike Paul Wolfowitz and Zalmay Khalilzad, Perle never wrote a dissertation under Albert's tutelage. But he was there at the creation, when "Delicate Balance" thrust Albert into the public eye. He may not have had the formal training of a PhD, but he was the ultimate apprentice, with insight into the mind of his mentor unsurpassed by others. The implication is that Perle was the genuine successor to the Wohlstetters. He was there when Albert initially entered the public domain; he was anointed to eulogize Albert in front of the nation; he had broken bread with the master.

The Perle Kitchen

"Not only two sinks but two dishwashers, fifty-five linear feet of butcher-block kitchen counter, handmade oak cabinets, a restaurant gas stove big enough to live in, four ovens, a huge gas grill with its own flue, enough copper pots and pans to cause a penny shortage." Somewhat overwhelmed with this exhibition of excess at the Perle's Chevy Chase abode, the *Washington Post*'s style correspondent noted that the gargantuan kitchen was "so big and important that the rest of the house seems to be an anteroom."[10]

The Perle kitchen was not merely the playroom of an overindulged epicurean. For Perle, the kitchen served as a stage for performative acts of cultural omniscience.

Bernard-Henri Lévy (known by all as BHL) was one of the many who nibbled at the bait cast out from the Perle kitchen. Perle's intellectual affectations—the portrait of Arthur Rimbaud, the light patter about Marxist philosopher Louis Althusser conducted over an espresso at the kitchen counter—were particularly appealing to the Frenchman. The kitchen itself, BHL conjectured, was "perhaps a discreet homage to Albert Wohlstetter, his intellectual master, whose fiercest passions, they say, included the culinary arts."[11] Within his kitchen, Richard Perle, the cultural omnivore, momentarily defied his demonization as "Prince of Darkness" or "neocon" (which, BHL pointed out, "can also mean, in French, 'neodummies.'"). After all, the French philosopher wondered, shouldn't the enlightened world "be delighted when in the most powerful democracy in the world there appears a generation of intellectuals who . . . can concretely work for the universalization of human rights and freedom?"[12] But then, as Perle and his guest left the magnificent kitchen and wandered out into the garden, the spell was broken. Outside his culinary comfort zone, Perle reincarnated as an "outraged old conservative" replete with gratuitous swipes at rivals and bilious politics. It is then, BHL recalled, "I swing over to the other side. . . . I tell myself that this man and I surely don't belong to the same family."[13]

This kitchen encounter with BHL—told this time from Perle's perspective—also made its way into *Hard Line*, Perle's fictionalized account of his role in the Cold War:

> Waterman led Arnaudet past the living room into the kitchen at the back of the house. It was here, in the huge terra-cotta-tile-floored and oak-countered kitchen, that Waterman sought refuge from the share of the world's ills that touched him. Unlike practically everything else he did, cooking promised instant gratification. No long-term projects, no protracted wars, no slowly evolving plans. In the space of a few hours a dinner could be conceived, cooked, and consumed. It was amazing how slicing, chopping, grating, and mixing, the least intellectual of activities, could force from one's mind the most intrusive concerns.
>
> "Formidable!" Arnaudet exclaimed. He peered at the professional kitchen, replete with indoor charcoal grill, restaurant stove, sixty linear feet of counter space, and a *batterie de cuisine* worthy of a good-sized restaurant. Recessed halogen lights played on a huge collection of brightly polished copper pots hanging from a large oval oak rack suspended from the ceiling. A copper marmite gurgled on the stove, the white porcelain tureen into which its contents would be placed by its side.
>
> "It keeps me sane," Waterman replied. "The last complete diversion."[14]

Hard Line is a thinly disguised account of Perle's aggressive action as the enforcer in a hard-fought mission to sabotage the arms reduction summit at Reykjavik in 1986. At the last moment, a team led by Perle and Wolfowitz and goaded on by Albert and Senator Henry "Scoop" Jackson managed to stymie what they considered to be dangerous American acquiescence to an arms reduction agreement that could not be enforced.[15]

Hard Line offers a fictionalized version of this defining moment in Perle's career. The hero of the novel is Michael Waterman, now a professor at Harvard, then an assistant secretary of defense. Waterman is a composite of Wohlstetter and Perle. At a personal level, as Robin Winks observes in his review of the book, the Waterman-Perle-Wohlstetter avatar "loves the perks of office, the limousines, the flights to Paris, the chance to eat in the best restaurants." Professionally, he is unwilling to entertain anything but his own views: "he undermines colleagues; he is intent on the triumph of his will, his ideas, his solutions."[16]

While Waterman-Perle is obviously quite proud of his triumph in sabotaging the deal with a duplicitous Soviet Union, the book is mostly an exercise in settling scores. For example, Perle portrays the President— unmistakably Ronald Reagan—as a dim-witted but mostly useful fool; if left to his own devices, he would have given away the farm. The nation's top military officers are nothing more than paper tigers who vacillate their way out of tough decisions. The derisive protagonist dismisses his fellow academics and intellectuals as clueless, unable to negotiate their own sabbatical, let alone forge agreements with a crafty enemy.

As for the policy disputes underlying the narrative, they are bereft of any intellectual content. Rather than engaging the principles of rival positions on arms reduction, Perle, the author, resorts to character assassination. Unwilling to portray opposing positions as merely wrong, and infuriated by their argumentation, Waterman-Perle falls back on the last resort of the cynic: patriotic damnation. Daniel Bennet—a fictional representation of assistant secretary of state Richard Burt—is savaged as both a dandy and a man of vacillating loyalties. Bennet-Burt is willing to destroy crucial evidence of Russian duplicity and entrap his president, although the reasons for his shocking deceit appear to amount to nothing more than his juvenile spats with Waterman-Perle.

At the end of the book one is left wondering who, in fact, the nation's enemies are, and whether the existential threat lurks in foreign lands or within the American body politic. In fact, the Soviets are mere background to a vicious attack on a liberal Beltway establishment accused of stopping at nothing to promote its dangerous worldview. Waterman's liberal nemesis willingly holds back intelligence from a gullible president, and exposes the nation to an existential threat in the service of a warped worldview never quite explained in the book.

In real life, Perle engaged his intellectual sparing partners with similar bursts of innuendo, contempt, and vilification. The conflict with Iraq offered an opportunity to attack a reigning president in a manner that cast doubt on his integrity, rather than on his judgment. Perle was somewhat indulgent of George H. W. Bush's strategic decision to limit American involvement in Iraq, reserving his scorn for Bill Clinton's refusal to "help the Iraqi opposition free their country from the totalitarian vise of Saddam Hussein's regime."[17]

Perle chided the Clinton administration for its Iraqi strategy of "containment."[18] For reasons that had to more with personality than policy, Perle accused Clinton of taking a patently treacherous policy route, reminiscent of the Cold War follies that Albert, his mentor, had managed to stymie. "Not since the Cold War, when the issue was whether to accept the permanence of the Soviet Union and find ways to get along with it, or challenge its legitimacy and develop policies to bring about its demise," he wrote, "has Washington seen two such starkly different approaches to a foreign country."[19]

Perle fully predicted that Clinton's version of containment would collapse under its own corrupt weight. The policy of sanctions and weapons inspections had already suffered serious blows from America's fickle allies, and as for Clinton's "pinprick military strikes," they had merely served to "bolster the myth of Saddam's invincibility."[20] Clinton's obsession with "stability," Perle argued, had provoked disastrous effects in other parts of the globe: Haiti, Bosnia, and Kosovo—not to mention North Korea. Given Iraq's geostrategic importance, the repetition of stability at any price would be catastrophic.[21] He condemned the CIA for its inability to find cooperative conspirators within the Baath regime, a failure reminiscent of the CIA's "similar error of judgment in its long-held belief that it could collaborate with Cubans close to Castro."[22]

Perle was particularly critical of what he called the "the Bay of Pigs Syndrome"—the fear among Clinton administration officials that a failed attempt to establish a homegrown, clean break from the Baath regime would lead to a protracted and costly American entanglement in the region. He dismissed as baseless and uninformed the "widespread fear" that an Iraqi alternative to Saddam, "even if it were well organized . . . would somehow be maneuvered into a situation where it would face annihilation unless U.S. forces were rushed to the rescue."[23]

Conjuring up images from the post–World War II period, Perle posited Iraq as a Persian Gulf version of the Soviet Union prior to its achievement of nuclear parity. Saddam's Iraq was on the verge of obtaining weapons of mass destruction, and an anemic, unimaginative policy of "containment" would surely hasten that goal. Once Saddam achieved such military prowess, the United States would be condemned to a new round of existential confrontations. He who ignores the past, Perle implied, was doomed to repeat it.

The key to a successful strategy in Iraq would be deliberate and forceful rollback, beginning with an extension of "liberated" zones within the country, the establishment of a provisional government in safe havens, a vigorous embargo against and delegitimation of Saddam and, finally, a military campaign bolstered by American ground forces and air strikes.[24] Some years later, an embittered Perle defended this policy by lashing out at George W. Bush for botching the historic moment. In a 2003 interview, Perle observed that "Bush never understood how to be President in my view. He thought it was enough to give a speech and action would follow." The ultimate insult was Perle's comparison of Bush and Obama. An "intensely ideological and very shrewd" Barack Obama, who embraced the decline of American influence lamented by others, was, in Perle's book, "far more effective as President than Bush was."[25]

Historical Analogy and Policy

Perle did not limit his attacks to the inhabitants of the Beltway. He also cheerfully savaged the representatives of an effete West writ large. In a 2003 encounter organized by *Foreign Affairs,* Perle taunted the faux innocence of the French-German libertarian Daniel Cohn-Bendit. The former leader of Europe's 1960s student protest movement and leader of Europe's Green Party alliance at the time of the interview, Cohn-Bendit became the target of Perle's insinuations of European feebleness and French duplicity. Europe's meddling was the reason the Middle East was in a mess, Perle lectured Cohn-Bendit. Europeans had undermined the Palestinian-Israeli peace process by showering unrestricted financial aid on a corrupt Yasser Arafat. Perle reserved particular scorn for France's "ambitions to build a Europe in opposition to the United States." Hence, "we, as Americans, will have to consider how we deal with this European departure from the trans-Atlantic axis."[26]

When all else failed in his efforts to cow his rivals, Perle invoked history—at least his own private version of the past—replete with contested analogies and misstatements of facts. Hitler's Germany made frequent appearances. In an interview with the Australian Broadcasting Company, Perle defended the idea of a preemptive strike against a nuclear-armed Saddam by proposing a counterfactual history of the Third Reich. "If Hitler had had a nuclear capability in the last days of the Reich, it's entirely possible . . . he would've used that nuclear weapon to attempt to intimidate the allied powers from liberating Europe." Perle pursued this line of thought with a rhetorical question: "Would we have liberated Kuwait if Saddam had had nuclear weapons?"[27]

Asked for his response to worldwide protests in early February 2003, when millions of demonstrators took to the streets to voice opposition to the invasion of Iraq, Perle cavalierly and insensitively played the Holocaust card. "I couldn't help but be struck by the irony because I saw the six million figure, that is the number of Jews who perished when well-meaning people, including peace demonstrators, failed to understand the threat that Adolf Hitler posed. . . . They just happen not to understand the balancing of risks and dangers that's entailed in a decision to leave Saddam Hussein defiantly rejecting the Seventeenth Resolution of the United Nations."[28]

The Chomsky Debate

On one notable occasion, Perle's historical manipulation and damnation of effete allies imploded with quite embarrassing results. In 1988 at Ohio State University, Perle encountered the renowned linguist and political activist Noam Chomsky at a debate held during Ramadan and sponsored jointly by the Arab-American Friendship Association and the Latin American Student Union.

In many ways, Chomsky was Perle's mirror image. Chomsky, too, methodically eviscerated opposing views with scorn and ridicule, often using historical conjecture to hammer home his fundamentalist critique of neoliberal capitalism. As Perle would discover, Chomsky's debating tactics were uncomfortably familiar. In the resulting heightened tension, Chomsky was able to goad Perle to enter a disputation beyond his comfort zone.

Chomsky began the encounter by citing a series of unspecified archival documents from the State Department and the National Security Council. The documents allegedly revealed deliberate attempts to destroy budding democracies in Latin America, while sustaining their economic dependency on the United States. Anticipating Perle's pieties on the benign nature of market democracies, Chomsky argued that the documentary record indicated otherwise. "The United States fosters stability and prosperity—of a very special kind, the kind in which we can prosper. The kind of stability in which, for example, Honduras exports snow peas and beef, but does not feed its own population—and also foster[s] democracy, namely, the kind that we like."[29] In Latin America, U.S.-orchestrated formal elections "are often farcical . . . a tactical device to ensure the dominance of 'private capitalistic enterprise linked to the U.S.'"[30] As far as Chomsky was concerned, "the term 'communist' has lost any substantive meaning in U.S. political rhetoric, referring to anyone who stands in our way."[31]

In the Middle East, "the primary concern was the same. The fear that indigenous nationalism might threaten their effective control over one of the greatest material prizes in world history, that was understood since the 1940s to provide us with a leverage over Europe and Japan."[32] Fearing the disruptive nature of Arab nationalism in any form or fashion, the United States sustained Israel's consistent policy to deny Palestinian self-determination, while aiding and abetting Israel's expansionist impulses.

Chomsky mentioned no names. There was no need to attribute authorship; the personal opinions of policy makers were irrelevant. In Chomsky's version of history, as Larisa Macfarquhar has observed, the economic interests of elite institutions were the main drivers of power politics. Individual motives and elaborate ideologies were merely masks for institutional maximization of profit to the exclusion of any other motives. Elites, in Chomsky's world, "act selfishly, on their own behalf, but this selfishness follows an institutional logic rather than an individual one. They are morally culpable, and yet they can scarcely act otherwise."[33]

Perle countered with sarcastic barbs at Chomsky's extrapolations from documentary shards. "Unless I am mistaken, you have never served in government, because anyone who would attempt to derive the conclusions you do from the kind of documents you have been reading simply does not understand what it means to formulate policy in a real government."[34] Facts and actions, Perle rejoined, belied Chomsky's bookish revelations of an American behemoth beholden to the corporate world rather than to its citizens. American efforts to transform its Second World War adversaries into thriving democracies provided ample evidence of an American desire to spread the benefits of a benign market economy throughout the world.

As for Chomsky's accusations of a regressive American role in the Middle East, Perle referred to the Israeli-Egyptian rapprochement as evidence to the contrary. "As we look at the recent history of the Middle East, perhaps the only progress toward stability . . . has been that diplomatic activity that was nurtured by the United States." He mentioned, in particular, the Camp David accord, "which at least ended the mortal hostility of Israel and Egypt," and the threats of recurring wars of even greater severity and destruction.[35]

Chomsky responded in sarcastic kind, hinting at Perle's cognitive and linguistic limitations. Referring to documentary evidence that Israel was less concerned with security than with holding territory, the Hebrew-speaking Chomsky observed that "you learn a lot from the fact that certain people do not want you to look at it. There is a very extensive documentary record in Hebrew (if any of you have access to it) of Israeli government planning and thinking, cabinet meetings, etc., from 1967 to 1973."[36]

Perle and his ilk, Chomsky argued, had invented new concepts in the world of global politics in order to stymie a two-state solution. It was not enough for the Palestinians "to recognize Israel: they had to recognize the legitimacy of Israel, or the right to exist of Israel. Now 'right to exist' is something that does not exist in international law. No state recognizes the right of any other state to exist. . . . Mexico does not recognize the right of the United States to exist within its present borders, which happen to include a third of Mexico. In fact, in the international system, there is a notion of recognition of a state, but there is no notion of recognition of the legitimacy of a state."[37] Citing the Israeli strategist Yehoshua Harkabi, Chomsky dismissed the connection between Israel's stubborn rejection of Palestinian statehood and the Jewish state's security concerns. The Israeli occupation, he declared with dogmatic certitude, was a simple land grab, part of the Israeli elite's institutional drive to maximize its political and economic gains at the expense of Palestine's indigenous citizens.

The Ohio State debate swiftly turned into a discussion on the nature of capitalism. Chomsky and Perle were the respective guardians of two extreme visions of American global leadership. In essence, the discussion confronted Perle's narrative of the ideological struggle with the Soviet Union with Chomsky's political cartography of U.S. global domination.[38] The crux of their disagreement was on the direction of the axis of global power plays. For Chomsky, the Cold War was essentially a confrontation along North-South lines rather than an East-West polarity. In his condemnation of Western imperialism and its contemporary American manifestation, the specter of predatory communism appeared as a propaganda ploy, a fear tactic instrumentalized by the West in its quest to control Third World economies. By contrast, Perle presented communism as a nefarious ideology thwarting the beneficial spread of an unfettered global market. Neither Chomsky nor Perle made reference to the impending crisis in the Soviet Union. They both appeared quite comfortable with its permanent presence.

Is It Really, Really Over?

Perle's reluctance to dwell on the fragile nature of the Soviet Union in this 1988 debate was, perhaps, understandable. Communism, as a clear and present danger, served a purpose of galvanizing a fainthearted American political establishment. When the Soviet Union eventually imploded, he responded with ambivalence to the successful conclusion of the Cold War. As one of the chief architects of a confrontational policy that had, in his view, brought the Soviet Union to its knees, the "Prince of Darkness" was obviously triumphant. After all, his worldview had been vindicated. Predictably, he lashed out at hapless intellectual rivals who were frantically scavenging for alternative explanations for the swift and unheralded demise of the Soviet Union. It "amuses me how the Left, in particular, which was never keen to engage in the Cold War, which was ready to accept the permanence of the Soviet Union and Communist ideology—now believes the Soviet Union collapsed under its own weight."[39]

Despite this celebratory tone, Perle was haunted by an underlying sense of a Pyrrhic victory. The disappearance of a mortal enemy threatened to provoke the ghosts of American isolationism and induce a merciless reduction of defense expenditures, all of which would lead to the ensuing rise of emboldened, predatory rogue states. "In the absence of a threat as profound and fundamental as that once posed by the Soviet

Union, the willingness of Americans and Europeans alike to sustain large defense expenditures and combat casualties has diminished significantly and will surely decline further," he predicted.[40]

Alluring overtures of peace masked the existential dangers facing the now triumphant yet unimaginative leadership of the Western world. Danger lurked in the inaction of complacent leaders. Lulled by peace, Western leaders ignored at their own peril a series of recurrent challenges of a frighteningly unknown quality.

Over the course of his career, Perle had demonstrated an aversion to international agreements of any shape or form. During the Cold War he had earned his "Prince of Darkness" nickname through consistent and unremitting sabotage of arms reductions negotiations with the Soviet Union. Perle was equally derisive of addressing other foreign policy challenges by compromise. In some future war of still unknown dimensions, Perle envisioned the United States as the intrepid guardian of Western values, facing down its enemies with little or no assistance from its allies. Such "self-reliance," he hastened to observe, should not be mistaken for isolationism; it was merely a realistic acknowledgment of the fecklessness of allies. Leadership meant acting alone if necessary. In fact, a credible "readiness to act alone has often been the decisive factor in obtaining coalition support" from those who appeared ready to jump on the bandwagon once victory seemed assured.[41]

Perle argued against the blunder of organizing the future in accordance with simple recourse to history. Writing in June 2000, he contended that the post–Cold War challenges in Iraq and the Balkans demonstrated that while political circumstances would have a familiar ring, the battlefields of the future "will be unlike those of the past."[42] The worst possible mistake would be to envision engagement with the enemy as a rerun of the Cold War. The weaponry, tactics, and challenges of the future were unclear; but they would definitely not be repeat performances of Cold War scenarios.

Perle therefore advocated preparation for all conceivable contingencies, ranging from missile defense to a rapid deployment force capable of handling low-intensive warfare anywhere and immediately. One of the great future advantages of the United States, he believed, would be its great technological prowess and its ability to operate with precision weapons "from beyond the lethal range of the enemy." Armed with the advantages of mobility, "reach, and stealth, our forces must be able to operate beyond the range of the enemy; and they must be capable of destroying enemy targets most of the time without relying on nearby bases, large quantities of heavy weapons, or favorable weather."[43] Precision would be the hallmark of future warfare, he maintained.

More than any other Wohlstetter acolyte, Perle was an unremitting advocate of unilateralism—most memorably manifested as an American-led "coalition of the willing" during the Iraq incursion. A "parting irony" of Saddam Hussein's downfall, Perle remarked, was that the Iraqi dictator would "take the United Nations down with him." Even if "the looming chatterbox on the Hudson" would "continue to bleat," the "intellectual wreckage of the liberal conceit" that had enabled the likes of "Syria, Cameroon, Angola, Russia, China, and France" to control global enforcement had been removed unceremoniously to the dust heap of history.[44] And yet, he warned, multinational coalitions of equal partners "can easily become a disabling encumbrance when the resolve of its weakest members falters."[45]

Perle expressed clear opposition to the concept of "managing" crises or simply arresting development of dangerous trends.[46] Instead, he advocated a policy of delegitimating, destroying, and dismantling the support systems of rival upstarts, rogue or otherwise. The Cold War had ended in the total collapse of the communist vision, he explained, because a group of fearless Western leaders had ignored ill-conceived advice suggesting that they should compromise or accommodate. It is precisely because of such resolute policies that the Cold War had ended "not with a bang but a whimper."[47] The postcommunist challenges, he argued, would have to be met with the same triumph of will. Reagan and his trusted lieutenants—Perle not the least—had not sought to merely control or contain communism. By the same logic, Perle argued, one should not try to "manage" the new breed of threats.[48]

Perle was particularly censorious about the role of academic superstars in politics, who seemed to have an ingrained aversion to resolving great existential struggles. Perle derided the likes of Harvard's John Kenneth Galbraith and his predictions of economic parity between the United States and the Soviet Union. Those, like Perle, who questioned such predictions, were reciprocally "scorned in academic circles."[49]

The ultimate example of the indulgent academic was Henry Kissinger and his "profoundly mistaken way to approach the Soviet Union." Perle described Kissinger's policy as a fantastically presumptuous attempt to "tie the Soviets down, Gulliverise them . . . with a thousand threads" made up of "agreements on science and technology and economics . . . the theory being that if we interacted on a broad enough front, it would somehow socialize, by which I mean civilize" the Soviets. The USSR would thereby entrap itself in the golden cage of a world order "dominated by Western norms and values." Such conceits, Perle argued, were unhinged from reality. They were "highly theoretical" and counterproductive, providing an economic crutch to a failed system.[50]

Kissinger's theory of détente, Perle implied, had actually extended the duration of the Cold War, and, in the process, had compromised the security of the United States and its most trusted allies. In Perle's view, Kissinger was blindly enamored with his theoretical constructs to the point that contravening facts never confused him. In actual fact, the Soviet Union had not collapsed under the weight of theoretical glyphs hurled from Harvard Yard, but as a result of direct military and economic confrontation.

As an example of Kissinger's dangerous self-infatuation with pet theories, Perle harped on the statesman's unwillingness to resupply Israel with weaponry during a crucial seventy-two-hour period of the Yom Kippur War. Kissinger was willing to shove Israel to the brink of defeat in order to salvage a theory of détente that the Russians had clearly never intended to follow, and that "was clearly shattered by Soviet involvement in that war." Whether Kissinger had merely been indecisive or "was deliberately unwilling to assist the Israelis" was unclear to many, though quite clear to Perle.[51]

And yet—Perle would state emphatically at every opportunity—the security and integrity of the Jewish state was endangered not only by Soviet designs, recalcitrant neighbors, and vainglorious professors. The enemy was deeply embedded within the Jewish state's own political elite. Israel's traditional political establishment, especially those identified with the Labor Party, had a corrosive effect on Israeli culture and society.

Israel's Socialist Shackles

The bloody deposal of Prime Minister Yitzhak Rabin and the subsequent election of Benjamin Netanyahu as prime minister of Israel encouraged Perle to advocate for a radical transformation of Israel's political creed.

As team leader of a strategic plan prepared for Netanyahu, Perle and a band of like-minded colleagues called for a revolutionary restructuring of Israeli society, or, as its title put it, "A Clean Break" from the defeatist policies associated with Rabin and his center-left predecessors. Using language previously reserved for enemy entities, this 1996 document described the Israeli Labor Party's "seventy-year" stranglehold on Israeli politics as undermining the very essence of a Jewish national homeland.

Labor's adherence to socialism had created a "stalled and shackled economy" in Israel, not unlike the planned economic vision of the Soviet Union. Much like the Soviet Union, according to Perle and colleagues, Labor had pursued a vision of "supranational over national sovereignty" that had undermined the "legitimacy of the nation" and had led Israel into "strategic paralysis."[52] Above all, Labor had openly displayed *"moral ambivalence* between the effort to build a Jewish state and the desire to annihilate it by trading *'land for peace.'"* Under the slogan of a "new Middle East," Labor had agreed to barter away "sovereignty over its capital" while responding "with resignation to a spate of terror." Having rid itself of a Soviet-like superstructure and freed itself from the bonds of appeasement promoted by Labor, Netanyahu's Israel would "no longer simply manage the Arab-Israeli conflict" it would "transcend it."[53]

Transcending the Arab Israeli conflict involved abandoning the corrupt two-state formula advocated by the intellectual bankrupt Labor Party and its PLO mirror image. While alleged Palestinian treachery was reason enough for rejecting a partition plan, the Perle plan preferred to base its designs on a biblical legacy that trumped all other claims to the territorial dispute. "Our claim to the land—to which we have clung for hope for 2,000 years—is legitimate and noble. . . . Only the unconditional acceptance by Arabs of our rights, *especially* in their territorial dimension . . . is a solid basis for the future."[54]

The road to a new Middle East, therefore, did not lead through territorial compromise in Israel-Palestine, but rather through a redrawing of Middle Eastern alliances. The transformation of Iraq from intractable enemy to central ally played center stage in this effort. The deposing of Saddam Hussein and the restoration of the Hashemite dynasty in Iraq, with intimate ties to the Hashemite Kingdom of Jordan—an Israeli client state—was key to creating a favorable pro-Western climate in the

Middle East. "Jordan has challenged Syria's regional ambitions recently by suggesting the restoration of the Hashemites in Iraq. . . . Syria recently signaled that it and Iran might prefer a weak, but barely surviving Saddam, if only to undermine and humiliate Jordan in its efforts to remove Saddam."[55]

The major impediment to implementing this new Middle Eastern map, the authors of "A Clean Break" stated, had been the Israeli labor leadership, encrusted with layers of duplicitous loyalties. The manifesto quoted "a senior Iraqi opposition leader," presumably Ahmed Chalabi, Perle's preferred pretender to post-Saddam Iraqi leadership, who said that "Israel must rejuvenate and revitalize its moral and intellectual leadership. It is an important—if not the most important—element in the history of the Middle East."[56] The downfall of Labor and the installation of a new Israeli government represented a historical break with the past and a new beginning that would alter the fate of the entire region.

Some years later, an incredulous reporter questioned the propriety of former administration officials taking part in this partisan promotion of change in an allied sovereign state. Jonathan Holmes of the Australian Broadcasting Corporation wondered whether it was "strange that a group of people including officials like yourself who were senior in the United States Defense Department, presumably privy to all kinds of United States policies and secrets and so on should be giving open strategic advice to foreign governments?"[57]

Perle replied that his participation had been quite minor. Somewhat flustered, he denied that he had prepared the paper at the behest of the Likud. "No; there was a research center, I've forgotten the name of it now that pulled together a team of people and actually I wasn't involved in the drafting of it but I read it through and I thought it made sense." In fact, Perle was far from being an accidental signatory. According to the published document, he was the report's team leader.[58]

When pressed further, Perle acknowledged, "I don't think we should be impartial; we should have a point of view about what is in the best interests of the things that we value. We value stability, we value peace, we value democracy and I believe that the leaders of this country, of either party are going to promote those values and I don't see any reason to apologize for that."[59]

"A Clean Break" offers a glimpse of a subtext on faith that would later come to dominate Perle's thoughts. The document explicitly pinpoints the combination of secularism and socialism in the Middle East as being at the heart of the region's pathologies. Prior to the rise of the Right, the Israeli political establishment appeared to be ensnared by the false consciousness of socialism, even to the point of compromising its historical, biblically based "2,000-year-old dream to live free in their own land."[60] The main Arab protagonists fomenting instability in the Middle East all professed some version of socialism and secularism: the Syrian and Iraqi Baath regimes, as well as the nominally secular Palestinian Liberation Organization. "A Clean Break" implied that the stranglehold of these vicious secular regimes would be broken by nurturing authentic religious sentiment in the region.

A malevolent Iraq would be neutered by empowering Jordan's King Hussein, whose religious pedigree appealed to both Sunnis and Shiites. "Were the Hashemites to control Iraq, they could use their influence over Najf to help Israel wean the south Lebanese Shia away from Hizballah, Iran, and Syria. Shia retain strong ties to the Hashemites: the Shia venerate foremost the Prophet's family, the direct descendant of which—and in whose veins the blood of the Prophet flows—is King Hussein."[61] Faux secularism had obfuscated the positive role that religion could play in the region. Secularism—both the Israeli-socialist and pan-Arab nationalist versions—had fanned the region's tensions. A counterintuitive embrace of true faith, Jewish and Muslim, could promote interfaith and intrafaith dialogue amenable to the strategic interests of the United States and its allies in the region.

An End to Evil

A more complex, if not contradictory, analysis of faith-based politics in the Middle East would burst onto the scene some eight years later in *An End to Evil*, Richard Perle's stab at modern-day eschatology. Coauthored with David Frum, a former George W. Bush speechwriter who helped create the "Axis of Evil" trope, the book presents contemporary global challenges in uncompromisingly Manichean terms. A specter of unadulterated "evil"—described as a malignant militant Islam—permeates the text: "Like communism, this ideology perverts the language of justice and equality to justify oppression and murder. Like Nazism, it exploits the injured pride of once-mighty nations."[62]

An End to Evil narrates an eschatological clash of civilizations, a zero-sum game between the Judeo-Christian West and a particularly obdurate Islamic enemy. This construct of a militant Islamic threat defies the conventional cartographic borders of global politics. A metastasizing, faith-based threat moves in multiple and unanticipated directions, infiltrating the stable havens of democratic regimes in the West, and spreading its malignant cells throughout the weak political structures of the Islamic world. While they ostensibly focus on a rogue version of Islam, Perle and Frum make no secret of their fundamental antipathy toward Islam in general. Militant Islam, which "seeks to overthrow our civilization and remake the nations of the West into Islamic societies . . . commands wide support, and even wider sympathy, among Muslims worldwide, including Muslim minorities in the West."[63] Islam's expansionist vision aggressively challenges the prevailing mores of civilized societies and displays no capacity to serve as a positive stabilizing force in global affairs. Islam's claim to truth, they argue, devalues reason, is premised on violence, and is sustained by the blind faith of believers.

An End to Evil's radical Islamic legions, Lance Morrow and other theologians have argued, suggest John Milton's defiant army of Lucifer, a malevolent entity "condemned to lose the fight (eventually) but nonetheless powerful" enough to wreak havoc on unsuspecting innocents.[64] The book's Manichean imagery rejects truce or compromise. The struggle with radical evil can only end with the annihilation of either side. The civilized world would do well, urge Perle and Frum, to acknowledge the civilizational clash with the militant legions of Islam. A sanguine understanding of the theological nature of the dispute is, they insist, a necessary condition for its suppression. As the nation had realized in the 1940s, "there is no middle way for Americans" when confronting unadulterated Evil. "It is victory or holocaust."[65]

An End to Evil is devoid of introspection or self-doubt. The forces of Judeo-Christianity, as embodied in the American body politic, are presented as innately virtuous, the mirror image of the Islamic variant of totalitarianism threatening peace-loving nations. The United States' growing entanglement in the Islamic world is that of the altruistic "would-be rescuer in the grip of a drowning man." Seeking to contain the cycle of violence convulsing through the region, "the United States was pulled deeper and deeper into the region's vortex of paranoia and hatred."[66] As for actions, such as the Iraq invasion, Perle and Frum claim "we have no choice. The enemy attacked us."[67]

An End to Evil presents spatial, temporal, and cognitive divides between Islam and Judeo-Christianity. Western civilization is oriented to the present; Islam derives its power from an idealized past, characterized by a "yearning for the Caliphate state . . . regaining Andalusia and establishing an Islamic regime in France." Western societies thrive on inclusiveness and cosmopolitanism; militant Islam embraces fundamentalism, exclusiveness and a furious "contempt for the rational, for women, and for non-Muslims."[68] The "Arab world produces virtually zero scientific papers and patents," and the "nations that constitute the Arab League, total population more than 300 million, annually translate about 330 books, one fifth the number translated by Greece, population less than three million."[69] Islam had ensnared the entire Arab world in an oppressive culture of "medieval theology and a smattering of Third World nationalist self-pity." This lethal combination inevitably created "an enraged populace ready to transmute all the frustrations in its frustrating daily life into a fanatical hatred of everything 'un-Islamic.'"[70]

Perle and Frum identify strong ties between the region's ostensibly secular regimes and the military arm of radical Islam. These two different strands of "radicals may detest one another, but their murderous hatred of the United States pushes all lesser animosities aside."[71] In the surrealistic Middle East, "religious extremists and secular militants; Sunnis and Shiites; communists and fascists . . . blend into one another. All gush from the same enormous reservoir of combustible rage. And all have the same target: the United States."[72]

The metaphor and imagery of *An End to Evil* evoke existential warfare, somewhere between *War of the Worlds* and the struggle with totalitarian powers. While the Soviet Union makes cameo appearances, the authors rely primarily on imagery from World War II. Militant Islam, they argue, cannot be contained through the type of crisis management that had characterized the Cold War. Those who advocated patience in anticipation of a Soviet-style implosion of its source were entangled in a web of denial.

Rather than confronting the Muslim enemy, Perle complained elsewhere, weak-kneed politicians from both parties sought refuge in futile international collaborations that merely provided covert support for the most dangerous strains of the Islamic threat. In his attack on the international effort to stymie Iran's nuclear program, Perle invoked *Hamlet.* In a 2008 article on "the coalition of the ineffectual," Perle impugned Angela Merkel and the "born-again" multilateralist Condoleezza Rice in the role of King Claudius whose words "fly up while her . . . government's thoughts remain below." Like Claudius, who understands that his insincere prayers and faux remorse will not open the gates of heaven, these two women leaders of the Western political class should have recognized that the pieties of multinational efforts to thwart Iran's nuclear ambitions were an "unforgivable betrayal." Despite protestations to the contrary, broad-based coalitions would ultimately acquiesce to the mullahs who supported "terrorism and subversion in Afghanistan, Iraq, Lebanon, Syria and Israel" while pursuing the acquisition of nuclear weapons.[73]

The only way to fight fire, Perle mused in response to this chorus of insincere nostrums, was with fire. "What did we learn from 11 September?" Perle asked an audience at Brown University in April 2003, in the midst of the American campaign in Iraq. "We learned that it is possible to wait too long before dealing with an observable threat." Instead, like the tragic Hamlet, "we didn't act . . . we waited" until it was too late to avoid a bloodbath of the innocent. "I don't know whether the administration that waited was hoping for the best or simply didn't know what to do or couldn't summon the will to do it."[74]

Perle's impulse to intervene forcefully—to lead history rather than follow it—knew no borders and rarely acknowledged a clear divide between friend and foe. Was Congress "Friend or Foe in Foreign Policy?," Perle queried rhetorically in a visceral attack on congressional attitudes toward the Soviet Union on the eve of its demise.[75] "It is difficult to describe the frustrations associated with sitting across the table from Soviet negotiators and knowing that the Congress has adopted resolutions, and in some cases, even endeavored to pass statutes, that favor the Soviet position and criticize the American position that is on the negotiating table."[76] European duplicity, in particular in Germany and France—two nations that, according to Perle, should have known better given their experiences in World War II—were borderline traitors to the post–Cold War cause. "Someday, the Western world will look back on its failure to deal decisively with Saddam Hussein and realize that it made a serious mistake of historic proportions," Perle observed in 1998. "At that moment, the French and others . . . may find themselves having second thoughts about whether the empowerment of Saddam Hussein . . . was a good idea."[77] How difficult it must have been for Perle and his kindred souls to be contrarians in a world dominated by small-minded and fraudulent allies seeking to snatch defeat from the mouth of what could have been a great victory.

Epilogue

The Hamlet of Nations?

O N NOVEMBER 7, 1985, President Ronald Reagan bestowed the Presidential Medal of Freedom—the U.S. government's highest civilian honor—on three recipients: Paul Nitze, Roberta Wohlstetter, and her spouse, Albert. A photograph encapsulates the moment. Roberta stands off center, beaming at her husband, who is basking in the aura of presidential approval. By their side stands Paul Nitze, their ideological comrade-in-arms and corecipient. Nitze appears puzzled; his eye is fixed on some distant point of reference.

The president's implicit ranking of the recipients may have induced Nitze's baffled demeanor. Reagan lauded Nitze for his unstinting public service since the Truman administration. As "principal architect of our security strategy after World War II," Nitze had helped "us understand what it would take in resources and commitment to meet the new challenges emerging in the postwar world." The president addressed Nitze with just a tinge of condescension toward an old man past his prime: "Paul, we may need to call on you to give our current foreign assistance program the same boost that you gave to Harry Truman's."[1] He complimented Nitze as an exemplary adviser who had "brought unmatched experience and expertise to his current responsibilities," and had served "so faithfully in the highest councils of state that his presence has been almost taken for granted." The president failed to mention Paul Nitze's major claim to fame as lead author of NSC 68, the planning document that had guided the nation's massive military buildup throughout the Cold War.

President Ronald Reagan awards the Medal of Freedom to Paul Nitze (center), Roberta Wohlstetter, and Albert Wohlstetter, 1985. *Photograph by Diana Walker/The LIFE Images Collection.*

As for Roberta, Reagan lingered on how she had shattered the glass ceiling separating women from the male titans of national security. Reagan mentioned Roberta's work on "terrorism, intelligence, and warning" prior to acknowledging her seminal collaboration with Albert on issues of nuclear deterrence. "I daresay that she has frankly enjoyed posing the same penetrating questions to her husband that she has to the intellectual and political leaders of the country. And that is certainly one explanation for the clarity and persuasiveness of his own voluminous words on strategy, politics, and world affairs."[2]

The president reserved special praise for Albert. Reagan lauded Albert's prescription for making the nation's strategic forces safe from surprise attacks, less indiscriminately destructive, "and thereby less dangerous to us all." Albert had advocated for strategic "choices for our society where others saw none." Together with Roberta, Albert had "taught us that there is an escape from fatalism."[3]

An outsider would have been forgiven for assuming that Roberta and Nitze were the supporting cast for a celebration of Albert's unparalleled greatness. Nitze was the loyal and persevering civil servant, Roberta the smiling helpmate who posed "penetrating questions to her husband." Albert was "brilliant" with "enormous strength of character." His "intellectual integrity is renowned," and his "analytical standards have been increasingly and unceasingly rigorous." Nitze, by contrast, was merely "erudite" and "immensely dignified, yet never stuffy."[4]

Although Reagan had explicitly recognized Roberta's contribution to Albert's design of an escape hatch from nuclear "fatalism," Albert did not reciprocate. In his acceptance remarks, he avoided any specific intellectual debts, preferring instead to dispense faint praise on unspecified collaborators "with whom I've been lucky enough to work for nearly thirty-five years." Even as Roberta stood by his side, Albert alluded only to an anonymous army of "devoted research men and students."[5] His most intimate debt remained unacknowledged. As she had throughout their partnership, Roberta stood quietly on the sidelines, conceding the center of attention to Albert.

Albert may as well have written the script for this ceremony himself. Experiencing not a moment of hesitation, he clearly believed that he had indeed moved the nation beyond a fatalistic global policy paralyzed by the fear of an impending clash between the superpowers. Never in doubt about his singular wisdom, prescience, and unique role as the primary proponent of an aggressive, data-driven strategy for U.S. global preeminence, Albert had founded his public career on a deep contempt for the pieties of liberalism and the moral caveats of realism. Albert, Jacob Heilbrunn has observed, "was no brooding émigré from Germany who scented the decline of the West around every corner and viewed democracy itself with apprehension."[6] He refused to suffer lightly those whom he considered to be the intellectual prisoners of "declinism" or compromise. Despite tepid Western responses to global security challenges, Albert dismissed concerns of the "inevitable" demise of the West.[7]

Albert did not shrink from confronting those he deemed either fainthearted or lacking in rigor, often choosing to ridicule, hector, and denounce. He usually placed his intellectual rivals on the defensive through the sheer weight of his argumentation. Failing that, he found other means to win the day. He had no qualms about transforming the principle into the personal or belittling his opponents. He was a prolific and persuasive writer, a formidable debater, and a compulsive verbal brawler. Albert was the mercurial spokesperson and promoter of the Wohlstetter Doctrine; casting a shadow over others came naturally to him.

"In Hamlet's Shade"

In 1967 at a military technology conference in Denmark, Albert gave a speech at Hamlet's own Elsinore (Kronborg Castle), standing literally "in Hamlet's shade." It was an "appropriate" occasion to invoke the indelible imprint the Prince of Denmark had made on the Wohlstetters' epistemology. The specter of Hamlet's tragic procrastination, Albert said, offered a timeless warning "that decision cannot be postponed indefinitely, that putting off the awful day frequently makes things still more awful; that we must commit ourselves."[8] Imperfect information, he explained, was a poor excuse for avoiding the necessary actions for maintaining the nation's preeminence in a harsh world.

Yet as we fast-forward through Albert's career, a different interpretation of the Shade—the ghost of Prince Hamlet's father—comes to mind. Shakespeare's *Hamlet,* Harold Bloom reminds us, is "a meditation upon fathers and sons."[9] One might say the same about the Wohlstetter estate and their community of intellectual heirs. The constant presence of Albert and Roberta as parental apparitions demands some concluding remark on the filial piety of those anonymous toilers briefly mentioned by Albert during his 1985 Medal of Freedom ceremony.

The historian Andrew Bacevich has tackled this fascinating tale of lineage by focusing predominantly on the legacy of Albert, the father figure. He describes Albert as the hovering, overbearing progenitor (mis)guiding his intellectual scions in their formulation of a post–Cold War strategy for global domination. His disciples, Bacevich explains, emulated their mentor's contempt for the pervasive "optimistic expectation that the world will embrace a set of common norms to achieve peace," which they contrasted with Albert's own grim representation of global power struggles.[10]

Over the years, Albert mesmerized his students with his choreographies for proactive displays of might aimed at eliminating the enemy threat "before it materializes."[11] With the passing of the Cold War, Bacevich argues, Albert's followers detected a momentary opportunity for achieving stable hegemonic dominance. The unipolar moment led Albert's students to translate his teachings into a moral justification of permanent political inequality among nations. They professed "an obligation that the nation needed to seize, for its own good as well as for the world's."[12] Inspired by Albert, the Wohlstetter disciples in government argued that the short, nasty, and brutal cycles of global conflict could be transformed into stable American dominance.[13]

Iraq became the hapless pilot project for this experiment in translating the theory of unipolar dominance into practical power politics. The motives behind the Iraq invasion, Bacevich argues, had little to do with WMD or with state-sponsored terrorism. The Bush administration's grim warnings resided somewhere on a continuum between wishful thinking and deliberate lies. The principals of the Wohlstetter school used any means possible—including nuclear scare tactics—to foist victory on a foreign policy establishment that had no stomach for this eschatological moment.

Bacevich, like most chroniclers of the Wohlstetters, belatedly airbrushes Roberta into the picture as the creator of a seminal—albeit logically inconsistent and factually erroneous—study of military surprise. Roberta, he argues, abused key military terminology, imputing "strategic significance to actions that occur in the realm of tactics." Worse, she blithely ignored the historical roots of conflicts leading up to the assault on Pearl Harbor. "To characterize the Pearl Harbor attack as a strategic failure—whether of 'warning' or 'decision' . . . is to abuse and misconstrue the word 'strategy.'" The real strategic failure, he insists, lay in the nation's inability to create a political modus vivendi with Japan in the Pacific by means other than an armed conflict. And yet, much to Bacevich's frustration, Roberta's problematic study of military surprise became the proverbial "ur text" of intelligence failure.[14]

The Wohlstetters' students and admirers in government did, indeed, canonize Roberta's book on Pearl Harbor. In two major congressional testimonies, both Paul Wolfowitz and his boss, two-time defense secretary Donald Rumsfeld, offered Roberta the opportunity to step outside of Albert's shadow. Rumsfeld has been her most fervent admirer. Well before 9/11, he enshrined Roberta's "brilliant" *Pearl Harbor: Warning and Decision* as the sacred text of his philosophy.[15] Appearing before a closed-door hearing of the House Armed Services Committee in May 2001, he distributed copies of Thomas Schelling's introduction to the book—a species of CliffsNotes for congressional leaders.[16] Rumsfeld's embrace of Roberta Wohlstetter's insight on anticipating the unexpected—the subject of a briefing he held on the very morning of September 11, 2001—did not prevent its sudden arrival.[17]

The events of 9/11, the first major enemy assault on American soil since Pearl Harbor, only deepened Donald Rumsfeld's commitment to Roberta's doctrine. It served not only as his model for explaining the 9/11 intelligence failure, but also as his justification for trying to apply the lesson proactively in Iraq. He declared that a fixation on routine and familiar dangers—the "poverty of expectations" that Roberta had identified at Pearl Harbor—was responsible not only for the 9/11 "defeat" but also for a misreading of Iraqi intentions. In a less-than-oblique criticism of the CIA analysis of the Iraqi threat, Rumsfeld recalled Roberta's dictum that we "tend to hear what we expect to hear." Surprise would always strike those who worked in a deductive manner, constructing their views based on the collection of evidence in familiar, comfortable ways. Unlike such unimaginative intelligence analysts, Rumsfeld declared, the Bush administration had studied Roberta's lessons and had "recalibrated" its thinking.[18]

Paul Wolfowitz, too, gave lavish credit to Roberta on the eve of the Iraq invasion. Appearing before a congressional committee in 2002, Wolfowitz bemoaned the fact that Roberta's work was still depressingly relevant. The intelligence community, Wolfowitz complained, had never emerged from the Pearl Harbor fog of war. Intelligence gathering remained compartmentalized; information sharing between different intelligence agencies continued to be clumsy and ridden with mutual suspicion. Crucial intelligence data followed a tortuous route from pertinent agencies to their destinations. Pleading the case Roberta had articulated more than fifty years earlier, Wolfowitz concluded that any form of intelligence reform—in addition to addressing issues of distracting "noise," analytical routine, and compartmentalization—would have to "accelerate the speed" and clear the routes "with which information is passed to policy makers and operators."[19]

Much like Pearl Harbor, Wolfowitz complained, the nation's strategic community clung to irrelevant analytical paradigms. "First, for [the] past fifty years, U.S. intelligence has concentrated on defeating external, nation-state threats," even though the main threat to the nation emanated from "nonstate actors," some of whom appeared "within our borders." The nation's intelligence community would have to develop "aggressive . . . ways to discern terrorist 'signals' from the background 'noise' of society. But we must also recognize that enemies will deliberately create 'noise' in our system, in order to conceal the real signals."[20] Finally, Wolfowitz rebuked both the intelligence community and civilian overseers for an unrealistic faith in military intelligence. "We should never allow ourselves to believe that we can rely exclusively upon intelligence for our security. We should expect surprises and have capabilities that do not depend on perfect intelligence to defend the nation."[21]

It was Roberta, Wolfowitz implied through his effusive praise of her work, who had provided the foundation for the most salient of Wohlstetter themes: the urgent need to prepare the nation for possibilities rather than probabilities. Albert often attacked the "Western-preferred" Soviet designs of policy makers—the lazy idea that the enemy would obligingly attack in accordance with the wishful thinking of Western policy makers—no matter how outlandish it seemed. By his own admission, he had lifted that central theme from Roberta's Pearl Harbor study. The disastrous consequences of relying on subjective projections of enemy designs was one of Roberta's major contributions to security studies, in general, as well as to the fraught reality of post-9/11 American warfare.

The Hamlet of Nations

In order to fully comprehend Roberta's impact on statecraft in the post–Cold War years, we return to President Reagan's remarks, where he singled out her work on terror prior to enumerating her other contributions to strategic studies.

Given the events of the early 1980s, the president's comments on Roberta's work on terrorism were not very surprising. The awards ceremony took place on November 7, 1985. On June 14 of that year, terrorists associated with Hezbollah had hijacked TWA Flight 847 between Athens and Rome, leading to the death of U.S. Navy Petty Officer Robert Stethem. This was the first time an American airliner had been hijacked in the Middle East since Ronald Reagan took office in January 1981. Nine days later, while the drama of Flight 847 continued to play out on television screens around the globe, a Sikh militant group detonated a bomb on Air India Flight 182 between Montreal and Delhi, killing all 329 passengers and crew. A month before the awards ceremony, on October 7, four heavily armed Palestinians hijacked the cruise ship *Achille*

Lauro in the Mediterranean Sea and killed Leon Klinghoffer in a particularly memorable act from the annals of the theater of terror. The events of 1985 were preceded by incidents in Lebanon in 1983 and 1984. Among the worst were the U.S. embassy car bombing of April 18, 1983, where more than forty people, including seventeen Americans, lost their lives, and the spectacular car bombing of the marine barracks at Beirut airport on October 23, 1983, in which 241 U.S. Marines were killed. Eleven months later, on September 20, 1984, the new U.S. embassy annex north of Beirut was attacked in a similar style, leading to the death of twenty-four persons, two of them Americans.

Reagan's introductory remarks at the Medal of Freedom ceremony presumably alluded to Roberta's role in formulating policies for the growing threat of anti-American terror. According to a 1984 report from Pan Heuristics—the Wohlstetters' consulting firm—Roberta was involved in several governmental antiterror initiatives. Most notably, she served as an adviser to Admiral Robert Long, the chairman of the Department of Defense committee investigating the attack on the Marine barracks in Beirut.[22] Some ten years earlier, Roberta had indeed made a number of important observations that seemed particularly pertinent to the rising threat of terror in the Middle East.[23] In fact, Roberta's 1976 analysis on "Terror on a Grand Scale" was firmly embedded in the findings of the Long Commission.[24]

Roberta's original article had asserted that transnational terror networks were intimately tied into, and dependent on, the lifeline of host states. They had no independent existence and therefore their actions were contained and constrained by state sponsors. Nevertheless, Roberta had raised the possibility that the "careless slaughter of innocents" she had observed in the Middle East of the 1970s "may indeed be an omen of the sort of random killing" that terrorists might use in the future. Such malevolent intentions, she cautioned, could not occur without essential support from rogue nation-states.[25]

The Long Commission reached almost identical conclusions. To begin with, its authors defined the bombing as a textbook surprise attack, a modern-day Pearl Harbor (although the term was never used). An ill-protected task force, clustered in one building, provided a tempting opportunity to incapacitate a mighty enemy. "From a terrorist perspective, the true genius of this attack is that the objective and the means of attack were beyond the imagination of those responsible for Marine security. As a result, the attack achieved surprise and resulted in massive destruction."[26] Once again, a Pearl Harbor–like failure of imagination had led to disastrous results.

The perpetrators of the deed were members of a Shiite terror group, but, as the Long Report noted, the attack was "an act of war" that was "sponsored by sovereign states or organized political entities."[27] The report therefore urged a policy aimed at state enablers rather than a narrow focus on the actual perpetrators. Acts of terror constituted war by other means, "warfare 'on the cheap'" permitting "small countries to attack U.S. interests in a manner, which if done openly, would constitute acts of war and justify a direct U.S. military response." Pointing a finger at Iran and Syria, the commission underscored the absurdity of discovering that a state "is conducting a terrorist campaign" without confronting "that government with political or military consequences."[28]

Little had changed eleven months later, when a car bomb exploded at the entrance to the new U.S. embassy annex in Lebanon. The only noticeable change was in Secretary of State George Schultz's furious and emotional response, later toned down by Reagan, Secretary of Defense Caspar Weinberger, and others. Frustrated by the nation's lack of response to the spate of terrorist attacks in Lebanon, Schultz argued that the only way to reassert American dominance in the region was to avoid endless debates and, instead, launch aggressive punitive measures against both the subnational perpetrators and their state enablers.[29] Terror, by its very definition, left no smoking gun, Schultz acknowledged. "But we cannot allow ourselves to become the Hamlet of nations, worrying endlessly over whether and how to respond."[30]

Speaking at the Park Avenue Synagogue in Manhattan, Schultz argued for "active prevention, pre-emption and retaliation" even before "every fact is known" and even at the risk of collateral damage to innocent bystanders. "Fighting terrorism will not be a clean or pleasant contest, but we have no choice but to play it."[31]

Wohlstetter protégés Wolfowitz, Iklé, and Khalilzad were serving under Schultz at the time and presumably did little to tone down the vitriol of their superior. This task fell on the shoulders of another RAND alumnus, who cautioned against radical shifts in the struggle against terrorism. Commenting on Schultz's remarks, the strategic analyst Robert Hunter agreed that the United States should take steps to avoid needless procrastination, but pointed out that "it is also important that it not become Othello, overreacting out of misrepresentation, or Lear," madly railing against "cataracts and hurricanoes" over which he had no control.[32]

Schultz's soliloquy on the war against terror was accompanied by a bizarre twist when the Baathist state of Iraq, a constant exemplar of state-enabled terror, received an unexpected American reprieve. In 1982, responding to Iraq's rapidly diminishing fortunes in its war against Iran, the Reagan administration dropped Iraq from the list of countries that supported terrorism, thereby opening the door to a massive infusion of arms and aid from both East and West. President Reagan then appointed Donald Rumsfeld as his emissary to the Iraqi regime. Rumsfeld visited Iraq, where he met with Saddam Hussein in December 1983 and March 1984. The Rumsfeld mission led to the expansion of military and civilian American aid to the embattled Baathist regime.[33] As for Secretary of State George Schultz, he held secret meetings with Iraqi foreign minister Tariq Aziz in Paris on several occasions in 1983. In May 1983 Schultz summarized one of these meetings in a cable to Aziz in which he pleaded for diminished Iraqi support for "international terrorism" in exchange for warmer relations with the United States. Terrorism, Schultz explained, posed a menace to both the United States and Iraq as it "emanates at times from the same [Iranian-inspired] sources." Schultz promised that "any new evidence that Iraq has decisively rejected international terrorism as an instrument of its foreign policy would have immediate positive effects" on the Reagan administration's policy toward Iraq.[34]

Laurie Mylroie

One of the most outspoken proponents of positive relations with Iraq during these years was Laurie Mylroie, a Wolfowitz confidante and an avid Saddam watcher. During the final phases of the Iran-Iraq War, Mylroie—at the time an assistant professor of government at Harvard—promoted Saddam as a constructive force in the region and a possible conduit for brokering an Israeli-Palestinian deal. In an article coauthored with Daniel Pipes, son of Harvard historian Richard Pipes and director of the conservative Middle East Forum, she argued that "seven years of bloody and inconclusive warfare" with the Islamic Republic of Iran had "changed Iraq's view of its Arab neighbors, the United States, and even Israel. Iraq restored relations with the United States in November 1984. Its leaders no longer consider the Palestinian issue their problem. Iraq's allies since 1979 have been those states—Kuwait, Saudi Arabia, Jordan, and Morocco—most threatened by revolutionary upheaval, most friendly to the United States, and most open to negotiations with Israel." War, argued Mylroie and Pipes, had imposed moderation on Iraqi ambitions.[35]

As late as 1989, Mylroie still hailed Saddam as a positive force for American interests in the Middle East. Saddam's regional ambitions in the aftermath of war were manifestly benign, if not constructive, she remarked. "Today, Iraq is closely aligned with the moderate Arab states. . . . The change in Iraq's alignment has implications for its posture toward the Arab-Israeli conflict, entailing an end to Iraqi rejectionism." She described Iraq's posture as "more 'moderate' than it was at any time before or during the war or any time during the Baathist rule."[36] Saddam Hussein's mass slaughtering of Kurds in 1987 and 1988 did not strike Mylroie as a reason to revise her position. According to multiple reports, Mylroie launched her own private mission of shuttle diplomacy between Iraq and Israel, confident in her ability to channel the energies of a reformed Saddam Hussein into a peace agreement with Israel.[37]

In 1990, the campaign for détente with Iraq self-destructed when Iraq invaded its Kuwaiti neighbor. Mylroie adjusted swiftly, transforming Saddam overnight from a scheming yet useful pragmatist to an unreconstructed demon. In a 1997 article published under the auspices of the Rubin Center for Research in International Affairs at the IDC (Interdisciplinary Center) in Herzliya, Israel, Mylroie enumerated a litany of Iraq's acts of defiance against UN weapons inspectors. The Clinton administration's effete policies, Mylroie warned, had enabled Iraq to arrive on the cusp of producing a formidable arsenal of WMD that would capsize the delicate balance of Middle Eastern power politics. The only way to thwart Saddam's nuclear ambitions was by forcible removal. The "late Professor Albert Wohlstetter had maintained that it was impossible to eliminate Saddam's weapons of mass destruction without eliminating Saddam himself. Wohlstetter has certainly been proven right."[38] A post-Saddam Iraq, deprived of its WMD, "would have a salutary effect on the Arab-Israeli peace process, as countries like Saudi Arabia would cease to turn to countries like Syria or Iran for help in dealing with an increasingly resurgent Iraq."[39]

In a July 2003 e-mail to a participant on right-wing conspiracy web-site Free Republic, Mylroie explained the importance of linking WMD to Saddam Hussein's ambitions for international terrorism. "I'm most appreciative that you picked up that remark: *You can go to war on the basis of the WMD, but not on the basis of terrorism.* That is why Bush has been unable to explain why we fought this war." As for the reason underlying Bush's tongue-tied response to criticism of his Iraqi policy, Mylroie added: "You're absolutely right about the enemy within," by which she meant senior administration officials who were allegedly sabotaging the Bush Doctrine.[40]

Mylroie's sensationalist image of an Iraqi mastermind of global terror was part of a process that Chaim Kaufmann has described as threat inflation and an addiction to threats where none existed.[41] "The shock of Saddam Hussein's invasion of Kuwait left Mylroie with a monomania about the Iraqi dictator that encroached on her judgment and eventually overturned her good sense," observed Daniel Pipes, who turned from collaborating with her to criticizing her. "After the invasion, she self-hijacked a hitherto-promising career to prove two bizarre assertions: that Saddam Hussein had a hand in virtually every terrorist incident and, conversely, that Islamists and others did not have a part in them."[42]

In her newly found invective against Saddam Hussein, CNN analyst Peter Bergen later concluded, Mylroie produced "what amounts to the discovery of a unified field theory of terrorism." She insisted that "Saddam was not only behind the '93 Trade Center attack, but also every anti-American terrorist incident of the past decade, from the bombings of U.S. embassies in Kenya and Tanzania to the leveling of the federal building in Oklahoma City to September 11 itself. She is, in short, a crackpot."[43]

Appearing before the 9/11 Commission during the Iraq War in 2003, Mylroie remained unrepentant, further sharpening her portrayal of Saddam's global reach. Al Qaeda, she announced, "was a front for Iraqi intelligence in much the same way that Hizbollah is a front for the Iranians and the Syrians." Senior administration officials were alarmed, she told the commission, at this "nexus between terrorist states and terrorist groups," as they feared "terrorism using weapons of mass destruction, including biological weapons."[44]

Mylroie informed the 9/11 committee members that there had been a conspiracy of government obstructionists who were allegedly undermining efforts to reveal this uncomfortable truth. "We went to war because senior administration officials believe Iraq was involved in 9/11. But as we did that and they tried to articulate it, they heard, and it would come out in the form of disgruntled individuals within the bureaucracies, including the CIA, leaking to the press 'there is no evidence.'" While refusing to name her source, Mylroie still went on record stating that a "senior administration official told me in specific that the question of the identities of the terrorist masterminds could not be pursued because of bureaucratic obstructionism."[45]

Mylroie's gyrations might have warranted nothing beyond an obscure footnote but for the presence of her influential mentors. By Mylroie's own admission, her representation of the Iraqi dictator as über-terrorist was not a solitary creation. In the introduction to her book-length diatribe portraying Saddam as the enabler of global terror, she all but admitted that her Al Qaeda–Iraq thesis was a joint creation engaging a powerful Beltway family. Mylroie singled out Clare Wolfowitz, Paul Wolfowitz's recently divorced spouse, as an adviser "who fundamentally shaped this book, infusing it with her wisdom, prudence, and very considerable talent for expression."[46] As for Clare's former spouse—all three were alumni of Cornell University's elite Telluride House—Mylroie noted that "Paul Wolfowitz was kind enough to listen to this work presented orally and then later read the manuscript. At critical times, he provided crucial support for a project that is inherently difficult."[47] The dust jacket contained some self-serving praise from Paul Wolfowitz, endorsing Mylroie's assertion that Iraqi intelligence had masterminded the 1993 attack. Wolfowitz pleaded that Mylroie's conclusion should, by necessity "change our views on Iraq's continuing efforts to retain weapons of mass destruction and to acquire new ones." Richard Perle added his own insight. "If Mylroie is right," he wrote, "we would be justified in concluding that Saddam was probably involved in the September 11, 2001, attack." By Perle's account, Mylroie had demonstrated that "there can be no war against terrorism that is not also a war against Saddam Hussein."[48]

Perle did not, however, maintain this conviction in public. In a verbal exchange with Stacey Bannerman, an activist for the families of returning veterans of the war in Iraq, Perle denied ever hearing, and by implication ever supporting, the theory of a connection between Saddam Hussein and Al Qaeda. "I didn't hear statements to the effect that Iraq was responsible for 9/11," he informed an incredulous Bannerman.[49] Perle's short-term memory appeared to have failed him. In a November 2006 interview on National Public Radio, Perle stated categorically that "the intelligence about Saddam's stockpiles appears certainly to have been wrong. I don't believe it's correct to say that his ties to terrorists have been discredited. There were numerous links between Iraqi intelligence and various terrorist organizations, including al Qaeda. Those have been documented. And I frequently hear people say that there's no evidence. It's simply wrong. I've seen the evidence."[50]

Perle's endorsement of the Saddam–Al Qaeda connection received assists from close colleagues. Richard Clark, the national coordinator for counterterrorism during the administration of George W. Bush, recalls a sharp confrontation with Paul Wolfowitz in April 2001 surrounding the Mylroie thesis. Wolfowitz accused Clark of giving bin Laden "too much credit" and ignoring the fact that bin Laden could not have pulled off his spectacular feats without state sponsorship. "Just because FBI and CIA have failed to find the linkages does not mean they don't exist," an angry Wolfowitz argued. "I could hardly believe it," Clark recalled, "but Wolfowitz was actually spouting the totally discredited Laurie Mylroie theory."[51]

Mylroie's observations on the triangular threat of terrorism, nuclear weapons, and Saddam Hussein bear a striking resemblance to Paul Wolfowitz's comments in the infamous May 2003 *Vanity Fair* interview. His narrative is worth repeating. Toward the tail end of the interview, Wolfowitz was distracted by a phone call. He appeared to lose his concentration, and, much to the concern of his senior adviser, Kevin Kellems, who was listening in to the interview, Wolfowitz became unusually candid. Between competing phone calls, Wolfowitz enumerated the three main challenges posed by Saddam Hussein: "There have always been three fundamental concerns. One is weapons of mass destruction, the second is support for terrorism, the third is the criminal treatment of the Iraqi people." The U.S. government decided to place WMD as its main concern because "the truth is that for reasons that have a lot to do with the U.S. government bureaucracy we settled on the one issue that everyone could agree on, which was weapons of mass destruction as the core reason" for the invasion. "The third one by itself, as I think I said earlier, is a reason to help the Iraqis, but it's not a reason to put American kids' lives at risk, certainly not on the scale we did it. That second issue about links to terrorism is the one about which there's the most disagreement within the bureaucracy, even though I think everyone agrees that we killed a hundred or so of an al Qaeda group in northern Iraq in this recent go-around, that we've arrested that al Qaeda guy in Baghdad who was connected to this guy Zarqawi whom Powell spoke about in his UN presentation."[52] In other words, the threat of Iraqi WMD was privileged for purposes of gaining public support.

Wolfowitz and Perle were by no means the only disseminators of Mylroie's linkage between state-enabled global terrorism and WMD. Following Iraq's invasion of Kuwait, Donald Rumsfeld presented Mylroie's thesis as the foundation for U.S. policy in the Gulf. Having transitioned from friendly envoy to Saddam Hussein to secretary of defense and a lead proponent of the invasion, he enthusiastically demonized Saddam, placing particular emphasis on the threat of Iraqi WMD. After 9/11, Rumsfeld implicated Iraq as the quintessential example of state-enabled terror. The threat of terrorism was not independent of the system of states, he declared. It was, instead, an effective tool employed by malevolent rogue states to consolidate their influence by remote control. Iraq, for Rumsfeld, had "relationships with terrorist networks. . . . They also have Al Qaida currently in the country." The potential to "use terrorist networks to dispense weapons of mass destruction is what's qualitatively different in our current circumstance."[53]

By Rumsfeld's account, the fateful day had arrived with all the telltale signs of a Roberta-style surprise attack. Rogue states, Iraq being a prime example, had discovered a new means of delivering the modern-day equivalent of Pearl Harbor by employing terrorist networks. In contrast to the Beirut events of the early 1980s but very much in character with Roberta's early observations, Rumsfeld predicted a quantum leap, with rogue states concealing "their responsibility for attacks on our people" by transferring WMD to terrorist clients. In the case of Iraq, Rumsfeld said, there was a clear "nexus between a country that is actively developing weapons of mass destruction, that is known as a terrorist state, and the use of those weapons, whether by them or, through a proxy, a terrorist network."[54] Roberta's 1976 "glimmer of interest in massive terror among terrorists" had turned into a blinding light.[55]

Writing in the aftermath of the First Gulf War, Zalmay Khalilzad concurred. He argued "that terrorists might gain access to and use WMD in the region or even in the U.S. Although terrorists have not used WMD so far, it could change."[56] Ten years after the 2003 invasion of Iraq, Richard Perle continued to insist that collaboration between a nuclear-armed Iraq and terrorist organizations was a legitimate possibility. "Having failed to anticipate any attack on the scale of 9/11 . . . we were suddenly faced with the danger of the next attack, perhaps with weapons of mass destruction," he observed. He asked of Saddam: "Could he—would he—make WMD available to terrorists for use against the United States? The question had become urgent."[57]

Branding Iraq as a nuclear threat poised to use its terrorist proxies for extending its nuclear arm may have been a tactic designed to cower opposition through fearmongering. It may also have been a delusionary self-fulfilling prophecy. Terror on a grand scale was first raised by a charismatic parent figure. A Pearl Harbor in modern times, Roberta had warned in her original study, might eventually involve WMD, and a terrorist event involving WMD would preclude any meaningful attempt to recuperate losses and respond in an effectual manner.[58] And yet a prudent Roberta found such a chain of events highly improbable. Roberta's faithful followers exhibited no such caution. On the eve of the Iraq invasion, they resurrected her 1976 warning, blew it out of its original proportions, and superimposed their iteration of her thoughts on Iraq.

As for Laurie Mylroie, her theories continued to percolate through government channels long after she had been discredited. The Defense Department's Office of Net Assessment (ONA) provided her a particularly important platform. In 2005 ONA published her extended history of Al Qaeda, basically a regurgitation of her previous theories.[59] In 2007 ONA published two additional reports written by Mylroie: "Saddam's Strategic Concepts: Dealing with UNSCOM" and "Saddam's Foreign Intelligence Service."[60] Established during the Nixon administration, ONA's first and only director until January 2015 was Andrew Marshall, a member of the Wohlstetter inner circle.[61] According to his biographers, Andrew considered himself a loyal apprentice to Albert.[62] Moreover, Roberta had described Andrew as an intimate friend and the inspiration for her Pearl Harbor study.

ONA's safe haven for the discredited theories of Wohlstetter acolytes was all the more remarkable given the U.S. Senate's Intelligence Committee's unequivocal conclusion, published in 2006. "Postwar findings indicate that Saddam Hussein was distrustful of al Qa'ida and viewed

Islamic extremists as a threat to his regime, refusing all requests from al Qa'ida to provide material or operational support. Debriefings of key leaders of the former Iraqi regime indicate that Saddam distrusted Islamic radicals in general, and al Qa'ida in particular. . . . Debriefings also indicate that Saddam issued a general order that Iraq should not deal with al Qa'ida. No postwar information suggests that the Iraqi regime attempted to facilitate a relationship with bin Laden."[63]

Farewell, but Not Goodbye

In May 2015, one-time Republican presidential hopeful Jeb Bush announced that his team of foreign advisers included Paul Wolfowitz.[64] As a visiting scholar at the American Enterprise Institute (AEI), Wolfowitz has had an active retirement. In fact, his writing and media appearances provide a glimpse of the Wolfowitz world since his hasty retreat from the World Bank. His ruminations, posted on the AEI website, are dedicated almost exclusively to pointing out gaping holes in logic and imagination in the Obama administration's nuclear agreement with Iran.[65]

Wolfowitz's AEI papers suggest that the nuclear accord with the Islamic Republic will actually make further military intervention in the Gulf inevitable. The imminent removal of economic sanctions, "as well as the commitment by the EU and the U.S. to refrain from any actions that would adversely affect the normalization of trade and economic relations with Iran, will effectively disable the use of economic leverage to respond to Iranian provocations." By removing the threat of economic sanctions, Wolfowitz writes, "the agreement disables the principal soft power instrument of U.S.-Iranian policy. It is particularly ironic, when President Obama is presenting the agreement as the only alternative to military action, that future presidents will find themselves effectively deprived of non-military instruments for dealing with Iran."[66]

Zalmay Khalilzad, who has demonstrated an attraction to presidential contender Donald Trump, has similarly faulted the Obama administration for ignoring the glaring and not-so-unanticipated consequences of the accord. "The Obama administration assumes that a nuclear agreement will strengthen moderates in Iran. Yet it is equally if not more likely that the agreement will strengthen the current regime." Rather than encouraging moderation, the economic infusion of funds following the lifting of sanctions would allow the regime to "resist political change, calculating that economic improvements will lower the demand for political reform."[67]

Neither Wolfowitz nor Khalilzad assign evil intentions to the Obama administration. Instead they describe the accord as a road of good intentions paved with flawed imagination and bureaucratic inertia. Richard Perle—he, too, found refuge at the AEI—tends to agree. "President Obama, who is the most risk-adverse figure in a risk-averse administration, brings the idea of acting as a last resort to new heights," Perle observes. "The result is that America, with an accumulation of scorned entreaties behind it and no strategy going forward, has become a bystander nation, cloaked in passivity, paralyzed with indecision. When President Obama said in his first Inaugural Address, 'We are ready to lead once more,' he might have added, 'maybe, as a last resort.' "[68] As far as Wolfowitz, Khalilzad, and Perle are concerned, the Iranian nuclear crisis was an immaculate conception, the result of Democratic mismanagement of affairs of state. By virtue of their silence, we are led to believe that their own actions in Iraq had no meaningful connection with Iran's rising fortunes. Given such breathtaking historical amnesia, we can only commiserate with Albert Wohlstetter, who once said that "it would be a terrible irony if our historic military success" in Iraq "were to end in an equally historic political and human disaster."[69]

The Theater of War

Pearl Harbor remained the fount of the Wohlstetter Doctrine, and *Hamlet* was its inspiration. It is therefore appropriate to return to both tropes for the final scene. In late December 1944, fifteen hundred GIs filled the camp theater at Schofield barracks, the secondary target of the Japanese surprise attack situated some eighteen miles north of the attack's epicenter, to witness a rendition of *Hamlet* for the military masses. "Neither planes, bugles," nor other disruptive noises of camp life distracted the "enraptured" audience from what the distinguished war correspondent Quentin Reynolds described as a masterpiece.[70]

The production was the labor of love of noted Shakespearean actor Maurice Evans—"the greatest living Hamlet," according to Reynolds—and at the time the commander of army entertainment in the Pacific theater.[71] The Evans version was edited for both time considerations and for content, much of which ironed out the Prince of Denmark's existential anguish. In fact, this condensed format produced an unambivalently heroic Hamlet, a man of action. Evans deleted the parts of the play that showed the character as emotionally unstable, paralyzed by procrastination, or beset by "unmanly grief." His Hamlet was challenged not by doubt but by exterior circumstances. The Evans Hamlet was "a character in whom every GI would see himself vaguely reflected—a man compelled to champion his conception of right in a world threatened by the domination of evil."[72] This Hamlet was a goal-oriented, ordinary person, who chose the difficult but righteous path when confronted with unmitigated evil. The exigencies of war, Todd Landon Barnes notes in another context, had resolved Hamlet's dilemmas. The idea that "wartime—as a time of exception—forecloses indecision" was "perhaps best articulated by Joyce's Stephen Daedalus who, in an oblique reference to the Boer War, sadly observes, 'Khaki Hamlets don't hesitate to shoot.' "[73]

Evans's Pearl Harbor *Hamlet* had a mesmerizing conclusion. In the final scene, as Hamlet expires in the arms of Horatio, the theater was plunged into darkness. The empty silence of the night was broken only by Horatio's words: "Now cracks a noble heart. Good night, sweet prince." Reynolds was moved by the astonishing theatrical device of having Hamlet die in pitch-black emptiness; the symbolism was evocative and bold, never before seen. The crowd of GIs roared its approval, only to discover that this electrifying finale was the result of a power failure.[74] A technical glitch had added a level of faux depth to this highly redacted performance of the "Mona Lisa of literature."[75]

American politicians and pundits have long labored with literary metaphors to add color, depth, and meaning to exigencies of war, with a thoroughly Americanized representation of Hamlet leading the pack. The results have most often been shallow and ridden with platitude. Fred Iklé, a Wohlstetter confidante, knew why. In a 1991 homage to the Wohlstetters, Iklé observed that an application of the arts to the grim world of global confrontation could be accomplish only by intellectual giants. In blurring the distinction between life and the arts, Iklé explained, the Wohlstetters had dispelled the fog of war that often precluded decision making under conditions of uncertainty and partial information. The Wohlstetters appeared to be in a league of their own because only the chosen few could hope to match their broad education and knowledge. They were the ultimate champions of a mixed-methods approach in strategic studies, a fusion of mathematical rigor with the complex amalgam of culture and politics undergirding global power plays. The key to their success, Iklé argued, was in their educations and life journeys. The culturally impoverished could never become great strategists, Iklé submitted. Quite the contrary: great strategists must "appreciate different cultures and good art . . . have, perhaps, an eye for architecture or painting, an ear for the best music . . . a broad understanding of philosophy, literature and, of course, history." Their "talent for creative work in security strategy goes together with a heart that clings to the beauty and values of our civilization."[76]

The Wohlstetters' accomplishments were, indeed, derived from their commodious understanding of American culture and their uncanny ability to tap into the nation's most inchoate fears. Edward Albee's critically acclaimed 1966 drama, "A Delicate Balance," demonstrates the confluence of culture and politics harnessed by the Wohlstetters. This appropriately named play unveils a comfortable and confident American couple who are forced to confront a mysterious existential threat brought into their home by unexpected guests, who flee in response to this unnamed but incapacitating terror. The tranquility of the couple's home is further disrupted by their impulse to sweep the unhappiness of their daughter under the domestic carpet until such time as it can no longer be ignored. In a 1996 preface, Albee wrote that "the play concerns . . . the rigidity and ultimate paralysis which afflicts those who settle in too easily, waking up one day to discover that all the choices they have avoided no longer give them any freedom of choice, and that what choices they do have left are beside the point."[77] The Wohlstetters could not have said it better.

While Roberta and Albert will always be remembered first and foremost as strategists for the nuclear age, the full gamut of their writings exposes their own anxieties over disruption and loss of control in the second half of the twentieth century. Through their own contributions to the collective fears and phobias of this epochal period in the nation's history, they affected and reflected the multiple sources of disruption rippling through the nation. They argued that any form of Hamlet-like procrastination in countervailing these supreme challenges—whether domestic or external—would tip the West into an abyss of dissembling mayhem.

Urged on by their mentors, the Wohlstetters' disciples in government advocated the very same vigilant concern for potential threats, brushing aside the allegedly timid paradigms of the establishment rivals. They adopted their mentors' foreboding that hesitancy or retreat would logically invite an enemy to pursue its ambitions at the expense of the United States.

The essence of deterrence theory, as the Wohlstetters passed it on to their followers, was the attempt to see the world through the lens of the Enemy Other, and thereby to anticipate the conclusions and actions of adversarial forces. Their intimate disciples, however, lacked the epistemological breadth of their mentors.

The three close collaborators presented in Chapters 9, 10, and 11 were, in essence, institutional gate-crashers proclaiming questionable omniscience: an academic bereft of the trappings of peer-reviewed publications, a sword bearer who cowed opponents through scare tactics, and an ambitious immigrant from the ethnic peripheries of American society who skillfully rode the coattails of his mentors to the center of American power.

They filled the public sphere with predictions about the impact of their mentors' discoveries on the future of humankind, affecting an air of knowledge while constantly courting disaster. Showing little concern for empirical evidence aside from the odd historical anecdote, the Wohlstetters' mentees promoted an arbitrary and contested construction of the enemy. In place of the "Western-preferred" strategies they so maligned, they concocted an irrational choice theory for an imaginary nightmare involving oil and nuclear terrorism that could only be averted by voiding the routine of incapacitating procrastination. Their prognostications were saturated with a species of eschatology that Albert had denounced, in a 1963 takedown of his rivals, as the vague tonalities of "the prophecies of Nostradamus"—more like "scattered shots in the dark" than "predictions deduced from a finished scientific theory."[78] Albert's second-generation followers claimed the very sort of false knowledge that Albert had denounced in his many diatribes against conventional expertise.

This litany of duplicities and factoids on WMD and Iraqi-inspired terror is a popular explanation for the debacle, but it is an unsatisfactory one, because it tends to deflect attention from the flawed sociological foundation of this crusade manqué. The Iraq invasion was much more than a great lie. It was the culmination of a great cultural delusion, as well. Its architects, in general, and its Wohlstetter-inspired promoters, in particular, trivialized and dismissed the role of faith-based politics in the Middle East and the attendant functional role of authoritarian regimes in containing pan-Islamic radicalism. As Francis Fukuyama, a former ally, has remarked, the Wohlstetters' acolytes were first and foremost poor historians who drew facile analogies between the collapse of the Soviet empire and the very different challenges of the Middle East. Having witnessed the remarkable spread of democratic currents in the Eastern bloc following the collapse of the Soviet Union, they erroneously concluded that the removal of regional despots would lead to similar results. Their fatal flaw, Fukuyama observed, was their assumption "that democracy was a default condition to which would revert once liberated from dictators."[79] Indeed, the post-Soviet experience itself has hardly been one of a seamless transition to democracy.

The advocates of the Iraqi invasion trivialized religious identity politics of the region in general and of Iraq in particular. Having willingly fallen under the spell of a small and inconsequential group of secular Iraqis in exile, they eagerly fell into a trap of their own making, believing that a small group of secular Iraqis in exile could tame the sectarian behemoth that, up to that point, had been ruthlessly contained by the Baathist regime. Contrary to their expectation, the separation of mosque and state—an essential ingredient in the seeding of democratic self-government—was rejected by all parties, other than the deposed Baathists, in the Iraqi civil war that ensued under their watch.

The great delusion was the creation of ideological "simplicists," by which I mean a cadre of individuals driven by a pervasive suspicion of complexity, rather than some slight on the intelligence of its perpetrators.[80] The Wohlstetter students regarded with contempt their colleagues who beat winding paths through dense brush in order to get a closer view of complicated problems. In the end, they argued, these dense journeys produced dense solutions. Wolfowitz, Perle, and their kind preferred the crisp geometric path, usually the straight, uncluttered line. They insisted on following the shortest link between two points, even when these dyads produced unrelated, and occasionally disastrous, combinations. Circuitous routes, they argued, bred doubt and inertia, which, in turn, would spawn a proverbial nation of Hamlets.

In 2004, while he was still the deputy secretary of defense in the George W. Bush administration, Paul Wolfowitz shared an anecdote illustrating what he described as the debilitating weight of convention in moments of crisis. The vignette concerned the British army's efforts to address the slow rate of artillery fire in its frontline units during World War II. Called in to observe an artillery battery in action, an efficiency expert noticed that, prior to firing, "two members of the gun crew would cease all activity and come to attention for a period of three seconds. Then the gun would be fired." Seeking to understand this enigmatic freeze, the expert consulted a veteran artillery officer. Upon hearing the story, "the old colonel brightened up, and he said, 'I have it. They're holding the horses.'"[81] Having ridden the storm, the Wohlstetter cavalry now paces impatiently in the wings of the next theater of war, hoping for a second chance to unbridle their phantom horses.

Notes

Introduction

1. Both quotations are from Fred M. Kaplan, *The Wizards of Armageddon* (Stanford, CA: Stanford University Press, 1983), title and 11, respectively.
2. A pictorial essay on the Wohlstetter home appears in Timothy Braseth, "Joseph Van der Kar: Building Architectural Bridges," *Modernism*, Summer 2011, 44–53, www.artcrafthomesla.com/Modernism_Magazine_-_Van _der_Kar.pdf.
3. Kaplan, *Wizards of Armageddon*, 122.
4. Deborah Welch Larson, "Deterrence Theory and the Cold War," *Radical History Review* 63 (1995): 109.
5. Jude Wanniski, "Albert Wohlstetter, RIP," January 16, 1997, in *Polyconomics: The Works and Life of Jude Wanniski*, www.polyconomics.com/fyi/fyi -970116.htm.
6. More admiring studies include Robert Zarate's introduction in Albert Wohlstetter and Roberta Wohlstetter, *Nuclear Heuristics: The Selected Writings of Albert and Roberta Wohlstetter*, ed. Zarate and Henry Sokolski (Carlisle, PA: Strategic Studies Institute, U.S. Army War College, 2009); Richard Rosecrance, "Albert Wohlstetter," in *Makers of Nuclear Strategy*, ed. John Baylis and John Garnett (London: Pinter Publishers, 1991), 57–69. More condemnatory studies include Andrew Bacevich, "Tailors to the Emperor," *New Left Review* 69 (May–June 2011): 100–124; Fred Kaplan, *Daydream Believers: How a Few Grand Ideas Wrecked American Power* (Hoboken, NJ: Wiley, 2008).
7. Richard Klein, "The Future of Nuclear Criticism," *Yale French Studies* 97 (2000): 83.
8. Major accounts of the Wohlstetters and their impact include Kaplan, *Wizards of Armageddon*; Bruce Kuklick, *Blind Oracles: Intellectuals and War from Kennan to Kissinger* (Princeton, NJ: Princeton University Press, 2006); Craig Unger, *The Fall of the House of Bush: The Untold Story of How a Band of True Believers Seized the Executive Branch, Started the Iraq War, and Still Imperils America's*

Future (New York: Scribner, 2007); Alex Abella, *Soldiers of Reason: The RAND Corporation and the Rise of the American Empire* (New York: Houghton Mifflin Harcourt, 2009); Jacob Heilbrunn, *They Knew They Were Right: The Rise of the Neocons* (New York: Doubleday, 2008); Kaplan, *Daydream Believers;* Andrew J. Bacevich, *The New American Militarism: How Americans Are Seduced by War*, rev. ed. (New York: Oxford University Press, 2013); Bacevich, "Tailors to the Emperor"; Muhammad Idrees Ahmad, *The Road to Iraq: The Making of a Neoconservative War* (Edinburgh: Edinburgh University Press, 2014). One particularly fascinating exception to the rule of avoiding the Wohlstetter world beyond strategic studies is Pamela Lee, "Aesthetic Strategist: Albert Wohlstetter, the Cold War, and a Theory of Mid-Century Modernism," *October* 138 (Fall 2011): 15–36.

9. Scholarship that recognizes the fundamental influence of Roberta's *Pearl Harbor* thesis includes Bacevich, "Tailors to the Emperor"; Kaplan, *Wizards of Armageddon,* 92–94; Kuklick, *Blind Oracles,* 59; and Zarate, "Introduction."

10. Anthony David, "The Apprentice," *American Prospect*, May 19, 2007, http://prospect.org/article/apprentice.

11. Patricia Sullivan, "Roberta Wohlstetter; Military Intelligence Expert," *Washington Post*, January 10, 2007, www.washingtonpost.com/wp-dyn/content/article/2007/01/09/AR2007010901741.html.

12. Roberta Morgan and Albert Wohlstetter, "Observations on 'Prufrock,'" *Harvard Advocate* 124 (December 1938): 27–40.

13. Albert Wohlstetter, "Strength, Interest and New Technologies" (Santa Monica, CA: RAND Corporation, January 24, 1968), www.rand.org/about/history/wohlstetter/DL16624/DL16624.html.

14. Albert Wohlstetter, "Bishops, Statesmen, and Other Strategists on the Bombing of Innocents," *Commentary* 75, no. 6 (1983): 596. Albert was punning on a line from *Hamlet,* act 2, scene 2.

15. Roberta Wohlstetter and Albert Wohlstetter, "On Dealing with Castro's Cuba" (Santa Monica, CA: RAND Corporation, January 16, 1965), www.rand.org/about/history/wohlstetter/D17906/D17906.html.

16. Ibid.

17. The Wohlstetters' writings on Cuba include Roberta Wohlstetter, "Notes on Castro and Oswald: The Maximo Lider on the Assassination," February 1964, Wohlstetter Papers, box 381, folder 7; Roberta Wohlstetter, "Cuba and Pearl Harbor: Hindsight and Foresight," *Foreign Affairs* 43, no. 4 (July 1965): 691–707; Roberta Wohlstetter, "Little War in a Big Shadow: Ties of Castro's Insurrection to the United States," September 1972, Wohlstetter Papers, box 381, folder 11; Albert Wohlstetter and Roberta Wohlstetter, "Notes on the Cuban Crisis" (Santa Monica, CA: RAND Corporation, D[L]-10647-ISA, October 28, 1962), www.rand.org/about/history/wohlstetter/DL10647/DL10647.html; Wohlstetter and Wohlstetter, "On Dealing with Castro's Cuba."

18. Robert Wohlstetter, "Kidnapping to Win Friends and Influence People," *Survey* 4, no. 93 (Autumn 1974): 1–40; Roberta Wohlstetter, "Terror on a Grand Scale," *Survival: Global Politics and Strategy* 18, no. 3 (1976): 98–104. On the "Theater of Terror," see Gabriel Weimann, "The Theater of Terror: Effects of Press Coverage," *Journal of Communication* 33 (1983): 33–45. Weimann accords authorship of the term to Brian Jenkins of the RAND Corporation.

19. James Digby and Joan Goldhamer, "The Development of Strategic Thought at RAND, 1948–63: A Mathematical Logician's View—an Interview with Albert Wohlstetter" (Santa Monica, CA: RAND Corporation, July 5, 1985), 60; Albert Wohlstetter and Henry Rowen, "Objectives of the United States Military Posture" (Santa Monica, CA: RAND Corporation, RM 2373, May 1, 1959), www.rand.org/about/history/wohlstetter/RM2373/RM2373.html.

20. Nathan Leites, "The New Economic Togetherness: American and Soviet Reactions," *Studies in Comparative Politics* 7, no. 3 (Autumn 1974): 246–285.

21. Bruce Kuklick, "H-Diplo Roundtable—*Blind Oracles*, Author's Response," ed. Thomas Maddux, 2006, http://h-diplo.org/roundtables/PDF/Kuklick-Response.pdf.

22. Mary Kaldor, *The Baroque Arsenal* (New York: Hill and Wang, 1981).

23. On strategists' search for a new enemy to replace the Soviet Union, see Andrea Lueg, "The Perceptions of Islam in Western Debate," in *The Next Threat: Western Perceptions of Islam*, ed. Jochen Hippler and Andrea Lueg, trans. Laila Friese (London: Pluto Press, 1995), 4.

24. Scholars have previously noted Albert Wohlstetter's advocacy of regime change. See Peter Minowitz, *Straussophobia: Defending Leo Strauss and Straussians against Shadia Drury and Other Accusers* (Lanham, MD: Lexington Books, 2009), 26; Bacevich, *New American Militarism*, 165; Abella, *Soldiers of Reason*, 286.

25. On democracy theory, see Michael W. Doyle, "Kant, Liberal Legacies, and Foreign Affairs," parts 1 and 2, *Philosophy and Public Affairs* 12, nos. 3 and 4 (Summer and Fall 1983): 205–235; Michael W. Doyle, "Kant: Liberalism and World Politics," *American Political Science Review* 80, no. 4 (December 1986): 1151–1169; Francis Fukuyama, "Liberal Democracy as a Global Phenomenon," *Political Science and Politics* 24, no. 4 (1991): 662; Jack S. Levy, "Domestic Politics and War," in *The Origin and Prevention of Major Wars*, ed. Robert I. Rotberg and Theodore K. Rabb (Cambridge: Cambridge University Press, 1989), 88. For an opposing view, see Christopher Layne, "Kant or Cant: The Myth of the Democratic Peace," *International Security* 19, no. 2 (Fall 1994): 5–49.

26. Evan Thomas, *Ike's Bluff: President Eisenhower's Secret Battle to Save the World* (New York: Little, Brown, 2012), 272.

27. For treatments of Wolfowitz and Perle, see Lewis D. Solomon, *Paul D. Wolfowitz: Visionary Intellectual, Policymaker, and Strategist* (Westport, CN: Praeger

Security International, 2007); Alan Weisman, *Prince of Darkness: Richard Perle: The Kingdom, the Power, and the End of Empire in America* (New York: Union Square Press, 2007). Khalilzad is discussed at length in Sonali Kolhatkar, *Bleeding Afghanistan: Washington, Warlords, and the Propaganda of Silence* (New York: Seven Stories Press, 2010); David L. Phillips, *Losing Iraq: Inside the Postwar Reconstruction Fiasco* (New York: Basic Books, 2009); and Michael R. Gordon and Bernard E. Trainor, *The Endgame: The Inside Story of the Struggle for Iraq, from George W. Bush to Barack Obama* (New York: Vintage Books, 2013). For a general discussion of Albert Wohlstetter's impact on the blueprints for an American empire, see Bacevich, *New American Militarism,* chaps. 6 and 7.

28. Francis Fukuyama, "After Neoconservatism," *New York Times Magazine,* February 19, 2006, www.uvm.edu/~wgibson/Of_interest/Fukuyama.pdf.

29. On the terrorist as a "smart bomb," see Bruce Hoffman, "The Logic of Suicide Terrorism," *Atlantic,* June 2003, www.theatlantic.com/magazine/archive/2003/06/the-logic-of-suicide-terrorism/302739/.

30. Kaplan, *Daydream Believers,* 194.

31. Michael Lind, "The Weird Men behind George W. Bush's War," *New Statesman,* April 7, 2003, www.newstatesman.com/node/145148.

32. Alan Wald, "Are Trotskyites Running the Pentagon?," *History News Network,* June 27, 2003, http://hnn.us/article/1514.

33. The rumor that Albert Wohlstetter was influenced by Strauss began with James Atlas, "A Classicist's Legacy: New Empire Builders," *New York Times,* May 4, 2003, WK1. Robert Bartley debunked the claim a month later in "Joining Larouche in the Fever Swamps," *Wall Street Journal,* June 3, 2003, www.wsj.com/articles/SB105513011183328200. See also Anne Norton, *Leo Strauss and the Politics of the American Empire* (New Haven, CT: Yale University Press, 2004), 182; Minowitz, *Straussophobia,* 27–28; Catherine H. and Michael P. Zuckert, *The Truth about Leo Strauss: Political Philosophy and American Democracy* (Chicago: University of Chicago Press, 2008), 11–12.

34. Thomas Farr, *World of Faith and Freedom: Why International Religious Liberty Is Vital to American National Security* (New York: Oxford University Press, 2008), 70.

35. Kuklick, *Blind Oracles.*

36. Scholars who argue that Albert Wohlstetter had a decisive impact on American military strategy include Marc Trachtenberg, *History and Strategy* (Princeton, NJ: Princeton University Press, 1991), 19; Morton H. Halperin, "The Gaither Committee and the Policy Process," *World Politics* 13, no. 3 (April 1961): 366n21. See Paul C. Avey and Michael C. Desch, "Why the Wizards of Armageddon Ran into an Intellectual Dead-End: And What That Tells Us about the Relevance of Academic Nuclear Strategy Today," draft paper, December 2014, https://data.itpir.wm.edu/trippub/images/NuclearWeaponsAndStrategy.pdf.

37. Sharon Ghamari-Tabrizi, *The Worlds of Herman Kahn: The Intuitive Science of Thermonuclear War* (Cambridge, MA: Harvard University Press, 2005).

38. Ibid., 5; Louis Menand, "Fat Man; Herman Kahn and the Nuclear Age," *New Yorker,* June 27, 2005, www.newyorker.com/magazine/2005/06/27/fat -man.

39. Ghamari-Tabrizi, *The Worlds of Herman Kahn,* 248.

40. Herman Kahn, quoted in ibid., 17.

41. Albert Wohlstetter, "The Structure of the Proposition and the Fact," *Philosophy of Science* 3, no. 2 (April 1936): 167–184. Quotations from Charles Wohlstetter, *The Right Time the Right Place* (New York: Applause, 1997), 13–14.

42. Albert Wohlstetter, "Scientists, Seers, and Strategy," *Foreign Affairs* 41, no. 3 (April 1963): 466–478.

43. Barry Scott Zellen, "Bernard Brodie: A Clausewitz for the Nuclear Age," *Strategic Innovator,* January 1, 2009, http://securityinnovator.com/index.php ?articleID=15954&sectionID=43.

44. Michael Howard, "Brodie, Wohlstetter and American Nuclear Strategy," *Survival* 34, no. 2 (Summer 1992): 113.

45. Gertrude Himmelfarb, *On Looking into the Abyss: Untimely Thoughts on Culture and Society* (New York: Knopf, 1994), 27.

1. The Wohlstetter Partnership

1. Robert Kirsch, "Trouble Shooter Aims High: 1963 Times Woman of the Year," *Los Angeles Times,* January 15, 1964, D1.

2. Art Seidenbaum, "U.S. History: Have We Learned Our Lesson? Southlanders Give History Lessons," *Los Angeles Times,* May 5, 1963, L2, 27.

3. Kirsch, Trouble Shooter Aims High."

4. Seidenbaum, "U.S. History."

5. "Edmund Morgan of Harvard Dies," *New York Times,* February 1, 1966, 35.

6. G. Louis Joughin and Edmund M. Morgan, *The Legacy of Sacco and Vanzetti* (New York: Harcourt, Brace, 1948), 157.

7. Edmund S. Morgan, quoted in David Courtwright, "Fifty Years of American History: An Interview with Edmund S. Morgan," *William and Mary Quarterly* 42, no. 2 (April 1987): 343–344.

8. See the biographical notes on Roberta Wohlstetter in "A Register of the Albert J. and Roberta Wohlstetter Papers," Online Archive of California, http://pdf.oac.cdlib.org/pdf/hoover/wohlstet.pdf.

9. Jerome Michael and Mortimer Adler, *Crime, Law, and Social Science* (New York: Harcourt, Brace, 1933), 69.

10. Ibid., 315.

11. Ibid., 210.

12. Ibid., 92.

13. Roberta Morgan, "One Approach to the Problem of Institutional Behavior of Delinquent Women" (MA thesis, Columbia University, 1936), 39.

14. Ibid., 35–36.

15. Ibid., 44.

16. Ibid.

17. Roberta Morgan, "Introduction" in draft dissertation, page i, Wohlstetter Papers, box 357, folder 5.

18. Quote is paraphrased from ibid.

19. Ibid., p. ii.

20. Roberta Morgan, draft dissertation, chapter 1 (untitled), p. 1, Wohlstetter Papers, box 357, folder 5.

21. Roberta Morgan, chapter 3 (untitled), p. 19, Wohlstetter Papers, box 356, folder 4.

22. Ibid., p. 43.

23. Ibid., p. 49.

24. Some biographic information on Theodore Spencer can be found in "Theodore Spencer Journals, 1937–1947: Finding Aid," Princeton University Library, Department of Rare Books and Special Collections, http://findingaids .princeton.edu/collections/C1056.pdf.

25. Theodore Spencer, "Miss Morgan's Thesis" (n.d.), Wohlstetter Papers, box 357, folder 13.

26. Letter to Roberta Morgan (n.a., n.d.), Wohlstetter Papers, box 357, folder 13.

27. See, for example, Theodore Spencer, "The Responsibility of the English Teacher," *College English* 1, no. 7 (April 1940): 589–594.

28. Roberta Morgan to "Howard," draft for a letter mailed February 26, 1942, Wohlstetter Papers, box 357, folder 13.

29. Theodore Spencer, "Hamlet and the Nature of Reality," *Journal of English Literary History* 5, no. 4 (December 1938): 258, 263–264.

30. Spencer, "The Responsibility of the English Teacher," 589.

31. Ibid., 590.

32. Ibid., 594.

33. Roberta Morgan, "The Philosophical Basis of Coleridge's Hamlet Criticism," *Journal of English Literary History* 6, no. 4 (December 1939): 256–270; Roberta Morgan, "Some Stoic Lines in Hamlet and the Problem of Interpretation," *Philological Quarterly* 20, no. 4 (October 1941): 549–558.

34. Morgan, "The Philosophical Basis of Coleridge's Hamlet Criticism," 258.

35. Samuel Taylor Coleridge, *Coleridge's Shakespearean Criticism,* ed. Thomas Middleton Raysor (Cambridge, MA: Harvard University Press, 1930), 2:197–198, quoted in ibid., 268.

36. Morton White, *A Philosopher's Story* (University Park: Pennsylvania University Press, 1999), 35.

37. Albert Wohlstetter, in Jim Digby and Joan Goldhamer, "The Development of Strategic Thinking at RAND, 1948–1963: A Mathematical Logician's View—an Interview with Albert Wohlstetter, July 5, 1985" (Santa Monica, CA: RAND Corporation, 1997), 4.

38. White, *Philosopher's Story,* 35.

39. Digby and Goldhamer, "The Development of Strategic Thinking at RAND," 8.

40. Jim Digby, in ibid.; Richard M. Cook, *Alfred Kazin: A Biography* (New Haven, CT: Yale University Press, 2007), 24. See also Robert Vanderlan, *Intellectuals Incorporated: Politics, Art, and Ideas inside Henry Luce's Media Empire* (Philadelphia: University of Pennsylvania Press, 2010), 273.

41. Albert Wohlstetter, in Digby and Goldhamer, "The Development of Strategic Thinking at RAND," 8. Some purport that Albert had been a member of the Socialist Workers Party before 1932, while at City College. See, for example, Robert L. Richardson Jr., "Neoconservatism: Origins and Evolution, 1945–1980" (PhD diss., University of North Carolina–Chapel Hill, 2009), 97.

42. Cook, *Alfred Kazin,* 25.

43. Digby and Goldhamer, "The Development of Strategic Thinking at RAND," 10.

44. White, *Philosopher's Story,* 36.

45. W. V. Quine, *The Time of My Life: An Autobiography* (Cambridge, MA: MIT Press, 2000), 124, 147, 184, 198.

46. Albert Wohlstetter, in Digby and Goldhamer, "The Development of Strategic Thinking at RAND," 14.

47. White, *Philosopher's Story,* 125.

48. Roberta Morgan and Albert Wohlstetter, "Observations on 'Prufrock,'" *Harvard Advocate* 124 (December 1938): 27–29.

49. Ibid., 38.

50. Albert Wohlstetter, "Strength, Interest, and New Technologies" (Santa Monica, CA: RAND Corporation, D[L]-16624-PR, January 24, 1968), www.rand.org/about/history/wohlstetter/DL16624/DL16624.html.

51. Albert Wohlstetter, in Digby and Goldhamer, "The Development of Strategic Thinking at RAND," 12.

52. White, *Philosopher's Story,* 37.

53. On Schapiro, art, and politics, see two articles in *Oxford Art Journal* 17, no. 1 (1994): Andre Hemingway, "Meyer Schapiro and Marxism in the 1930s," 13–29, and Patricia Hills, "1936: Meyer Schapiro, 'Art Front' and the Popular Front," 30–41, as well as other articles in this issue.

54. Wayne Anderson, "Marx and the Reacting Sensibility of Artists," *Social Research* 45, no. 1 (Spring 1978): 68.

55. See Peter Berkowitz, *Varieties of Conservatism in America* (Stanford, CA: Hoover Institution Press, 2004), 112; Jacob Heilbrunn, *They Knew They Were Right: The Rise of the Neocons* (New York: Doubleday, 2008), 99.

56. On Schapiro's use of this pseudonym, see Alan M. Wald, *The New York Intellectuals: The Rise and Decline of the Anti-Stalinist Left from the 1930s to the 1980s* (Chapel Hill: University of North Carolina Press, 1987), 212.

57. David Merian [Meyer Schapiro], "Socialism and the Failure of the Nerve—the Controversy Continued: Reply to Sidney Hook," *Partisan Review* 10, no. 5 (September–October 1943): 474.

58. David Merian [Meyer Schapiro], "The Nerve of Sidney Hook," *Partisan Review* 10, no. 3 (May–June 1943): 251–252.

59. Ibid., 256.

60. Sidney Hook, "The Politics of Wonderland," *Partisan Review* 10, no. 3 (May–June 1943): 258.

61. Sidney Hook, "Faith, Hope, and Dialectic: Merian in Wonderland," *Partisan Review* 10, no. 5 (September–October 1943): 479.

62. Albert Wohlstetter and M.G. White, "Who Are the Friends of Semantics?," *Partisan Review* 6, no. 5 (Fall 1939): 53.

63. Stuart Chase, *The Tyranny of Words* (New York: Harcourt, Brace, 1938), 22.

64. Wohlstetter and White, "Who Are the Friends of Semantics?," 53. Emphasis in original.

65. Ibid., 50–55. See also Sidney Hook, "Some Social Uses and Abuses of Semantics," *Partisan Review* 4, no. 5 (April 1938): 14–25.

66. On the Wohlstetters' youthful leftist connections, see, for example, Wald, *The New York Intellectuals,* 107; Alex Abella, *Soldiers of Reason: The RAND Corporation and the Rise of the American Empire* (New York: Houghton Mifflin Harcourt, 2009), 75–78; Heilbrunn, *They Knew They Were Right,* 100.

67. White, *Philosopher's Story,* 37.

68. Lionel Abel, *The Intellectual Follies: A Memoir of the Literary Venture in New York and Paris* (New York: Norton, 1984), 37.

69. Robert J. Alexander, *International Trotskyism, 1929–1985: A Documented Analysis of the Movement* (Durham, NC: Duke University Press, 1991), 773–774.

70. Albert Wohlstetter, "Economic and Strategic Considerations in Air Base Location: A Preliminary Review" (Santa Monica, CA: RAND Corporation, D-1114, December 29, 1951), www.rand.org/about/history/wohlstetter /D1114.html.

71. Albert Wohlstetter, in Digby and Goldhamer, "The Development of Strategic Thinking at RAND," 32–33.

72. William Barrett, *The Truants: Adventures among the Intellectuals* (Garden City, NY: Anchor Press/Doubleday, 1982), 92.

73. Wald, *The New York Intellectuals,* part 3.

74. Barrett, *The Truants,* 94, 96.

75. Biographical notes on Roberta Wohlstetter in "A Register of the Albert J. and Roberta Wohlstetter Papers."

2. Roberta Wohlstetter

1. Robert L. Richardson, "Neoconservatism: Origins and Evolution" (PhD diss., University of North Carolina, 2009), 99. See also Charles Wohlstetter, *The Right Place, The Right Time* (New York: Applause, 1997), 116.

2. Albert Wohlstetter, in Martin Collins and Joseph Tatarewicz, *National Air and Space Museum and RAND Corporation, Joint Oral History Project on the History of the RAND Corporation, Santa Monica, July 29, 1987* (National Aerospace Museum, Washington, DC: RAND Oral History Series, 1989), 3.

3. The story of the GPC is the subject of Gilbert Herbert, *Dreams of the Factory-Made House: Walter Gropius and Konrad Wachsmann* (Cambridge, MA: MIT Press, 1984). Albert Wohlstetter called Wachsmann a "mad genius" in Jim Digby and Joan Goldhamer, "The Development of Strategic Thinking at RAND, 1948–1963: A Mathematical Logician's View—an Interview with Albert Wohlstetter, July 5, 1985" (Santa Monica, CA: RAND Corporation, 1997), 29.

4. Digby and Joan Goldhamer, "The Development of Strategic Thinking at RAND," 26–31.

5. Roberta Wohlstetter and Joseph Goldsen, "American and British Protests against Allied Bombing in World War II," in RAND Social Science Division, "The Warning of Target Populations in Air War; an Appendix of Working Papers," Appendix O 1–11. See Andrew David May, "The RAND Corporation and the Dynamics of American Strategic Thought, 1946–1962" (PhD diss., Emory University, 1998), 106–108.

6. See the biographical notes on Albert Wohlstetter in "A Register of the Albert J. and Roberta Wohlstetter Papers," Online Archive of California, http://pdf.oac.cdlib.org/pdf/hoover/wohlstet.pdf.

7. On RAND's founding, see Alex Abella, *Soldiers of Reason: The RAND Corporation and the Rise of the American Empire* (New York: Harcourt, 2008); David Hounshell, "The Cold War, RAND, and the Generation of Knowledge, 1946–1962," *Historical Studies in the Physical and Biological Sciences* 27, no. 2 (1997): 237–267.

8. Hounshell, "The Cold War, RAND," 243.

9. Ibid., 241.

10. James A. Smith, *The Idea Brokers: Think Tanks and the Rise of the New Policy Elite* (New York: Free Press, 1991), xiii.

11. Morris Janowitz, "Remarks," in *Symposium Proceedings: The U.S. Army's Limited-War Mission and Social Science Research,* ed. William Lybrand (Washington, DC: Special Operations Research Office, 1962), 147.

12. Philip Green, "Science, Government, and the Case of RAND: A Singular Pluralism," *World Politics* 20, no. 2 (January 1968): 312.

13. Ibid., 317.

14. Roberta Wohlstetter, review of John McDonald, *Strategy in Poker, Business, and War,* 1950, Wohlstetter Papers, box 112, folder 19. Mills's understanding of the "sophisticated conservatives"—a precursor to his "power elites"—appears in C. Wright Mills, with Helen Schneider, *The New Men of Power: America's Labor Leaders* (New York: Harcourt, Brace, 1948).

15. The initial study for RAND was Roberta Wohlstetter, "Signals and Decisions at Pearl Harbor" (Santa Monica, CA: RAND Corporation, R-331, 1958). It was published as *Pearl Harbor: Warning and Decision* (Stanford, CA: Stanford University Press, 1962).

16. Roberta Wohlstetter, "Chronology on Pearl Harbor Study," n.d., Wohlstetter Papers, box 377, folder 1.

17. Various letters from Roberta in Wohlstetter Papers, box 377, folder 2. Emphasis in original.
18. Roberta Wohlstetter to John Chamberlain, December 28, 1962, Wohlstetter Papers, box 377, folder 5.
19. Roberta Wohlstetter, letter to the editor, *Wall Street Journal,* October 18, 1962, 12. "Day of Infamy" is the title commonly given to December 7, 1941.
20. Wohlstetter to Chamberlain.
21. Warner Schilling, "Surprise, Attack, Death, and War: A Review," *Journal of Conflict Resolution* 9, no. 3 (September 1965): 386.
22. Wohlstetter, *Pearl Harbor,* 384.
23. Ibid., 349.
24. Ibid., 55. The expression appears to originate in William James's 1890 *Principles of Psychology,* in which he wrote of "the baby, assailed by . . . one great blooming, buzzing confusion"; William James, *Principles of Psychology* (New York: Henry Holt, 1890), 1:488.
25. Wohlstetter, *Pearl Harbor,* 393.
26. Michael Handel, "The Yom Kippur War and the Inevitability of Surprise," *International Studies Quarterly* 21, no. 3 (September 1977): 462.
27. Edward Luttwak and Dan Horowitz, *The Israeli Army* (London: Allan Lane, 1975), 340. Emphasis in original.
28. Wohlstetter, *Pearl Harbor,* 230.
29. Ibid., 152–159.
30. Ibid., 356.
31. Ibid., 357.
32. Ibid., 355.
33. Ibid., 396.
34. Ibid., 389.
35. Ibid., 397.
36. Ibid., 304.
37. Ibid., 397.
38. Stephen Chan, "The Intelligence of Stupidity; Understanding Failures in Strategic Warning," *American Political Science Review* 73, no. 1 (March 1979): 175.
39. Wohlstetter, *Pearl Harbor,* 399.
40. MacArthur cited in Harvey A. DeWeerd, "Strategic Surprise in the Korean War," *Orbis* 6, no. 3 (Fall 1962): 440.
41. Ibid., 441.
42. Ibid., 445.
43. Ibid., 446.
44. Ibid., 451.
45. Wohlstetter, *Pearl Harbor,* 399.
46. Ibid., 397.
47. Ibid., 399.

48. Ibid., 287, 395.

49. Ibid., 70, 382.

50. Ibid., 400–401.

51. Ibid., 401.

52. See for example, Johan Jorgen Holst, "Surprise, Signals, and Reaction: The Attack on Norway, April 9, 1940—Some Observations," *Cooperation and Conflict* 2, no. 1 (March 1967): 31–45; Barton Whaley, *Codeword Barbarossa* (Cambridge, MA: MIT Press, 1973).

53. The battle lines separating the orthodox school from revisionists are delineated in Richard K. Betts, "Surprise, Scholasticism, and Strategy: A Review of Ariel Levite's *Intelligence and Strategic Surprises*," *International Studies Quarterly* 33, no. 3 (September 1989): 329–343. Some of the primary proponents of the orthodox school, in addition to those cited here, include Alexander George and Richard Smoke, *Deterrence and American Foreign Policy* (New York: Columbia University Press, 1974); Klaus Knorr, "Failures in National Intelligence Estimates: The Case of the Cuban Missiles," *World Politics* 16, no. 3 (April 1964): 455–467; and Harold Wilensky, *Organizational Intelligence* (New York: Basic Books, 1967).

54. See, for example, Avi Shlaim, "Failures in National Intelligence Estimates: The Case of the Yom Kippur War," *World Politics* 28, no. 3 (April 1976): 348–380.

55. Critics include Eliot Cohen and John Gooch, *Military Misfortunes: The Anatomy of Failure in War* (New York: Free Press, 1990); Irving Janis, *Victims of Groupthink: A Psychological Study of Foreign-Policy Decisions and Fiascoes* (Boston: Houghton-Mifflin, 1972); and David Kahn, "The Intelligence Failure of Pearl Harbor," *Foreign Affairs* 70, no. 5 (Winter 1991): 138–152.

56. Ariel Levite, *Intelligence and Strategic Surprises* (New York: Columbia University Press, 1987), 52.

57. Ibid., 65.

58. Ibid., 82. Emphasis in original.

59. Ibid., 93.

60. Ariel Levite, "Intelligence and Strategic Surprises Revisited: A Response to Richard Betts' 'Surprise, Scholasticism, and Strategy,'" *International Studies Quarterly* 33, no. 3 (September 1989): 349.

61. Wohlstetter, *Pearl Harbor*, 398–399.

62. Robert Jervis, "Hypothesis on Misperception," in *Readings in American Foreign Policy*, ed. Morton Halperin and Arnold Kanter (Boston: Little, Brown, 1973), 134.

63. Chan, "The Intelligence of Stupidity," 175.

64. Levite, "Intelligence and Strategic Surprises Revisited," 349.

65. Michael Howard, "Military Intelligence and Surprise Attack: The 'Lessons' of Pearl Harbor," *World Politics* 15, no. 4 (July 1963): 701–711.

66. Ibid., 705.

67. Bernard Brodie, *Strategy in the Missile Age* (Princeton, NJ: Princeton University Press, 1959), 397.

68. Howard, "Military Intelligence," 709, 711.

69. Schilling, "Surprise, Attack, Death, and War," 390.

70. Ibid., 389.

71. Ibid., 387.

72. Ibid., 389.

73. Richard Betts, *Surprise Attack: Lessons for Defense Planning* (Washington, DC: Brookings Institution, 1982).

74. Robert Jervis, Richard Ned Lebow, and Janice Gross Stein, eds., *Psychology and Deterrence* (Baltimore, MD: Johns Hopkins University Press, 1985).

75. Roger Dingman, "Reflections on Pearl Harbor Anniversaries Past," in "December 7, 1941: The Pearl Harbor Attack," ed. Roger Dingman, special issue, *Journal of American–East Asian Relations* 3, no. 3 (Fall 1994): 284–285.

76. Bernard Brodie, "Implications for Military Policy," in *The Absolute Weapon: Atomic Power and World Order,* ed. Bernard Brodie (New York: Harcourt, Brace, 1946), 76.

77. George Kennan, quoted in David Allan Mayers, *George Kennan and the Dilemmas of U.S. Foreign Policy* (New York: Oxford University Press, 1988), 308.

78. Albert Wohlstetter, in Office of the Secretary of Defense, Historical Office, oral history interview with Professor Albert Wohlstetter by Dr. Maurice Matloff, January 30, 1986, 21, http://history.defense.gov/Portals/70/Documents/oral_history/OH_Trans_WohlstetterAlbert1-30-1986.pdf.

79. Albert Wohlstetter and Roberta Wohlstetter, "Notes on the Cuban Crisis" (Santa Monica, CA: RAND Corporation, D(L)-10647-ISA, October 28, 1962), www.rand.org/about/history/wohlstetter/DL10647/DL10647.html.

80. Wohlstetter, in Office of the Secretary of Defense, oral history interview, 18–19.

81. Ibid., 20. Emphasis in original.

82. Dominic Tierney, "'Pearl Harbor in Reverse': Moral Analogies in the Cuban Missile Crisis," *Journal of Cold War Studies* 9, no. 3 (Summer 2007): 49–77. The history of the ExComm tapes is the subject of Sheldon Stern, *The Cuban Missile Crisis in American Memory: Myths versus Reality* (Palo Alto, CA: Stanford University Press, 2012).

83. Tierney, "'Pearl Harbor in Reverse.'"

84. Roberta Wohlstetter, "Cuba and Pearl Harbor: Hindsight and Foresight," *Foreign Affairs* 43, no. 4 (July 1965): 707.

3. "In Dubious Battle"

1. John Milton, *Paradise Lost,* quoted in Bernard Brodie, "The Atomic Dilemma," *Annals of the American Academy of Political and Social Science* 248 (January 1947): 32.

2. Ibid.

3. Bernard Brodie, "The Development of Nuclear Strategy," *International Security* 2, no. 4 (Spring 1978): 66.

4. Bernard Brodie, "Implications for Military Policy," in *The Absolute Weapon: Atomic Power and World Order,* ed. Bernard Brodie (New York: Harcourt, Brace, 1949), 76.

5. Bernard Brodie, "War in the Atomic Age," in *The Absolute Weapon,* 63.

6. Ibid., 83.

7. Robert Jervis, "Variation, Change and Transitions in International Politics," in *Empires, Systems, and States: Great Transformations in International Politics,* ed. Michael Cox, Tim Dunne, and Ken Booth (Cambridge: Cambridge University Press, 2001), 290; Barry Scott Zellen, *State of Doom: Bernard Brodie, the Bomb, and the Birth of the Bipolar World* (New York: Continuum, 2012), 145; Bruce Kuklick, *Blind Oracles: Intellectuals and War from Kennan to Kissinger* (Princeton, NJ: Princeton University Press, 2006), 59–60.

8. Brodie, "Implications for Military Policy," 76.

9. Alex Abella, *Soldiers of Reason: The RAND Corporation and the Rise of the American Empire* (New York: Harcourt, 2008), 41.

10. Albert Wohlstetter, "Theory and Opposed-Systems Design," *Journal of Conflict Resolution* 12, no. 3 (September 1968): 328. Marianne Moore, quoted by Bonnie Costello, *Marianne Moore: Imaginary Possessions* (Cambridge, MA: Harvard University Press, 1981), 21. Moore was paraphrasing Yeats in the last phrase.

11. Laurence Stapleton, cited in Elizabeth Gregory, *Quotation and Modern American Poetry: Imaginary Gardens with Real Toads* (Houston, TX: Rice University Press, 1996), 157.

12. Deborah Welch Larson, "Deterrence Theory and the Cold War," *Radical History Review* 63 (1955): 86–109.

13. Most of Albert's writings for RAND are available at www.rand.org/about /history/wohlstetter.html. The article is Albert Wohlstetter, "The Delicate Balance of Terror," *Foreign Affairs* 37, no. 2 (January 1959): 211–234.

14. See Robert Zarate's introduction in Albert Wohlstetter and Roberta Wohlstetter, *Nuclear Heuristics: The Selected Writings of Albert and Roberta Wohlstetter,* ed. Zarate and Henry Sokolski (Carlisle, PA: Strategic Studies Institute, U.S. Army War College, 2009), 26; Rajesh Basrur, "Nuclear Deterrence: The Wohlstetter-Blackett Debate Re-Visited," S. Rajaratnam School of International Studies Working Paper, April 15, 2014, 3–4, www.rsis.edu.sg/rsis -publication/rsis/280-nuclear-deterrence-the-wohlst/#.VX4jsvlVhBc.

15. Albert Wohlstetter, in James Digby and Joan Goldhamer, "The Development of Strategic Thinking at RAND, 1948–1963: A Mathematical Logician's View—an Interview with Albert Wohlstetter, July 5, 1985" (Santa Monica, CA: RAND Corporation, 1997), 57. Brackets and emphasis in original.

16. Albert Wohlstetter, "The Delicate Balance of Terror" (Santa Monica, CA: RAND Corporation, P-1472, November 6, 1958, rev. December 1958), www

.rand.org/about/history/wohlstetter/P1472/P1472.html. Hereafter, all references to "Delicate Balance of Terror" are to the RAND version.

17. Ibid., endnote 6.

18. Ibid., part 5.

19. Albert's first reference to the example of Pearl Harbor is in Albert Wohlstetter et al., "Selection and Use of Strategic Air Bases" (Santa Monica, CA: RAND Corporation, April 1954, R-266), 18, www.rand.org/pubs/reports/R0266.html.

20. Ibid.

21. Ibid.

22. Secretary of State Dean Acheson, Secretary of the Navy Francis Matthews, and President Harry Truman all advocated or considered first strikes on the Soviet Union. Abella, *Soldiers of Reason,* 43.

23. Wohlstetter, "Delicate Balance of Terror." Emphasis in original.

24. Wohlstetter et al., "Selection and Use of Strategic Air Bases," esp. 299–307. See also Albert Wohlstetter and Fred Hoffman, "Defending a Strategic Force after 1960," (Santa Monica, CA: RAND Corporation, D-2270, 1954), www.rand.org/about/history/wohlstetter/D2270/D2270.html.

25. Wohlstetter et al., "Selection and Use of Strategic Air Bases."

26. Scholars who have credited Wohlstetter as the inventor of "second-strike capability" include Robert Ayson, *Thomas Schelling and the Nuclear Age: Strategy as Social Science* (London: Frank Cass, 2004), 60; Patrick Coffey, *American Arsenal: A Century of Waging War* (New York: Oxford University Press, 2014), 221. The RAND Corporation itself credits Wohlstetter's studies as having "led to the 'second strike' and 'Fail-Safe' concepts." See the introduction to "Writings of Albert Wohlstetter," website of the RAND Corporation, www.rand.org/about/history/wohlstetter.html.

27. Albert Wohlstetter, "Diversity in Interactions at the 1950s RAND," November 4, 1991, Wohlstetter Papers, box 120, folder 27.

28. Richard Rosecrance, "Albert Wohlstetter," in *Makers of Nuclear Strategy,* ed. John Baylis and John C. Garnett (London: Pinter, 1991), 57. Other authors who support the Brodie claim to originality include Fred Kaplan, *The Wizards of Armageddon* (Stanford, CA: Stanford University Press, 1991), 122; Scott Ritter, *Dangerous Ground: America's Failed Arms Control Policy, from FDR to Obama* (New York: Nation Books, 2010), 67–68.

29. Kaplan, *Wizards of Armageddon,* 121; Andrew May, "The RAND Corporation and the Dynamics of American Strategic Thought" (PhD diss., Emory University, 1998), 132.

30. Wohlstetter, "Delicate Balance of Terror."

31. Mark Rix, "The Games Grown-Ups Play: The Disciplinary Formation of Strategic Studies, 1946–1960" (2000), 12–13, Global Site. Originally available at www.theglobalsite.ac.uk/010rix.pdf. Currently available via the Internet Archive, at https://web.archive.org/web/20030321180937/http://www.theglobalsite.ac.uk/press/010rix.pdf.

32. Brodie, "Development of Nuclear Strategy," 68.

33. Richard Curl, "Strategic Doctrines in the Nuclear Age," *Strategic Review* 3 (Winter 1975): 48.

34. Rix, "The Games Grown-Ups Play," 2.

35. Winston Churchill, "The Deterrent—Nuclear Warfare," speech to the British House of Commons, March 1, 1955, in *Winston S. Churchill: His Complete Speeches, 1897–1963*, vol. 8: *1950–1963*, ed. Robert Rhodes James (London: Chelsea House, 1974), 8629.

36. John Lewis Gaddis, "The Long Peace: Elements of Stability in the Postwar International System," *International Security* 10, no. 4 (Spring 1986): 99–142.

37. Henry Kissinger, *Diplomacy* (New York: Simon and Schuster, 1994), 714.

38. Wohlstetter, "Delicate Balance of Terror."

39. Ibid., 231.

40. Albert Wohlstetter and Henry Rowen, "Objectives of the United States Military Posture" (Santa Monica, CA: RAND Corporation, RM 2373, May 1, 1959), www.rand.org/about/history/wohlstetter/RM2373/RM2373.html. Emphasis in original.

41. Wohlstetter, "Delicate Balance of Terror."

42. On rational choice theory at RAND, see Sonja Michelle Amadae, *Rationalizing Capitalist Democracy: The Cold War Origins of Rational Choice Liberalism* (Chicago: University of Chicago Press, 2003), chap. 1.

43. Wohlstetter, in Digby and Goldhamer, "The Development of Strategic Thinking at RAND," 21. Emphasis in original.

44. Wohlstetter and Rowen, "Objectives of the United States." Emphasis in original.

45. Ibid. On Kahn's influence on Wohlstetter, see Kaplan, *Wizards of Armageddon*, 368.

46. On advocacy for MAD, see Henry D. Sokolski, *Getting MAD: Nuclear Mutual Assured Destruction, Its Origins and Practice* (Carlisle, PA: Strategic Studies Institute, U.S. Army War College, 2004).

47. Albert expressed his critique of the "cities only" approach most fully in his article "Bishops, Statesmen, and Other Strategists on the Bombing of Innocents," *Commentary* 75, no. 6 (June 1983): 15–35. See also his comments in Digby and Goldhamer, "The Development of Strategic Thinking at RAND," 43–45. On the "cities only" versus counterforce debate, see Paul Ramsey, "The Limits of Nuclear War: The Do-Able and the Un-Do-Able," in *Moral Dimensions of American Foreign Policy*, ed. Kenneth Winfred Thompson (New Brunswick, NJ: Transaction, 1984), 105–152.

48. See especially Wohlstetter's articles "Analysis and Design of Conflict Systems," in *Analysis for Military Decisions*, ed. E. S. Quade (Chicago: Rand McNally, 1964), 103–48; "Theory and Opposed-Systems Design." The quotation is from Albert Wohlstetter, "Strategy and the Natural Scientists," in *Scientists and National Policy-Making*, ed. Robert Gilpin and Christopher Wright (New York: Columbia University Press, 1964), 238.

49. Wohlstetter, "Strategy and the Natural Scientists," 195. Emphasis in original.

50. Wohlstetter, "Theory and Opposed-Systems Design," 306.

51. Ibid., 304.

52. Ibid., 307.

53. Ibid., 314.

54. Davis Bobrow, "Strategies beyond Followership," in *Hegemony Constrained: Evasion, Modification, and Resistance to American Foreign Policy,* ed. Bobrow (Pittsburgh, PA: University of Pittsburgh Press, 2008), 9.

55. Roberta Wohlstetter, "Nathan Leites, Always Surprising," in *Remembering Nathan Leites,* ed. Charles Wolf (Santa Monica, CA: RAND Corporation, 1988), 73.

56. Nathan Leites, *The Operational Code of the Politburo* (New York: McGraw-Hill, 1951). For more on this subject, see Ron Robin, *The Making of the Cold War Enemy: Culture and Politics in the Military-Intellectual Complex* (Princeton, NJ: Princeton University Press, 2003), 131–134.

57. Nathan Leites, *A Study of Bolshevism* (Glencoe, IL: Free Press, 1953), 21.

58. Leites, *The Operational Code of the Politburo,* xii.

59. Ibid., xv.

60. Nathan Leites, "Panic and Defense against Panic in the Bolshevik View of Politics," in *Psychoanalysis and the Social Sciences,* ed. Geza Roheim (New York: International Universities Press, 1955), 4:138.

61. Leites, *A Study of Bolshevism,* 403.

62. Leites, *The Operational Code of the Politburo,* 78.

63. Roberta Wohlstetter, "Draft for Chapter V: Some French Hamlets: Delacroix, Manet, and Odilon Redon." Sent to Sheldon Meyer, Oxford University Press, October, 15, 1959, Wohlstetter Papers, box 356, folder 4.

64. Roberta Morgan, "Notes for a Chapter on Melville: Hamlet in America," pp. 7–8, Wohlstetter Papers, box 356, folder 4.

65. Wohlstetter, in Digby and Goldhamer, "The Development of Strategic Thinking at RAND," 58.

66. Wohlstetter, "Analysis and Design of Conflict Systems," 131.

67. Wohlstetter, "Delicate Balance of Terror."

68. Ibid.

69. Roberta Wohlstetter, "The Pleasures of Self-Deception," *Washington Quarterly* 2, no. 4 (Autumn 1979): 61–62.

70. Wohlstetter, "Theory and Opposed-Systems Design," 311.

71. Ibid., 309.

72. Wohlstetter, "Strategy and the Natural Scientists," 228–229.

73. Ibid., 230.

74. Ibid., 197.

75. Wohlstetter, "Theory and Opposed-Systems Design," 319. The original Kennan quotation appears in George Kennan, *Russia and the West under Lenin and Stalin* (New York: New American Library, 1962), 261.

76. Wohlstetter, "Theory and Opposed-Systems Design," 324. Emphasis in original.

77. Ibid., 322.

78. Ibid., 324.

79. Ibid., 326.

4. *"He Is but MAD North-North-West"*

1. Michel Lefebvre, "Constantin Melnik (1927–2014), figure des services secrets," *Le Monde*, September 18, 2014, www.lemonde.fr/disparitions/article /2014/09/18/constantin-melnik-1927-2014-figure-des-services-secrets _4490305_3382.html. Melnik authored an influential RAND study of the Algerian War, "Insurgency and Counterinsurgency in Algeria" (Santa Monica, CA: RAND, D[L]-10671-1, April 23, 1964), www.rand.org/content /dam/rand/pubs/documents/2006/D10671-1.pdf. For a history of RAND counterinsurgency thinking that includes Melnik's work, see Austin Long, "Lessons from Five Decades of RAND Counterinsurgency Research" (Santa Monica, CA: RAND, MG-462, 2004), www.rand.org/content/dam/rand /pubs/monographs/2006/RAND_MG482.pdf.

2. Alex Abella, *Soldiers of Reason: The RAND Corporation and the Rise of the American Empire* (New York: Harcourt, 2008), 129–130, 196–197.

3. Barry Scott Zellen, *State of Doom: Bernard Brodie, the Bomb, and the Birth of the Bipolar World* (London: Continuum, 2012), 169, 233.

4. Albert Wohlstetter, in James Digby and Joan Goldhamer, "The Development of Strategic Thinking at RAND, 1948–1963: A Mathematical Logician's View—an Interview with Albert Wohlstetter, July 5, 1985" (Santa Monica, CA: RAND Corporation, 1997), 85–88.

5. For a popular history of Fawn Brodie, see Newell Bringhurst, *Fawn McKay Brodie: A Biographer's Life* (Norman: University of Oklahoma Press, 1999).

6. Ibid., 187.

7. Brodie cited in Zellen, *State of Doom,* 91–92.

8. Brodie cited in Fred Kaplan, *Wizards of Armageddon* (Stanford, CA: Stanford University Press, 1983), 222–223.

9. Bernard Brodie, *Strategy in the Missile Age* (Princeton, NJ: Princeton University Press, 1959), 314–315.

10. On psychopolitics and psychoculture, see Ron Robin, *The Making of the Cold War Enemy: Culture and Politics in the Military-Intellectual Complex* (Princeton, NJ: Princeton University Press, 2003), 127–136.

11. On Brodie and Leites, see Zellen, *State of Doom,* 280–283. On the Wohlstetters and Leites, see Roberta Wohlstetter, "Nathan Leites; Always Surprising," in *Remembering Nathan Leites: An Appreciation,* ed. Charles Wolf Jr. (Santa Monica, CA: RAND Corporation, 1988), 73–78; Wohlstetter, in Digby and Goldhamer, "The Development of Strategic Thinking at RAND," 58.

12. See, e.g., David R. Jardini, "Out of the Blue Yonder: The RAND Corporation's Diversification into Social Welfare Research" (PhD diss., Carnegie Mellon University, 1996).

13. Bernard Brodie, "The Development of Nuclear Strategy," *International Security* 2, no. 4 (Spring 1978): 68–69.

14. Ibid., 69.

15. Ibid.

16. Bernard Brodie, "The Scientific Strategists," in *Scientists and National Policy*, ed. Robert Gilpin and Christopher Wright (New York: Columbia University Press, 1964), 252.

17. Bernard Brodie, *War and Politics* (New York: Macmillan, 1973), 380. Emphasis in original.

18. Ibid., 462.

19. Ibid., 127.

20. Brodie, "Development of Nuclear Strategy," 69.

21. Ibid., 68.

22. Ibid., 11. On the Committee for Present Danger, see John Boies and Nelson A. Pichardo, "The Committee on the Present Danger: A Case for the Importance of Elite Social Movement Organizations to Theories of Social Movements and the State," *Berkeley Journal of Sociology* 38 (1993–1994): 57–87.

23. Brodie, "Development of Nuclear Strategy," 72. Emphasis in original.

24. Brodie, *War and Politics*, 126.

25. Ibid., 81.

26. Ibid., 78.

27. Ibid., 80.

28. Brodie, "Development of Nuclear Strategy," 76.

29. Ibid., 77. Emphasis in original.

30. P. M. S. Blackett, *Studies of War: Nuclear and Conventional* (Edinburgh: Oliver and Boyd, 1962), 92.

31. Ibid., 139.

32. Colin Gray, "What RAND Hath Wrought," *Foreign Policy* 4, no. 1 (Autumn 1971): 111.

33. Philip Green, "Strategy, Politics, and Social Scientists," in *Strategic Thinking and Its Moral Implications*, ed. Morton Kaplan (Chicago: University of Chicago, Center for Policy Study, 1973), 41.

34. Ibid., 42–43.

35. Philip Green, *Deadly Logic: The Theory of Nuclear Deterrence* (New York: Schocken, 1968), 37.

36. Green, "Strategy, Politics, and Social Scientists," 44. Emphasis in original.

37. Green, *Deadly Logic*, 268.

38. Albert Wohlstetter, quoted in ibid., 264.

39. Green, *Deadly Logic*, 264.

40. Ibid., 272.

41. Ibid., 261.

42. Gray, "What RAND Hath Wrought," 112.

43. Albert Wohlstetter, "Is There a Strategic Arms Race?," *Foreign Policy* 15 (Summer 1974): 3–20.

44. Michael Nacht, "The Delicate Balance of Error," *Foreign Policy* 19 (Summer 1975): 163–177.

45. Green, "Strategy, Politics, and Social Scientists," 50.

46. Ibid., 61.

47. Ibid., 62.

48. Green, *Deadly Logic,* 72.

49. Ibid., 77.

50. Green, "Strategy, Politics, and Social Scientists," 52n17.

51. Ibid., 52n16. Paul Wolfowitz uses the phrase *cities only* in his response to Green in the same volume, "The Pot and the Kettle, or Rationality within Reason: Mr. Green's Deadly Logic," in *Strategic Thinking and Its Moral Implications,* 95–96.

52. Green, *Deadly Logic,* 265.

53. Albert Wohlstetter, "Strategy and the Natural Scientists," in *Scientists and National Policy-Making,* ed. Robert Gilpin and Christopher Wright (New York: Columbia University Press, 1964), 208, quoted in ibid., 75.

54. Green, *Deadly Logic,* 261.

55. Ibid., 262–263.

56. Ibid., 90.

57. This elegant expression belongs to Richard Neustadt and Ernest May, *Thinking in Time: The Uses of History for Decision Makers* (New York: Free Press, 1986).

58. Albert Wohlstetter, "Bishops, Statesmen, and Other Strategists on the Bombing of Innocents," *Commentary* 75, no. 6 (June 1983): 27.

59. Brodie, "Development of Nuclear Strategy," 68–69.

60. Blackett, *Studies of War,* 135.

61. Roberta Wohlstetter, "Slow Pearl Harbors and the Pleasures of Deception," in *Intelligence Policy and National Security,* ed. Robert L. Pfaltzgraff Jr., Uri Ra'anan, and Warren H. Milberg (London: Macmillan, 1981), 23–34.

62. Roberta Wohlstetter, "Surprised by the Obvious," speech at the National Press Club, December 7, 1988, p. 16, Wohlstetter Papers, box 373, folder 14.

63. Roberta Wohlstetter, "The Pleasures of Self Deception," *Washington Quarterly* 2, no. 4 (1979): 55, 57, 62.

64. Robert Zarate's introduction to Albert Wohlstetter and Roberta Wohlstetter, *Nuclear Heuristics: The Selected Writings of Albert and Roberta Wohlstetter,* ed. Zarate and Henry Sokolski (Carlisle, PA: Strategic Studies Institute, U.S. Army War College, 2009), 61.

65. Wohlstetter, "Scientists, Seers, and Strategy," 474, 470.

66. Ibid., 468.

67. Ibid., 471.

68. Albert Wohlstetter, in Office of the Secretary of Defense, Historical Office, oral history interview with Professor Albert Wohlstetter by Dr. Maurice Matloff, January 30, 1986, 18–20, http://history.defense.gov/Portals/70/Documents/oral_history/OH_Trans_WohlstetterAlbert1-30-1986.pdf.

69. Wohlstetter, "Bishops, Statesmen, and Other Strategists," 32. Albert was quoting from *Hamlet,* act 2, scene 2.

70. National Conference of Catholic Bishops, *The Challenge of Peace: God's Promise and our Response; Pastoral Letter of the National Conference of Catholic Bishops on War and Peace, Second Draft* (Washington, DC: United States Catholic Conference, 1983).

71. Albert reacted to the pastoral letter in Wohlstetter, "Bishops, Statesmen, and Other Strategists," 15–35.

72. Francis X. Winters, letter to the editor, in "Letters from Readers: Morality and Deterrence; Albert Wohlstetter & Critics," *Commentary* 76, no. 6 (December 1983): 4.

73. National Council of Catholic Bishops, *The Challenge of Peace,* 1. The bishops are quoting from a statement made by the Second Vatican Council.

74. Ibid., 80 (paragraphs 259 and 260).

75. Ibid., 75 (paragraph 243).

76. Ibid., 83 (paragraph 270).

77. Ibid., 50 (paragraph 161).

78. Michael Walzer, *Just and Unjust Wars: A Moral Argument with Historical Illustrations* (New York: Basic Books, 1977), 282, quoted in James Blight, "'Limited' Nuclear War? The Unmet Psychological Challenge of the American Catholic Bishops," *Science, Technology & Human Values* 10, no. 4 (Autumn 1985): 8.

79. Bruce M. Russett, "Ethical Dilemmas of Nuclear Deterrence," *International Security* 8, no. 4 (Spring 1984): 39–40.

80. Winters in "Letters from Readers," 5.

81. Ibid., 5–6.

82. Wohlstetter, in "Letters from Readers," 16.

83. Wohlstetter, "Strategy and the Natural Scientists," 222.

84. Wohlstetter, "Bishops, Statesmen, and Other Strategists," 29.

85. Ibid., 23.

86. Pope John XXIII, "Pacem in Terris: Encyclical of Pope John XXIII on Establishing Universal Peace in Truth, Justice, Charity, and Liberty," April 11, 1963, http://w2.vatican.va/content/john-xxiii/en/encyclicals/documents/hf_j-xxiii_enc_11041963_pacem.html.

87. Wohlstetter, "Bishops, Statesmen, and Other Strategists," 15.

5. Castrophobia and the Free Market

1. Roberta Wohlstetter, "Notes on Castro and Oswald: The Maximo Lider on the Assassination," February 1964, 3 and 10–11, Wohlstetter Papers, box 381, folder 7.

2. Ibid., 11, quoting Teresa Casuso, *Cuba and Castro*, trans. Elmer Grossberg (New York: Random House, 1961), 188. On Roberta's work with Leites on Castro, see her "Nathan Leites: Always Surprising," in *Remembering Nathan Leites: An Appreciation*, ed. Charles Wolf Jr. (Santa Monica, C A: RAND Corporation, 1988), 73–78.

3. Albert Wohlstetter and Roberta Wohlstetter, "Notes on the Cuban Crisis" (Santa Monica, CA: RAND Corporation, D[L]-10647-ISA, October 28, 1962), www.rand.org/about/history/wohlstetter/DL10647/DL10647.html.

4. Wohlstetter, "Nathan Leites," 76.

5. Wohlstetter, "Notes on Castro and Oswald," 7.

6. Ibid., 4, citing Jules DuBois, *Fidel Castro: Rebel—Liberator or Dictator?* (Indianapolis: Bobbs-Merrill, 1959).

7. Wohlstetter, "Notes on Castro and Oswald," 11.

8. Ibid., 17.

9. Ibid., 11.

10. Ibid., 2–3.

11. Ibid., 5.

12. Albert Wohlstetter and Nancy Virts, "Armenian Terror as a Special Case of International Terror," in *Symposium on International Terrorism: Armenian Terrorism, Its Supporters, the Narcotic Connection, the Distortion of History* (Ankara: Ankara University, 1984), 274–275. On Joseph Sobran, see Joseph Sobran, "For Fear of the Jews," September 2002, www.sobran.com/fearofjews.shtml; Deborah Lipstadt, " 'Skeptical' on Holocaust?," *New York Times*, October 4, 2010.

13. Albert Wohlstetter, "No Highway to High Purpose" (Santa Monica, CA: RAND Corporation, P-2084-RC, June 1960), www.rand.org/about/history/wohlstetter/P2084/P2084.html. Published versions include "National Purpose: Wohlstetter View: Appraisal of the Need to Examine Means as Well as Ends," *New York Times*, June 16, 1960, 30; "A Purpose Hammered Out of Reflection and Choice," *Life*, June 20, 1960, 115 and 126–134; and "No Highway to National Purpose," in *The National Purpose*, ed. John Knox Jessup et al. (New York: Holt, Rinehart and Winston, 1960), 95–108.

14. Wohlstetter, "No Highway to High Purpose."

15. Ibid.

16. Albert Wohlstetter and Roberta Wohlstetter, " 'Third Worlds' Abroad and at Home," *Public Interest* 14 (Winter 1969): 90–91. An earlier, unpublished version was Albert Wohlstetter and Roberta Wohlstetter, "Metaphors and Models: Inequalities and Disorder at Home and Abroad" (Santa Monica, CA: RAND Corporation, D-17664-RC/ISA, August 27, 1968), www.rand.org/about/history/wohlstetter/D17664/D17664.html. The Wohlstetters were citing Gary Becker, *The Economics of Discrimination* (Chicago: University of Chicago Press, 1957).

17. Wohlstetter and Wohlstetter, " 'Third Worlds' Abroad and at Home," 99.

18. Albert Hirschman, *The Rhetoric of Reaction: Perversity, Futility, Jeopardy* (Cambridge, MA: Belknap Press, 1991).

19. Michael Walzer cited in Joseph Dorman, *Arguing the World: The New York Intellectuals in Their Own Words* (Chicago: University of Chicago Press, 2001), 169.

20. Albert Wohlstetter and Sinclair Coleman, "Race Differences in Income: Summary and Conclusions" (Santa Monica, CA: RAND Corporation, R578-OEO, October 1970), 101–102, www.rand.org/content/dam/rand/pubs/reports/2006/R578.pdf.

21. Wohlstetter and Wohlstetter, "'Third Worlds' Abroad and at Home," 98–99.

22. Quoted in ibid., 98. See also Ralph Ellison, Whitney M. Young Jr., and Herbert Gans, *The City in Crisis* (New York: A. Philip Randolph Educational Fund, 1966).

23. Wohlstetter and Wohlstetter, "'Third Worlds' Abroad and at Home," 99.

24. On antiblack racism in the Vietnam War, see James E. Westheider, *Fighting on Two Fronts: African Americans and the Vietnam War* (New York: New York University Press, 1997); Herman Graham, *The Brothers' Vietnam War: Black Power, Manhood, and the Military Experience* (Gainesville: University of Florida Press, 2003); Natalie Kimbrough, *Equality or Discrimination: African Americans in the U.S. Military during the Vietnam War* (Lanham, MD: University Press of America, 2007); and James E. Westheider, *The African American Experience in Vietnam: Brothers in Arms* (Lanham, MD: Rowman and Littlefield, 2008).

25. On black radicals and Cuba, see Cynthia Young, "Havana Up in Harlem: LeRoi Jones, Harold Cruse, and the Making of a Cultural Revolution," *Science and Society* 65, no. 1 (Spring 2001): 12–38.

26. Wohlstetter and Wohlstetter, "'Third Worlds' Abroad and at Home," 94–95.

27. Ibid.

28. Ibid.

29. Ibid.

30. Gunnar Myrdal, *An American Dilemma: The Negro Problem and Modern Democracy,* 2 vols. (New Brunswick, NJ: Transaction, 1996). Myrdal's other major works include *Economic Theory and Underdeveloped Regions* (New York: Harper Touchbooks, 1956); *Challenge to Affluence* (New York: Pantheon, 1962); *Asian Drama: An Inquiry into the Poverty of Nations* (New York: Twentieth Century Fund, 1968).

31. Wohlstetter and Wohlstetter, "'Third Worlds' Abroad and at Home," 90. For a comparison of Becker and Myrdal, see Steven Shulman, "Metaphors of Discrimination: A Comparison of Gunnar Myrdal and Gary Becker," *Review of Social Economy* 50, no. 4 (1992): 432–452.

32. Becker, *Economics of Discrimination,* 11.

33. Wohlstetter and Wohlstetter, "Metaphors and Models."

34. Ibid.

35. Ibid.

36. Ibid.

37. Kenneth B. Clark, *Dark Ghetto: Dilemmas of Social Power* (New York: Harper and Row, 1965), 11.

38. Wohlstetter and Wohlstetter, "'Third Worlds' Abroad and at Home," 88.

39. Ibid., 89.

40. Ibid., 102.

41. See, for example, Dorman, *Arguing the World;* Neil Jumonville, *Critical Crossings: The New York Intellectuals in Postwar America* (Berkeley: University of California Press, 1991); Peter Steinfels, *The Neoconservatives; The Men Who Are Changing America's Politics* (New York: Simon and Schuster, 1979).

42. Roberta Wohlstetter and Albert Wohlstetter, "On Dealing with Castro's Cuba, Part 1" (Santa Monica, CA: RAND Corporation, D[L]-17906-ISA, January 16, 1965), www.rand.org/about/history/wohlstetter/D17906/D17906 .html.

43. Jeffrey Engel, "Of Fat and Thin Communists; Diplomacy and Philosophy in Western Economic Warfare Strategies toward China (and Tyrants, Broadly)," *Diplomatic History* 29, no. 3 (June 2005): 445–474.

44. For contemporary definitions of modernization theory, see Daniel Lerner, "Modernization: Social Aspects," in *International Encyclopedia of the Social Sciences,* ed. David L. Sills (New York: Macmillan, 1968), 9:386–394; James Coleman, "Modernization: Political Aspects," in ibid., 395–402. See also Michael Latham, "Ideology, Social Science, and Destiny: Modernization and the Kennedy-Era Alliance for Progress," *Diplomatic History* 22, no. 2 (Spring 1998): 202.

45. Engel, "Of Fat and Thin Communists," 468.

46. Ibid.

47. Albert Wohlstetter, "Their Pain and Ours in Far and Close Prospects: Economic, Political, and Military Parallel and Interactions," January 1982, Wohlstetter Papers, box 116, folder 37.

48. Wohlstetter and Wohlstetter, "On Dealing with Castro's Cuba."

49. Ibid.

50. Ibid.

51. Ibid.

52. Engel, "Of Fat and Thin Communists," 462.

53. Wohlstetter and Wohlstetter, "On Dealing with Castro's Cuba."

54. Ibid.

55. Ibid. Emphasis in original.

56. Roberta Wohlstetter, "Little War in a Big Shadow: Ties of Castro's Insurrection to the United States," September 1972, 7, Wohlstetter Papers, box 381, folder 11.

57. Ibid., 19.

58. Anthony dePalma, *The Man Who Invented Fidel* (New York: Public Affairs, 2006). For Matthews's own version of his Castro scoop, see Herbert Matthews, *The Cuban Story* (New York: George Braziller, 1961).

59. Herbert L. Matthews, "Cuban Rebel Is Visited in Hideout: Castro Is Still Alive and Still Fighting in Mountains," *New York Times,* February 24, 1957, 1, quoted in ibid., 9.

60. Wohlstetter, "Little War in a Big Shadow," 10.

61. Ibid., 12.

62. A clip from this documentary is on YouTube.com at www.youtube.com /watch?v=DT04DugUkRM.

63. Wohlstetter, "Little War in a Big Shadow," 13–16.

64. Castro, quoted in ibid., 15.

65. Ibid., 21. Emphasis in original.

66. Ibid., 36.

67. Robert Wohlstetter, "Kidnapping to Win Friends and Influence People," *Survey* 4, no. 93 (Autumn 1974): 1–40; Wohlstetter, "Little War in a Big Shadow."

68. Albert Wohlstetter, "The Fax Shall Make You Free," unpublished speech for the Prague Conference, July 23, 1990, in *Nuclear Heuristics: Selected Writings of Albert and Roberta Wohlstetter,* ed. Robert Zarate and Henry Sokolski (Carlisle, PA: Strategic Studies Institute, U.S. Army War College, 2009), 639.

69. Ibid., 646.

70. Ibid., 648.

6. Discriminate Interventionism

1. Albert Wohlstetter, "Strength, Interest, and New Technologies" (Santa Monica, CA: RAND Corporation, D[L]-16624-PR, January 1968), www .rand.org/about/history/wohlstetter/DL16624/DL16624.html.

2. Alfred [*sic*] Wohlstetter, "Making Peace and Keeping It," *New York Times,* January 28, 1979, E17.

3. Albert Wohlstetter, "Between an Unfree World and None: Increasing Our Choices," *Foreign Affairs* 63, no. 5 (Summer 1985): 994.

4. Albert Wohlstetter, "Impressions and Appraisals in Hong Kong, May 19– May 23, 1962" (Santa Monica, CA: RAND Corporation, D[L]-10364-ISA, August 20, 1962), www.rand.org/about/history/wohlstetter/DL10364/DL 10364.html.

5. Ibid.

6. Ibid.

7. Albert Wohlstetter, "Impressions and Appraisals in Japan, May 8–May 19, 1962" (Santa Monica, CA: RAND Corporation, D[L]-10391-ISA, August 27, 1962), www.rand.org/about/history/wohlstetter/DL10391/DL10391.html; Albert Wohlstetter, "Impressions and Appraisals in Singapore, May 18– May 29, 1962" (Santa Monica, CA: RAND Corporation, D[L]-10399-ISA, August 28, 1962), www.rand.org/about/history/wohlstetter/DL10399/DL 10399.html.

8. Roberta Wohlstetter, "Terror on a Grand Scale," *Survival* 18, no. 3 (1978): 98. For contemporary studies of nuclear weapons in the hands of terrorists, see Augustus Norton and Martin Greenberg, eds., *Studies in Nuclear Terrorism* (Boston: G. K. Hall, 1979); Thomas Schelling, "The Terrorist Use of Nuclear Weapons," in *National Security and International Stability,* ed. Bernard Brodie, Michael Intriligator, and Roman Kolkowicz (Cambridge, MA: Oelgeschlager, Gunn and Hain, 1983), 209–225.

9. Wohlstetter, "Terror on a Grand Scale," 99.

10. Ibid.

11. Ibid., 101.

12. Gabriel Weimann, "The Theater of Terror: Effects of Press Coverage," *Journal of Communication* 33 (1983): 33–45. Weimann accords authorship of the term to Brian Jenkins of the RAND Corporation.

13. Roberta Wohlstetter, "Kidnapping to Win Friends and Influence People," *Survey* 20, no. 4 (Autumn 1974): 2.

14. Wohlstetter, "Terror on a Grand Scale," 102.

15. Ibid., 99.

16. Wohlstetter, "Kidnapping to Win Friends and Influence People," 31.

17. Ibid., 11, 28–31.

18. Albert Wohlstetter, "Viet Nam and Bureaucracy," in *Great Issues of International Politics: The International System and National Policy,* ed. Morton Kaplan (Chicago: Aldine, 1970), 281.

19. The charge of isolationism is particularly pronounced in Albert Wohlstetter, "Illusions of Distance," *Foreign Affairs* 46, no. 2 (January 1968): 242–255.

20. Wohlstetter, "Viet Nam and Bureaucracy," 280–281.

21. Wohlstetter, "Illusions of Distance," 244.

22. Ibid., 246.

23. Ibid., 288. The article Albert praised was Hans Morgenthau, "To Intervene or Not to Intervene," *Foreign Affairs* 45, no. 3 (April 1967): 425–436.

24. Morgenthau, "To Intervene or Not to Intervene," 432.

25. Wohlstetter, "Viet Nam and Bureaucracy," 289.

26. Albert Wohlstetter, "Comments on the Wolf-Leites Manuscript: 'Rebellion and Authority'" (Santa Monica, CA: RAND Corporation, D[L]-17701-ARPA/AGILE, August 30, 1968), www.rand.org/about/history/wohlstetter/DL17701/DL17701.html.

27. Ibid.

28. Ibid.

29. Wohlstetter, "Viet Nam and Bureaucracy," 289.

30. Nathan Leites and Charles Wolf Jr., "Rebellion and Authority: Myths and Realities Reconsidered" (Santa Monica, CA: RAND Corporation, P3422, 1966), www.rand.org/pubs/papers/P3422.html. Leites and Wolf later enlarged this paper into a book, *Rebellion and Authority: An Analytical Essay on Insurgent Conflicts* (Chicago: Markham, 1970).

31. Charles Wolf Jr., "Insurgency and Counterinsurgency: New Myths and Old Realities," *Yale Review* 56, no. 2 (Winter 1967): 225–241. On "constructive counterinsurgency" and the critique of it that Leites, Wolf, and their RAND colleagues elaborated, see Ron Robin, *The Making of the Cold War Enemy: Culture and Politics in the Military-Intellectual Complex* (Princeton, NJ: Princeton University Press, 2003), chap. 9.

32. Leites and Wolf, *Rebellion and Authority,* 2.

33. Ibid., 17–18.

34. Ted Gurr with Charles Ruttenberg, *Cross-National Studies of Civil Violence* (Washington, DC: CRESS, 1969), 6. Gurr later published his studies as *Why Men Rebel* (Princeton, NJ: Princeton University Press, 1970).

35. Carl F. Rosenthal, *Phases of Civil Disturbances: Characteristics and Problems* (Washington, DC: American University, Center for Research in Social Systems, 1969). See also Guy J. Pauker, "Black Nationalism and Prospects for Violence in the Ghetto" (Santa Monica, CA: RAND Corporation, P-4118, 1969), www.rand.org/pubs/papers/P4118.html; Tracy Tullis, "A Vietnam at Home: Policing the Ghettos in the Counterinsurgency Era" (PhD diss., New York University, 1999).

36. Wohlstetter, "Comments on the Wolf-Leites Manuscript."

37. Wohlstetter, "Viet Nam and Bureaucracy," 280–281.

38. Ibid., 290.

39. Ibid., 289–291.

40. Richard Perle, "Launching the Right Answer at the Right Question," *U.S. News and World Report,* January 25, 1988, 47.

41. Department of Defense, Commission on Long Term Strategy, *Discriminate Deterrence: Report of the Commission on Integrated Long-Term Strategy,* ed. Daniel Seligman (Washington, DC: Department of Defense, 1988). See also *The Future of Containment: America's Options for Defending Its Interests on the Soviet Periphery: Report of the Offense–Defense Working Group, Submitted to the Commission on Integrated Long-Term Strategy* (Washington, DC: Department of Defense, 1968); *Technology for National Security: Report by the Working Group on Technology, Submitted to the Commission on Integrated Long-Term Strategy* (Washington, DC: Department of Defense, 1988).

42. Paul Kennedy, "Not So Grand Strategy," *New York Review of Books,* May 12, 1988.

43. Henry Trewhitt, "Uncle Sam in a Grave New World," *U.S. News and World Report,* January 25, 1988, 46.

44. *Discriminate Deterrence,* 63.

45. Ibid., 60.

46. Ibid., 1.

47. Ibid., 14–15.

48. Ibid., 5.

49. Ibid., 3.

50. Ibid., 39.

51. Ibid., 7.
52. Ibid., 63.
53. Trewhitt, "Uncle Sam in a Grave New World," 45.
54. *Discriminate Deterrence,* 33–34.
55. Ibid., 1.
56. Ibid., 23.
57. Ibid., 1.
58. Ibid., 33.
59. Ibid., 27.
60. Ibid., 49.
61. Ibid., 30.
62. Ibid., 65.
63. Ibid., 29.
64. Ibid., 40.
65. Ibid., 21.
66. Ibid., 6.
67. Henri Eyraud, cited in Keith Armes, "*Discriminate Deterrence:* Western European Comment," *Atlantic Community Quarterly* 26, no. 3 (Fall–Winter, 1988): 250.
68. Ibid., 251, 252, 261. The table is found in *Discriminate Deterrence,* 7.
69. Albert Wohlstetter, "Overseas Reactions to *Discriminate Deterrence,*" *Atlantic Community Quarterly* 26, no. 3 (Fall–Winter 1988): 236.
70. *Der Spiegel,* paraphrased in Armes, "*Discriminate Deterrence,*" 253.
71. Ibid.
72. Ibid., 254.
73. Ibid.
74. Ibid., 256.
75. Michael Quinlan, quoted and paraphrased in Wohlstetter, "Overseas Reactions to *Discriminate Deterrence,*" 239.
76. *The Economist,* February 27, 1988, quoted in ibid., 240–241.
77. Ibid., 243.
78. Bernard E. Trainor, "Another U.S. Study Down the Drain?" *New York Times,* January 13, 1988, A16.
79. "More Vietnams?," *The Nation,* January 23, 1988, 75–76.
80. Martha Little, "It's Time to Break Up the 40-Year-Old Concrete of 'Containment,'" *Christian Science Monitor,* May 18, 1988.
81. Kennedy, "Not So Grand Strategy."
82. Ibid.
83. Ibid.
84. Ibid.
85. Ibid.
86. Trewhitt, "Uncle Sam in a Grave New World," 46.
87. State Department press guidance cited in Wohlstetter, "Overseas Reactions to *Discriminate Deterrence,*" 235.

88. Albert Wohlstetter, "The Uses of Irrelevance," *New York Times,* February 25, 1979, E17. Emphasis in original.

89. Paul Edwards, *The Closed World: Computers and the Politics of Discourse in Cold War America* (Cambridge, MA: MIT Press, 1996).

90. Albert Wohlstetter, "Theory and Opposed Systems Design," *Journal of Conflict Resolution* 12, no. 3 (September 1968): 302.

7. Slow Pearl Harbors

1. Roberta Wohlstetter, "Surprised by the Obvious," speech at the National Press Club, December 7, 1988, and "Surprised by the Obvious: Pearl Harbor with Minimal Shock," talk for National Security Forum, December 9, 1988, Wohlstetter Papers, box 373, folder 14.

2. Wohlstetter, "Surprised by the Obvious," talk, 1.

3. Ibid., 1–2.

4. Ibid., 5.

5. Roberta Wohlstetter, "The Pleasures of Self-Deception," *Washington Quarterly* 2, no. 4 (Autumn 1979): 54–63.

6. Wohlstetter, "Surprised by the Obvious," speech, 16.

7. Ibid. Emphasis in original.

8. Ibid., 22.

9. Ibid., 17.

10. Ibid.

11. Ibid., 19.

12. Ibid., 20. Emphasis in original.

13. Wohlstetter, "Surprised by the Obvious," talk, 26.

14. Ibid., 26–27.

15. Wohlstetter, "Surprised by the Obvious," speech, 4, 7.

16. Ibid., 9–10.

17. Wohlstetter, "Surprised by the Obvious," talk, 2.

18. Wohlstetter, "Surprised by the Obvious," speech, 2.

19. Albert Wohlstetter, "The Fax Shall Set You Free," speech, July 1990, in *Nuclear Heuristics: The Selected Writings of Albert and Roberta Wohlstetter,* ed. Robert Zarate and Henry Sokolski (Carlisle, PA: Strategic Studies Institute, U.S. Army War College, 2009), 641. Emphasis in original.

20. Albert Wohlstetter in James Digby and Joan Goldhamer, "The Development of Strategic Thinking at RAND, 1948–1963: A Mathematical Logician's View—an Interview with Albert Wohlstetter, July 5, 1985" (Santa Monica, CA: RAND Corporation, 1997).

21. Ibid., 59.

22. Albert Wohlstetter and Henry Rowen, "Objectives of the United States Military Posture" (Santa Monica, CA: RAND Corporation, RM-2373, May 1, 1959), www.RAND.org/about/history/wohlstetter/RM2373/RM2373.html. Emphasis in original.

23. Albert Wohlstetter, in Digby and Goldhamer, "The Development of Strategic Thinking at RAND," 33.
24. Ibid., 57.
25. Ibid., 60.
26. Ibid., 58.
27. Ibid., 67. Emphasis in original.
28. Ibid., 58.
29. Wohlstetter and Rowen, "Objectives of the United States Military Posture."
30. Albert Wohlstetter, "The Forces of Change: Technology, Prediction, and Disorder," *Vanderbilt Law Review* 17, no. 1 (December 1963): 9, 11.
31. Wohlstetter and Rowen, "Objectives of the United States Military Posture."
32. Albert Wohlstetter, in Digby and Goldhamer, "The Development of Strategic Thinking at RAND," 58.
33. Ibid. Emphasis in original.
34. Ibid. Emphasis in original.
35. Henry Rowen and Albert Wohlstetter, "Varying Responses with Circumstance," in *Beyond Nuclear Deterrence: New Aims, New Arms,* ed. Johan Holst and Uwe Nerlich (New York: Crane, Russak, 1976), 227.
36. Albert Wohlstetter, "End of the Cold War? End of History and All War? Excerpt from an Outline for a Memoir" (1989), in *Nuclear Heuristics,* 637.
37. Ibid.
38. Ibid. Emphasis in original.
39. Ibid., 638.
40. Ibid.
41. Albert Wohlstetter, "Spreading the Bomb without Quite Breaking the Rules," *Foreign Policy* 25 (Winter 1976–1977): 165.
42. Ibid., 89–93.
43. Albert Wohlstetter, "Strength, Interest, and New Technologies" (Santa Monica, CA: RAND Corporation, D[L]-16624-PR, January 1968), www .rand.org/about/history/wohlstetter/DL16624/DL16624.html.
44. Albert Wohlstetter, "Nuclear Sharing: NATO and the N+1 Country," *Foreign Affairs* 39, no. 3 (April 1961): quotes from 363 and 356, respectively.
45. Ibid., 358.
46. Ibid., 361.
47. Ibid., 363. Albert was paraphrasing François Mauriac here.
48. Roberta Wohlstetter, *The Buddha Smiles: Absent-Minded Peaceful Aid and the Indian Bomb* (Los Angeles, CA: PAN Heuristics, 1977); see also Wohlstetter, *Nuclear Heuristics,* 339–356.
49. Wohlstetter, "The Pleasures of Self-Deception," 55.
50. Albert Wohlstetter, ed., *Swords from Plowshares: The Military Potential of Civilian Nuclear Energy* (Chicago: University of Chicago Press, 1979).
51. Wohlstetter, *The Buddha Smiles,* 340.

52. Albert Wohlstetter, "RPM or Revolutions by the Minute," address to the American Enterprise Institute for Public Policy Research, June 1992, in *Nuclear Heuristics*, 619.

53. Wohlstetter, "End of the Cold War?," 637.

54. Quoted in ibid., 637. See also Albert Wohlstetter, "The Delicate Balance of Terror," *Foreign Affairs* 37, no. 2 (January 1959): 234.

55. Wohlstetter, "End of the Cold War?," 638.

56. Albert Wohlstetter, "No Highway to High Purpose" (Santa Monica, CA: RAND, P-2084-RC, June 1960), www.rand.org/about/history/wohlstetter /P2084/P2084.html.

57. Albert Wohlstetter, comments in "How Has the United States Met Its Major Challenges since 1945?," *Commentary* 80, no. 5 (November 1985): 107.

8. *"Do Not Go Gentle into That Good Night"*

1. Senator Jon Kyl, in "Remembering Albert Wohlstetter," *Congressional Record—Senate*, February 6, 1997, 105th Congress, 1st Session; Vol. 143, No. 14—Daily Edition, S1112, www.congress.gov/crec/1997/02/06/CREC -1997-02-06.pdf.

2. Ibid.

3. Dylan Thomas, quoted by Richard Perle, in ibid., S1113.

4. On the Senate ABM debate, see Johan J. Jolst, William Schneider, and Frank E. Armbruster, eds., *Why ABM? Policy Issues in the Missile Defense Controversy* (New York: Pergamon Press, 1969); Edward Randolph Jayne, "The ABM Debate: Strategic Defense and National Security" (PhD diss., Massachusetts Institute of Technology, 1969); Charles A. Rees, "ABM: A Study of Legislative Decision Making," *American Bar Association Journal* 56, no. 5 (May 1970): 475–477; Thomas Halsted, "Lobbying against the ABM, 1967–1970," *Bulletin of the Atomic Scientists* 27, no. 4 (April 1971): 23–28; Paul Doty, "Can Investigations Improve Scientific Advice?," *Minerva* 10, no. 2 (April 1972): 280–294; Geoffrey Till, "The Safeguard Debate: Image and Reality," *RUSI Journal* 119, no. 4 (1974): 40–46; Robert A. Bernstein and William W. Anthony, "The ABM Issue in the Senate, 1968–1970: The Importance of Ideology," *American Political Science Review* 68, no. 3 (September 1974): 1198–1206; Alan Platt, *The U.S. Senate and Strategic Arms Policy, 1969– 1977* (Boulder, CO: Westview Press, 1978); Graham Spinardi, "The Rise and Fall of Safeguard: Anti-Ballistic Missile Technology and the Nixon Administration," *History and Technology* 26, no. 4 (2010): 313–334; Rebecca Slayton, *Arguments That Count: Physics, Computing, and Missile Defense, 1949– 2012* (Cambridge, MA: MIT Press, 2013), chap. 6.

5. See the following letters and articles in the *New York Times:* William Beecher, "Scientist Rebuts Criticism of ABM; Wohlstetter Sees Mistakes in Some Foes' Arguments," May 26, 1969, 13; George W. Rathjens and Albert Wohlstetter, letters under the title "Safeguard Missile System Is Evaluated by Two

Scientists," June 15, 1969, E17; George W. Rathjens, "Calculations on ABM," June 22, 1969, E15; Albert Wohlstetter, "Minuteman Costs," June 29, 1969, E11; William Beecher, "Report on Safeguard ABM Testimony Finds Unprofessional and Misleading Comments on Both Sides," October 1, 1971, 23.

6. Ad Hoc Committee on Professional Standards, "Appendix III: Treatment of Operations-Research Questions in the 1969 Safeguard Debate," *Operations Research* 19, no. 5 (September 1971): 1185.

7. Truman Botts, Douglas L. Brooks, Leslie C. Edie, and T. E. Compton, et al., "Reactions to the Guidelines for the Practice of Operations Research," *Operations Research* 20, no. 1 (January–February 1972): 208–209.

8. See the reference to the work of Thomas Kuhn in D. Carpio, B. Cohen, J. Eldred, and V. Gangavane, et al., "A Student Appraisal of the Proposed Guidelines for Operations Research," *Management Science* 18, no. 10 (June 1972): B621n6. The authors refer to Kuhn's seminal *The Structure of Scientific Revolutions* (Chicago: University of Chicago Press, 1962).

9. Botts et al., "Reactions to the Guidelines," 231–237.

10. Carpio et al., "A Student Appraisal," B619.

11. Perle, in "Remembering Albert Wohlstetter," S1113.

12. George Orwell, quoted in Albert Wohlstetter, "Creating a Greater Serbia: Clinton's Final Sell-Out of Bosnia," *New Republic*, August 1, 1994, 22.

13. Ibid., 24.

14. Ibid.

15. Ibid., 27.

16. Albert Wohlstetter and Gregory S. Jones, "Beyond the Cold War—Foreign Policy in the 21st Century: Alternatives to Negotiating Genocide," *Wall Street Journal*, Europe, May 12, 1995, 6, quoted in Neil Swidey, "The Analyst," *Boston Globe*, May 18, 2003.

17. Albert Wohlstetter, "Genocide by Mediation," *New York Times*, March 3, 1994, A21.

18. Ibid.

19. Albert Wohlstetter, "Notes to Clinton on Bosnia," *Wall Street Journal*, June 10, 1994, A14.

20. Wohlstetter, "Genocide by Mediation."

21. Paul Wolfowitz, "Statesmanship in the New Century," in *Present Dangers: Crisis and Opportunity in American Foreign and Defense Policy*, ed. Robert Kagan and William Kristol (San Francisco, CA: Encounter Books, 2000), 323.

22. Wohlstetter, "Genocide by Mediation."

23. Albert Wohlstetter, quoted in Marshall Freeman Harris and Stephen Walker, "Remembering Albert Wohlstetter," *Bosnia Report*, February–May 1997, www.bosnia.org.uk/bosrep/febmay97/remember.cfm.

24. Quoted in Swidey, "The Analyst."

25. Albert Wohlstetter and Fred Hoffman, "The Bitter End: The Case for Re-Intervention in Iraq," *New Republic*, April 29, 1991.

26. Richard Perle, quoted in Swidey, "The Analyst."

27. Paul Wolfowitz, quoted in Sam Tanenhaus, "Bush's Brain Trust," *Vanity Fair,* July 2003.

28. Wohlstetter and Hoffman, "The Bitter End."

29. Ibid.

30. Ibid.

31. Albert Wohlstetter, "Wide Open Secret Coup," *National Review,* March 16, 1992, 35–36.

32. Wohlstetter and Hoffman, "The Bitter End."

33. Albert Wohlstetter, "A Vote in Cuba? Why Not in Iraq?," *Wall Street Journal,* May 24, 1991, A10.

34. Wohlstetter and Hoffman, "The Bitter End."

35. Ibid.

36. Albert Wohlstetter, "High Time," *National Review,* February 15, 1993, 32.

37. Albert Wohlstetter, "A Clear Win, Bearable Cost," *Wall Street Journal,* January 10, 1991, A14.

38. Albert Wohlstetter, "Help Iraqi Dissidents Oust Saddam," *Wall Street Journal,* August 25, 1992, A14.

39. Wohlstetter, "High Time," 30.

40. Wohlstetter, "Help Iraqi Dissidents Oust Saddam."

41. Wohlstetter, "Clear Win."

42. Wohlstetter and Hoffman, "Bitter End."

43. Wohlstetter, "High Time," 33.

44. Robert Jervis, "Understanding the Bush Doctrine," *Political Science Quarterly* 118, no. 3 (Fall 2003): 367.

45. Kenneth N. Waltz, *Man, the State, and War: A Theoretical Analysis* (New York: Columbia University Press, 1959).

46. Kenneth N. Waltz, *Theory of International Politics* (Reading, MA: Addison-Wesley, 1979).

47. Kenneth N. Waltz, "The Spread of Nuclear Weapons: More May Better," in *Adelphi Papers 171* (London: International Institute for Strategic Studies, 1981), https://www.mtholyoke.edu/acad/intrel/waltz1.htm. Emphasis in original.

48. Ibid.

49. Ibid.

50. Ibid.

51. Jervis, "Understanding the Bush Doctrine," 369.

52. Waltz, "The Spread of Nuclear Weapons."

53. Brodie, quoted in ibid.

54. Paul Johnson, "Leviathan to the Rescue: The Responsibility of the United States," *National Review,* October 14, 2002, 20.

55. Lee Harris, "Our World-Historical Gamble," March 11, 2003, www.ideasinactiontv.com/tcs_daily/2003/03/our-world-historical-gamble.html. Emphasis in original.

56. Ibid.

57. Paul Wolfowitz, "Remembering the Future," *National Interest* 59 (Spring 2000): 36, 45.

58. Roberta Wohlstetter, "From Pearl Harbor to the Gulf: When to Worry," *Wall Street Journal*, December 5, 1991, A14.

9. Paul Wolfowitz

1. Andrew W. Marshall, J. J. Martin, and Henry S. Rowen, eds., *On Not Confusing Ourselves: Essays on National Security Strategy in Honor of Albert and Roberta Wohlstetter* (Boulder, CO: Westview Press, 1991).

2. Richard Perle, *Hard Line* (New York: Random House, 1992).

3. Wolfowitz discusses his *Ravelstein* cameo appearance in Paul Wolfowitz, "News Transcript: Deputy Secretary Wolfowitz Interview with Sam Tanenhaus, *Vanity Fair*," May 9, 2003, U.S. Department of Defense, www .defense.gov/transcripts/transcript.aspx?transcriptid=2594. See also Gary J. Dorrien, *Imperial Designs: Neoconservatism and the New Pax Americana* (New York: Routledge, 2004), 52, citing Diana West, "Paul Wolfowitz: Superpower Strategist," *M 9*, May 1992, 60; Saul Bellow, *Ravelstein* (New York: Viking, 2000).

4. American Enterprise Institute, "Paul Wolfowitz, Visiting Scholar," www .aei.org/scholar/paul-wolfowitz/.

5. Telluride Association, "About Us: History," www.tellurideassociation.org /about/history.html

6. Lewis D. Solomon, *Paul D. Wolfowitz: Visionary Intellectual, Policymaker, and Strategist* (Westport, CT: Praeger, 2007), 16.

7. Anne Hessing Cahn, *Killing Détente: The Right Attacks the CIA* (University Park: Pennsylvania State University, 1998), 151–153.

8. Richard H. Immerman, *Empire for Liberty: A History of American Imperialism from Benjamin Franklin to Paul Wolfowitz* (Princeton, NJ: Princeton University Press, 2012), 207–208.

9. Paul Wolfowitz, "Surprise . . . and Courage," *Executive Speeches* 16, no. 2 (October–November 2001): 20.

10. Paul Wolfowitz, "Bridging Centuries: Fin de Siècle All Over Again," *National Interest* 47 (Spring 1997): 3–8.

11. Ibid., 4–5.

12. Ibid., 6.

13. Norman Angell, *The Great Illusion: A Study of the Relation of Military Power to National Advantage* (New York: G. P. Putnam's Sons, 1910), 56.

14. Wolfowitz, "Bridging Centuries," 6.

15. Francis Fukuyama, *End of History and the Last Man* (New York: The Free Press, 1992) and John Mueller, *Retreat from Doomsday: The Obsolescence of Major War* (New York: Basic Books, 1989).

16. Wolfowitz, "Bridging Centuries," 7.

17. Ibid., 8.

18. Paul Wolfowitz, "Remembering the Future," *National Interest* 59 (Spring 2000): 45.

19. Paul Wolfowitz, "Managing Our Way to a Peaceful Century," in *Managing the International System over the Next Ten Years: A Report to the Trilateral Commission,* ed. Bill Emmott, Koji Watanabe, and Paul Wolfowitz (New York: Trilateral Commission, 1997), 48.

20. Wolfowitz, "Remembering the Future," 37–38.

21. Paul Wolfowitz, "The Greatest Deeds Are Yet to Be Done," *Naval War College Review* 57, no. 1 (Winter 2004): 17–18.

22. Ibid., 18.

23. Wolfowitz, "Surprise . . . and Courage," 20.

24. Paul Wolfowitz, "Statesmanship in the New Century," in *Present Dangers: Crisis and Opportunity in American Foreign and Defense Policy,* ed. Robert Kagan and William Kristol (San Francisco, CA: Encounter Books, 2000), 314.

25. Charles Fairbanks, quoted in Michael Hirsh, "Neocons on the Line: Welcome to the Real World," *Newsweek,* June 23, 2003, 28.

26. Edward Gibbon, *The History of the Decline and Fall of the Roman Empire* (New York: Macmillan, 1914), 3:136n137.

27. This theme of warrior politics, including the quote from Livy, appears in Robert Kaplan, *Warrior Politics: Why Leadership Demands a Pagan Ethos* (New York: Vintage Books, 2002), 25.

28. Paul Wolfowitz, "Courage and Freedom: Address at Warsaw University," October 5, 2004, U.S. Department of Defense, www.defense.gov/Speeches /Speech.aspx?SpeechID=159.

29. Wolfowitz, quoted in "News Transcript."

30. Wolfowitz, "Courage and Freedom."

31. Eric Schmitt, "The Busy Life of Being a Lightning Rod for Bush," *New York Times,* April 22, 2002, A3.

32. Bill Keller, "The Sunshine Warrior," *New York Times,* September 22, 2002, E49.

33. Wolfowitz, quoted in "News Transcript."

34. Paul Wolfowitz, quoted in "Interview: Paul Wolfowitz," *Frontline,* April 22, 2002, www.pbs.org/wgbh/pages/frontline/shows/campaign/interviews/wol fowitz.html.

35. Donald Rumsfeld, "Prepared Testimony of U.S. Secretary of Defense Donald Rumsfeld before the House and Senate Armed Services Committees Regarding Iraq, as Delivered by Donald Rumsfeld," September 18, 2002, U.S. Department of Defense, www.defense.gov/Speeches/Speech .aspx?SpeechID=283.

36. On the contemporary attraction to the Carthage analogy in the post–Cold War period, see Richard Miles, *Carthage Must Be Destroyed: The Rise and Fall of an Ancient Civilization* (New York: Viking, 2011); Thomas H. Henriksen, *America and the Rogue States* (New York: Palgrave Macmillan, 2012), 55.

37. Examples include Paul Wolfowitz, "On Iraq," speech, Washington, DC, October 16, 2002, www.defense.gov/Speeches/Speech.aspx?SpeechID=295;

Paul Wolfowitz, "Building the Bridge to a More Peaceful Future," speech, San Francisco, CA, December 6, 2002, www.defense.gov/speeches/speech .aspx?speechid=310.

38. Paul Wolfowitz, interviewed by Nathan Gardels, "Deputy Secretary Wolfowitz Interview with *Los Angeles Times,*" May 9, 2002, http://209.157.64.200 /focus/f-news/680860/posts.

39. Paul Wolfowitz, "Remarks at the Defense Forum Foundation, Rayburn House," October 18, 2002, Homeland Security Digital Website, www.hsdl .org/?abstract&did=2640.

40. Ibid.

41. John F. Kennedy, quoted in ibid.

42. Ibid.

43. On Roberta and Fidel, see Roberta Wohlstetter, "Notes on Castro and Oswald: The Maximo Lider on the Assassination," February 1964, 3, Wohlstetter Papers, box 381, folder 7.

44. Wolfowitz, quoted in Mark Bowden, "Wolfowitz: The Exit Interviews," *Atlantic Monthly,* July–August 2005, 114.

45. Wolfowitz, "Remarks at the Defense Forum Foundation."

46. Ibid.

47. Wolfowitz, quoted in Bowden, "Wolfowitz," 122.

48. Paul Wolfowitz, "Nuclear Proliferation in the Middle East: The Politics and Economics of Proposals for Nuclear Desalting" (PhD diss., University of Chicago, 1972).

49. Zach Levey, "The United States, Israel, and Nuclear Desalination, 1964–1968," *Diplomatic History* 39, no. 5 (2014): 14.

50. Wolfowitz, "Nuclear Proliferation in the Middle East, 36.

51. André Beaufre, *Deterrence and Strategy,* trans. R. H. Barry (New York: Praeger, 1966), cited in Wolfowitz, "Nuclear Proliferation in the Middle East," 29, 35.

52. Ibid., 36.

53. Ibid., 35.

54. Ibid., 378–379.

55. Wolfowitz, quoted in "News Transcript."

56. Joan Wohlstetter, conversation with the author, March 13, 2008.

57. On Strauss's admiration for Ze'ev Jabotinsky, a founding father of Zionist Revisionism, see K. H. Green, "Introduction: Leo Strauss as a Modern Jewish Thinker," in Leo Strauss, *Jewish Philosophy and the Crisis of Modernity: Essays and Lectures in Modern Jewish Thought,* ed. K. H. Green (Albany: State University of New York Press, 1997), 3.

58. Leo Strauss, "What Is Political Philosophy?," *Journal of Politics* 19, no. 3 (August 1957): 356–357.

59. Richard Perle and David Frum, *An End to Evil: How to Win the War on Terror* (New York: Random House, 2003).

60. Steven Smith, *Reading Leo Strauss: Politics, Philosophy, Judaism* (Chicago: University of Chicago Press, 2007), 200.

61. Leo Strauss, *The City and Man* (Chicago: University of Chicago Press, 1977), 127.

62. Strauss, "What Is Political Philosophy?," 356.

63. Francis Fukuyama, *America at the Crossroads: Democracy, Power, and the Neoconservative Legacy* (New Haven, CT: Yale University Press, 2001), 28.

64. Paul Wolfowitz, "Realism," *Foreign Policy* 174 (September–October 2009): 67.

65. Ibid.

66. Ibid.

67. Wolfowitz, quoted in Bowden, "Wolfowitz," 112.

68. Paul Wolfowitz, "Rising Up," *New Republic,* December 7, 1998, 14.

69. Paul Wolfowitz, "Clinton's Bay of Pigs," *Wall Street Journal,* September 27, 1996, A18.

70. Wolfowitz, quoted in Bowden, "Wolfowitz," 119.

71. Wolfowitz, "Statesmanship in the New Century," 315.

72. Paul Wolfowitz, "Support Our Troops," *Wall Street Journal,* September 2, 2003.

73. On Wolfowitz's role in U.S.-Philippine relations, see Solomon, *Paul D. Wolfowitz,* 30–40; Amy Blitz, *The Contested State: American Foreign Policy and Regime Change in the Philippines* (Lanham, MD: Rowan and Littlefield, 2000), chap. 6.

74. Wolfowitz, "Remembering the Future," 39.

75. Albert Wohlstetter, "Wide Open Secret Coup," *National Review,* March 16, 1992, 34–37.

76. Albert Wohlstetter, "A Vote in Cuba, Why Not in Iraq?," *Wall Street Journal,* May 24, 1991, A10.

77. Wohlstetter, "Notes on Castro and Oswald," 3.

78. Wolfowitz, "Statesmanship in the New Century," 308.

79. Paul Wolfowitz, "American Power for What? A Symposium," *Commentary* 109, no. 1 (January 2000): 47.

80. Wolfowitz, "Remarks at the Defense Forum Foundation."

81. Ibid.

82. Wolfowitz, "Remembering the Future," 39.

83. Paul Wolfowitz, "Remarks as Delivered by Deputy Secretary of Defense Paul Wolfowitz, the Pentagon, Washington, DC, Friday, November 30, 2001," in *Wolfowitz On Point: Recognizing World Reality,* ed. Lee Crane (Philadelphia: Pavilion Press, 2004), 85.

84. For the argument that nation-states are often motivated by concerns of justice as well as power, see David Welch, *Justice and the Genesis of War* (New York: Cambridge University Press, 1993).

85. "Remarks by Deputy Secretary of Defense Paul Wolfowitz at the Lighting of the National Menorah, The Ellipse, Washington DC, Sunday, December 9, 2001," in *Wolfowitz on Point,* 87.

86. Sam Tanenhaus, "Bush's Brain Trust," *Vanity Fair,* July 2003.

87. Wolfowitz, quoted in "News Transcript."

88. William Kristol, "What Wolfowitz Really Said: The Truth behind the *Vanity Fair* 'Scoop,'" *Weekly Standard,* June 9, 2003, www.weeklystandard.com /Content/Public/Articles/000/000/002/757wzfan.asp.

89. Paul Wolfowitz, "Remarks as Delivered by Deputy Secretary of Defense Paul Wolfowitz, Westin Fairfax Hotel, Washington, DC, Monday, October 22, 2001, to the American Jewish Congress," in *Wolfowitz on Point,* 69.

90. Wolfowitz, quoted in "News Transcript."

91. Ibid.

10. Zalmay Khalilzad

1. Anne Norton, *Leo Strauss and the Politics of American Empire* (New Haven, CT: Yale University Press, 2004), 185. In his memoir, Khalilzad remembered being "fascinated with Nasser." Zalmay Khalilzad, *The Envoy: From Kabul to the White House, My Journey through a Turbulent World* (New York: St. Martin's Press, 2016), 44.

2. Khalilzad, *Envoy,* 46.

3. Ibid., 46–48.

4. Ibid., 9.

5. Ibid., 44.

6. "Alumni in the News: Ambassador Zalmay M. Khalilzad, PhD '79," https://web.archive.org/web/20070402043348/http://ihouse.uchicago .edu/alumni/alumni_inthenews.shtml.

7. John Lee Anderson, "American Viceroy: Zalmay Khalilzad's Mission," *New Yorker,* December 19, 2005, www.newyorker.com/magazine/2005/12 /19/american-viceroy.

8. Khalilzad, *Envoy,* 36–44; Anderson, "American Viceroy."

9. Anderson, "American Viceroy."

10. Khalilzad, *Envoy,* 45–48.

11. Ibid., 48.

12. Zalmay Khalilzad, "The Political, Economic and Military Implications of Nuclear Electricity: The Case of the Northern Tier" (PhD diss., University of Chicago, 1979).

13. Norton, *Leo Strauss,* 184.

14. Khalilzad, "Implications of Nuclear Electricity," 321.

15. Ibid., 268.

16. Sonali Kolhatkar and James Ingalls, *Bleeding Afghanistan: Washington, Warlords, and the Propaganda of Silence* (New York: Seven Stories Press, 2010), 128; Anderson, "American Viceroy."

17. Anderson, "American Viceroy."

18. Zalmay Khalilzad, "Afghanistan: Time to Reengage," *Washington Post,* October 7, 1996, www.washingtonpost.com/archive/opinions/1996/10/07 /afghanistan-time-to-reengage/300b1725-8d30-4b98-a916-03f7b588bb2c/.

19. Khalilzad's publications in the 1980s include: "Afghanistan and the Crisis in American Foreign Policy," *Survival* 22, no. 4 (1980): 151–160; "The Strategic Significance of South Asia," *Current History* 81, no. 475 (1982): 193; *Security in Southern Asia* (New York: St. Martin's Press, 1984); "Islamic Iran: Soviet Dilemma," *Problems of Communism* 33, no. 1 (1984): 1–20; "The Politics of Ethnicity in Southwest Asia: Political Development or Political Decay?," *Political Science Quarterly* 99, no. 4 (1984): 657–679; "The Soviet Dilemma in Afghanistan," *Current History* 84, no. 504 (1985): 334; "Moscow's Afghan War," *Problems of Communism* 35, no. 1 (1986): 1–20; "Afghanistan: Anatomy of a Soviet Failure," *National Interest,* no. 12 (Summer 1988): 101–108.

20. Zalmay Khalilzad, "Afghanistan in 1994: Civil War and Disintegration," *Asian Survey* 35, no. 2 (February 1995): 147–152. See also Zalmay Khalilzad, "Afghanistan in 1995: Civil War and a Mini–Great Game," *Asian Survey* 36, no. 2 (February 1996): 190–195.

21. Zalmay Khalilzad, "Anarchy in Afghanistan," *Journal of International Affairs* 51, no. 1 (Summer 1997): 37–56.

22. Ibid., 48.

23. See, for example, Zalmay Khalilzad, "The Superpowers and the Northern Tier," *International Security* 4, no. 3 (Winter 1979–1980): 6–30.

24. Ibid., 8.

25. Ibid., 7.

26. Ibid.

27. Ibid., 15.

28. Ibid., 28.

29. See, for example, Cheryl Benard and Zalmay Khalilzad, *"The Government of God": Iran's Islamic Republic* (New York: Columbia University Press, 1984), 1–24.

30. Cheryl Benard and Zalmay Khalilzad, "Secularization, Industrialization, and Khomeini's Islamic Republic," *Political Science Quarterly* 94, no. 2 (Summer 1979): 229.

31. Ibid., 231.

32. Quoted in ibid., 234. See also Samuel Huntington, "The Change to Change: Modernization, Development, and Politics," in *Comparative Modernization: A Reader,* ed. Cyril Edwin Black (New York: Free Press, 1976), 43.

33. Benard and Khalilzad make this case in *"Government of God."*

34. Zalmay Khalilzad, "How to Nation Build: Ten Lessons from Afghanistan," *National Interest* 80 (Summer 2005): 19–27.

35. Zalmay Khalilzad, quoted in James Kitfield, "Difficult, but Not Impossible," *National Journal,* October 13, 2007, 52.

36. Ibid., 51–53.

37. Khalilzad, "How to Nation Build," 19.

38. Ibid., 20.

39. Ibid., 22.

40. Ibid., 25.

41. Jonathan Stevenson, *Learning from the Cold War: Rebuilding America's Strategic Vision in the 21st Century* (New York: Penguin Books, 2008), 259.

42. Cheryl Benard, *Moghul Buffet* (New York: Farrar, Straus and Giroux, 1998); Cheryl Benard, *Turning on the Girls* (New York: Farrar, Straus and Giroux, 2001).

43. Cheryl Benard, *Civil Democratic Islam: Partners, Resources, and Strategies* (Santa Monica, CA: RAND Corporation, 2003), 3–4.

44. Ibid., xi.

45. Ibid., 46.

46. Angel Rabasa, Cheryl Benard, Lowel Schwartz, and Peter Sickle, *Building Moderate Muslim Networks* (Santa Monica, CA: RAND Center for Middle East Public Policy, 2007), 2.

47. Benard, *Civil Democratic Islam*, 14.

48. Cheryl Benard, "Caution Nation Builders: Gender Assumptions Ahead," *Fletcher Forum of World Affairs* 2, no. 1 (Winter 2008): 26–28.

49. U.S. Department of State Archive, "U.S. Ambassador to Iraq on MSNBC," August 16, 2005, http://2001-2009.state.gov/r/pa/prs/ps/2005/51119.htm.

50. Zalmay Khalilzad, "Afghan Women Have Limitless Opportunities," March 9, 2004, http://iipdigital.usembassy.gov/st/english/texttrans/2004/03/20040309150232esnamfuak0.7954828.html#axzz3rhHAR6SU.

51. Nicholas Lemann, "The Next World Order: The Bush Administration May Have a Brand-New Doctrine of Power," *New Yorker,* April 1, 2002.

52. A highly redacted version of the original memorandum appears on the National Security Archives website: "Memorandum from Principal Deputy, Undersecretary of Defense; Subject: FY 94-99 Defense Planning Guidance: Section for Commentary," February 18, 1992, http://nsarchive.gwu.edu/nukevault/ebb245/doc03_full.pdf.

53. On Shulsky's involvement in preparing the document, see the commentary attached to the collection of documents at National Security Archives, " 'Prevent the Reemergence of a New Rival': The Making of the Cheney Regional Defense Strategy, 1991–92," http://nsarchive.gwu.edu/nukevault/ebb245/.

54. Lewis D. Solomon, *Paul D. Wolfowitz: Visionary Intellectual, Policymaker, and Strategist* (Westport, CT: Praeger, 2007), 51; Richard H. Immerman, *Empire for Liberty: A History of American Imperialism from Benjamin Franklin to Paul Wolfowitz* (Princeton, NJ: Princeton University Press, 2012), 217.

55. Patrick Tyler, "Senior U.S. Officials Assail Lone-Superpower Policy" and "Lone Superpower Plan: Ammunition for Critics," *New York Times,* March 11 and 12, 1992. For a concise summary of the controversy, see James Mann, "The True Rationale? It's a Decade Old," *Washington Post,* March 7, 2004, http://nsarchive.gwu.edu/nukevault/ebb245/wp_true_rationale.pdf.

56. Zalmay Khalilzad, *From Containment to Global Leadership? America and the World after the Cold War* (Santa Monica, CA: RAND Corporation, 1995).

57. Ibid. See also Robert Jervis, "The Future of World Politics: Will It Resemble the Past?," *International Security* 16, no. 3 (Winter 1991–1992): 47.

58. Zalmay Khalilzad, "Losing the Moment? The United States and the World after the Cold War," in *Order and Disorder after the Cold War,* ed. Brad Roberts (Cambridge, MA: MIT Press, 1995), 60.

59. Jervis, "Future of World Politics," 71.

60. Khalilzad, "Losing the Moment?," 61.

61. Ibid., 64.

62. Ibid., 65.

63. Zalmay Khalilzad, "Strategy and Defense Planning for the Coming Century," in *Strategy and Defense Planning for the Coming Century,* ed. Khalilzad and David A. Ochmanek (Santa Monica, CA: RAND Corporation, 1997), 8.

64. Ibid., 10.

65. Ibid., 11.

66. See, e.g., Kenneth Waltz, "Structural Realism after the Cold War," *International Security* 25, no. 1 (Summer 2000): 5–41.

67. Zalmay Khalilzad, Abram N. Shulsky, Daniel L. Byman, Roger Cliff, David T. Orletsky, David Shlapak, and Ashley J. Tellis, *The United States and a Rising China: Strategic and Military Implications* (Santa Monica, CA: RAND Corporation, 1999), esp. 72, www.rand.org/content/dam/rand/pubs /monograph_reports/2007/MR1082.pdf.

68. Zalmay Khalilzad, "The United States and the Persian Gulf: Preventing Regional Hegemony," *Survival* 37, no. 2 (Summer 1995): 118.

69. Ibid.

70. Khalilzad, "Anarchy in Afghanistan," 53.

71. Zalmay Khalilzad and Daniel Byman, "Afghanistan: The Consolidation of a Rogue State," *Washington Quarterly* 23, no. 1 (Winter 2000): 71–72.

72. Frank Carlucci, Robert Hunter, and Zalmay Khalilzad, "A Global Agenda for the New President," *RAND Review* 25, no. 1 (Spring 2001): 10–23, www .rand.org/content/dam/rand/pubs/corporate_pubs/2006/RAND_CP22 -2001-03.pdf.

73. Frank Carlucci, Robert Hunter, and Zalmay Khalilzad, *Taking Charge: A Bipartisan Report on Foreign Policy and National Security to the President-Elect* (Santa Monica, CA: RAND Corporation, 2000), 55, www.rand.org/pubs /monograph_reports/MR1306.html.

74. Zalmay Khalilzad to Albert Wohlstetter and the Power Projection Group, "Security Contingencies for the Persian Gulf and the Northern Tier States," June 7, 1979, p. 1, Wohlstetter Papers, box 174, folder 1.

75. Ibid., p. 4.

76. Khalilzad, "The United States and the Persian Gulf," 95–120.

77. Benard and Khalilzad, *"Government of God,"* 115–117, 146–148.

78. Khalilzad, "The United States and the Persian Gulf," 112.

79. Ibid.

11. Richard Perle

1. Cheryl Benard and Zalmay Khalilzad, *"The Government of God": Iran's Islamic Republic* (New York: Columbia University Press, 1984), 74.

2. Ibid., 83.

3. Ibid., 77.

4. Ibid., 76.

5. The unofficial biography of Richard Perle is Alan Weisman, *Prince of Darkness; Richard Perle, the Kingdom, the Power and the End of Empire in America* (New York: Union Square Press, 2007).

6. These revelations appeared first in Seymour Hirsch, "Lunch with the Chairman," *New Yorker,* March 17, 2003, www.newyorker.com/magazine /2003/03/17/lunch-with-the-chairman.

7. Richard Perle, "Albert Wohlstetter, 1913–1997," in "Remembering Albert Wohlstetter," *Congressional Record—Senate,* February 6, 1997, 105th Congress, 1st Session; Vol. 143, No. 14; Daily Edition, S1113, www.congress.gov /crec/1997/02/06/CREC-1997-02-06.pdf.

8. See the retraction of these multiple errors in "Corrections," *New York Times,* June 22, 2003, WK2.

9. Annahrae White, "The House That Hangs in the Sky," *Los Angeles Examiner,* August 7, 1955, 14–22.

10. Sarah Booth Conroy, "Amazing Feats of Kitchen Magic," *Washington Post,* October 5, 1980, E1–2.

11. Bernard Henri Levy, *American Vertigo: Traveling America the Footsteps of Tocqueville,* trans. Charlotte Mandell (New York: Random House, 2005), 188.

12. Ibid., 188–190.

13. Ibid.

14. Richard Perle, *Hard Line* (New York: Random House, 1992), 68–69.

15. Ibid.

16. Robin Winks, "Cold Warrior Stirring the Pot," *Washington Post,* June 9, 1992, E1.

17. Richard Perle, "Iraq: Saddam Unbounded," in *Present Dangers: Crisis and Opportunity in American Foreign and Defense Policy,* ed. Robert Kagan and William Kristol (San Francisco, CA: Encounter Books, 2000), 99.

18. Weisman, *Prince of Darkness,* 162.

19. Perle, "Iraq: Saddam Unbounded," 99.

20. Ibid., 100.

21. Ibid., 101–102.

22. Ibid., 373n6.

23. Ibid., 104.

24. Ibid.

25. Alan Mendoza, "'We Should Still Be Prepared to Intervene': Richard Perle on George W. Bush, Barack Obama and the Arab Spring," *Fathom,* Summer 2013, http://fathomjournal.org/we-should-still-be-prepared-to-intervene -richard-perle-on-george-w-bush-barack-obama-and-the-arab-spring/.

26. Daniel Cohen-Bendit and Richard Perle, "Blessed are the Warmakers?," May 1, 2003, https://foreignpolicy.com/2003/05/01/blessed-are-the-warmakers/.

27. Richard Perle, quoted in Chris Masters, interview with Richard Perle, August 6, 2001, *Rogue State,* Australian Broadcasting Company, www.abc.net .au/4corners/roguestate/interviews/perle.htm.

28. Richard Perle, quoted in Jonathan Holmes, "Interview with Richard Perle," February 18, 2003, *Four Corners,* Australian Broadcasting Company, www .abc.net.au/4corners/content/2003/20030310_american_dreamers/int _perle.htm.

29. Noam Chomsky, speaking in "The Perle-Chomsky Debate: Noam Chomsky debates with Richard Perle (Ohio State University, 1988)," https://chomsky .info/1988____-2/.

30. Ibid.

31. Ibid.

32. Ibid.

33. Larisa Macfarquhar, "The Devils Accountant," *New Yorker,* March 31, 2003, 66.

34. Richard Perle, speaking in "The Perle-Chomsky Debate."

35. Ibid.

36. Chomsky, speaking in "The Perle-Chomsky Debate."

37. Ibid.

38. Nanda Shrestha and Kenneth Gray, "Clash of Civilizations or Cartography of U.S. Global Domination," *International Journal of World Peace* 23, no. 3 (September 2006): 33–44.

39. Perle, in Masters, interview with Richard Perle.

40. Richard Perle, "The Cold War: Is it Really, Really, Really Over?," The Ruttenberg Lecture, June 23, 2000, http://hotcopper.com.au/threads/neo-cons -post-cold-war-doctrine.58548/#.VL-5lUfF9Og.

41. Ibid.

42. Ibid.

43. Ibid.

44. Richard Perle, "United They Fall," *Spectator,* March 22, 2003, 22–26.

45. Richard Perle, "How America Could Lose," *U.S. News and World Report,* September 24, 1990, 45.

46. Richard Perle and David Frum, *An End to Evil: How to Win the War on Terror* (New York: Random House, 2003), 7.

47. Perle, "The Cold War."

48. Perle and Frum, *An End to Evil,* 7.

49. Richard Perle, "In the Dark," review of *Secrecy: The American Experience,* by Daniel Patrick Moynihan, *Commentary,* December 1, 1996, 79.

50. Richard Perle, in "Interview with Richard Perle," March 30, 1997, National Security Archive, Georgetown University, www2.gwu.edu/~nsarchiv /coldwar/interviews/episode-19/perle2.html.

51. Ibid.

52. Richard Perle, James Colbert, Douglas Feith, Robert Loewenberg, et al., "A Clean Break: A New Strategy for Securing the Realm," July 8, 1996, www.informationclearinghouse.info/article1438.htm.

53. Ibid. Emphasis in original.

54. Ibid.

55. Ibid.

56. Ibid.

57. Perle, quoted in Jonathan Holmes, "Interview with Richard Perle."

58. Ibid.

59. Ibid.

60. Perle et al., "A Clean Break."

61. Ibid.

62. Perle and Frum, *An End to Evil,* 35.

63. Ibid.

64. Lance Morrow, *Evil: An Investigation* (New York: Basic Books, 2003), 15–16.

65. Perle and Frum, *An End to Evil,* 7.

66. Ibid., 47.

67. Ibid., 124.

68. Ibid., 50.

69. Ibid., 132–133.

70. Ibid., 137–138.

71. Ibid., 40.

72. Ibid., 50.

73. Richard Perle, "Coalition of the Ineffectual," *Washington Post,* June 26, 2008, www.washingtonpost.com/wp-dyn/content/article/2008/06/25/AR20080 62501943.html?hpid=opinionsbox1.

74. Richard Perle, in Paul Kennedy, Richard Perle, and Joseph Nye, "The Reluctant Empire: In a Time of Great Consequence," *Brown Journal of World Affairs* 10, no.1 (Summer–Fall 2003): 19–20.

75. Richard Perle, "The Congress: Friend or Foe in Foreign Policy?," *University of Miami Law Review* 43, no. 91 (September 1988): 91–99.

76. Ibid., 92.

77. Richard Perle, "Is the United States Turning Inward?," *International Journal* 54, no. 1 (Winter 1998–1999): 4.

Epilogue

1. Ronald Reagan, "Remarks at the Presentation Ceremony for the Presidential Medal of Freedom," November 7, 1985, Ronald Reagan Presidential Library and Museum, www.reagan.utexas.edu/archives/speeches/1985/110785a.htm.

2. Ibid., but as quoted in Henry Rowen, "Commentary: How He Worked," in *Nuclear Heuristics: Selected Writings of Albert and Roberta Wohlstetter,* ed. Robert Zarate and Henry Sokolski (Carlisle, PA: Strategic Studies Institute, U.S. Army War College, 2009), 102.

3. Ibid.

4. Ibid.

5. Ibid.

6. Jacob Heilbrunn, *They Knew They Were Right* (New York: Random House, 2008), 98.

7. Albert Wohlstetter, "Making Peace and Keeping It," *New York Times,* January 28, 1979, E17.

8. Albert Wohlstetter, "Strength, Interest, and New Technologies" (Santa Monica, CA: RAND Corporation, D[L]-16624-PR, January 24, 1968). The text was "presented at Elsinore, September 28, 1967"; see www.rand.org /about/history/wohlstetter/DL16624/DL16624.html.

9. Harold Bloom, *Hamlet* (Philadelphia: Chelsea House, 2003), 43.

10. Andrew Bacevich, "A Letter to Paul Wolfowitz: Occasioned by the Tenth Anniversary of the Iraq War," *Harper's Magazine,* March 2013, 49, http:// harpers.org/archive/2013/03/a-letter-to-paul-wolfowitz/.

11. Ibid.

12. Ibid.

13. Andrew Bacevich, "Tailors to the Emperor," *New Left Review* 69 (May– June, 2011), http://newleftreview.org/II/69/andrew-bacevich-tailors-to -the-emperor.

14. Ibid.

15. Donald Rumsfeld, "Surprise, Surprise: When It Comes to Ballistic Missile Proliferation, Expect the Worst," *National Review,* December 7, 1998, 51–52.

16. Associated Press, "Rumsfeld Says the Pentagon Must Plan for the Unexpected; He Also Assures Lawmakers He Has Made No Decision on New Strategies," *St. Louis Post-Dispatch,* May 24, 2001, A8; Leila Hudson, "The New Ivory Towers: Think Tanks, Strategic Studies and 'Counterrealism,'" *Middle East Policy* 12, no. 4 (Winter 2005): 123.

17. Donald Rumsfeld, *Known and Unknown: A Memoir* (New York: Penguin, 2011), 334; Errol Morris, "The Certainty of Donald Rumsfeld, Part 3: A Failure of Imagination," *New York Times,* March 23, 2014, http://opinionator .blogs.nytimes.com/2014/03/27/the-certainty-of-donald-rumsfeld-part-3/? _r=0#ftn2.

18. Jeffrey Goldberg, "The Unknown," *New Yorker,* February 10, 2003, 40–47.

19. Paul Wolfowitz, "Prepared Testimony of Deputy Secretary of Defense Paul Wolfowitz for the Senate Select Committee on Intelligence and the House Permanent Select Committee on Intelligence, Joint Inquiry Hearing on Counterterrorist Center Customer Perspective, September 19, 2002," Federation of American Scientists, Intelligence Resource Program, http://fas .org/irp/congress/2002_hr/091902wolfowitz.pdf.

20. Ibid.

21. Ibid.

22. Pan Heuristics, "Quarterly Progress Report; Integrated Long-Term Defense Strategy," Marina Del Ray, CA, November 1984, 3, www.dod.gov/pubs/foi/Reading_Room/Other/80.pdf.

23. Roberta Wohlstetter, "Terror on a Grand Scale," *Survival: Global Politics and Strategy* 18, no. 3 (1976): 98–104.

24. "Report of the DoD Commission on Beirut International Airport Terrorist Attack, October 23, 1983," December 20, 1983, https://fas.org/irp/threat/beirut-1983.pdf.

25. Wohlstetter, "Terror on a Grand Scale," 102.

26. "Report of the DoD Commission," 123.

27. Ibid., 4.

28. Ibid., 128.

29. Heilbrunn, *They Knew They Were Right,* 179–180.

30. "Excerpts from Shultz's Address on International Terrorism," *New York Times,* October 26, 1984, A12.

31. Ibid.

32. Robert Hunter, "Can U.S. Muster the Will, Master Ways to Use Force?," *Los Angeles Times,* October 30, 1984, C5. Hunter was quoting *King Lear,* act 3, scene 2.

33. On Rumsfeld's role in Iraq during the 1980s, see the collection of documents collated in Joyce Battle, ed., *Shaking Hands with Saddam Hussein: The U.S. Tilts toward Iraq, 1980–1984,* National Security Archive Electronic Briefing Book no. 82, February 23, 2003, http://nsarchive.gwu.edu/NSAEBB/NSAEBB82/.

34. Secret cable from Secretary of State George Schultz to Foreign Minister Tariq Aziz, May 23, 1983, http://nsarchive.gwu.edu/NSAEBB/NSAEBB82/iraq18.pdf.

35. Daniel Pipes and Laurie Mylroie, "Back Iraq: It's Time for a U.S. 'Tilt,'" *New Republic,* April 27, 1987, www.danielpipes.org/5330/back-iraq. See also Laurie Mylroie, "After the Guns Fell Silent: Iraq in the Middle East," *Middle East Journal* 43, no. 1 (Winter 1989): 51–67.

36. Laurie Mylroie, "Iraq's Changing Role in the Persian Gulf," *Current History* 88, no. 535 (February 1989): 89, 92.

37. An account of Mylroie's shuttle diplomacy appears in Michael Isikoff and David Corn, *Hubris: The Inside Story of Spin, Scandal, and the Selling of the Iraq War* (New York: Crown, 2006), 68–72.

38. Laurie Mylroie, "Iraq's Weapons of Mass Destruction and the 1997 Gulf Crisis," *Middle East Review of International Affairs* 1, no. 4 (December 1997), www.rubincenter.org/category/1997-12-01-04/.

39. Ibid.

40. Laurie Mylroie to Matchett-PI, quoted in blog post, July 15, 2003, www.freerepublic.com/focus/news/947251/posts.

41. Chaim Kaufmann, "Threat Inflation and the Failure of the Marketplace of Ideas: The Selling of the Iraq War," *International Security* 29, no. 1 (Summer 2004): 5–48.

42. Daniel Pipes, "Laurie Mylroie's Shoddy, Loopy, Zany Theories—Exposed," April 30, 2008, www.danielpipes.org/blog/2008/04/laurie-mylroies-shoddy -loopy-zany-theories.

43. Ibid. See also Peter Bergen, "Armchair Provocateur; Laurie Mylroie: The Neocon's Favorite Conspiracy Theorist," *Washington Monthly,* December 2003, www.washingtonmonthly.com/features/2003/0312.bergen.html.

44. Testimony of Laurie Mylroie, National Commission on Terror Attacks upon the United States, Public Hearing, Panel 2: States and Terrorism, July 9, 2003, http://govinfo.library.unt.edu/911/archive/hearing3/9-11Commission _Hearing_2003-07-09.htm.

45. Ibid.

46. Laurie Mylroie, *Study of Revenge: The First World Trade Center Attack and Saddam Hussein's War against America* (Washington, DC: American Enterprise Institute, 2001), xvii.

47. Ibid. On the Telluride connection, see Isikoff and Corn, *Hubris,* 73.

48. Comments by Richard Perle and Paul Wolfowitz on Mylroie, *Study of Revenge,* dust jacket.

49. Public Broadcasting System, "The Case for War; In Defense of Freedom" (Washington, DC, PBS, April, 2007), www.youtube.com/watch?v=9T3a NvSf8mo.

50. Amanda Terkel, "Richard Perle Insists That Saddam Had Ties to Al Qaeda Because He's 'Seen the Evidence,'" ThinkProgress, November, 13, 2006, http://thinkprogress.org/politics/2006/11/13/8613/perle-saddam-al -qaeda/ (contains the transcript as well as the actual soundtrack of the interview).

51. Richard A. Clarke, *Against All Enemies: Inside America's War on Terror—What Really Happened* (New York: Free Press, 2004), 232.

52. Paul Wolfowitz, quoted in "News Transcript: Deputy Secretary Wolfowitz Interview with Sam Tanenhaus, *Vanity Fair,*" May 9, 2003, U.S. Department of Defense, /www.defense.gov/transcripts/transcript.aspx?transcriptid =2594.

53. Donald Rumsfeld, "Testimony of U.S. Secretary of Defense Donald H. Rumsfeld before the House Armed Services Committee Regarding Iraq (Transcript)," September 18, 2002, U.S. Department of Defense, www .defense.gov/Speeches/Speech.aspx?SpeechID=284.

54. Ibid.

55. Wohlstetter, "Terror on a Grand Scale," 102.

56. Zalmay Khalilzad, "The United States and WMD: Missile Proliferation in the Middle East," in *Weapons of Mass Destruction: New Perspectives on Counterproliferation,* ed. William H. Lewis and Stuart E. Johnson (Washington, DC: National Defense University Press, 1995), 129.

57. Richard Perle, "Lessons Learned: The Iraq Invasion," *World Affairs,* May–June 2013, www.worldaffairsjournal.org/article/lessons-learned-iraq -invasion-4.

58. On the connection among rogue states, terrorism, and nuclear weapons, see Michael Klare, *Rogue States and Nuclear Outlaws: America's Search for a New Foreign Policy* (New York: Hill and Wang, 1995); Raymond Tanter, *Rogue Regimes: Terrorism and Proliferation*, rev. ed. (New York: St. Martin's Griffin, 1999).

59. Laurie Mylroie, "The History of Al Qaida" (Washington, DC: Office of Net Assessment, W7 4V8H-04-P-0187, September 1, 2005). The executive summary is available at www.google.com/url?sa=t&rct=j&q=&esrc=s&source =web&cd=1&cad=rja&uact=8&ved=0CB4QFjAAahUKEwikvOOk9pLIAhU GeT4KHayZB5k&url=http%3A%2F%2Fwww.oss.net%2Fdynamaster %2Ffile_archive%2F091213%2F5dac88914b0c094889fba7343df379dd%2 FPart%25201%2C%2520Executive%2520Summary%2520and%2520Othe r%2520Front%2520Matter.doc&usg=AFQjCNFxUVZwaDCtWtnaGjht7S0P NkdZNA&sig2=kDhmEb83-lkwVuEPiXsV4g.

60. Mylroie's reports for ONA are listed on pages 8 and 12 of the Office of the Secretary of Defense, "Net Assessment Reports" (ND), www.dod.gov/pubs /foi/Reading_Room/Other/OSD_Net_Assessment_Log.pdf.

61. Roberta Wohlstetter, *Pearl Harbor: Warning and Decision* (Palo Alto, CA: Stanford University Press, 1962), xi.

62. Andrew Krepinevich and Barry Watts, *The Last Warrior: Andrew Marshall and the Shaping of Modern American Defense Strategy* (New York: Basic Books, 2015), 37–39.

63. United States Senate, *Report of the Select Committee on Intelligence on Post War Findings about Iraq's WMD Programs and Links to Terrorism and How They Compare with Prewar Assessments* (Washington, DC: Government Printing Office, 2006), 105, https://fas.org/irp/congress/2006_rpt/srpt109-331.pdf.

64. David Corn, "The Jeb Bush Adviser Who Should Scare You," *Mother Jones,* May 13, 2015, www.motherjones.com/politics/2015/05/jeb-bush-adviser -paul-wolfowitz.

65. A full list of Wolfowitz's recent AEI contributions is found at www.aei.org /scholar/paul-wolfowitz/.

66. Paul Wolfowitz, "Is the U.S. Now Committed to Removing Iran from the Terrorism List?," American Enterprise Institute, July 24, 2015, www.aei .org/publication/is-the-us-now-committed-to-removing-iran-from-the -terrorism-list/.

67. Zalmay Khalilzad, "Congress Must Strengthen Iran Deal," *National Interest,* July 14, 2015, http://nationalinterest.org/feature/congress-must-strengthen -iran-deal-13335. On Trump and Khalilzad, see Fareed Zakaria "Would Former Ambassador Khalilzad Work for Trump?," CNN, April 15, 2016, http://www.cnn.com/videos/tv/2016/04/15/exp-gps-khalilzad-sot.cnn.

68. Richard Perle and Jonathan Perle, "Leadership as a Last Resort," American Enterprise Institute, April 20, 2014, www.aei.org/publication/leadership-as -a-last-resort/.

69. Albert Wohlstetter and Fred Hoffman, "The Bitter End: The Case for Re-Intervention in Iraq," *New Republic,* April 29, 1991, 20.

70. Quentin Reynolds, "GI Hamlet," *Collier's Weekly,* March 24, 1945, 14, 27.

71. Ibid.

72. Evans quoted in Anne Russell, "Maurice Evan's GI Hamlet; Analogy, Authority, and Adaptation," in *Shakespeare and the Second World War: Memory, Culture, Identity,* ed. Irene Rima Makaryk (Toronto: University of Toronto Press, 2012), 237–238.

73. Todd Landon Barnes, "Hamlet on the Potomac: Anti-Intellectualism in American Political Discourse before and after 'the Decider,'" in *Hamlet Handbook: Subject Matter, Adaptations, Interpretations,* ed. Peter W. Marx (Stuttgart: J. B. Metzler, 2013), 347. Barnes quotes James Joyce, *Ulysses,* ed. Hans Walter Gabler (New York: Vintage, 1986).

74. Reynolds, "GI Hamlet."

75. T. S. Eliot, quoted in Roberta Morgan, "Introduction," in draft dissertation, page ii, Wohlstetter Papers, box 357, folder 5.

76. Fred Charles Iklé, "The Role of Character and Intellect in Strategy," in *On Not Confusing Ourselves: Essays on National Security Strategy in Honor of Albert and Roberta Wohlstetter,* ed. Andrew W. Marshall, J. J. Martin, and Henry S. Rowen (Boulder, CO: Westview Press, 1991), 315.

77. Albee cited in Hilton Als, "Just the Folks: Edward Albee's Bad Marriages," *New Yorker,* December 1, 2014, www.newyorker.com/magazine/2014/12 /01/just-folks-4.

78. Albert Wohlstetter, "Technology, Prediction, and Disorder," *Vanderbilt Law Review* 17, no. 1 (December 1963): 3–4. See also Albert Wohlstetter, "Scientists, Seers and Strategy," *Foreign Affairs* 41, no. 3 (April 1963): 466–478, 3–4.

79. Francis Fukuyama, *America at the Crossroads: Democracy, Power, and the Neoconservative Legacy* (New Haven, CT: Yale University Press, 2001), 116.

80. I have extracted this concept from Norman Moss, letter to the editor, *Bulletin of the Atomic Scientists,* October 1, 1965, 28–29.

81. Paul Wolfowitz, "Remarks on Defense Transformation," speech, February 27, 2004, www.defense.gov/Speeches/Speech.aspx?SpeechID=101.

Acknowledgments

The gestation of this project began some twelve years ago when I was fortunate to be a research fellow at NYU's International Center for Advanced Studies (ICAS), a gem that sadly no longer exists. My Wohlstetter project did not exactly receive a warm welcome. Many of my fellow scholars at ICAS rejected my approach, which, truth be told, is perforated with begrudging admiration for this intimidating couple. Admiration for intellectual achievements is not synonymous with an endorsement of their views, and I am grateful to colleagues and critics who recognized and accepted my attempt at guarded objectivity. Along the way, I have received encouragement and constructive criticism from a host of colleagues, including Marilyn Young, Bruce Kuklick, Marc Trachtenberg, and many anonymous readers. As always, I have benefited from the sharp eye of David Hollinger and my good friend Richard Hill, an attorney who definitely missed his vocation in life.

I have been a beneficiary of NYU's tremendously supportive Department of Media Culture and Communication. I was recruited to the department by the Steinhardt school's former dean, Mary Brabeck. After a couple of years I left for the provost's office, where I have assisted Provost David McLaughlin in the challenging mission of building NYU's global portals in Abu Dhabi and Shanghai. Both Mary and Dave encouraged me to continue my work in the few furtive moments I was able to find during my globetrotting. Fabio Piano and Al Bloom, my principals at NYU Abu Dhabi, offered constant and generous financial support for this project. I could never have completed this task without the services of an outstanding scholar and editor, Paul Sager, a fearless intellectual who kept me honest throughout the project. Nic Dobja-Nootens and Nick Heller completed the many thankless tasks of bringing the manuscript to the production stage.

My editor at Harvard, Kathleen McDermott, demonstrated infinite patience and perseverance. Her ability to forgive my tardiness was nothing less than saintly.

My spouse and partner in life, Livi Wolf-Robin, provided me with the necessary peace of mind to write by dragging me to isolated corners of the world with poor phone reception and sporadic email. I feel blessed to have such a companion.

I am dedicating this book to our grandchildren, Shachar, Eli, and Aviv. I hope one day they may live in a world where strategists have no place.

Index